Psyche's Veil

Historically, the language and concepts within clinical theory have been steeped in linear assumptions and reductionist thinking. Because the essence of psychotherapy involves change, *Psyche's Veil* suggests that clinical practice is inherently a nonlinear affair.

In this book Terry Marks-Tarlow provides therapists with new language, models, and metaphors to narrow the divide between theory and practice, while bridging the gap between psychology and the sciences. By applying contemporary perspectives of chaos theory, complexity theory, and fractal geometry to clinical practice, the author discards traditional conceptions of health based on ideals of regularity, set points, and normative statistics in favour of models that emphasize unique moments, variability, and irregularity. *Psyche's Veil* further explores philosophical and spiritual implications of contemporary science for psychotherapy.

Written at the interface between artistic, scientific, and spiritual aspects of therapy, *Psyche's Veil* is a case-based book that aspires to a paradigm shift in how practitioners conceptualize critical ingredients for internal healing. Novel treatment of sophisticated psychoanalytical issues and tie-ins to interpersonal neurobiology make this book appeal to both the specialist practitioner, as well as the generalist reader.

Terry Marks-Tarlow, Ph.D., a Research Associate at the Institute for Fractal Research in Kassel, Germany, works in private practice in Santa Monica, California.

Psyche's Veil

Psychotherapy, fractals and complexity

Terry Marks-Tarlow

Routledge
Taylor & Francis Group

LONDON AND NEW YORK

First published 2008
by Routledge
27 Church Road, Hove, East Sussex BN3 2FA

Simultaneously published in the USA and Canada
by Routledge
711 Third Avenue, New York, NY 10017, USA

Routledge is an imprint of the Taylor & Francis Group, an informa business

© 2008 Terry Marks-Tarlow

Typeset in Times by RefineCatch Limited, Bungay, Suffolk
Paperback cover design by Lisa Dynan

British Library Cataloguing in Publication Data
A catalogue record for this book is available from the British Library

Library of Congress Cataloging-in-Publication Data
Marks-Tarlow, Terry, 1955–
    Psyche's veil: psychotherapy, fractals and complexity / Terry
Marks-Tarlow.
        p. cm.
    Includes bibliographical references and index.
    ISBN 978-0-415-45544-2 (hardback) – ISBN 978-0-415-
45545-9 (pbk.) 1. Psychotherapy. 2. Nonlinear theories. I. Title.
    RC437.5.M367 2008
    616.89′14–dc22   2007048945

ISBN: 978-0-415-45544-2 (hbk)
ISBN: 978-0-415-45545-9 (pbk)

To my husband, Buzz, and children, Cody and Darby, guardians of my roots, inspiration for my wings.

Contents

Figures

Science boxes

Foreword

Daniel J. Siegel

Psyche's Veil is not your average book about the mind and healing. Terry Marks-Tarlow invites us into a new world – one worth diving into and relishing for its fresh and important approach that can expand how we understand our lives. This is not a straightforward, logical, linear analysis that the left hemisphere of our brain longs to read. Instead, the pages ahead are best ingested by the totality of our brains, both the linguistic, logical, linear left and the often under-appreciated, less utilized right side of the cortex. The author indeed beckons each of our right-brains to participate: we can ignore the invitation, reading these words with the mindset of a usual logical analysis. Or, if we have the kind of courage in the reading that the author reveals in the writing, we can bring the nonlinear perception of these stories and ideas as our guide along this journey into the world of psychotherapy complexity and fractals.

I ask you this: how often have you encountered the challenge of a linear, linguistic product – a book that requires you to use more than just the dominant response of your logical and literal left hemisphere? "In books of poetry or art, in novels, in personal memoirs," you might say. "Yes!" I'd respond. This is a book with many of these elements of personal reflection, narrative and visual art. Indeed, the beauty of this book is that it is filled with artful poetry that requires we use a more integrated ear to hear the music of the author's mind. If you try to read this work with *only* the common, professional, everyday point of view, you will metabolize little of the rich meal in this banquet. You may even come to feel out of place, a guest at a strange dinner you never were fully informed you would be attending. And so my role in offering you this foreword is to forewarn you very directly: without informed consent, you may try to read this important new material only through the lenses of familiar linear perceptual pathways. Such an experience may make you become confused, irritated, or even bored. But take a deep breath, or two, and consider this: the world of the mind and the way we develop and live is much more interesting than the usual and familiar patterns we see through logical lenses. Terry Marks-Tarlow has had the daring to lay down in print a journey into what for many is a new realm. No one claims that this is the "absolute truth" or some kind of reality-as-it-truly-is. But this journey offers the unusual opportunity for you to consider a new way of viewing your old ways of seeing and doing. In fact, you may even find that stretching your mind in this way by opening the doors of perception into the complex and fractal nature of reality also creates a new way of being – with yourself, with others, and with the world. I join the author in inviting you to experience this journey directly for yourself.

But this invitation is not a simple, "Let's go!" I've had enough experience working with poets and poetry alongside those in the fields of psychotherapy, business, and science to know that communication in one mode that requires an integration of left and right – such as with poetry and nonlinear thinking – falls on deaf ears for primarily left-linear thinkers without preparation. In readying yourself for this experience, if that is where your usual perceptual biases rest, here are a few issues that you may wish to consider to enrich the reading.

First, our left-brains love lists – and hence here is a kind of list right now to invite your left side into the party.

Second, "nonlinear" is not the purview of the left, but rather a specialty of right-sided perceptual processing. When we try to see the nonlinearity in the world, the left is blind but the right comes alive.

Third, the left loves certainty while the right relishes the unknown. Clinical practice, and perhaps everyday life itself, is enriched in many ways when we embrace the reality of uncertainty and keep the admonishment of "Don't be too sure" in the front of our minds. We can develop the art of not knowing, of not clinging on to prior expectations. In many ways this is the important role of being "mindful" in clinical practice. This does not mean we become stupid or ignorant, but rather have the openness and receptivity to truly see things as they are, not as our brains wish they would be.

Fourth, so many people these days long for a "simpler life." When those of us working to reveal the role of complexity in human development and psychotherapy raise this concept, many respond with "Life is too complicated as it is, why do you bring in more complexity?" This concern is understandable, but the reality is that complexity is quite simple, and very different from the notion of things being complicated. Complexity is like harmony: when we maximize complexity we flow in a river banked on either side by chaos and by rigidity. We achieve a harmonious flow as we come to integrate elements of a system – to link differentiated parts. This integration – parallel to what Marks-Tarlow terms "complexifying" – leads to a flow toward mental health.

Fifth, the human mind's ability to comprehend reality is constrained by the neural circuitry of perception. When we see only through the linear lens of the left side, we come up with a cause–effect set of explanations of a limited and linguistically delineated world. Naturally the way we think from only this vantage point is lopsided, in this case toward a left, linear mode of thinking. We can widen our receptivity to the world as it is by actively inviting a different mode of perception: the nonlinear, holistic, imagery-based, somatic, sensual and affective world of the right hemisphere. Not usually a part of formal education or professional training, this emphasis on the right is a vital part of seeing a fuller picture of the nature of reality. It is perhaps an important step in becoming more mindful, in accepting things as they are, of seeing things with curiosity, openness, acceptance and kind regard.

Sixth, scientists seeking visions of the world beyond Newtonian physics embrace a perception of the world marked by probabilities and contradictions. This view into the microstructure of quantum reality reverberates with a macro-systems view in which patterns of functional interrelations of energy, matter, and information repeat like ripples on the surface of a pond. These "self-similar" patterns are embedded within layers of a system, or fractals, which repeat and reveal the nature of the whole in the fractional dimensions that form the embedded structure of reality.

Seventh, the left hemisphere may cringe at this notion that elements of a whole are not in linear, causal relationship with each other. Though the left may protest, you can invite your right hemisphere to *feel* its way into seeing the world through these descriptions of the fractal nature of reality. You can *sense* in your own personal, direct, subjective experience the ways fractal patterns become revealed within your own nonlinear awareness. Your left hemisphere, loving linearity, may filter these sensations away from consciousness, appraising them as irrelevant or even just not seeing them at all. But bringing the right hemisphere into alignment with the linguistic analyses of the left is important to weave a tapestry of the whole. Take for example the ways in which attachment research reveals layers of the narrative themes that emerge within an individual that influence affect regulation, interpersonal communication, family function, and even larger cultural dimensions within a society. A strict geneticist searching for simple linear causality might say, "Oh, this is the nature of how DNA leads to familial transmission" and miss the fractal reality that we see experientially derived self-similar patterns rippling throughout relationships. These fractal patterns are enacted within our relationships with ourselves, with others, and with the world. The wise therapist, open to this fractal reality, does not point the finger of causal accusation, but sees the larger systems view of each member of the family playing out this familiar and fractal cross-generational drama.

Eighth, when we see the nature of our intersubjective lives unfolding in this nonlinear way, we can relax into an integrated right–left mode of embracing uncertainty while at the same time actively constructing worlds of overlapping patterns. It is these fractal patterns that Marks-Tarlow delineates so beautifully in these stories and scientific explorations ahead. In science we say that "chance favors the prepared mind." *Psyche's Veil* prepares our minds to see the fractal, nonlinear complex nature of our lives with more receptivity and clarity.

Finally, here is my suggestion: kick off your shoes, sit back, and let the fullness of the words, images, and stories in the following pages just sift through your mind. Let your body feel the fullness of these tales. If and when your left mode protests, let these linear concerns have their say – but do not give up. See if your right hemisphere can have a voice as well. The key is integration, not the dominance of one mode to the exclusion of another. In between chapters, as you live your life and work your work, notice if in fact you begin to sense fractal patterns of self-similar ripples in your personal, inner world, your interpersonal relationships, and your own connection with the world-at-large. Our guide on this journey herself has had the insight to share parts of her own internal journey, serving as a role model for us in revealing how to be alert to fractal patterns in all of these dimensions of our lives that before may have remained hidden beneath the often dominant left linear logical mode of day-to-day processing. Immersing yourself in an integrated way is an opportunity to try on something fresh and new – something that can only help us and help others in this journey of being human.

Preface

Within psychology, clinical theory is tricky business. Ideas and practices come and go like fads or fashions based as much on cultural trends as on empirically grounded truths. No wonder many people question whether psychotherapy is a science at all. This book emerges out of my own growing excitement that nonlinear dynamics offers a framework broad and flexible enough to capture such elusive qualities as emotional sensitivity, clinical intuition, relational empathy, and the genius of timing.

In the spirit of Allan Schore's approach, this book strives to merge artistic aspects of psychotherapy with its technical and spiritual dimensions. In embracing such lofty goals, I do not aim to supersede previous clinical theories so much as to contextualize them. I firmly believe in a multiverse of perspectives; each theory is valid in its own way. There is a time and a place for every clinical formulation, not as a preset generalization or mechanical formula, but as a living process emerging out of unique interpersonal chemistry and "moments of meeting."

Within the history of psychology there is a broad evolution from using static, linear, mechanistic metaphors to dynamic, holistic, nonlinear ones. A key goal of mine is to help make this trend more conscious and explicit, partly by introducing new metaphors. Regardless of theoretical orientation, these additional tools may help to lessen the gap between theory and practice, to enhance our conception of what we actually do and how we do it. Happily, readers might discover that new concepts often feel old, as they challenge the mind to stretch in ways compatible with previous formulations and resonant with the "psycho-logic" of holistic intuition.

Early chapters highlight fundamental uncertainty and complexity at the edge of chaos. Middle chapters introduce metaphor as a nonlinear means for driving complexity within psychotherapy. Later chapters utilize fractal geometry as a source for new metaphors surrounding the psyche. This book combines model, myth, and metaphor to align scientific dimensions of psychotherapy with artful and the spiritual in hopes of weaving an essential new narrative for clinical practice.

I adopt a show-and-tell style, wherever possible beginning with a real life example to flesh out ideas later framed within the context of nonlinear science. Because nonlinear science is highly visual and spatial and primarily a right-brain affair, multiple images punctuate the text to inform, illustrate and inspire the reader. A glossary towards the end of the book tracks technical terms, whether psychological, mathematical or scientific.

Some books are about one thing. They start with an idea and build a case with examples and evidence. This book differs, by moving dynamically with its subject matter. For readers new to nonlinear science, the ideas at first may seem overwhelming, especially those steeped in paradox. I offer the option to skip technical aspects altogether by boxing off much of the science from the clinical material. Or when encountering unfamiliar terms and ideas, new material can be treated like a long dream, with the goal of absorbing it into the unconscious and figuring it out later.

For those more versed in contemporary science, this book is less rather than more technical in nature. Although I do my best to avoid inaccuracies and cite up-to-date research, my purpose is to engage the right-brained, intuitive side more than the left-brained, logic-driven side. The first few chapters may appear to cover old territory, but I hope they offer enough novelty within their cased-based application to retain the technical reader's interest. Early chapters lay conceptual foundations for the final three chapters, which contain my most original contribution to clinical theory, in the form of fractals as model and metaphor for psychological complexity.

All the clinical material in this book is based on my personal and professional experience, including twenty-odd years of long-term psychotherapy. Where appropriate, cases have been read, critiqued, and incorporated by patients in our ongoing explorations. I thank Mike Eigen for the courage to utilize case material in this therapeutic manner. Most of the cases reflect psychotherapy with single individuals, although in two instances, the cases represent composites.

Acknowledgments

If it takes a village to raise a child, it took a community to bring this book to fruition. Ten years after conception and three versions later, I acutely recognize my personal and professional growth along the way. I extend my deep gratitude to all my patients, whether they grace the following pages or not, for the privilege of transforming along with them.

I extend warm gratitude to Daniel Siegel for guidance and enthusiasm in writing a foreword and to Allan Schore for invaluable professional mentorship. Special thanks to John Howie for unwavering emotional and intellectual support; to Grant Brenner for a deep and thoughtful critique; to Michael Summerlin for a careful read and guidance at a crossroads; and to Irina Kerdman for envisioning the finished product all along. This project was deeply nourished by years of discussion with the Chaos Study Group: Ishai Almog, Todd Burley, Bonnie Burstein, Lou Jenkins, Daphne Lee, and David Rapkin.

Deep appreciation to Nicolas Desprez, David Wexler, Susan Mirow, and Fred Abraham for custom-made, computer graphics, to Georgianne Cowan for such lovely photographs, to Megan Williams for paintings from a former life, and to Myrna Katz for her evocative drawing. Other people with significant contributions to this book include: Wade Anderson, Richard Bird, Sandy Brown, Ronit Davidyan, Kristina Diener, Michael Eigen, Ben Goertzel, Patricia Greenfield, Patrick Grim, Steven Guastello, Raphael Gunner, John Holgate, William Jackson, Larry Starr-Karlin, Matthijs Koopmans, Lubomir Kostron, Susan B. Krevoy, Ivelisse Lazzarini, William McCown, Valerie Maxwell, Teena Moody, Jim Morris, Stephen Oyer-Owens, Katherine Peil, David Pinkus, Robert Porter, Ruth Richards, Carolyn See, Doug Seelig, Sarah Seyler, Frank Suzzoni, Norma Tracey, Susie Vrobel, Rita Weinberg, Bruce West, and Tobi Zausner. My apologies to anyone I inadvertently omitted.

Chapter 1

The nonlinear paradigm

The map is the treasure.

Will Rood, mathematician

Psychotherapy is a complex affair. Consider what it means to be human: each body capitalizes on millions of years of biological evolution to form the most complicated object in the known universe, the human brain. Each brain supports consciousness by parallel processing 100 billion neurons, an amount that approaches the number of stars in the Milky Way. Each neuron communicates with approximately 100,000 of its near and distant neighbors to result in more neuronal synaptic interconnections in a single human brain than the number of known particles in the universe – 10 followed by a million zeros (Edelman, 1992).

The biology of the isolated brain is just the beginning. In life, the brain and psyche develop out of a tangle of relationships with others. Give an infant all she needs physically, but deprive her of loving touch and she will wither as if starving. From the moment of conception, complicated feedback loops link mind to mind, mind to brain, and mind to body. Multiple, parallel interactions continually connect self with other, self with self, and self with world, each level operating according to intrinsic dynamics on different time scales. From infancy on, ongoing interactions with family, friends, strangers, and culture at large lead to *absolute uniqueness* in the minute-to-minute cocreation of self and other. Yet the uniqueness of each moment is easy to overlook. Ongoing consciousness is based on language that categorizes by similarities and analyzes by breaking experience down into digestible bits. Linear thinking characterizes ordinary logic and the working of the brain's left, more verbal hemisphere.

By contrast the nonlinear perspective characteristic of contemporary science is more typical of the nonverbal, pattern-seeking, right hemisphere and reveals a different universe. In the midst of staggering complexity, system parts are inseparable from the whole. Holistically perceived, each moment contains an infinite amount of information for which words do little justice.

With interdependence and open boundaries between one complex system and another, distinct borders dissolve. Dancing in continual flux, each part is fully enfolded by dynamics of the whole. No wonder the nonlinear realm is where mystics have played for millennia (see Figure 1.1).

Given such a kaleidoscope of flux and entanglement, how do therapists converge to clear vision? How do we distinguish body from mind, inner beliefs from outer reality, one psyche from another, personality from culture? How do we put together an infinite amount of information to do our job? Must we even answer such questions to work effectively?

Secretly most clinicians know that the work can proceed beautifully

Figure 1.1 The dance of Shiva.

Whereas the logical, rational style of the left-brain short circuits in the face of extreme complexity, the nonlinear, synthetic style of the right-brain is undaunted. This image of Shiva, derived from ancient Hindu mythology, portrays the continual dance of creation and destruction in the flux of the whole of Atman. The surrounding ring represents the universe with all its illusion, suffering and pain. The outer circle constitutes the fire of cosmos and consciousness, its inner edge lined with ocean waters. Shiva stands on the demon of illusion and ignorance. His dance is intended not only as a symbol, but also as a literal depiction of what takes place within us all at each moment, at invisible levels at the heart of consciousness. Like this book, Shiva dances at the intersection of art, science and spirituality.

without our ever knowing exactly what is going on or what will happen – sometimes maybe even because we do not "know." Contemporary clinical thinkers such as Allan Schore (1999, 2003a, 2003b) attend to right-brain, implicit, nonconscious processes underlying psychotherapy. At this level, body-based responses underlying the attachment dynamics of an attuned relationship between therapist and patient can proceed without our awareness or even understanding.

Despite its underlying physiological complexity, *being* in relationship and *doing* psychotherapy does not always *feel* complex. When we operate smoothly, in a state of flow (Csikszentmihalyi, 1990), or with hovering attention (Freud) resembling a moving meditation, the work can seem downright simple, almost as if it completes itself. How does so much complexity translate into something so simple? What is this paradox? If formulas and templates do not easily capture the essence of human transformation, what can? Despite a process plagued by messiness, fits and starts, and frequent setbacks, how do competent therapists manage to get the job done?

The science of change

In line with the interdisciplinary field of interpersonal neurobiology (e.g., Cozolino, 2002, 2006; Ogden et al., 2006; Schore, 2003a, 2003b; Siegel, 2001, 2006, 2007, 2008; Siegel and Hartzell, 2003; Solomon and Siegel, 2003) and those who have recognized the importance of nonlinear science to psychology (e.g., Abraham and Gilgen, 1995; Abraham et al., 1990; Barton, 1994; Bütz, 1997; Combs, 1997; Dauwalder and Tschacher, 2003; Goertzel, 1993, 1994, 1997; Grisby and Stevens, 2000; Guastello, 2001, 2006; Kelso, 1995; Lewis and Granic, 2002; Mac Cormac and Stamenov, 1996; Piers et al., 2007; Robertson and Combs, 1995; Shelhamer, 2006; Sulis and Combs, 1996; Thelen and Smith, 1993, 1994; Vallacher and Nowak, 1994; Van Orden, 2002) and to clinical practice specifically (e.g., Bütz et al., 1996; Chamberlain and Butz, 1998; Gottman et al., 2002; Levenson, 1994; Masterpasqua and Perna, 1997; Miller, 1999; Orsucci, 1998; Palombo, 1999; Pizer, 1998; Rossi, 1996; Seligman, 2005), I offer nonlinear science as a framework to understand how such questions relate to issues of clinical intuition, complexity, and creativity. Nonlinear dynamics represents the science of change, and offers metaphors and models closer to embodied experience while refining the therapist's eye to detect complex patterns. Nonlinear science specializes in facets of nature that are idiosyncratic, spontaneous, irregular, emergent, discontinuous, and unpredictable.

One important premise is that a nonlinear paradigm helps to conceptualize the early attachment dance between infant and caretaker that coordinates physiology, choreographs movements, tunes brains, and ultimately sculpts the minds of each. These ideas are especially important to Schore's regulation theory (e.g., Schore, 1999, 2001, 2003a, 2003b) and its sister science, attachment theory (e.g., Bowlby, 1969; Fonagy et al., 1995; Main and Hesse, 1990; Sroufe, 1983; Stern, 1985). Such theories reverse how we normally conceptualize development. Rather than viewing separate individuals as they come together to form relationships, these perspectives examine how the individual psyche emerges out of relationship as the basic building block.

The precise way in which developing brains, bodies and minds self-organize in response to attuned caretaking requires nonlinear conceptions. This framework is ideal to model the implicit, often nonverbal, unconscious levels of emotional and ideational exchange. Nonlinear techniques capture coupled dynamics between people at multiple descriptive levels (e.g., Guastello et al., 2006; Levinson and Gottman, 1983). Precise, idiographic methods track unique physiological events, including significant therapeutic moments (e.g., Pincus, 2001; Shockley, 2003).

Before introducing a detailed clinical case to offer major book themes, first I present a brief overview of nonlinear science.

Nonlinear science in a nutshell

Nonlinear dynamics spans the spectrum from the microscopic to macroscopic, from physics to biology, from neuroscience to economics. Scores of disciplines, most highly specialized and mathematically rooted, sport arcane names like "nonequilibrium thermodynamics," "cellular automata," and "free agent modeling." Though initially we may feel apprehensive about unfamiliar, technical or mathy sounding terms, they are easier to grasp than on first blush. Because the ideas align with clinical intuition already developed, to grasp them at more conscious, formal levels can prove especially powerful.

I draw primarily from three areas of contemporary science most relevant to clinicians – chaos theory, complexity theory, and fractal geometry. Chaos theory grounds us in the inevitable turmoil, discontinuities, and limited predictability of ordinary life. Complexity theory reveals how development, new order and creative change self-organize, spontaneously emerging at the edge of chaos. Fractal geometry detects complex patterns of the whole as they extend through a system's parts, including paradoxical boundaries simultaneously open and closed, bounded and unbounded. Taken together, these sciences model the deep and mysterious interpenetration between self, world, and other.

We can understand the essence of nonlinear dynamics by contrasting contemporary with traditional paradigms. Much of classical science, like Newtonian physics, is linear. In linear systems or states small inputs give rise to small outputs, while large inputs give rise to large outputs. The relationship between variables is additive, and given the relative independence of underlying aspects, cause relates to effect in ways that are dependable, repeatable, and predictable.

Science box 1.1 Linear versus nonlinear science

Linear ideas and methods are the foundation for the empirical method of classical science, where predictions are formulated and hypotheses tested in replicable designs. In linear systems or realms, simple cause and effect relationships hold because the contribution of each part is independent and additive, such that the whole is exactly the sum of the parts. Classical statistics within social sciences and clinical psychology specifically often are based on linear, normative assumptions. As we shall see, the falsity of underlying assumptions might explain why experimental results in the social sciences are often hard to replicate, and why so many experimental outcomes account for so little of the variance.

Linear dynamics	Complex, nonlinear dynamics
Output proportional to input	Small changes diverge over time
Elements are additive	Elements are multiplicative
Simple interaction rules – simple results	Simple interaction rules – complex results
Stable, predictable	Unstable, limited predictability
Normal distributions	Inverse power law distributions

Nonlinearity is at the heart of all fields of modern science, permeating the curved geometry underlying Einstein's formulation about spacetime, the strange world of quantum dynamics, small world network dynamics and other types of highly uneven distributions by which a few people do most of the work, carry most of the power, and why the rich often get richer.

With the advent of modern computers and brain imaging, methods for capturing subtle and unique nonlinear interactions get more sophisticated. New techniques allow us to get ever closer to quantifying the complex and normally invisible ways that people's brains and bodies lock in together and influence one another, often below the threshold of consciousness. In

continued

nonlinear systems or realms, due to interdependent parts whose contribution to the whole is multiplicative, simple cause-and-effect relationships break down. The time-honored Gestalt formulation, of the whole as more than the sum of its parts, perfectly characterizes nonlinearity.

When approaching contemporary science, the question is not whether to go linear *or* nonlinear. Nonlinear methods do not replace linear ones. Nonlinear results are not more true or descriptive than linear ones. This is not an either/or issue partly because linear realms are included within the nonlinear. Linear states can emerge under certain, well-constrained conditions. Because the nonlinear is the broadest reaching realm, through its understanding, we gain a more direct window into life's ongoing complexity.

Everyday logic, by which we use left-brain thinking to pick apart experience, discern cause and effect, and mentally calculate our next move, is both linear and reductionistic. Reductionism involves the analysis of complex problems by breaking them down into simpler components. Imagine a mechanic who trouble-shoots a car by dismantling it, finding and replacing faulty parts, and then putting the parts back together to reconfigure the whole. Because of the repeatability of links between cause and effect, time drops out as a factor in reductionistic thinking. Whether the car is fixed now, in a week or in a month is irrelevant to the mechanics of the process

The application of the reductionistic paradigm to therapy is severely limited. We cannot take people or relationships "apart" at any level, either literally or symbolically, without destroying their wholeness. Timing is everything; the same intervention that in one moment is welcome and incisive, in the next may be intrusive and injurious. Nor can we exactly repeat the magic of a therapeutic moment, either in action or with words. Yet when Freud popularized psychoanalysis, the field emerged politically as a subdiscipline of medicine during an era when medicine was deeply steeped in reductionism. Because of these historical roots, plus persistent cultural agendas demanding predictability and control, most therapists are only dimly aware of how steeped in linear paradigms we remain.

It is my belief that human undertakings of emotional healing and psychological transformation are quintessentially nonlinear and dynamic affairs.

Dynamic implies movement; and movement implies motion over time. Simply put, dynamical systems theory examines how systems change *over time*. Time has all too often been ignored in clinical theory, where static conceptualizations abound, such as diagnosis as a one-time, one-body, static affair or the classical conception of the unconscious where there is no time. Lack of attention to the centrality of context as well as to unique, moment-to-moment dynamics can lead to poorly designed outcome studies that attempt to reduce healing to therapeutic modalities rather than to focus on idiosyncratic elements, dynamic state changes, and nonlinear moments where real change emerges.

In nonlinear systems or states, small inputs often give rise to unexpectedly large consequences, while huge inputs sometimes have little or no impact at all. Imagine a pivotal moment during a therapy session when a tiny remark can trigger an avalanche of repercussions or surprising progress. Or consider the opposite, when what seems like a "highly significant" interpretation falls on unflappable ears. Day in and day out, these two extremes of tiny and huge inputs having disproportionate outputs constitute the nonlinear rule in contrast to the linear exception.

The nonlinear in action

With this bit of technical explanation under the belt, I turn next to a clinical case chosen specifically for its nonlinear aspects. With Sabina, no single, logical chain of thought seemed to work based on the "traditional" model of diagnosis, treatment plan, implementation and evaluation. As the reader will see, my understanding of Sabina's problems kept shifting kaleidoscopically, along with implications for intervention and criteria for judging outcomes. As the case took unexpected twists, success depended critically upon my ability to feel my way through dynamics on a minute-to-minute basis, by operating in the dark as I struggled toward a coherent understanding of the whole. The highly nonlinear nature of Sabina's case renders it an ideal springboard to introduce three major themes of this book:

- the certainty of uncertainty
- the natural evolution in psychotherapy from chaos to complexity
- fractal conceptions of psychological patterns and boundaries.

A full discussion of each nonlinear component follows the case presentation.

Straddling worlds

From the moment I set eyes on Sabina, I was struck by her dark exotic beauty so tightly concentrated into a petite frame. In her mid twenties, recently married and arrived from India, Sabina left behind the world she knew too

well in search of a new life. As I soaked in this initial feeling of richness, I mused:
*Here is a culture I know little about. I sense adventure ahead . . . even if I have to fly
by the seat of my pants.*

Sabina was visibly upset in my office, her torso and limbs vibrating in tiny,
frantic motions. Emotion poured out of every pore. Sabina's body seemed to
take on its own life as she relayed her tale. This young woman had gone for an
advanced degree in English from abroad, and was now supplementing her
education locally with technical courses taken in film. Despite knowing she
was married, one of her professors reportedly was communicating with sexual innuendo, maneuvering her into private conversations, while streaming
her with vaguely suggestive emails.

As I listened I noticed my split attention: on the one hand I felt empathy for
Sabina, detecting the young woman's sincerity while appreciating her immediate, open trust. Yet I was also aware that she trusted me "too" quickly, before
I had earned this trust. So on the other hand, my clinical intuition started
tugging and nudging me away from the surface.

*Something's missing. Something doesn't make sense here. Why the mismatch
between the details of this story and the intensity of Sabina's emotionality? A
professor shows poor taste by flirting. He's low key, not demanding or threatening.
She's not scared of him physically. What's going on?*

Uncertainty streamed inside me in the form of a flood of questions.

- *Is there some religious dilemma?*
- *Perhaps a moral one?*
- *Trouble at home?*
- *Pressures from Sabina's husband?*
- *Could it be jealousy?*

While religious issues proved a dead end, questions concerning Sabina's home
life opened up a floodgate, slowly at first, then with increasing speed. Her
head hung low, Sabina revealed that during arguments with her husband, also
of Indian origin, occasionally he would strike her. Sabina struggled with low
self-esteem and a misogynist cultural background. She felt confused about
whether the violence was wrong or deserved. To complicate the picture further, Sabina was not a passive victim, but an active participant who occasionally broke a vase or struck her husband back or even first.

Over the course of several sessions, intimate disclosures spilled like fine
wine finally uncorked. During her childhood Sabina's father hit her whenever he disapproved of her behavior, sometimes punishing her severely with a
belt and often misusing his parental authority. Sabina's mother lashed out

primarily with her tongue, accusing her daughter of "laziness" and "ingrati-
tude," or ridiculing her appearance, especially her "straggly" hair.

Eventually the unspeakable poured out. When Sabina was 5 years old her
father forced her to touch his penis while he fingered her vagina. When she
was 14 her father capitalized on her mother's absence by hungrily groping his
daughter's unusually large breasts. Sabina later described the full context for
her father's sexual frustration. Sabina's mother not only denied her husband
sex, but also during the full length of their marriage she had flaunted favor
upon her husband's brother, a Catholic priest. Throughout the girl's
childhood, rumors flew of the scandalous union between mother and priest.
Over and over Sabina felt inexplicably shunned by classmates.

At age 16, Sabina's upset peaked by translating into self-destructive impulses.
Among several suicide gestures she once ingested pesticide that caused lasting damage to her kidneys. The attempt left Sabina with an ongoing feeling of
vulnerability and conflict around doctors – should she tell her embarrassing
story or continue to hide her shame? To date she had not mentioned her
history to anyone.

With memories known but unspoken, they were less repressed than purposefully suppressed. Between the ages of 16 and 26, Sabina tried both to live
with her horror by holding it close inside, and yet not to live with it by evacuat-
ing all the painful memories. As a result Sabina was haunted by nightmares
of bloody monsters and shadowy figures chasing her. Even after her dreams
dissipated, once awake, Sabina continued to fear what lurked under her
bed, refusing to touch the floor at night, even if this meant occasional
bedwetting.

Much of the time Sabina was reluctant to drive or be alone. She responded
to painful memories and personal ghosts by an internal running – staying busy,
keeping her mind occupied with creative fantasies and perfectionist strivings.
Sabina also ran on the outside. After all she had emigrated from her country
of birth, leaving behind every cultural mooring she had plus nearly every
friendship. Here she was, tens of thousands of miles away from home, telling
her story to a stranger.

In the context of this full history, Sabina's initial intense upset now made
complete sense. Her distress was not born of oversensitivity to one professor's lustful fantasies, but instead was the cumulative outpouring of more than
a decade of sexual shame. As Sabina and I sat together amidst her pain and
humiliation, I was struck by her courage to attempt self-empowerment so
consciously. She had resisted any hint of an arranged marriage. Instead she
had found a man she loved and intended to make the marriage work. Now she
had also chosen the path of psychotherapy. Rather than to deal with inner

pain by making outer changes, she selected self-reflection no matter how culturally alien the process. To share so many secrets so quickly was an immediate bond between us. Sabina was relieved finally to talk. I was gratified to work with someone so thankful for my active interest.

Yet even as good feelings were generating in both directions, Sabina became instantly symptomatic, perhaps related to the immediate and unprecedented trust and intimacy. She began to suffer from physical pain that roved through her body. Her husband faithfully at her side, Sabina started to rush to hospital emergency rooms at all hours of the day or night. Here an ovarian cyst; there a kidney infection. Upon ceasing to run emotionally, Sabina's internal disorder found the only outlet still available by funneling through her body. This young lady was now completely in crisis – emotionally, physically and financially. Sabina could hardly have felt more out of control.

What next? We have an excellent relationship. Psychotherapy is the right track . . . but neither her physical body nor the framework of our relationship can contain this outpouring. Time to consider psychotropic medication? Don't really like this alternative . . . prefer to work issues from the inside. Still, feels prudent about now. Perhaps a little medication will turn down the volume of the upset enough to bring body and mind back under control.

Sabina readily agreed to visit a psychiatrist, quickly finding one through a trusted family doctor. Imagining a scenario of calm containment to emerge from this plan, I felt little prepared for what happened next. Over the next several months Sabina responded extremely poorly to every medication the psychiatrist attempted. Her tiny body buckled under the smallest doses, as if reeling under whopping amounts of narcotics. More than once, she literally stumbled into and out of my office as if about to fall. Not at all present mentally, Sabina's symptoms dominated and interfered with her psychotherapy. Meanwhile she became confused about whom to call in an emergency. Were these medical crises under the bailiwick of the psychiatrist or emotionally driven episodes better suited for her psychologist?

The psychiatrist proved to be an extremely busy man, often slow to respond to Sabina's distress calls. As she continued to respond poorly to the medication, he began actively questioning the utility of her psychotherapy. Sabina felt increasingly defensive about our work and increasingly frightened to meet with the psychiatrist. When she did keep appointments, she became more hesitant to discuss her symptoms or her psychotherapy. Eventually another full-blown crisis ensued, this time surrounding her relationship with her psychiatrist. A negative cycle was in full force between them: the psychiatrist viewed Sabina and her therapy increasingly negatively, while Sabina steadily lost trust and confidence in the doctor.

In pondering my own reactions, I emptied my mind of all previous mental constructions, letting a voice deep inside me hold its own dialogue. *Now what? Again my gut tells me something more is going on than meets the eye. Why isn't this a medically straightforward situation of symptom and relief? What other dynamics are at play?*

Once again questions burned. I felt an increasing polarization within the therapeutic triangle – between patient, psychologist, and psychiatrist. As Sabina's symptoms and side effects worsened, the psychiatrist began to pathologize his patient ever more to me, speculating about her borderline personality. As he grew frustrated with her lack of progress, he expressed doubts more vocally to Sabina about my competence as a psychotherapist. These judgments scared me. They taunted my defenses. My self-doubts howled. Meanwhile the rebel in me wanted to point a finger back at the psychiatrist for *his* role in escalating the drama. At the same time my urges to make someone wrong – whether my self or the psychiatrist – *felt wrong*. Again that inner tug to go *deeper* came, this time pulling me to intuit an underlying transference dimension. The inner silence into which my questions poured was rewarded yet again with greater clarity.

Ah, now I see it! Transference is brewing within this therapeutic triangle.

- *Psychiatrist = Father*
- *Psychologist = Mother*
- *Sabina = Child.*

Sabina's crisis with the psychiatrist echoes that with her father. Another man in authority who is supposed to help, but instead is hurting her. And look at my role as the enabling mother . . . ignoring the abuse . . . allowing it to continue.

Meanwhile something else compounded Sabina's relational distress. Using her computer, Sabina had entered the psychiatrist's name into an Internet search engine. Sabina wound up so horrified at what she found, she could barely glance at the screen: the man appeared involved in a high profile case of child abuse. What was worse, Sabina announced shrilly, he is participating *on the side of the alleged abuser.*

That was the last straw – Sabina felt she could no longer work with this psychiatrist. She had the impulse to flee immediately, without saying a word. Together we examined the transference crisis, how the relationships between Sabina, her psychiatrist and her psychologist repeated the original trauma of abuse with her parents. Given her panic I supported Sabina's intention to leave. But I also pointed out that she intensified her own disempowerment by choosing to leave in silence. I suggested an alternative: during our next session, together we could write the psychiatrist a termination letter. Visibly relieved Sabina readily agreed.

I felt confident in my interpretation and the good sense of our plan, anticipating that my patient would remain fairly stable until our next session. Once again, I could not have been more mistaken. Sabina entered my office announcing that she had just visited the emergency room again following the worst bout of physical pain to date.

Something's wrong here. I sense Sabina unconsciously trying to speak to me through these symptoms. The plan's no good. I shouldn't be helping her to write this letter. But why not?

Suddenly in a flash I saw the big picture. In my eagerness to help my patient avoid further repetition of the original trauma with her parents, unwittingly I ushered in the repetition even deeper by enacting my countertransference. I was playing the good mother that Sabina never had, who was not in denial, but instead actively willing to step in and protect her innocent daughter from actions of the bad father. However to leave the psychiatrist now was merely another act of demonizing and running. This was not a path true towards healing, but a false one towards more symptoms, amidst even less support.

Clearly Sabina needed the opposite action from me – assistance *not to leave.* In over twenty years of practice, what happened next was one of my most concentrated experiences of professional "magic." First I admitted the "badness" of our plan to Sabina. Next I pointed out that her intentions to leave the psychiatrist were not relieving her, but instead were intensifying her feelings of internal fragmentation. To heal these inner splits, it appeared that Sabina had to face her fears. To do this, she needed her symbolic "parents" to heal their outer divisions by displaying a united front.

This new understanding of the transference triangle – between psychiatrist/father, psychologist/mother, and Sabina/child – made perfect sense to Sabina. The interpretation hit home precisely. Sabina's sense of understanding and being understood instantly bound and contained most of her symptoms. Not only did Sabina's visits to the hospital stop, but also, under medical supervision, she weaned herself off all psychotropic medication and has not returned since.

When I called the psychiatrist to discuss matters he was open to my interpretation of events. Upon hearing that Sabina had done an Internet search on him, he verified his involvement in the high profile case but clarified a distortion in Sabina's perceptions. The psychiatrist had not been retained by the alleged abuser, but was hired on the side of the victims instead.

How fascinating! In her haste to run away from information related to her fears, Sabina had completely reversed her facts. What a tragic feedback loop. Getting scared made her want to run, but the very act of running made her more scared and symptomatic. Could the universe have concocted a more fitting lesson? What invisible hand crafted such a perfect illumination of the dangers of Sabina's impressionistic, impulsive style?

Sabina, the psychiatrist and I were all struck by the cogency of events. As we reviewed the convoluted course of inner and outer events, Sabina saw how her impulses to flee, even from relevant information, caused her to seize upon bits of it to exaggerate the dangers. Terrified of the trees, she had lost sight of the forest, to the point of "delusion." As Sabina took in the truth, the air streamed right out of her inner representation of the psychiatrist as a looming menace. The man even began to seem downright decent and compassionate. The central transference crisis was over. Meanwhile, driven by all the stress, Sabina's husband entered individual therapy with a colleague of mine. The violence and drama drained not only out of Sabina's body and psyche, but also mostly out of her marriage.

Sabina's nightmares are a telling gauge of her transformation over the months. The nightmares continued, but grew steadily more infrequent. As Sabina calmed down, their content morphed. The horrific monsters no longer chased, caught or killed her so often. This indicated to me that Sabina felt less haunted. As her defenses grew less primitive and lodged in her body the monsters took more human form. From time to time Sabina's mother and other family members even appeared directly, reminiscent of Stephen Mitchell's "transformation of ghosts into ancestors."

Ever less caught by amygdala-driven, fight/flight impulses of trauma-based physiology, Sabina stopped running in response to inner horrors. A recent dream was revealing: a werewolf lay dead in the middle of the road, its fur ripped open to reveal blood and guts utterly disgusting to Sabina. Yet she felt *drawn toward* the beast, struck by the saw tooth shape of its wounds. While talking about it to me, the jagged pattern inspired Sabina to imagine a similar design emblazoned artistically on a canvas, painted in bold colors. This was the point in psychotherapy where I knew Sabina was fully captivated by the path of self-reflection. Not just consciously, but unconsciously as well, Sabina now embraced the beauty of her own experience, no matter how painful (see Figure 1.2).

A nonlinear interpretation

With this case in hand we turn next to a nonlinear understanding. In sections to follow, as I return to Sabina's case in order to outline nonlinear themes, the reader is sure to notice my use of language. With terms like "chaos" and "complexity" I ricochet from technical meanings to everyday vernacular. By

Figure 1.2 Sabina's animation.

   In line with Sabina's fantasy of emblazoning her saw tooth wound design from a nightmare onto a canvas, in real life Sabina conceived and created an animated short called *Flight of the Bumblebee*. Portrayed with music and without words, originally Sabina had no inkling that this story of trauma and healing was auto-biographical in any way. Depicted here are several scenes with self-referential significance to psychotherapy. Based on actual storyboards and redrawn by the author with the patient's permission, the main character, Bumble, has run away from a fire in which he lost his home, family, friends and the capacity to fly. On his journey Bumble meets a series of helpers, culminating in the fan-waving Ladybug, illustrated with Bumble in the first frame. After Ladybug places a cold pack on the Bumble's wings, the bee has a flashback that draws him into the alchemical fire of change and allows him to re-emerge as whole. In the last frame, Bumble is able to fly once again, while the delighted Ladybug bears witness.

mixing scientific with colloquial usages I risk the ire of hardcore scientists who demand more precision. In deference to them I distinguish between technical and metaphorical usages wherever possible. However, I admit purposely conflating scientific with non-scientific usages at times as a device to encourage creative thought, especially among less scientifically minded therapists who wish to embody these ideas and develop a more scientifically grounded clinical intuition (see Figure 1.3).

Figure 1.3 Chaos everywhere.

Courtesy of Megan Williams/Collection of Dean Valentine

One compelling facet of chaos theory is its name. Despite the lack of technical knowledge, most of us resonate intuitively to the idea of chaos in life. A continuum exists – from "chaos" as metaphorically used in everyday vernacular to chaos as technically defined. Early interpretations of chaos by social scientists as "anxiety" or "internal crisis" were clumsy, if not inaccurate. Yet at the practical level, therapists interested in the new sciences need not always make a clear distinction between metaphorical and technical use. This is partly because clinical practice involves dealing with the emotional and cognitive impact of living in a chaotic world. In this painting, *Twister* by Megan Williams, there is a confluence between a literal, outer depiction of chaos and a figurative, inner description.

Uncertainty at the core

The first theme of this book is the certainty of uncertainty, a feeling tone that punctuated my inner experience throughout Sabina's case. Over and over I was as interested in what I *did not* know as in what I did know. During the initial stage of treatment I harbored the disconcerting sense of information missing. As this gap filled but Sabina's symptoms increased, I was uncertain our relationship alone could contain the dynamics. After help from a psychiatrist was enlisted, without medications successfully stemming the tide of symptoms, I became uncertain about the utility of a straightforward medical model. I deepened my sensibilities to consider the transference triangle between psychiatrist/father, psychologist/mother, Sabina/child. While a premature sense of certainty caused me concoct a poor plan of action based on overly reductionist thinking, ultimate success required a more complex picture based on my continued openness to indirect feedback signals surrounding what I did not know.

In the history of clinical theory, many highly respected therapists have emphasized the importance of not-knowing. Sigmund Freud encouraged the cultivation of "evenly hovering attention." Wilfred Bion entreated us to face each session anew, "without memory, intent or desire." Marion Milner emphasized the centrality of the "pregnant void" and "creative chaos." Maurie Pressman called for "knowing beyond knowing." Michael Eigen likened psychoanalysis to mystical prayer, both sharing "openness to the unknown." Common to these approaches is the loosened grip on the clinician's "certain" knowledge while recognizing the attendant danger of premature, excessively rigid or narrow formulations.

The notion that informed uncertainty can be a higher state of consciousness, enabling us to stay present, alert, and ready dovetails with the history of Eastern martial arts and the meaning of being a warrior continually ready for action. The history of esoteric spiritual practices likewise reveals a pattern of placing value in not-knowing. The *Advaita* and *Vedanta* of Hinduism strive towards "pure consciousness." Taoism and mystic Christianity aspire to a state of "silence." Zen Buddhism reaches towards "emptiness," while honoring the "beginner's mind." Vipassana Buddhist meditators speak of "pausing" amidst relationships of "insight dialogue." Within Buddhism most broadly, empty mental states promote the flow of "loving-kindness" and "compassion."

I add to this venerated tradition by juxtaposing an old message next to contemporary science. The certainty of uncertainty is the subject of Chapter 2. The central theme is as follows: because psychological functioning and especially processes of change are fundamentally nonlinear processes borne of coupled dynamics, no matter how complete our understanding of a person's psyche, history or current day situation, we cannot predict or control with certainty what will happen in the future especially during times of crisis or emotional instability. Given this existential truth pervading nature at large, we must ground ourselves within the holistic, often nonverbal intuition of our right-brain, as we draw upon faith and operate at times in the dark.

The scientific part of Chapter 2 traces shattered hopes of certain knowledge in the history of science broadly, and chaos theory specifically, drawing implications for the field of clinical psychology. The first of many paradoxes in this book reveals itself here: contrary to fears that uncertain knowledge will be our undoing, I hope to show that to unseat the "expert authority" in favor of reasonable doubt is to provide the most solid foundations of all. How ironic that uncertainty at one level can lead to increased certainty at others. And in fact chaos theory frequently allows us to predict some things with greater certainty than previously.

For therapists, a stance of not-knowing keeps us flexible and creative. It ensures that we remain in a state of openness with our patients, rather than closing down with certainty or pre-established beliefs and formulations. Not-knowing stimulates the senses, prevents closure of thought, eggs us towards new information, forces us beyond our comfort zone, invites us to regulate our own difficult emotions, and helps to avert the complacency premature certainty can bring. For patients a stance of not-knowing lessens pathological levels of anxiety and guilt born of futile, self-defeating attempts to be certain about what cannot be known. For both, not-knowing limits left-brain cognitive analyses that run the risk of being cut off from right-brain, body, relationship, and emotion-based states at the heart of attachment dynamics that drive psychotherapy. For anyone, a stance of not-knowing is open and emotionally healthy, and often spiritually blended with fruits of esoteric practices cultivated throughout the millennia.

From chaos to complexity

A second major theme of this book is nature's evolutionary path from chaos to complexity. Sabina's case characterized this trajectory in psychotherapy. Upon choosing a path of self-reflection, Sabina's world spun rapidly out of control. After speaking the unspoken, first Sabina was engulfed by torrents of uncontained emotion, and then her body was deluged with untreatable physical symptoms. As Sabina struggled consciously to make room for her emotions by making sense of memories only now expressed, unconsciously she attempted to flee from all disruptive feelings.

Not only was there chaos metaphorically and perhaps literally within Sabina's internal world, but also chaos interpersonally, reflected by disrupted relations within the transference triangle. As effective communication broke down, inner object representations between patient, psychologist, and psychiatrist became more demonic and distorted. Out of this initial chaotic stew a higher state of complexity eventually did self-organize. Self-organization is a key feature of nonlinear science, through which changes in complex, nonlinear systems seem to direct themselves according to their own intrinsic dynamics and time scales. In systems far from equilibrium, where there is a continual exchange of matter, energy or information across open boundaries, change tends to arise suddenly and spontaneously as a bifurcation. Sometimes triggered by inside and sometimes outside events, bifurcations arise from the bottom-up out of the dynamics of the whole system.

That is why the implicit, non-conscious level by which brain and body are coupled proceeds on rapid timescales that precede or even bypass the much slower time scales of conscious awareness altogether. The emergence of new wholes occurs via reciprocal interactions between basic elements. These elements are bootstrapped together, a term that highlights the interdependence of constituent parts in nonlinear systems. This contrasts to change within linear systems where constituent elements are relatively independent and more amenable to top-down direction and control. Unfortunately, left-brained, linear thinking often falls short, because it depends upon false presumptions of closed systems composed of independent elements that can be manipulated apart from one another.

In the case of Sabina, although I worked hard to use top-down reasoning to understand and control the escalating crisis, especially during initial stages my good intentions not only backfired, but also served to intensify the pace of the mounting problem. Yet despite all the disorder within the case, even before its final resolution, an underlying order became apparent through bifurcations to a new set of underlying attractors, as complexity mounted with each step:

- Step 1: Sabina needed psychotherapy for past traumas reactivated by current professor.
- Step 2: Sabina needed medication as crisis crosses the mind/body boundary.
- Step 3: Medication regime did not work because Sabina unconsciously viewed the psychiatrist as her abusive father.
- Step 4: Efforts to leave the psychiatrist did not work due to fragmentation accompanying further flight.
- Step 5: Each participant became fully conscious of enactment within the transference triangle.

All three major players in this case contributed both consciously as well as *unconsciously and necessarily* to its progression. Eventually out of complete chaos metaphorically speaking, a bifurcation arose with the self-organization of greater order. At this change point, higher inner and outer complexity signaled shared awareness of core dynamics between all three parties, but only after the fact. Clear cognitive understanding appeared to be impossible at the outset.

Chapter 3 echoes these themes by addressing the evolution from chaos to complexity as a universal principle of nature. No matter how a system is constituted, similar dynamics often occur at various levels of biological, psychological, social and cultural observation. Whether we consider the apparently random movements of a flailing infant or neuronal noise in the background EEG (electroencephalogram) readings of ordered perception, human development self-organizes from a fundamental substrate of generative chaos.

Whether we observe huge expanses of evolutionary time or tiny windows of developmental time, nature tends to spontaneously self-organize from the bottom up rather than from top down, in directions of greater complexity. In line with Siegel's approach to mindfulness and well-being (Siegel, 1999, 2007, 2008; Siegel and Hartzell, 2003), Chapter 3 conceives of mental health as self-organized complexity at the edge of chaos. This view suggests mental health is less a static or optimal state and more a *dynamic range of possibilities*. Within this range we possess fully differentiated but integrated faculties plus ready access to our full repertoire of emotions, thoughts and behaviors, along with the flexibility to change course according to changing circumstances.

Mental health conceived as the delicate but resilient edge of chaos provides enough order for stable, integrated foundations, plus sufficient disorder to keep things flexible, fluid and creative. This stands in contrast to derailed or pathological conditions characterized either by too much stagnant order or overly destructive disorder.

Both Chapter 3 and the broad progression of ideas in this book illustrate the self-organization of complex formulations from the chaos of initially "unformulated experience," to use Donnel Stern's evocative phrase (Stern, 2003). Within the psyche, developmentally later capacities for complexity are intimately tied to metaphor and meaning-making in the form of a coherent, internal narrative, not so much articulating the *why*, but more the *what* of ongoing experience. Both metaphor and meaning-making require an integration of right-hemisphere, visual, emotional and spatial processing with left hemispheric verbal skills. The whole brain integration of both sides is indispensable for achieving the key developmental goals of symbolization in the context of secure attachment.

Chapter 4 traces metaphors underlying psychotherapy as they have evolved from static and linear in nature towards dynamic and nonlinear. Being largely a verbal and dialogical affair, metaphor lurks at the narrative base of how we understand our selves, our patients and our work. The art and science of psychotherapy merge within our metaphors to frame how we look at and with our patients. Early clinical metaphors tended to promote simplistic, static images plus dualistic conceptions of the psyche as a container separating inner from outer processes. More contemporary neurobiological, attachment and, intersubjective perspectives, including mechanisms of projective identification, require subtle, sophisticated metaphors to capture open psychological boundaries and coupled interpersonal dynamics that operate simultaneously at multiple levels of description (see Figure 1.4).

Figure 1.4 After Magritte.

We most readily associate metaphor-making with left-brain, verbal capacities to manipulate language. Yet metaphor arises primarily from the divergent and synthetic processing of the right-hemisphere. Developmentally our first metaphors emerge concretely through the body, preceding the development of language, as when a toddler takes flight on a broom. Art is filled with visual metaphor, especially when it is humorous. Psychotherapy too is filled with concrete and visual metaphors that arise through mind/body work, the symbolism of dream imagery or spontaneous, waking associations during sessions. This cartoon, as conceived by the author, conflates the three realms of art, humor and psychotherapy.

From the beginning of humankind, not to mention clinical theory, one rich source for psychological metaphors has come from ancient mythology. Chapter 5 revisits the Oedipus myth as the originating myth and cornerstone for Freud's classical psychoanalysis. Through nonlinear lenses the riddle of the Sphinx appears as a paradox of self-reference that propels humankind from concrete to metaphorical thinking. Metaphor is inherently paradoxical through juxtaposing differences with similarities. All truly creative metaphor heightens psychological complexity by integrating right-brain, nonverbal, imagistic modes and left-brain, verbal and logical formulations (see Modell, 2003).

Chapter 6 carries these themes further by examining paradoxes of self-reference as they emerge to taunt and tickle us in everyday life. Within psychotherapy, wherever paradox appears complexity is likely to follow. From a linear perspective it is easy to assume that paradox is pathological, as in those double-binds surrounding Borderline Personality Disorder. But from a nonlinear perspective where paradox abounds, the capacity to hold ambiguities and contradictions proves as defining of genius as madmen. In Chapter 6, I claim that paradox resides at the edges, if not at the core of us all. I also claim that the primary difference between conditions of pathology and those of mental health lies in rejection versus acceptance of this primary state of being.

Fractal geometry: self-similarity in psychological boundaries

The third major theme explored in these pages involves the use of fractal metaphors to understand complexity within the self-organizing psyche, including its ever-shifting boundaries between self, other and the world at large. I partition psychological complexity into three, intertwined aspects – self–self relations, self–other relations, and self–world relations. I devote a chapter to fractal dynamics within each of these three aspects of inner complexity. Fractal geometry, a new branch of mathematics, is filled with paradoxes, like open yet closed boundaries, finite yet infinite processes, offering some highly effective tools to model natural complexity and enhance clinical practice and theory.

There are many ways to understand a fractal, but regardless of which we use, fractals involve the emergence of complex detail on multiple levels as arises from very simple rules. One hallmark of a fractal is self-similarity, where the pattern of the whole is reflected in the form of its recursively enfolded parts. A spatial example is a series of nested Russian dolls, each tinier than the last, each resembling the largest in which all are encased (Figure 1.5). A temporal example of self-similarity is a moody character whose emotional fluctuations are self-similar, with instability as reflective of minute-to-minute dynamics as those on a broader time scale.

To understand metaphorically how patterns can be recursively enfolded, consider problems that arose for philosophers who logically tried to deconstruct the "I" of consciousness. In answer to a linear conception of "Who runs the show?" philosophers conceived a homunculus, or "little man." But this led only to postulating yet another homunculus in charge of the first. And so on, ad infinitum, in an endless regress of little men running little men (Figure 1.6).

Fractals do apply to the "I" of consciousness, but not in the form of little men. Self-similarity is a newly discovered symmetry in Nature related to how the wholeness of identity gets cobbled across the pieces of experience within the flux of time and change. Fractals also relate to the interface where dynamics cross from brain to mind or body and back again. Through their evolution over time, fractals reveal the intersection between process and structure. In Chapter 8, I claim our inner selves to possess fractal structure. To illustrate, consider the logo for Susan B. Krevoy Eating Disorder Program at the Wright Institute Los Angeles (Figure 1.7).

T. Marks-Tarlow
6·07

Figure 1.5 Nested dolls.

Children are inherently drawn to the self-similar forms related to fractal geometry, where the pattern of the whole reflects itself on various size or time scales.
Perhaps this has to do with how intuition works, by tapping into the whole of
things, and in through the parts. As a fifth grader I struggled to understand the
term "infinity" and spontaneously generated a fractal image. I envisioned our
universe in a shoe box of the closet of a giant, whose universe in turn was in an
even larger shoe box of the closet of yet a larger giant, etc. As we shall see, there
may even be a developmental stage of children's art consisting of experimentation
with self-similar form.

For most of us fractal thinking already occupies an important, implicit
part of our clinical toolbox. We understand fractals intuitively when we sense
how an initial interchange between patient and therapist reflects dynamics
of the rest of the session or the case as a whole. We use fractal thinking
when interpreting the meaning of a single dream to reflect the entire psyche.
Returning to the case of Sabina, there is self-similarity in the repetition of
dream images involving scary monsters. Successful dream interpretation lies

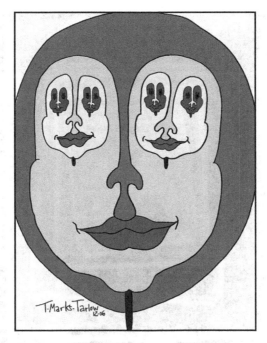

Figure 1.6 Homunculus.

The I/eye of consciousness, here depicted as a fractal, with smaller and smaller faces rendered in the eyes of still larger ones.

precisely in fractal thinking that seeks isomorphism, or structural similarities, to link various formal features, such as the presence of animals versus humans or avoidance versus approach of scary objects, to changing intrapsychic and interpersonal dynamics on a grander scale.

Self-similarity also comes into play in Freud's "repetition compulsion" and how the countertransference-transference/experiential matrix reflects earlier, family of origin dynamics. The case of Sabina reveals self-similar dynamics within her "repetition compulsion" to replay the same old trauma with a new cast of players. Throughout this case we see repeatedly how unconscious elements first get enacted and then are made conscious. This occurs not just within Sabina, but also within each of the three main players. As Sabina's unconscious dynamics spill across interpersonal boundaries to trigger feelings, issues and concerns within others, each player becomes an instrument for a melody that clearly transcends the individual.

During these exciting times, psychoanalytic thought dovetails with contemporary neuroscience in the neurobiology of attachment and emotional regulation. Most therapists now recognize how the minds and brains of individuals co-emerge and co-develop inside the fluid medium of other minds

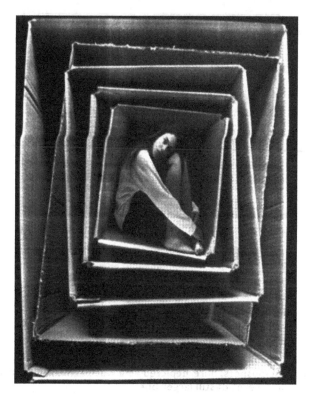

Figure 1.7 Logo for the Susan B. Krevoy Eating Disorder Program.

Courtesy of Susan B. Krevoy

A girl with an eating disorder embodies a visual metaphor for her problems. Here she is cornered and trapped, huddling miserably within the smallest of a series of nested boxes. This logo is so effective because it literally depicts a symbolic process by which this girl remains isolated and hermetically sealed within a mental maze. How much the maze is an internal construction versus an external constriction is unclear. This very ambiguity amplifies the hopeless and helpless state the girl has reached. For even if the girl breaks through one layer of defense, there are so many left to tackle. And so with eating disorders, where layer after layer of physical, emotional, social and cultural issues exist.

and brains. Many pioneers, such as Daniel Stern, call out for a language of intersubjectivity, which I believe can be partly answered by nonlinear science. Chapter 8 tackles fractals in the self–other dimension of psychological complexity. Because fractal boundaries are paradoxical with infinitely enfolded detail, they possess an outside that is readily discernible on the inside and an inside replicated over and over on the outside. This helps to model complex, intersubjective fields of interpenetration between self and other. Fractals contribute to understanding how self-similar resonances exist as multiply linked dynamics, from subcortical, physiological, implicit levels to cortical, emotional, and symbolic levels.

As Sabina's psychotherapist, I held her symptoms partly through a boundary "transgression" by which I remained "blind" to my role in perpetuating the crisis. Ultimately my ability to make my own unconscious conscious, as well as to see my countertransferential role in the drama paved the way for Sabina to do the very same. Fractal patterns are not only self-similar but also self-referential. Self-reference is a broad quality of the universe that implicates the *observer in the observed*.

In much the same way that Oedipus self-referentially enacted the Oracle's predicted fate, so did I in the case of Sabina. Only after becoming fully aware of the true nature of my entwinement with Sabina could resolution of these dynamics proceed. There is self-similarity in the resonances and expanding consciousness between us, as each of us moved from the implicit to the explicit, from unconscious to conscious levels, from enactment to symbolization.

Within contemporary psychoanalytic thought, Stephen Mitchell (1997) speaks of "bootstrapping" when therapists get caught in the very dynamics they attempt to step apart from and analyze. The bootstrapping problem, part of the more general problem of "repetition compulsion," constitutes a central dilemma for psychotherapists. In Chapter 8, I show how nonlinear science affords some fresh tools to address these issues. A totally relational perspective has the disadvantage of getting trapped in the infinite regress of two subjectivities. With nothing to privilege the reality of therapist over patient, there is no recourse to find the "real" truth. One advantage of a nonlinear scientific paradigm, anticipated by Levenson (1983), is its grounding in "objectively" discernible fractal patterns that transcend the particulars of space, time and even subjectivity.

In Chapter 8, I offer the notion of "interobjectivity" to get at truth about the external world as intersubjectively perceived. The notion of interobjectivity segues into Chapter 9, which examines fractal dynamics in patterns of fate. An important example of self-similar interpenetration between self and world is synchronicity, the occurrence of meaningful coincidences (see Jung, 1973). This final chapter models synchronistic events in light of open, paradoxically entwined boundaries, by which "inner world" and "outer world" events get mixed up.

The case of Sabina reveals a minor synchronicity when circumstances took a curious turn that played upon her fears, yet seemed custom designed to teach this young woman a critical lesson. Upon feeling mistrustful of her psychiatrist and deciding to check him up on the Internet, Sabina jumped to the erroneous conclusion that he was aiding and abetting sexual predators. The truth was just the opposite – he was the psychiatrist hired for the defense by the victims. Within therapy, we later made important meaning out of this event as a "sign" from the universe that Sabina needed to slow down and stop running in order to ease traumatic residues from the past and recognize the support, caring and help available in her present surroundings.

When examining the topic of synchronicity, it is important to make a distinction between authentically uncanny coincidences of "true synchronicity" from overinterpreted or misperceived faulty pattern recognition born of the expectation or desire to see patterns where there are none. While Sabina's case can be interpreted both ways, two factors mitigate against this. First, the cosmic irony of this course of events was evident to both of us, not just to Sabina. Second, the event itself proved a powerful bifurcation, or point of sudden change, where Sabina's emotional or cognitive style suddenly self-organized. In the years since this event, I have not witnessed Sabina reacting to frightening events or unpleasant information by running away or avoiding information. Quite the opposite: she has been very careful. That this change reached deep unconscious levels is confirmed by the dramatic shift in manifest content of Sabina's dreams: rather than running away from scary objects, she now approaches them.

For psychotherapists and patients alike, the authentic experience of synchronistic events can evoke spiritual resonances in the awe and thirst to know the genesis of such patterns and to understand seemingly inexplicable, uncanny events of everyday life. This includes the certainty of uncertainty as well as unexpected resonances between inner and outer realms. In order to explore these themes further, I return to the mythological origins of the very word "psyche" in the ancient Greek myth of Psyche.

Viewed from a contemporary neurobiological perspective, the tale of Psyche and Eros illuminates the foundation in us all of fractal boundaries between self, world and other, which are dynamic, fluid and eternally mysterious, yet ordered and infinitely and infinitesimally detailed. Fractal consciousness helps us to find ourselves in others, while understanding synchronicity as a natural part of everyday existence, including the occasional "magic" of psychotherapy when the universe continually lets slip the pattern of the whole in both the rending and mending of its parts.

Chapter 2

The certainty of uncertainty

Knowledge is proud because She knows so much.
Wisdom is humble because She understands so little.

Old British saying

As far as the laws of mathematics refer to reality, they are not certain, and as far as they are certain, they do not refer to reality.

Albert Einstein

I would like to beg you dear Sir, as well as I can, to have patience with everything unresolved in your heart and to try to love the questions themselves as if they were locked rooms or books written in a very foreign language. Don't search for the answers, which could not be given to you now, because you would not be able to live them. And the point is to live everything. Live the questions now. Perhaps then, someday far in the future, you will gradually, without even noticing it, live your way into the answer.

Rainer Maria Rilke

Rita entered therapy for the first time, tense and apprehensive, having avoided the process for years. Everyone told her it would be a good idea. She had turned the possibility over a thousand times in her mind. Finally she hit a point so low she could no longer tuck away her distress. Now this young woman sat in my office, anguish gushing through every word, feeling no choice but to share her deepest intimacies with a stranger. After spilling out a flood of information, Rita turned her previously averted gaze to look me straight in the eyes: "Tell me, doctor, do you really think therapy can help? What will it be like? How long will it take?"

How many first-time patients like Rita do we encounter? How do therapists respond to questions whose answers cannot be precisely known? Do we all taste the same hollow edge of dread when faced with this task? How often do we tell the truth about natural ambiguity? When do we fudge with imprecise answers of our own? Who do we service by covering up – our patients or ourselves?

Pressures "to know" on therapists are enormous. They bombard us from all directions. Managed health panels demand transparency: What is the *exact problem*? What *specific methods* are planned? What *concrete outcomes* are expected? *Precisely how many* sessions will be needed? Some proponents of evidence based treatment even question whether open-ended therapies like psychoanalysis are ethical. Meanwhile patients like Rita abound. When feeling desperate, stuck, fragmented or emotionally lost, deep security rests in visions of an all-seeing, all-knowing Other.

Pressures towards certainty likewise compel therapists from the inside. As caring people, we set high standards for ourselves. We want to be effective as help-givers. Because our profession was spawned within the more general culture of the "expert authority," such feelings readily translate into internal urgency to diagnose quickly; produce a surefire treatment plan; deliver rapid results. We may cite statistics or answers based on working with similar patients. But normative statistics used traditionally in the social sciences do not work for the complex phenomena they attempt to capture. The art of psychotherapy rests not in central tendencies but at the extremes, in statistical tails where *differences* and unique events matter.

Most therapists begin our training knowing that we do not know. We elevate our mentors for the knowledge they appear to possess. We hope that with a little talent and lots of luck, eventually we too will ascend to similar heights. But what does it mean to arrive? Do we reach a safe professional plateau or keep ascending an endless series of challenges, blocks, risks, and openings? If the latter, what does it mean to become an expert? Does clinical competence surround certain knowledge or the maintenance of an open, flexible stance?

These choices are likely not mutually exclusive. Clinical competence comes out of accruing knowledge from books and experience *in service of* maintaining an open, flexible, relational stance. Both are the necessary ingredients. Both enable us to use both left- and right-brain skills to embrace the full complexity of the clinical encounter. After twenty-odd years of voracious study and practice, my professional doubts are *still* with me. They have not so much diminished as changed form, grown more multifaceted, pervasive and nuanced. Happily, feelings of uncertainty no longer automatically signal my deficiencies to me. I now readily accept them as part of the work, harboring no grand illusions about their disappearance. Paradoxically my certainty about uncertainty leads me to feel more secure as a clinician. No matter how experienced I become, no matter what my talent level, contemporary nonlinear science assures me that not-knowing will continue to punctuate, penetrate, hound, if not haunt my work.

This chapter concerns what can and cannot be known with certainty within psychotherapy in light of nonlinear science. I present the case of Rita to illustrate how not-knowing in patients and therapists alike can be pivotal towards deep transformation, representing both full engagement with another as well as the hero's journey into and out of darkness. Then I segue to a brief, developmental history of Western science, where a broad sea change has churned for over a century. The solid stance of predictability and certainty arising from the classical, Newtonian paradigm has dissolved into waves of indeterminacy characteristic of quantum physics and postmodern thought.

Next the chapter turns to chaos theory to bring uncertainty to the macroscopic level of everyday life. Whereas traditional Western thinking associates full understanding of a system with capacities to predict and control future behavior, findings from the new sciences require much more humility. In highly nonlinear realms characteristic of change points, complete knowledge about a complex system's current state does not grant capabilities for long-range prediction or control.

Yet the picture is mixed, for the signature of chaos includes the strange juxtaposition of uncertainty at the local level with certainty at the global one, where scientists can detect broad outlines of what is possible. Certainty lies partially in the scale of the beholder's eye. As clinicians, we do well to keep our eye on the big scale, while stealing sideways glances at local details. Only by patiently culling consciousness to a still, open point can each moment provide maximum grist for the mill. By lunging towards what cannot be known or by grabbing too tightly upon a single version of "the facts," even the best of intentions carries danger either of grinding the mill or ignoring the whole.

Fertile darkness

The minute that Rita, a 22-year-old Southerner, entered my office, my head began to swirl.

Wow! What's happening? What's all this darkness? So many layers of opacity. So deep, such movement . . . so quiet, something static. Reminds me of the scary feeling before a storm? I can almost smell it coming.

Rita was dressed in a creation of her own making, swathed in layers of stunning colors. Some materials were draped; others stuck out; some were tucked in. It was hard to keep track of all the layers dancing, hiding, revealing, shielding, wrapping Rita in mystery, teasing the eye. Around and around, my eyes followed the paths of cloth, until I could not take the visual journey any longer. I felt almost dizzy and had to look away. But just for a moment. Then I had to look back again. Throughout the session, I found my eyes shuttling back and forth between outer and inner layers.

Rita was raised by a stoic, depressed, chronically tired mother who methodically but robotically held herself together, going through the motions of life.

Father and mother contrasted like day and night. Rita's father, a military man, was bright and shining. He hung high in the family. Like the medals he wore, he towered above Rita and her downtrodden mother. More engaged with career than family, dad was absent much of the time.

For as long as her episodic memory coiled backwards, Rita possessed "just enough" to make due – enough clothes to be presentable, enough food not to whine, enough toys to be placated. To the degree Rita's physical needs were met, her emotional needs were "missed." Rita's mother was unable to tune into her own self, much less anybody else's. Rita's father did not seem to try. There were no brothers or sisters in whom to take refuge. Changing homes every year or two left few opportunities to cultivate friends. In time, Rita stopped making the effort.

Instead, blessed with a rich fantasy life, Rita retreated within her own mind. She huddled deep within a rickety inner shelter cobbled mostly out of thin air. In this frozen place of aloneness, Rita left her emotions outside this shelter, keeping feelings at a distance partly with an incredibly fertile imagination. Rita poured everything she might-have-felt-but-did-not-dare into mythic scripts concocted for her stuffed animals. Night after night Rita animated and launched these furry companions on epic journeys, forcing them to rally their courage, mobilize resources and discover helpmates, while facing impossible challenges, often hovering near-death (see Figure 2.1).

After barely making it through college, Rita now came to therapy to figure her self and her future out. As our work progressed, Rita slowly and steadily warmed in the heat and easy humor of our sessions. As Rita expanded, she began to take refuge in therapy. She discovered feelings that always had been there, but never had been named or expressed. However unpleasant these feelings were, at first, just to name and share them helped to thaw her psyche. As we huddled together in the safety of my empathy, Rita was able to study how her stories and words affected me. She affixed to tiny flexes and contractions in the muscles of my face. Through bonds of our mutual gaze, with waves of feeling shuttling back and forth, moving like threads of connection, all too often, I watched Rita watch me lament.

Her isolation is so poignant. My heart aches ... I'm throbbing inside. How she pulls at my breast; how she sucks at my attention like a vortex. I hang onto every word. Rita hangs onto every grimace on my face, every smile. Every twitch a lifeline. Can these tiny threads hold up in the storm to come?

In my own fascination with Rita's fascination, I felt the thrill of budding connection. In my own countertransference, I recognized a connection that never-was-but-might-have-been when I was a child held far away from my own mother's withheld breast. Years after my mother's death, inner work during

Figure 2.1 Fool's paradise.

Psychologically when dissociation is the driving force, fantasy can serve as a retreat from reality. And so the popularity of stories such as James Thurber's *The Secret Life of Walter Mitty*, where the internal motion of fantasy becomes a substitute for external action or real change. On the other hand, dissociation is also linked to increased creativity in artists and non-artists alike (e.g., Watson, 2001). When fantasy is fully harnessed through outer expression and discipline, it is channeled through the body and brought out into the world where it serves as a portal into reality rather than as a barrier from it.

When you first looked at this cartoon, how did you interpret its meaning? My intent was to portray defensive withdrawal from reality: instead of attending to the mounds of work in front of him, this man fantasizes about castles in the air. But the first person I showed the drawing to, another psychologist, viewed the cartoon in a very different light, as "making lemonade out of lemons," and so interpreting the potentiality rather than the defenses within this man's imagination.

Concerning the role of imagination in art, almost anything goes. By contrast, science is more rule-bound, "forcing imagination into a strait jacket," as physicist and artist Richard Feynman put it (personal communication). I maintain that the role of imagination is central within psychotherapy, which is an inherently creative enterprise. We may be effective as healers only when sitting right at that edge between science and art.

psychotherapy seemed to bring my mother back to life, leaving me with an intensity of feeling and empathy towards her that far exceeded what I had experienced in the flesh.

And now Rita was "feeling felt" for the first time, as psychiatrist Daniel Siegel might say. As psychotherapy proceeded, she became ever more responsive to my increasing responsiveness to her. Initially this felt good to us both. But as Rita continued to bring all of her feelings directly into the shelter of our work, the atmosphere shifted. The process stopped feeling so good. As Rita's inner life gained painful poignancy she paid less attention to my reactions and more to what she actually felt. As Rita thawed emotionally, her internal barometer shot from a state of frozen, through a warmed transition period, to a red-hot zone that reached an intensity threatening to break the very gauge itself.

After two years of our work, Rita's pain became excoriating, her emotions too much to bear. Rita became suicidal. All the richness of her inner life stormed the rickety shelter of her previous isolation, breaking it into pieces, fragmenting her, leaving her naked, vulnerable, throbbing. During this period, Rita brought in sexualized transference dreams, such as one dream where she sucked my dry breasts, followed by another where her bed was infested with spiders that circled her, wrapping her tightly in a silk cocoon.

Rita had a history of dangerous impulses. Starting in high school and increasingly in college, she cocooned herself with just enough drugs to self-medicate without developing an addiction. Passively self-destructive when "altered," she would hop into cars with strangers or walk a wee bit too close to a cliff's edge. Throughout her flirtations with danger, Rita remained lucky. Despite crossing over the line in fantasy, she had never crossed this line in real life – at least not yet.

During our psychotherapy, Rita was in a stage of refusing drugs. Her sobriety was one of her few sources of pride. Rita had read Kay Jamison's (1996) *Touched with fire: Manic-depressive illness and the artistic temperament*, documenting anecdotes and statistics about creative musicians and poets who suffered from mood disorders. Identified with their capacity for subtly nuanced feeling, Rita adamantly turned away from the potential path of psychotropic medication.

In my own life when facing the great Unknown, reflexively I reach inwards for vision and inspiration. Perhaps following suit, I have helped to launch many a patient onto sometimes halcyon, often turbulent, seas of self-expression (see Figure 2.2).

Given Rita's fabulous fantasy life and my own predilections towards creative self-expression, it is not surprising that Rita began drifting towards poetic dimensions of her pain. For months to come, as Rita slid emotionally, she metaphorically sliced herself on the infinitely thin, razor's edge where agony flows into ecstasy and back out again. Together we hovered in what truly felt like the edge of chaos. Later I would conceive of this period as a phase transition or bifurcation between two sets of state space – a lower,

Figure 2.2 Map of Islandia by Ortelius.

Contrary to popular belief, people during Columbus' times were less afraid of sailing off the edge of the earth than they were of encountering strange marine life. The medieval vision of uncharted waters was frequently inhabited by mythological monsters such as those that appear in this fragment of Ortelius' map, fashioned in 1570. Here we see a confluence between the technical sense of chaos in turbulent ocean waters and chaos in the metaphorical sense of the great unknown. Within mythology the world over, dragons represent chaos, though as other drawings in this chapter indicate, different cultures maintain different relationships between forces of chaos and order.

more primitive, dysregulated set and a higher, more complexly organized one. While hanging out in this agonizing transition phase between, at times Rita seemed totally out of control; at other times she seemed beautifully under control. More and more rapidly, she alternated between the two states.

Science box 2.1   Bifurcation

In dynamical systems, a bifurcation or sudden change occurs when a critical threshold is reached in underlying variables giving rise to a different attractor pattern (Figure 2.3). The capacity to model sharp discontinuities and irregularity in change is one strong advantage to nonlinear science. Researcher Scott Kelso

continued

(1995) is a pioneering psychological researcher who applies non-linear concepts to motor coordination. During normal locomotion in a horse, Kelso studied the control parameter of speed during transitions from a trot to a canter. At the phase transition zone between these two gaits, Kelso found evidence for both patterns mixed together, chaotically. The kind of rapid oscillation Rita demonstrated on the threshold of change is a pattern every clinician and patient knows, perhaps giving rise to the clinical cliché: "one step forward, two steps backward." One insight that nonlinear dynamics has to contribute to the clinician is the importance of attending to transition zones, as this is where lots of information is available and much of the action occurs. Many people function quite well once securely ensconced within a structured environment. The more emotionally dysregulated an individual is, the greater the likelihood problems will manifest in the spaces between activities.

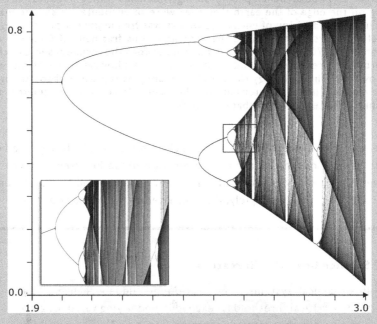

Figure 2.3 Bifurcation diagram.

Courtesy of Nicolas Desprez

During this middle phase of treatment, Rita read tales of tragic creators, like Dylan Thomas and Virginia Woolf. She was especially drawn to the verses of Sylvia Plath, including one written as she approached her own suicide. Called "Edge," a young woman is depicted as "perfected" by death. She wears a flowing white toga and a "smile of accomplishment," lying in her casket flanked by two dead children. Coiled at her side like white serpents, the children fold back into her body like rose petals.

Inspired by such verse, Rita's imagination became fertile with images of her own death and its grandeur. She listened to grunge rockers romanticize suicide, while pondering the "perfection" of her own demise. Given that Rita's mother actually did commit suicide in the face of irreversible illness, multigenerational strings of Fate tugged. Rita had little choice but to stare at her own cold, silent babies longing to fold back into the corpse. How could Rita not question the value of life itself? Would she ever peel back the dead layers to flower a new self? Who knew? But one thing was clear – a shift towards life could take root only in soil of our relatedness.

Oh my God! Rita is utterly obsessed with death. Such blackness to her thoughts. The air is so thick. I can hardly breathe. Is she safe? Can she hold on? Will the threads of trust between us hold? Something feels so fragile. Yet something else so strong. Am I strong enough? Am I too much? What is this unnamable thing? Can I trust it? Are we in too far? Can I get out? No . . . mustn't leave. Must calm my own frantic feelings. Must stop my own impulses to flee, my need to control, to get things under control. . . Don't alter a thing . . . Just wait . . . Hold on . . . Trust those tiny rays of hope.

Drenched in torrents of my own emotion and fragmented states, I swam mostly by instinct, the logic and reason of my left-brain "left behind" on dry shores. Amidst so much impulsivity with nowhere to go, a palpable sense of danger grew, yet never became so acute as to mandate action. I knew I could not predict the result of the various pushes and pulls on Rita's fluid psyche. I could not make her safe. Nor could I control what would happen next. Here was chaos theory in action within such a clear separation between understanding versus prediction and control.

I prayed the cords/chords of mutual caring were blending/binding enough to hold her/us together. I worried. I worried a lot. As the days drifted into weeks, honestly, part of me just wanted relief. I wanted to rein in all the emotion, both Rita's and my own. I wanted to eliminate all risk. I wanted to put Rita into some structured environment where I could be *certain* she was safe. This not-knowing stuff was *damned* uncomfortable. I wanted to shut down the storm of Rita's morbid thoughts, so I would not have to entertain my own.

The possibility that Rita might lose all the hard gains we had made felt excruciating. My selfish side resented the heightened sense of responsibility. I did not want to have to be so bloody careful. I resented monitoring my answering machine like a hawk. I was sick of pondering implications of every word. I wanted to be free of considering consequences for every decision. To hell with documenting all the gory details! Torrents of my own emotion watered tiny tendrils of doubt that threatened to creep over the threshold of my own inner sanctuary.

Maybe I'm a lousy therapist. If I really were doing things right, we wouldn't be in this mess. Am I missing something? Is there a simple solution? Something I'm not seeing? Some way back from this edge? Some less risky path? One not so filled with suffering and pain?

As these dark fears tried to take root, I also recognized the open boundaries between Rita and myself. I began to envision my own psyche as the necessary, though not sufficient, foundation for Rita's inner sanctuary. I understood my own feelings to be partly hers. I felt the urgency of fortifying my own foundation, for the survival of us both. In time, I saw my primary challenge as not the outer question of what to do or how to change courses, but the inner challenge of holding down my own being, my torrent of feelings with equanimity, grace and stillness.

In response to this inner mandate I used every resource I could seize. I sought the support of colleagues. I redoubled my own creative pursuits. I scrambled to do yoga, dance, and draw away Rita's pain on the canvas of my life, diffusing the toxins and attempting to reconnect with my own sources of joy (see Figure 2.4).

An understanding of nonlinear science also helped a great deal. The theory strengthened my sense of necessity, my resolve to hold up in the face of so much uncertainty and unpredictability. Nonlinear science proved an abstract anchor to moor my understanding of the instabilities and disorder inevitable at the threshold of change.

However shaky I sometimes felt, ultimately the therapy proved "good enough" to harbor Rita's growing sense of aliveness. Thankfully I met the challenges of containment partly by becoming secure enough in my insecurity intuitively to sense the big picture. In my best moments I knew that everything about this dark and stormy sea journey was just as it needed to be. In retrospect I believe the opaque, fertile state of not-knowing proved to be *the* most critical bond that existed between us – even if at times, I carried most of the hope.

I can mark Rita's evolution by the progression of poems drawing her interest. An early one of Emily Dickinson's, "No. 650," captured the paradox of putting into words a nameless feeling without clear boundaries of origin or end.

Figure 2.4 Yoga of psychotherapy.

Photo by Irina Kerdman

One of the values of yoga as a mind/body adjunct to psychotherapy is its capacity at a cellular level to teach non-reactivity in the face of pain. When a beginner attempts poses such as this, the body presents barriers and muscles or joints often ache. How to keep emotional equanimity in the face of these challenges is an important emotional goal. How to rein in the fury at the teacher for keeping students in a pose too long or contempt towards self for not being able to do something. Over time, yoga students learn not to direct a pinpoint focus towards pain. Instead, they make tiny micro-adjustments to their bodies allowing greater comfort. Eventually, even in really difficult poses, yogis retain calm and diffuse concentration, not unlike the evenly hovering attention considered ideal for therapists.

Pain – has an Element of Blank –
It cannot recollect
When it begun – or if there were
A time when it was not –

It has no Future – but itself –
Its Infinite contain
Its Past – enlightened to perceive
New Periods – of Pain.

A definite turning point came with Rita's delivery of Dickinson's poem "No. 599":

There is as pain – so utter –
It swallows substance up –
Then covers the Abyss with Trance –
So Memory can step
Around – across – upon it –
As one within a Swoon –
Goes safely – where an open eye –
Would drop Him – Bone by Bone.

As Rita came back to the surface from nearly drowning in her own torrents of emotion, she increasingly turned to art as a means of fortifying her psyche with words (see Figure 2.5). Professionally Rita began to edit the literary

Figure 2.5 Chaos on a dancing star.

Courtesy of Tobi Zausner

The artist of this painting, Tobi Zausner, also a psychologist, has intimate familiarity with the role that physical illness can play in creativity, and creativity can play in healing. Diagnosed with cancer many years ago, she turned to her art for inspiration. While a controversial topic how much suffering or psychopathology facilitates the artistic process, it is well known that many artists suffered the loss of a parent during childhood. Zausner (2006) has converted her insight about the role of physical illness in creativity into a book, called "*When walls become doorways.*"

works of others. Her good instincts for tearing down and resurrecting their verbal constructions laid foundations for her own continued healing.

Eventually Rita wrote plays of her own. As if to revisit and revise her early childhood play, Rita brought her stuffed animals to life in more mature, human form, while animating ever-deeper layers of her self in the process. One day about nine years after our work had begun, Rita brought in a review of her new play to share. Both Rita and I simultaneously recognized her psychotherapy was complete.

The heroine's journey

The pivotal point in Rita's therapy involved her willingness to descend into the deep black chasm of the unknown, plus my capacity to tolerate and contain Rita's emotions as well as my own. Where Rita submerged in her own dark, scary depths is precisely where she merged with me and the challenges I faced emotionally, each of us shading into and reflecting the other. This journey into darkness was the vehicle for Rita's re-emergence into lighter places (see Figure 2.6).

This clinical tale represents Allan Schore's (1999, 2003a, 2003b) regulation theory in action, at that pivotal point where regulation through relatedness gives way to a fledgling capacity for regulation by self. The tale also illustrates the extreme role doubt sometimes plays upon inner and outer stages of transformation. To descend with Rita into the unknown was to embrace the inner, feminine equivalent of the outer, hero's journey, whose stages of separation, initiation and return were initially popularized by Joseph Campbell (1949/ 1973) and then embraced by Carl Jung to define three stages of individuation, the process by which we articulate our selves:

1   Separation from known beliefs, teachings and authority figures.
2   Initiation into unknown, unknowable depths to face, fight and befriend inner demons.
3   Return to a more fully conscious, articulated sense of self (see Figure 2.7).

Rita's descent felt both mythic and inevitable. Her journey, like the fruits of chaos theory itself, represented a paradoxical juxtaposition of the unknown with the known. Rita's willingness to risk the dangers of her unknown, deep emotional self emerged out of feeling known in the first place. This was the cognitive part of our empathic connection: both of us knew exactly *what* Rita felt, *why* she felt it, plus the narrative thread of *how* her current experiences linked with early childhood precedents.

At the same time, the unknown part of the empathic connection was purely emotional: both of us felt varying degrees of fear, doubt, helplessness and uncertainty about what all this meant for the future. *All the cognitive*

Figure 2.6 Chinese dragon.

In Chinese art and mythology, the dragon is an important symbol of chaos. Unlike most Occidental myths, where the dragon embodies evil and must be slaughtered in order that civilized order may progress, Oriental mythology tends to portray a more harmonious relationship between chaos and order (e.g., Hayles, 1990). Dragons often live in the clouds where they create thunder with their movements and rain. Sometimes dragons like this Chinese one, guard a beautiful pearl, a marvelous treasure for whatever mortal might succeed in tricking or wresting it from the dragon's clutches.

understanding in the world couldn't lessen the pain or do away with the ambiguity of an unknown future. No sliver of knowledge guaranteed Rita's survival or erased the risks that not-knowing entailed during Rita's dark journey towards wholeness.

The two aspects of Rita's therapy – the cognitive, narrative figure and the implicit, emotional ground – represented mind to mind, brain to brain connections (see Schore, 1999, 2003a, 2003b). While an intact, left-brain narrative was important as a cognitive anchor for our empathic connection, the real action of the therapy involved reconnecting with the functioning of the right-brain, nonverbal, relational, emotional side of Rita's brain, whose operation previously had been dissociated from the whole. To work with this side of the brain is not to possess certain, word-based knowledge readily put

Figure 2.7 Western hero slaying the dragon.

In the hero's journey, we find the classic image of chaos represented as a dragon. In contrast to Eastern mythology where forces of chaos and order often work together, as mentioned Western mythology tends to pit one against the other. Often times the hero rescues the damsel from distress by defeating the dragon. We will revisit this theme again in Chapter 6 in the Oedipus story, interpreted by Jung more symbolically as killing the father in order to harvest the mother's bountiful fruits of the unconscious.

into action. The process is like swimming in an implicit soup, glimpsing and feeling one's way, dipping in and out of flotsam, amid moments of clarity and glimpses of safety.

The rapid shifts of emotion experienced both by Rita and myself were characterized by chaos, both metaphorically and technically. From a scientific point of view, the flux of emotion itself tends to be more or less nonlinear, especially compared to the logic of thought (e.g., Delignières et al., 2004). The flow of dysregulated emotion is even more chaotic than the sequence of regulated emotion, due to abrupt, unpredictable transitions.

Deep psychological change is inherently a nonlinear affair. Chapter 3 focuses on these processes of self-organization at the edge of chaos in service of greater complexity. The current chapter concentrates more on chaotic bases for self-organized change. One way to understand the emotional chaos in the case of Rita was as an intermediate transitional state between one mode of underlying organization and another. Phase transitions between one state and the next are often inherently chaotic (see Kelso, 1995). The hallmark of this kind of phase transition is a chaotic mixing of elements from both states.

As psychoanalyst Stuart Pizer (1998) illustrates eloquently, we see this kind of transitional chaos often during psychotherapy, especially once trust has established. Ironically patients progress far enough to feel as if they are moving backwards. They enter a kind of no-man's land where they have lost their previous defensive organization, and yet a new psychological organization is not yet firmly in place. This can leave people feeling extremely vulnerable and frightened. As with Rita, this transitional zone is often characterized by rapid shifts back and forth between two different internal organizations, whether in the form of old versus new defenses, defensive vs. expressive organization, or dysregulated versus regulated emotional and/or behavioral states.

Patients often express the yearning to return to the safety of old, familiar ways, combined with the perception of having gone "too far" to return successfully. The only choice is to wait out this horrific transition period. In the meantime, having a grasp of nonlinear theory provides a left-brain anchor to allow for right-brain, nonlinear shifts, both in therapist and patient alike.

The role of the therapist

In Freud's original model, at least in theory, the psychoanalyst was steeped in narrative clarity, possessing certain knowledge about interrelationships between a patient's past, present, and future. Armed with universal, psychosexual stages of development plus the Oedipus story as a mythic blueprint, early psychoanalysts sat out of sight of patients, who lay prone on the couch. Classical psychoanalysts enjoyed a bird's eye view, both literally and symbolically, hovering in body and mind in authoritative heights of neutrality and objectivity.

This left-brained, logical model of the therapist as "expert authority" fits nicely into the hierarchical structure of the medical model in which psychoanalysis was conceived. The model also fits well with the hierarchical, father/son struggles of the Oedipus story, as we shall examine in the middle chapters. At its extreme the model becomes authoritarian, if therapists adopt a rigid posture of certainty. Within psychotherapy, trouble often brews in the form of definitive claims of knowing the contents of a patient's unconscious better than the patient does herself. For a therapist to make assertions about matters outside of patient awareness, where not even vague emotional resonances exist, is to risk invalidating that person's experience, sense of autonomy, and/or feeling of agency.

In the history of psychotherapy, a number of therapeutic schools arose in rebellion to the authoritarian aspect of Freud's model. Carl Roger's client-centered therapy promoted a nondirective, active listening stance to replace an authoritarian, telling one. Other humanistic approaches, such as Gestalt, stressed authentic contact between equals. Over the past several decades contemporary psychoanalysts, such as Stephen Mitchell, have dethroned the therapist as expert authority by emphasizing a collaborative stance of open dialogue and mutual investigation. In *The art of unknowing*, New York psychoanalyst Stephen Kurtz (1989) likens psychotherapy to listening to a poem with multiple interpretations that cannot be immediately analyzed or understood.

Limits to logic and certainty

Trends in the history of psychoanalysis have moved from authoritarian models of therapist certainty based on universal, invariant one-person assumptions about development and change to more flexible, relational bases for help-giving based on two-person, intersubjective models and increasing recognition of the limitations of fixed assumptions. An interesting parallel exists culturally as Western science has also matured from its infancy to face clear limits on what can be known and controlled in nature (see Marks-Tarlow, 2003). Not just in practice, but also in theory, the naive, reductionist framework many held of strict determinism – of a future thoroughly predictable and controllable based on objectively understanding the present and past – appears an early illusion of a fledgling science.

Science box 2.2 A clockwork universe

Scientists such as Roger Bacon and René Descartes harnessed their open curiosity about the workings of nature into a formal dialogue known as the empirical method, based on close observation combined with hypothesis formulation and testing. Ironically, out of Descartes' open, philosophical stance emerged what later became a set of calcified assumptions:

- The more we can separate nature's workings into component parts, the more knowledge we will possess about nature's operations.
- The more underlying formulas we possess, including critical

continued

> variables and exact starting positions for each, the greater our capability to accurately and precisely predict nature's future workings.
> * The better we get at predicting nature, the more control we will gain over her course.
>
> This mechanistic vision of a "clockwork" universe emanated from linear thinking within a reductionistic, deterministic framework. These assumptions imply an authoritarian stance with an agenda to use science, whose blueprint for order depended upon the destruction of chaos.

Until recently within Western science, assumptions of absolute knowledge and logical bases for certainty seemed fail proof. For centuries, as scientific knowledge accrued, so did our capacity for certainty, prediction, and control. Wondrous technology emerged to extend the senses, enhance mobility, increase communication, and lighten our physical toil. All proceeded beautifully until the twentieth century when strange things began to happen. After much of the visible world had been well categorized, once researchers began fixing their sights on abstract realms related to cosmic or microscopic extremes, the bedrock of certainty started to crumble at the edges.

Science box 2.3 The end of certainty

When Einstein's theory of general relativity dissolved the absolute frame of reference of classical Newtonian physics, hopes for an immutable, objective framework for truth became shaky, and the precise stance of observers in nature began to make all the difference. Einstein's perspective on relativity seeped into psychotherapy through psychoanalyst Franz Alexander, a seminal figure in bringing psychoanalysis to the United States. Alexander rejected the metaphor of therapist as a "blank screen" (Schwartz, 1999). Rather then function as a passive, neutral, objective recipient of the projection of unconscious content by patients, Alexander argued for the therapist as an actively involved subject, who invariably influences the course of affairs. The idea of the therapist as a *participant-observer* was also prevalent in Harry Stack Sullivan's Interpersonal School, with a more contemporary variation found in John Fiscalini's (2004) *Coparticipatory psychoanalysis*.

Einstein's cosmology carried implications for the microscopic realm, and the burgeoning field of quantum mechanics dethroned scientific certainty still further. Werner Heisenberg was an early, foundational quantum physicist who demonstrated that when measuring a particle's properties, it was fundamentally impossible to achieve precision beyond a certain level. For example, to know the position of a subatomic particle precisely, we must give up knowing its precise momentum, and vice versa; to know its momentum, we must give up knowing its precise position. When multiplied together, position and momentum will exceed Heisenberg's number.

This limit to certainty in knowing a particle's properties is called Heisenberg's Uncertainty Principle. A particle's position and speed are "yoked" qualities, so that the more we know about position, the less we know speed, and vice versa. This is not intuitively obvious and can appear paradoxical and confusing to most people. To knock ordinary logic on the head further, the "wave-particle duality" revealed by the double slit experiment shakes our Boolean demands for either/or formulations – when measured in one particular experimental set-up, light behaves like a particle (or tiny billiard ball), whereas when measured in a slightly different way, light behaves more like waves in the ocean. The both/and qualities of light open the way for scientific models of mystical thought (see Capra, 1975; Zukav, 1979) as well as for fuzzy logic (Kosko, 1994) and the embrace of paradox pervasive in this book.

The quantum science of microscopic indeterminacy brought a statistical view that eroded the scientific capacity for making predictions. In the quantum realm, no matter how much information we possess, we can never know the precise instant a radioactive nucleus will decay. Again we find global certainty coupled

continued

> with local unpredictability. Even though quantum mechanics emerged directly from his work, Einstein, standing with one foot in the classical world and one foot in the world of modern physics, could not accept the outrageous, counterintuitive and disturbing conclusions his fellow physicists were reaching. An oft-quoted phrase reveals Einstein's unshakable faith that "God doesn't play dice with the universe." To this, an esteemed colleague Neils Bohr reputedly quipped, "Quit telling God what to do!"

In physics the solid world of our senses dissolved into a statistical sea of moving particles. In mathematics, problems were formulated that could neither be proved nor disproved. To glimpse a realm beyond the reach of reason was rather shocking. Then a blow came that proved fatal to establishing logical bases for all of mathematics. In the mid nineteenth century, a brilliant, Austrian-born mathematician Kurt Gödel used logic self-referentially to discredit its own use. When Gödel proved that all systems of sufficient complexity ultimately either are inconsistent or incomplete, suddenly logic became a very shaky, leaky container for certain knowledge.

Related conclusions about the limits of logic infiltrate neurobiology today. Whereas early theories of brain development privileged our cognitive capacities, contemporary theories do not. Consider one such early take on the brain – MacLean's triune model (1990) consisting of reptilian, mammalian and uniquely human elements. With each new stage of evolution, MacLean proposed a top-down model of control over the rest of the brain. Autonomic and instinctual responses of the reptilian brain stem were believed superceded by emotional and social aspects of the mammalian limbic system, in turn seen as regulated and controlled by symbolic aspects of the cerebral cortex. Of course exceptions to such neurology have existed always, evident in the work both of Sigmund Freud and William James.

MacLean's model of top-down control is brought to task by contemporary affective neurobiology (e.g., Damasio, 1999; Panksepp, 1998). These theorists dethrone the power of the linear left-brain with its Cartesian logic to dominate and control decision-making and intentional action within the body. With limbic areas of the brain the most centrally and extensively distributed, plus indications of action evident in the brain before conscious awareness (e.g., Libet, 2005), it appears that emotion rather than symbolic thinking, plus unconscious, implicit processes more than conscious, explicit ones, unify mind, body and spirit. The highest levels of neural and psychological integration necessarily involve the interplay between emotion and cognition, cortical and subcortical processes as orchestrated by right-brain processes.

Technical chaos

The current neurobiological emphasis on nonlinear emotional and relational processes comes to fruition in an age when chaos theory spans most of the hard sciences and has been steadily making its way into economics and organizational psychology. Chaos theory, which originated in the 1960s, addresses aspects of the environment previously thought too complex to pick apart with reductionistic means or linear logic. The emergence of chaos theory brings a shift in fundamental uncertainty from cosmic and microscopic levels, to the macroscopic realm of everyday existence in parallel with postmodernism and hermeneutics. Chaos theory clarifies limits to certainty (Barrow, 1999; Smith, 2007) in the understanding and prediction of complex systems. To understand this better, next I retell the story of the discovery of technical chaos as first popularized in James Gleick's (1987) book, *Chaos*. Readers already familiar with this story are welcome to skip to the next section.

Edward Lorenz was a rare breed of meteorologist who used the computer to model weather patterns. After isolating his critical variables, Lorenz ran a corresponding set of differential equations. Rather than solving such equations once and definitively as had been customary, Lorenz used a new method called iteration. When iteration is in use, an initial starting value for all variables is set, and then the equations are run again and again. With each new go-round, or iteration, the end results of the previous round are used as the new starting positions. When combined with the data crunching power of a computer, iteration is a recursive method that allows for complex simulations composed of thousands, if not millions, of go-rounds. End results are either charted or mapped visually.

Science box 2.4 Iteration

When iteration is in progress, a system's output for some algorithm, process or formula (c in Figure 2.8), is recycled back in as the new input. Iteration is linear when the output is proportionate to the input and nonlinear when the output is disproportionate. In both cases, iteration implies system memory, since the next round always starts over where the last one left off. In this

continued

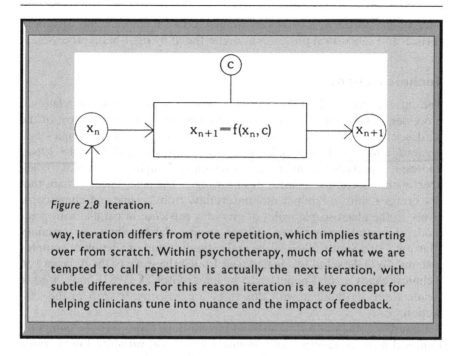

Figure 2.8 Iteration.

way, iteration differs from rote repetition, which implies starting over from scratch. Within psychotherapy, much of what we are tempted to call repetition is actually the next iteration, with subtle differences. For this reason iteration is a key concept for helping clinicians tune into nuance and the impact of feedback.

One day in the middle of a weather simulation, Lorenz left for a short coffee break. When he returned he became interested in rerunning some equations to duplicate previous findings. Much to his surprise, he could not reproduce his results, but instead kept achieving *entirely different* ones. After multiple trials and lots of consideration, Lorenz figured it out. When reinserting his numbers back into the equations, Lorenz had rounded them off slightly. Within a very short period of simulated time, approximating two weeks of "real" weather time, these tiny differences in initial conditions became amplified by positive feedback within his equations. The differences had reached such huge proportions as to yield an entirely new weather pattern that bore no resemblance to the original.

Another researcher might have dismissed the whole event as an unfortunate waste of time. Yet a mark of true genius is the capacity to capitalize on the unexpected. Recall Louis Pasteur's famous saying, "Chance favors the prepared mind." Pasteur embodied his own dictum by recognizing the significance of a mold that killed the bacteria he tried to cultivate. What began as the misfortune of toxic cells that threatened his whole experiment was transformed into Pasteur's good fortune of formulating the germ theory of disease. Although Pasteur had unwittingly come across the world's first antibiotic, penicillin, it took more than a decade for Sir Alexander Fleming to discover penicillin in the year 1928.

The ability to capitalize on chance events is especially important for therapists. Given the nonlinear nature, including fundamental unpredictability, of true change, movement is often triggered by tiny events that occur in wholly unpredictable ways. It might be an off-hand remark or a therapeutic boundary crossed, such as the therapist showing up late. It might be a nonverbal gesture or an aspect of prosody (voice rhythm and intonation). Because therapeutic change is rarely triggered by well-thought-out interpretations designed for this purpose, we must be ready and honed to capitalize on tiny relational shifts apparent only in the unique appearance of each moment.

Over a century after Pasteur welcomed the serendipity of chance, Lorenz's success also lay in his ability to capitalize on his failure. By recognizing and honoring the nonlinearity that foiled his intentions, Lorenz's seemingly "botched" experiment led him to envision a whole new science of chaos extending far beyond his own narrow field (see Figure 2.9). In decades to follow, technical chaos has infiltrated nearly every important subdiscipline of science – from material science, to medicine, to quantum theory itself.

Chaos theory and its relatives, complexity theory and fractal geometry, have been slow to penetrate the social sciences, and clinical psychology in particular, even though aspects of nonlinear science appeared even before Freud's time. Lorenz followed in the footsteps of a French mathematician named Henri Poincaré, who in the late 1880s created uproar (of academic sorts) by suggesting that the infamous "three-body problem" was insoluble. The three-body problem posed the challenge of using linear methods to

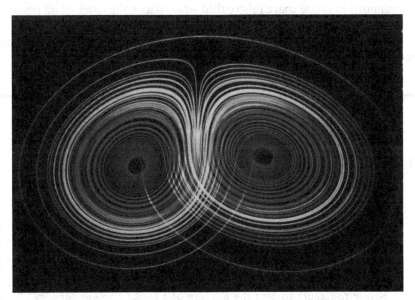

Figure 2.9 Lorenz attractor.

This chaotic attractor was discovered by Lorenz. This is what he might have seen were his numerical figures in visual form.

calculate the precise gravitational effects of three heavenly bodies in inter-action with one another. Whereas the orbits of two bodies in space demon-strate orderly and predictable trajectories, throw a third body into the mix and all chaos breaks loose, figuratively and technically speaking.

With childrearing epithets like "spare the rod and spoil the child" and Victorian society broadly preoccupied with taming disorder, cultural reasons may have contributed to why the detection of chaos literally drove Poincaré mad. Perhaps chaos, an idea whose time was yet to come, was more compat-ible with liberal childrearing and the culture of postmodernism that existed in the 1960s. Whatever the reasons, luckily Lorenz retained his sanity in the face of his discovery. He felt compelled neither to tame the beast nor to toss out the baby with the "noise" in service of preserving and amplifying a clear, orderly signal. In a turn of events that made scientific history, instead Lorenz recognized the value of the noise itself.

Hidden order

The hallmark of chaos is surface behavior that appears random, or without defined pattern. Yet underneath invisible order lurks in the form of strange attractors, whose pattern is revealed abstractly through mathematical analy-sis. An attractor maps the end-state of a system after it runs for a while. Linear systems, like clocks and cogs, move on regular and predictable tracks. When diagrammed in phase space (also called state space), the space of all possible system behavior, linear states form point and cyclic attractors that settle down to one or more points. The end-states of linear paths involve a simple underlying order, often appearing as a point, circle or spiral in phase space.

Science box 2.5 Variety of attractors

The study of system dynamics, or how a system changes over time, began centuries ago with Newton's laws of motion. Attractors map out where dynamical systems wind up over time. Attractors may be diagrammed in phase space, not a literal depic-tion of space and time, but rather an abstract map of all possible system behavior. Attractors may be portrayed as time series that show their step-by-step progression, whether in physical space or as a set of data points. They may likewise be graphed as a power spectrum to plot the portion of a signal's power (energy per unit time) that falls within given frequency bins.

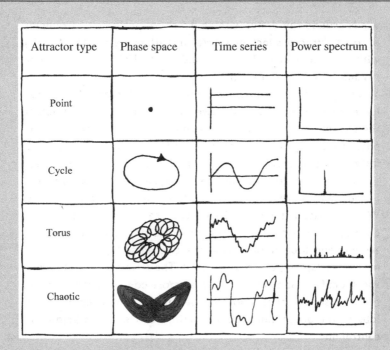

Attractor type	Phase space	Time series	Power spectrum
Point			
Cycle			
Torus			
Chaotic			

Figure 2.10 Variety of attractors.

Adapted from Abraham, Abraham and Shaw, 1990

Figure 2.10 depicts four attractor types in each of three ways.

A *point attractor* is the simplest of all, as it comes to rest at a single point. Imagine a 10 pound block tossed in the air and landing with a plunk. Depicted as a time series, a point attractor goes nowhere and so appears as a flat, horizontal line. With no energy in the system, the power spectrum for a point attractor is empty.

A *cycle attractor* oscillates between two or more states in a regular pattern. With only two states in the cycle attractor above, it appears as a smooth circle in phase space. Imagine a metronome swinging back and forth between two points. Shown as a time series, a cycle attractor with period 2 appears as a smooth sine wave, with a power spectrum that reveals a single frequency.

A *torus attractor* is quasi-periodical, because its trajectory

continued

winds around the donut with an irrational periodicity. Examples of torus attractors include ultradian rhythms (less than 24 hour) within the human body (Lloyd and Rossi, 1994). Because such rhythms do not entrain perfectly, they can remain flexible in adapting to changing circumstances. Despite increased complexity in their time series and power spectrum, we can still detect the two basic phases of their rhythms, corresponding to a slow phase that wraps longitudinally around the donut's hole versus a faster phase that wraps perpendicularly around the donut's core.

A *chaotic attractor* is completely irregular, as illustrated by the Lorenz mask here, which has two lobes like a butterfly's wings. Weather patterns studied by Lorenz are a good example of a chaotic attractor. The trajectory loops any number of times around one lobe until it switches unpredictably to the other, never overlapping or crossing itself. The time series and power spectrum for this attractor are even more complex. For example, the time series reflects no clear periodicity in moving from one lobe to the other, indicated by portions above versus below the central line.

By contrast chaotic systems, like smoke and wind, travel along irregular, nonlinear paths that never settle down to simple order. Instead their terminating sets reveal a complex underlying geometry. From a linear point of view, scientists previously declared turbulent features of nature like smoke or cascading water impossible to model. Before understanding technical chaos, they believed that such complexity arose from highly complicated interactions between huge numbers of variables. Nonlinear science reveals a very different picture. When technical chaos is present, complexity arises instead from as few as three underlying variables driving many local interactions.

When modeling the weather, Lorenz discovered one of many forms of strange attractors. All reveal beautifully complex shapes, usually possessing fractal structure, a topic explored more thoroughly in Chapters 7, 8 and 9. Despite multiple appearances, one common element to all strange attractors is the uniqueness of their paths – no matter how long they keep running, their paths will never repeat exactly or cross themselves even once. This speaks to the uniqueness of each moment, no matter how familiar the circumstances or events, when we are present with ourselves and with our patients.

Science box 2.6 Some strange attractors

All chaotic attractors (also called strange attractors) represent completely unique trajectories. All are characterized by a combination of positive and negative feedback understood concretely like the stretching and folding of dough by a baker. Positive feedback amplifies systems dynamics, stretching the system towards the edges of its containment area, before negative feedback kicks in to make sure the system is damped back down again and refolded within its outer boundaries. All complex systems operate according to a combination of positive and negative feedback. Unstable states occur when positive feedback outweighs the negative feedback term, while stable states occur when negative feedback outweighs the positive feedback term. No matter how far out of phase such trajectories might diverge, eventually they will return arbitrarily closely again, though their convergence in not causally meaningful.

There are a variety of chaotic attractors, other than the Lorenz mask (Figure 2.11): (a) Ueda attractor was discovered by Yoshisuke Ueda in 1961, the very same year of Lorenz's discovery. Ueda's supervising professor did not believe in chaos, and so Ueda was prohibited from publishing his findings until 1971; (b) Two plus two scroll attractor, relevant to engineering applications, such as secure communication and vibration analysis, as well as biometric identification applications, relevant to fingerprint patterns; (c) Hénon attractor, a two-dimensional quadratic map related to complicated trajectories of stars through a galaxy; (d) Two-well Duffing attractor, models chaotic vibrations in mechanical systems; (e) part of a Rössler funnel, which demonstrates more complicated motion than the Rössler band, both contributing to Otto Rössler's passion of constructing a taxonomy of chaotic motion; (f) Rössler band, illustrates the simplest form of continuous chaos, while demonstrating the motion of a Möbius strip with a single twist.

continued

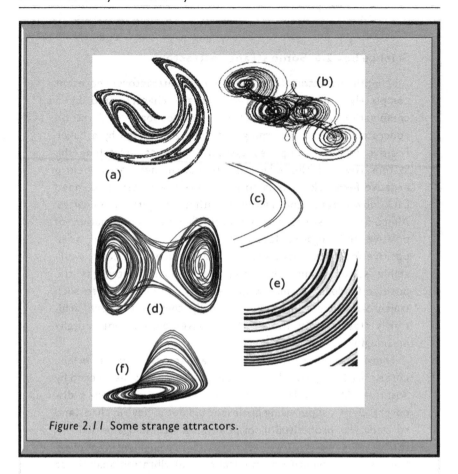

Figure 2.11 Some strange attractors.

The important point is this: it does not take complex underpinnings to produce complexity. Simplicity will due. From a developmental point of view, many parents understand instinctively that it takes the consistent application of some very simple ingredients to help babies and young children develop complex and integrated psyches.

Sensitive dependence

When it comes to highly nonlinear systems, what is more critical than the input of complexity is the use of iteration in combination with feedback. Iteration plus feedback is how nature recycles her procedures and habits, so that critical aspects either expand or contract, multiply or diminish. Iteration plus feedback is the engine by which nature uses simple building blocks to build increasingly complex structures, continually churning the known into the unpredictable.

The quality of unpredictable behavior in chaotic systems produced by iteration and feedback is called sensitive dependence on initial conditions. Sensitive dependence means that the tiniest change in initial conditions causes the system to career off in completely unexpected directions. This was the essence of Lorenz's original discovery, where slight difference in starting numbers shifted long-term system behavior so completely.

Science box 2.7 Sensitivity to initial conditions

This graph is much like what Lorenz might have seen, had his figures been graphed as time series trajectories. Here are the relevant differential equations:

$$dx/dt = s(y - x)$$
$$dy/dt = rx - y - xz$$
$$dz/dt = xy - bz$$

Whereas Lorenz initially tracked the x-variable, this graph tracks the z-variable, with the x-variable displayed. We see readily how the two different trajectories, whose initial position differs by a mere fraction, start almost completely coordinated with one another, but quickly move quite out of phase (Figure 2.12).

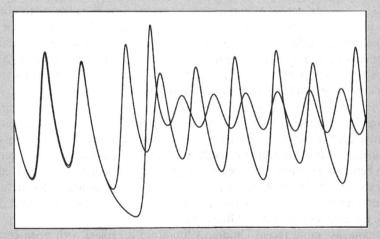

Figure 2.12 Sensitive dependence on initial conditions.
Courtesy of Fred Abraham

continued

In the chaotic realm, we see how rounding a single variable can shift weather conditions unrecognizably within a relatively short period of time. No wonder people make fun of meteorologists' limited forecasting abilities. At the same time, how real weather systems move in and out of nonlinear realms can be charted more precisely with methods such as ensemble forecasting. This is where chaos theory offers greater predictive power – by delineating degrees of certainty about the uncertainty. Clinicians readily understand this meta-level of operation. We continually use our intuition to feel out how stable or unstable particular patterns or time frames are in our patients' lives and in the therapeutic dynamics.

In the early lore of chaos theory the "butterfly effect" was the metaphor that arose to capture the idea of sensitive dependence on initial conditions: under just the right conditions, a butterfly flapping its wings in Japan could trigger a tornado in Kansas (Gleick, 1987). The butterfly effect is easy to recognize in everyday life. "But for the want of a nail, the kingdom was lost." So often those tiny, seemingly arbitrary details snowball completely to alter the face of our existence. A man returns to a store for a triviality – a forgotten stick of butter – only to discover a life-altering event – his soul mate in the checkout line. During times of major transition, it is especially easy to detect the butterfly effect. Consider the many "war tales" after September 11, 2001, where a missed clock alarm or a sick child caused tiny deviations from normal routines with big results of averting personal disaster.

Whereas the "for the want of a nail" story is very old, contemporary children's literature is also filled with nonlinear tales about the power of sensitive dependence to amplify tiny events. Contemporary cultural roots of nonlinearity can be detected broadly in children's literature about a generation before the science, although not empirically validated to my knowledge. Prior to the 1950s most American children's books contained well-structured stories with beginnings, middles, and ends that followed the standard dramatic formula dating back to Greek antiquity.

By contrast more recent children's literature is replete with open-ended, nonlinear adventures. Consider *Because a little bug went ka-choo*, by Rosetta Stone (1975), a book that epitomizes sensitive dependence on initial conditions. A tiny trigger – a bug's sneeze – cascades from a scale no bigger than a blade of grass into one mishap after another, until it finally unleashes a major social avalanche of circuses, helicopters and a myriad of folks running amok down city streets.

Another children's author brimming with nonlinear wisdom is the late Theodore Reisel, popularly known as Dr. Seuss. In *The cat in the hat comes back* (1958), a mere dirt ring from the naughty cat's bath is what eventually wreaks havoc. Inside the house first the pink stain spreads to mother's dress, then dirties the walls, tarnishes the carpet, and soils mother and father's bed (how Oedipal!), until the metaphorical chaos spills outside the house, turning an entire field of white snow into a pink mess. The disaster is both nonlinear in its escalating proportions and chaotic in its unpredictable course. Eventually this state of utter disorder is reversed by yet another nonlinear act – out of a cascade of self-similar cats within hats, only the cat so tiny as to be invisible is powerful enough to clean up the whole mess and restore the house to order.

While this sort of chaos in literature exists at the level of dramatic story line, which is more important, chaos in content or chaos in structure? This makes for an interesting philosophical dilemma, as contemporary society is also filled with unpredictability at the structural level. Examples include fusion jazz, avant-garde classical music such as Stockhausen, or improvisational performance art, like street mimes, where performances are sensitively dependent upon immediate, tiny reactions to and from local audiences.

The importance of feedback loops to chaos

Nonlinearity and chaos arise because of feedback loops, or self-interactions between system elements. The importance of feedback to coupled dynamics is where chaos theory dovetails with the neurobiology of attachment and regulation theories. By viewing emotional and behavioral development of babies in the context of their relationship with caregivers, these theories posit the coupled dynamics between bodies, brains, and minds to underlie development. Coupled bodies, brains, and minds use feedback loops in the mutual exchange of energy, matter and information across open borders. It is impossible to understand how coupled dynamics work without nonlinear models and methods of detection.

Nonlinearity that emerges out of different kinds of feedback loops is critical to psychotherapy. First, consider the meaning of attuned responses: through coupled dynamics of resonance and empathy, the caretaker amplifies positive emotional cycles of interest, excitement and joy, while dampening negative emotional cycles of fear, disappointment, and anger. When considering feedback cycles during psychotherapy, nonlinearity is also evident in disproportional outcomes that rarely match the degree of our effort as therapists. At times, as previously mentioned, a tiny almost incidental remark can spark a cascade of change in patients, while at other times, what may seem a brilliant and highly significant interpretation to us may hardly draw

Science box 2.8 Coupled dynamics

The notion of coupled dynamics is critical to the significance of nonlinear thinking both to developmental and clinical psychology. Dynamics become coupled when they share the same underlying attractors. Systems can either be strongly coupled if they move in lockstep, or loosely coupled if influenced by one another to a lesser degree. Dynamics can be coupled symmetrically if they share similar states, or asymmetrically if their states are opposite.

Although we are unaware of it, physiological coupling occurs between people all the time. Consider an experiment conducted by Guastello et al. (2006). These researchers examined electrodermal skin fluctuations between two strangers in conversation to determine whether people's physiological functions were entrained to one another, and if so, which person was driving the response of the other. Data revealed that even strangers had high levels of nonlinear coupling that sometimes operated with directional influence and sometimes without. Such measures could prove central to detecting critical right-brain to right-brain moments where implicit, nonverbal, emotional exchanges lie at the core of effective psychotherapy.

Research such as this measures subcortical processes that operate on time scales faster than those characteristic of language or conscious thought. Due to the recent revolution in interpersonal neurobiology, more and more people believe the critical action of psychotherapy exists in implicit, emotional exchanges registered in the body but not in conscious thought. To test this out, extensive research needs to be conducted on coupled physiology between therapists and patients.

Coupled nonlinear physiological responses are potential indicators of implicit processes and exchanges occurring within intersubjective realms. Since intersubjectivity ranges from shared conscious states to unconscious bodily based, physiological ones within the autonomic systems, techniques such as these are ideal for capturing processes related to clinical intuition as well as bottom-up, body and affect based work.

the flick of an eyebrow. And this is merely at conscious levels. Some theorists, like Allan Schore, believe that unconscious, implicit levels in both therapist and patient might prove even more significant in revealing the power of psychotherapy than any conscious level.

To understand such feedback loops clinically, recall the case of Rita. In my account of our early relationship, Rita was warmed by the empathy of feeling felt. I described her watching and reacting to me watching and reacting to her. Through mutual eye locks and face gazing a circuit of emotional exchange was established that passed back and forth rapidly between us, operating nonverbally, primarily beneath the level of conscious awareness. Eye contact and face gazing, along with smell and touch, are among the earliest, extra-uterine forms of establishing relationship between mother and child (e.g., Beebe and Lachmann, 2005; Schore, 1999). Ultimately shifts at this nonverbal level, in the quality and type of emotion exchanged, more than the words used or the logical narrative they signified, are likely what most facilitated Rita's therapeutic change.

In light of Lorenz's discovery of technical chaos, it is no coincidence that I sprinkled the clinical tale of Rita with weather metaphors. I likened the *dark stillness* when Rita first entered therapy to the feeling *before a storm*. I alluded to Rita's feeling *warmed* by our sessions, taking *refuge* from her isolation, as well as to our mutual plunge into *torrents* of emotion. Weather metaphors may speak to human emotions because their intersubjective trajectory may follow similar dynamics and principles as the weather, being sunny and stable or chaotic and unpredictable under just the right conditions.

To see how metaphor can shade into model, consider the research of psychologist John Gottman. After teaming up with James Murray, author of *Mathematical biology* (2004), Gottman et al. (2002) began conceiving of non-linear differential equations to capture the dynamics he and his students were observing in their couples. Some very simple equations proved incredibly powerful for describing the complex dynamics of marriage.

Gottman has become a cult figure in couples therapy partly because his nonlinear methods are much more powerful than the traditional psycho-logical research. Ironically Gottman enjoys greater than a 90 percent success rate in predicting long-term relationship stability – a statistic nearly unheard of in social science research – following a mere 15 minute discussion sur-rounding a conflict area. By using nonlinear, differential equations, Gottman discovered how some very complex interactions can be represented in very simple ways.

Gottman's methods tap right into the coupled dynamics of marriage. His critical variable proved the ratio of positive to negative emotion, with a 5 to 1 ratio of positive to negative affect in stable couples compared to a 0.8 to 1 ratio in couples headed for divorce. Gottman also explored physiological linkages between couples, finding that the higher the linkage evident in the form of bodily upset during discussions about conflict areas, the more unhappily married the couple. Gottman suggested that the diffuse physiological arousal of distressed couples was associated with decreased information-processing and increased reliance on overlearned patterns of behavior and thought associated with fight or flight.

Gottman's research illustrates the irony of chaos theory, the science of unpredictability, at times leading to increased rather than decreased predictability. High certainty is possible, even in the face of what remains uncertain, once we know what to pay attention to. Again we find that while "local" details may be unpredictable, the global pattern remains quite stable. Although Gottman might not be able to predict the gory details, he is amazingly perceptive about which couples will break up. This paradox – how uncertainty at the minute-to-minute level often goes hand-in-hand with certainty about the big picture – is but the first of many more to come.

Chapter 3

Complexity at the edge of chaos

I believe the next era is the age of complexity.

Stephen Hawking

Psychiatrist and educator Daniel Siegel likes to pose the question, "What is mental health?" to therapist audiences. His purpose is simple – to highlight how rarely we consider this issue despite working in the field of *mental health*. It is all too easy to become symptom focused, especially when most clinical trainings and third-party payers encourage attention to gross and subtle signs of psychopathology in order to diagnose and formulate treatment plans.

Our most highly validated clinical test, the MMPI (Minnesota Multiphasic Personality Inventory), refers to itself as a personality inventory, yet represents mental health by a flat, normative line, below which symptoms are clinically insignificant. The DSM IV, bible for clinical diagnosis, categorizes people entirely by a Chinese style menu of symptoms and stressors, without a single page devoted to a description of the healthy individual (American Psychiatric Association, 1994). In turn, clinicians all too readily conceptualize mental health as the *absence* of negative or debilitating symptoms. Prevailing perspectives on what it means to be "mentally healthy" seldom go beyond this exclusion of pathology, and therefore lack a positive vision. This state of affairs not only dehumanizes people, but also can widen the gap between clinical theory and clinical practice.

If mental health involves the presence of something, what might that something be? Around the turn of the twentieth century, Freud suggested *satisfaction in work and love*. During the 1960s, the humanistic movement offered up *self-actualization*. More recent movements towards positive psychology highlight *emotions* like happiness, contentment and love, including Siegel's (2007, 2008) most recent emphasis on *well-being*.

According to Siegel's view (e.g., 1999, 2007, 2008), interpersonal neurobiology involves the search for unity, or consilience (see Wilson, 1998) between all of the sciences, including chaos and complexity theory, as well other ways of knowing, such as mindfulness practices, in order to re-envision the concept of mental health within a framework that is holistic, descriptive, pathology-neutral and content free, using a flexible approach focused upon observable dynamics. By considering multiple levels of observation simultaneously – biological, psychological, social, cultural, and historical – we recognize that mental health does not reside in one particular part of a system, but depends upon the multidimensional interaction of its parts within an embedded context that includes culture and history.

Nor does mental health reside within any particular state of a system. Rather than to identify ideal or normative conditions by which regularity is sought, mental health is better detected within a system's capacity for variability and a wide range of states, plus the adaptive capability to transition flexibly between them. By focusing on unique dynamics of particular systems as they shift in context, evolving and self-organizing according to their own intrinsic space and time, a complexity approach to mental health celebrates multiple paths towards normal development. We enhance our clinical and theoretical skill set by tuning into unique individuals rather than normative levels, and by broadening our repertoire with precise language designed to capture what is irregular, discontinuous, and convoluted in nature. Whatever the path taken, complexity self-organizes at the edge of chaos, a dynamic zone with enough order to provide structure and transport information, yet enough disorder to keep things fluid, novel and creative.

Cases of Sabina and Rita discussed in the book so far attained greater complexity through similar paths of chaos constrained. The case example presented next mixes things up: Charlotte's dilemma illustrates what can happen when development becomes derailed towards the pole of excessive order, when therapy sometimes nudges and rebalances the system closer towards the edge of chaos.

Charlotte's cage

Charlotte was the child of a self-obsessed mother, who harbored little emotional room for her daughter in the guise of care taking. Suffocating inside, Charlotte recognized her need for help as a young adult, and consequently went through decades of psychotherapy. Her initial treatment with a psychiatrist afforded Charlotte a sympathetic ear, while she soothed herself more with medication than insight. Then under the tutelage of a Gestalt therapist, Charlotte identified the importance of feelings and began to articulate her inner states more fully. As she tuned into her feelings, Charlotte realized how unhappy she had always been married to a rich and successful, yet controlling and emotionally unavailable man. By outside appearances, Charlotte was well taken care of, yet upon deeper analysis, this occurred at the cost of great impoverishment inside.

Eventually Charlotte left the marriage. Under pressures to be self-supporting, she decided to become a therapist. After years of training, she now made her living in the field of mental health. Charlotte entered psychotherapy with me as a veteran of the process. For once, she was not desperate and did not have to come. Drawn by my emphasis on self-expression, Charlotte was motivated by a deep desire to live more creatively.

Given her immersion in psychotherapy from both ends of the couch, I was surprised by Charlotte's early admission of having little idea what psychotherapy really is or how the process works. Intellectually I could walk Charlotte through the facts of her own life. We could gather external evidence for huge changes made in the context of previous therapies. From the outside, Charlotte could deduce how her years invested in internal exploration had translated externally into huge differences in the quality of her life as well as those of her clients.

Yet on the inside, even after all this time and obvious change, Charlotte still *felt the same*. She experienced her self and life just as she always remembered. Charlotte felt stuck in every way – stuck in her relationships; stuck in her aloneness; stuck in her stifled creativity. Charlotte also felt stuck in her body. She had suffered physically for years. When first married, she had severe headaches. Later the pain spread throughout her entire frame until she was diagnosed eventually with fibromyalgia. Physical sensations of tiredness and pain merged with an emotional tangle of frustration and stagnancy.

Trapped within her own aching body, Charlotte was also burdened with a mother who incessantly complained, giving voice to all that Charlotte might have, had she not been so resistant to becoming like her mother. Charlotte understood her own internalized martyr dynamics quite consciously, as she wittingly and willingly put up with her mother by silencing herself. Ironically as merged as Charlotte felt, she was simultaneously locked up by loneliness. Charlotte had not been physically or emotionally touched by a man in the twelve years since her divorce. While aching for genuine emotional contact, Charlotte also feared getting lost in the Other, as had happened both in relation to mother and ex-husband.

As our therapy progressed I came to trust in the transformative power of Charlotte's imagery. Over time, more and more spontaneous waking images, as well as dream images, entered our work. The first one Charlotte brought in was well worn and in use with other healers. It revealed a Purgatory reminiscent of the ancient Greek myth of Sisyphus, condemned for his sins to roll a boulder up a hill through eternity. Charlotte imagined her own mind/body interface as a car stressing and straining to go uphill. No sooner did the car

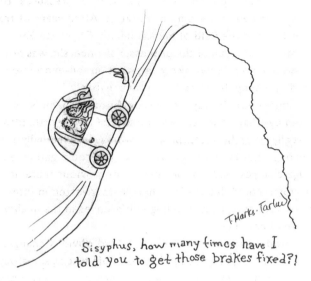

Sisyphus, how many times have I told you to get those brakes fixed?!

T.Marks. Tarlau

Figure 3.1 The marriage of Sisyphus.

reach the top, than it slid back down again, only to begin the same sequence anew (see Figure 3.1).

This image spoke miles to me. Despite the continual movement – up and down, back and forth – there was never any progress. The human element was lacking, lost in a mechanical grind of rote, routine, repetition, and restless revving. Yet side by side with this cold mechanical image, stood my experience of Charlotte's warm, open humanity, shining through like a beacon. The contrast seemed curious – why such a discrepancy between this cold imagery and Charlotte's warm presence?

Charlotte's so sincere and open. She means what she says, yet her truths subtly grate upon me . . . violate my sensibilities . . . strain my experience. Something I can't figure out here. . . . Charlotte feels stuck/I see movement. She feels stagnant/I see change. She feels empty/I see resources. She feels tired/I see activity. She feels stifled/I see originality. Why this discordance? What lies behind this mystery of opposites?

As therapy progressed, these musings continually tickled me. Over and over I noticed how Charlotte's very being seemed to sharpen my awareness, both of self and other. There were many similarities between us, although initially Charlotte was unaware of parallels as I digested them internally: both therapists; both interested in creativity; both spawned from martyr mothers stuck with partners due to dependency needs; both mothers suffered from autoimmune problems.

There were also marked differences: Charlotte felt trapped; I felt free. Charlotte was preoccupied with her body; I had been oblivious to mine. Charlotte's style was compulsive, organized, and rule-bidden; mine was impulsive, messy, and rule-breaking. Charlotte knew little about change; I felt like an expert on the topic. Even as a young adult I harbored illusions of daily self reinvention.

Filled with many unanswered questions, I began to understand my early countertransference reactions within an "edge of chaos" framework. Perhaps unlike/like her real mother I was containing forbidden parts of Charlotte which, if she could take up herself, would place her in a more healthy position at her own edge of chaos, more balanced in her internal struggles between excessive order and unbridled disorder.

Science box 3.1   Edge of chaos in human physiology

Visual recurrence analysis (VRA) is a method that reveals short- and long-term correlations in a nonlinear data set by finding patterns in the time series. On the left of Figure 3.2 is a computer-generated image of white noise ($1/f^0$) = 1. This image can be conceptualized as visualizing the sound of static generated by a white noise machine. White noise includes all frequencies, with a power spectrum equal to one. For white noise to occur, each frequency in a time series is completely uncorrelated to its predecessors, both short and long term. White noise produces wild fluctuations with each value containing no memory of the system's history.

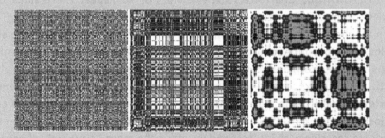

Figure 3.2 Edge of chaos in the motor system.
Courtesy of Susan Mirow, Department of Psychiatry, University of Utah

continued

By contrast, a computer-generated image of brown noise, shown on the right of Figure 3.2, has a power spectrum of $1/f^2$. Recall that the power spectrum reflects energy in the frequency spectrum. Brown noise is named for Robert Brown, who discovered Brownian motion. Brown noise, also known as a random walk, is characterized by randomness in each subsequent value in a time series, while the position the next value takes is correlated. This means that Brown noise shows bias to slow fluctuations. On a human level, the trajectory of the walk of a very drunk person is akin to brown noise.

In the middle of Figure 3.2 is real data derived from psychiatrist Susan Mirow, who studied movement variability in incarcerated teenage law offenders. The data illustrates complexity typical of virtually all physiological variability measures, as they arise at the edge of chaos. In contrast to the high disorder of white noise and stable order of brown noise, these measurements fall into the spectrum frequencies of pink noise ($1/f^1$), so named for its relevance to living systems. Within these incarcerated youth, Mirow discovered altered patterns of motion variability that correlated with clinical levels of physical reactivity to their own and others' emotional states.

At first I kept these comparisons to myself. I wanted neither to invalidate nor to crowd out Charlotte's experience, nor to repeat the trauma of a narcissistic mother. I wanted to ensure Charlotte felt my presence in the room as wholly in service of her needs rather than my own. But like the self-disclosure so prominent in this clinical write up, over time my self-disclosures became more prominent with Charlotte, moving from implicit to explicit levels, from unexpressed to expressed thoughts. Intuitively as I sensed Charlotte's full trust in me as a therapist, I inched my toe into waters of self-disclosure, while closely gauging Charlotte's responses. The more I sensed Charlotte reacting with interest and intimacy, the more comfortable I became using my perception of our similarities versus differences as a clinical tool.

From a complexity point of view, I noticed how my disclosures, both reinforced and triggered by Charlotte's recovery of detail, opened additional channels between us. There was more energy in the room. A greater flow of information was being exchanged. Sometimes this flow was based on negative events and emotions; sometimes it was based on positive ones. Always these exchanges seemed to push our collective system towards greater complexity. Intuitively and implicitly, I was responding to Charlotte's rigidity with fluidity, and this helped to shift our coupled system closer to the edge of chaos.

As I cautiously and carefully brought more of my full self into the room, I noticed Charlotte's open curiosity and sophisticated capacity for mutual exploration. As therapy progressed, we both became fascinated by our strange mirror reversals, intrigued to behold reflections of the other as if opposite cuts from similar cloth. Although we were not focusing exclusively or even always explicitly on the realm of the unconscious, still what Charlotte and I were attempting to do unwittingly was to unearth unconscious ground to unite our conscious differences. As our work continued, I had flashes of what it must have been like to be psychoanalyzed by Sándor Ferenzi, a disciple of Freud famed for his co-analysis with patients, each taking turns in search of the other's unconscious.

Complexity within psychotherapy

The complexity of psychotherapy is intimately bound with the wholeness of the endeavor. A view from the whole suggests intersubjective linkages characterized by open boundaries plus full interpenetration between self and other. In healthy states, these exchanges exist in conditions far-from-equilibrium where evolution naturally and spontaneously self-organizes. In unhealthy states, the collective system may exist in conditions too close to equilibrium, where system dynamics converge to static, stable states and change becomes unlikely, if not impossible, represented as the therapeutic impasse.

Science box 3.2 Homeostasis

Traditional models of physical health within Western medicine have rested upon assumptions of homeostasis. The word derives from Greek roots: "homeo," meaning the same or similar, and "stasis," meaning stable or standing still. When homeostasis is in play, systems operate near equilibrium where little, if any, open exchange of information, energy or matter crosses the boundaries. To understand this, imagine filling a cup with water and setting

continued

it on a table. When first placed, the water moves rhythmically, surging up the sides of the cup, maybe even sloshing over the rim. Eventually the water settles to stillness. Upon attaining this steady state, equilibrium is reached and there are no further exchanges between the inside and outside of the system (until it is time to wash or throw out the cup).

Western medicine has operated largely by assuming homeostasis in physiological systems. Consider body temperature as an example. We are taught that 98.7° is "normal," with all deviations potentially dangerous – the wider the deviation, the greater the pathology in need of correction. Yet research spearheaded by Bruce West (e.g., 1990, 2006; West and Deerling, 1995) among others reveals not homeostasis but natural variability that characterizes body temperature, along with other physiological systems, including heartbeat, breathing rate, and motor stride.

Along with natural variability in basic physiological systems, at higher levels of system coordination, something like homeostasis may operate. Recordati (2003) views the autonomic nervous system broadly as an open thermodynamic system in continual exchange with the environment. The sympathetic component acts as an accelerator, through its tight engagement with the outside world, where it gathers information, and utilizes lots of energy to ready the organism for action and novel tasks. By contrast, the parasympathetic component of the autonomic nervous system serves as the brakes, disengaging the organism from the outside world in order to attend to internal processes, utilizing low levels of energy in service of self-protection, recovery and restoration.

Recordati views the parasympathetic nervous system as bringing the organism back to homeostasis. While a useful formulation, it is important to remember that this is not homeostasis in its literal meaning of "standing still." Even here, physiological systems do not return to point attractors that correspond to idealized states. Given a continual flux in underlying neural components, homeostasis would be better conceptualized as a constrained range of normal variability.

The process of psychotherapy represents an open, coupled nonlinear system whose collective dynamic depends upon iteration and feedback. Complexity builds through a tangle of exchanges that occur simultaneously at multiple levels of observation. These exchanges span from unconscious, implicit levels connected to prosody (melody of the voice), mutual gaze, and body language, to conscious, explicit levels connected to verbal and symbolic flows of feelings and information. As with any highly nonlinear system, the entire history of the coupled system is enfolded in each moment, with each round capturing the whole by starting off where the last ended.

Science box 3.3 Self-organization far from equilibrium

In contrast to the sterile, tightly controlled conditions of the laboratory, where near to equilibrium conditions can be artificially created, most of nature operates under far from equilibrium conditions. Far from equilibrium, there is a continual flow of matter, energy and information across open borders. Complex feedback loops exist on multiple scales within these flows. Too close to equilibrium and a dynamical system is unlikely to change. Far from equilibrium, an optimal influx of energy, matter, and information allows complex systems to self-organize to greater complexity.

Ilya Prigogine received a Nobel Prize in chemistry for defining dissipative, or energy dissipating, structures operating in thermodynamic systems under far from equilibrium conditions (Prigogine and Stengers, 1984). Figure 3.3 illustrates patterns of the Belousov-Zhabotinsky (B-Z) reaction, an unusual chemical process demonstrating non-equilibrium dynamics. Rather than moving towards a single, equilibrium state, this chemical clock oscillates between two states, reflected by different colors when the experiment is done in a beaker. If instead a thin layer of fluid is trapped between two glass plates, beautiful patterns self-organize as shown here, oscillating both in space and time.

If a mere chemical reaction can self-organize under far from equilibrium conditions, imagine what higher order systems can do. Prigogine's pioneering work paved the foundation for the study of self-organization and complexity in biological and social systems, with the human brain by far the most complex self-organizing system.

continued

Figure 3.3 B-Z Reaction.

If all goes well, greater complexity can emerge out the process by integrating the system into a tighter unit. While the form this complexity takes can vary enormously, depending upon the precise details of coupled dynamics, as the system gets more tightly coupled, there are fewer degrees of freedom in underlying parameters. While seemingly paradoxical that fewer degrees of freedom in the collective system translate into a greater range of overt behavior, this occurs due to increased differentiation in combination with tighter and more efficient integration. For patients like Charlotte, this might be experienced as a greater sense of freedom, increased self-confidence, self-trust, self-awareness, greater cohesion of self, as well as bridges between dissociated aspects of self.

Opening doors

Through the iteration of continual feedback loops between self–other, self–world, and self–self, we become witnesses to countless cycles of action–reaction, cry–response, and experience–reflection. Out of these multiple iterations emerges the miracle of self-creation like an Uroboros, the mythological snake that swallows its own tail (Figure 3.4).

With each new turn of self-reflection, we swallow an old tail/tale to generate a new one. When this exchange primarily involves words and ideas, the

Figure 3.4 Uroboros.

When the snake of chaos bends round to ingest its own tail, the circle is closed. Through iterated feedback, chaos transforms into complexity. The Uroboros, an ancient symbol of self-fertilization and creative regeneration, captures this process beautifully. In his seminal book, *Origins and history of consciousness* (1954), Jungian psychologist Eric Neumann chose the Uroboros as the original symbol of self-creation. What a lovely depiction of chaos self-contained. An article commemorating the late and great neuroresearcher Francisco Varela (Marks-Tarlow et al., 2002) links the Uroboros to iteration as the basic process of life and to Varela and Maturana's ideas about autopoeisis (e.g., Varela et al., 1974), or the capacity for systems to self-create. In neurobiology the Uroboros also links to Edelman's (1992) ideas about re-entrant dynamics.

process is reminiscent of the "hermeneutic circle" as well as "narrative therapy," symbolization from British Object Relations, or a detailed inquiry from Interpersonalism. An advantage to the complexity perspective is the capacity to track multiple levels of coupled dynamics, including nonverbal, preverbal and unconscious levels characteristic of neural and physiological linkages as well as right-brain to right-brain processes gaining popularity among clinicians interested in the neurobiology of attachment and self-regulation (see Figure 3.5).

In complex systems that exist far from equilibrium, high exchanges of

Figure 3.5 Double Uroboros.

Within attachment and regulation theories, the double Uroboros beautifully represents regulation through relationship that enables physiological systems to run smoothly, both in pre- and post-natal conditions, providing a safe, secure emotional environment for children to internalize the care of parental figures necessary for self-regulation. As children mature and gain greater control over their own emotions and impulses, they may appear to function independently, yet this is largely an illusion. As open systems existing in far from equilibrium conditions, even if we attain functional independence, we remain structurally coupled throughout life. In the case of our bodies, openness means oxygen, water, nutrients, and waste must pass in and out of open borders. In the case of psyches, no matter how independent we appear, we remain embedded emotionally in a social and cultural matrix necessary to sustain independent and complex functioning. This image of the double Uroboros from ancient mythology reminds us both of opportunities and dangers that stem from coupled dynamics.

energy, information and/or matter across unfettered borders ensures some degree of novelty to emerge. Even a car that climbs the same hill over and over carries the potential for change. Microscopically it is never the same car; it is never the same hill. Tune into a fine-enough grain scale of observation, and we readily see how all remains in dynamic flux. As Heraclitus reflected, we can never step into the same river twice. His student responded that we cannot even step into the same river once; yet another observed the same thing about consciousness – it is not even the same "we" who does the stepping.

Over time with Charlotte, it was definitely a different "we" that detected some interesting distinctions upon the foundation of our similarities. As we examined the dynamic underpinnings to her stuck relationships, Charlotte's life and experience began to shift in an embodied way. Her ability to detect differences among similarities started with me and extended to her mother, allowing Charlotte to move beyond her fearful, merged position. Greater differentiation between herself and mother served as a more permeable, fluid psychological boundary. By establishing this sorely needed boundary with her mother, Charlotte found enough safety to break the bounds of her loneliness with men, without fearing or experiencing loss of self. Charlotte met and fell in love, and ultimately married a poor but highly supportive man who touched her emotionally and physically, both with joy and pain.

Meanwhile what was previously an undifferentiated block of sensation within Charlotte's body dissolved into subtler proprioception. The pain and tired-ness became less global, more localized and attenuated, as if fanning out into a multitude of different shades. Charlotte's body perceptions were becoming more differentiated, more complex. She could tune in to ever-finer scales of sensation. She could trust the spontaneous imagery that emerged in response to these sensations. An increased awareness of feedback cycles of action/reaction helped Charlotte to feel more confident about anticipating somatic and emotional consequences to plans she made, rather than continually to wonder if her body was going to cooperate with her schedule. Charlotte could distinguish between "good" pain, as when the body opens up from a work out, versus "bad" pain, as from an injury when body tissues break down.

Science box 3.4 Healthy chaos

Medical evidence rapidly accumulates that a host, if not most, of human physiological functions depend less on stable, ordered conditions, and more on irregularity and variability in the form of a system moving toward chaos in the process of reorganizing to a

continued

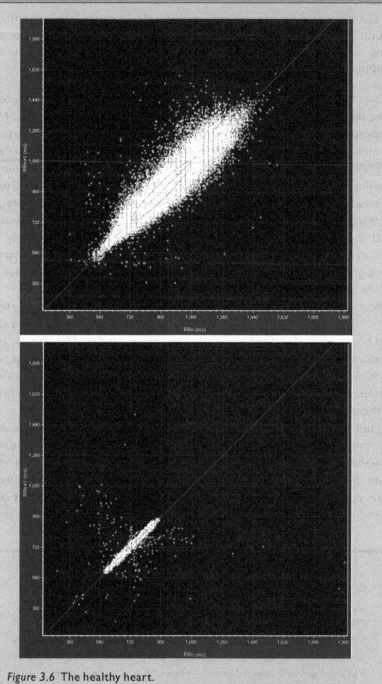

Figure 3.6 The healthy heart.

Courtesy of Susan Mirow, Department of Psychiatry, University of Utah

more adaptive state in response to a task. Consider the healthy heart, a fitting example since its rhythmic beat connects meta-phorically and maybe literally with the quality of our emotional health, e.g., "She died of a broken heart." Although physicians previously associated stable rhythm with cardiac health, too much regularity is associated with congestive heart failure, while too much irregularity is seen in fibrillation and heart attacks (see West, 2006). The healthy heart occupies a variable range of states between these extremes.

The revolution in medicine suggests that *dynamic variability rather than static order indicates health*. That is, some degree of unpredictability and irregularity indicate healthy and not patho-logical states. Research mounts that aging is characterized broadly as a loss of plasticity in physiological systems throughout the body (e.g., Lipsitz and Goldberger, 1992). Both images in Figure 3.6 portray heart rate variability, measured by comparing the spaces between heartbeats as compiled over a 24-hour period. The image at the top displays the baseball bat shaped variability typical of a healthy person. The bottom image displays the con-stricted range of heart rate variability in a man suffering from a rare cancer, called a carcinoid tumor. The man died six weeks after this tracing was made. Nonlinear measures of heart rate variability, like these recurrence plots, are highly accurate in short-term predictions of sudden death.

Out of this new awareness Charlotte came to appreciate her own creativity more directly. She watched herself transform along with her imagery. She was able to transfer this newfound skill to her clinical work with others. The pivotal image in Charlotte's therapy emerged one day while attending closely to her own mind/body interface. A familiar, constricted feeling kept tugging at the bottom of her chest. Charlotte spontaneously visualized a tiny, beautiful, winged woman locked inside a cage. This stunning "Wild Woman," as she came to be called, pressed her whole body against the bars, peeking through longingly (Figure 3.7). Charlotte immediately identified with the creature's plight – her trapped existence, her quest for freedom, her hidden potential for flight.

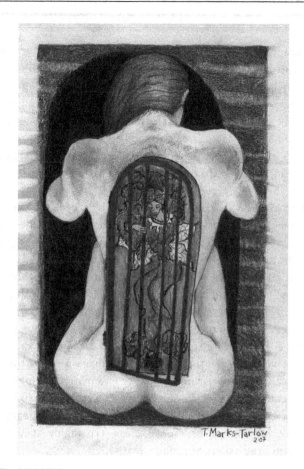

Figure 3.7 The Wild Woman.

After working with the image on numerous occasions, a shift occurred one day when, for the first time, Charlotte *considered the cage from all angles.* Previously she had stuck to appearances from the front of the cage. On that day Charlotte's attention wandered around to the back, where she noticed the entire side open, with a door that held no lock. The Wild Woman's imprisonment had been an illusion born of a limited perspective. Through continued work with the image, Charlotte's Wild Woman emerged from the cage shyly, in slow steps. Eventually this lovely creature opened her wings to take flight, knowing that her freedom to leave the cage was matched by the security of returning to its safe enclosure. How reminiscent of impossible figures in art, whose seeming impossibility is resolved with the addition of another dimension.

Science box 3.5 Impossible objects

Impossible objects, which make sense on the two-dimensional surface of a flat canvas, but not in the three-dimensional space we live in, were popularized by Maurice Escher, a master at combining artistic with mathematical ideas. The prototypical impossible object, a tri-bar, pictured in Figure 3.8, was borrowed by Escher for lithographs such as "Waterfall," a zig-zag, perpetual motion fountain in which water continually flows downhill, yet always winds up at the starting point. In the drawing pictured in this figure, not only the tri-bar but also how it fits into the room are impossible. The bar on the right appears to run towards us and away from us at the same time. Likewise, this same bar appears to recede out of the room and enter further forward into the room simultaneously.

What are we to make of such illusions? The facility of the human eye to accept impossible and ambiguous objects not only makes

Impossibility
T. Marks Tarlow
12-06
[After Bruno Ernst]

Figure 3.8 Impossible objects.

continued

for interesting art, but also for the kinds of soft calculations that occur during psychotherapy, sometimes reflecting ambiguity that already exists, sometimes driving ambiguity that opens internal space for novel emergence. While we readily accept the plausibility of the tri-bar when rendered in two-dimensional space, we easily detect its impossibility when cast as a sculpture or model within three-dimensional space. In life as in art, the dimensionality of one's perspective is critical, helping us to distinguish between ambiguity that opens up new possibilities and illusions that fly in the face of reality.

Paradoxically Charlotte entered therapy free in some ways without realizing it, while being constrained in other ways. She was so busy fighting to *not* be her mother that she could not notice the actual differences that already existed between them. She was so locked into repetitive experience as to be able to step back and gain a vantage point of the whole or the ability to articulate her understanding. No wonder my own initial experience of her seemed so paradoxical.

As a spontaneously arising, embodied image, the Wild Woman symbolically added an extra dimension to Charlotte's self-reflection that eventually allowed her inner world to grow more differentiated. From a complexity vantage point, the fractal consciousness detailed later means that the whole of a patient's life may be understood within a single narrative or poignant therapeutic moment. The shift in perspective on the Wild Woman's cage was such a moment for Charlotte. Her ability to perceive the open door at the back of the cage was a tiny difference that made all the difference in her personal sense of freedom.

Two-way doors

Within the intersubjective field of psychotherapy, fractal consciousness can work both ways. Not only can the therapist detect the whole of a patient's life within a moment of transference, but also the possibility exists that the whole of a therapist's life can be compacted into a significant moment with a patient. This happened to me during my work with Charlotte, one session a few months before the emergence of Charlotte's Wild Woman, though I waited to share my personal sense of transformation until the end of Charlotte's therapy, after I was sure that Charlotte had experienced the full freedom to revel in her own changes without becoming distracted by mine.

Here is the background to my insight. Charlotte's parents had had a terrible marriage and fought all the time. Their house was filled with negative emotions, continual accusations, much rage and disgust. Charlotte identified primarily with her mother who, as if a living enactment of Charlotte's car image, repeatedly climbed the same hill by trying to leave her husband over and over. Once she even required Charlotte to testify against her father in court, only to fall back down the hill again by returning to their horrific relationship, feeling ever more defeated, hopeless, and helpless.

Over time Charlotte became disgusted and disappointed with her mother. She adapted to this repetitive trauma first by ceasing to expect any change, and eventually by ceasing to recognize change. At this point Charlotte had moved more fully from dysregulated states of emotion into dissociated ones.

By comparison my parents, now both deceased, had an equally toxic marriage. There was never open conflict between them, just a sickly stagnant atmosphere that left me yearning always to play outside. Neither parent left the other, at least on the surface. My father frequently left underneath, refusing to be pinned down, either in body or spirit, by my mother's frustrated unhappiness and stifled aliveness. My mother also left underneath in a different way, as she slowly and painlessly became more and more isolated, trapped and immobilized by an undiagnosed autoimmune condition.

Like Charlotte, I felt great disappointment that my parents never resolved their smoldering conflict. Unlike Charlotte I adapted differently, primarily by identifying with my father and inheriting his tendencies to act out rather than act in. I responded to my own disappointment first by vowing never to get stuck in a stagnant relationship, and then by devoting myself to making sure others would not get stuck either.

In a sudden "aha!" moment, I had envisioned psychodynamic sources of my eagerness and intuitive skill in helping others to undergo the deep transformation that my mother/parents never had. I now understood the family origins of my acute sensitivity to minute changes in self and others, no matter how rigid the personality or stereotyped the interpersonal dynamics. I also understood the origins of my creativity as a therapist and my interest in creativity both personally and professionally, including how to capitalize on minute changes to jumpstart and drive the change process itself. Finally I recognized the perversity in my taking pleasure in people, including myself, going where my parents never could.

Within psychotherapy, such moments of self-awareness feel sacred. They energize and protect us therapists as "Wounded Healers." To be a Wounded Healer stands in contrast with others more like the "Walking Wounded." Too many patients and friends abound with horror stories about Walking Wounded therapists who are internally troubled, yet unaware of their blind spots and unable to control the leakage of their issues across interpersonal boundaries. The case presented next provides an illustration of this sort.

In many Native American cultures, the Wounded Healer carries the highest respect of all. This is the individual who possesses the courage to address life's inevitable wounds by taking the hero's journey into darkness and returning again. Like many wonderful addiction specialists who are recovered addicts themselves, Wounded Healers have a unique perspective and a special set of tools sometimes possible only with first-hand experience, a badge of "been there, done that" (see Figure 3.9).

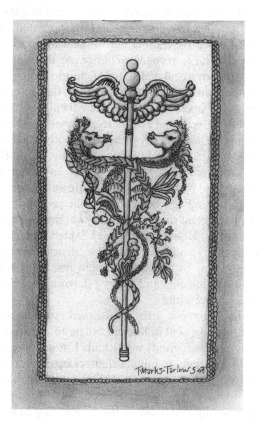

Figure 3.9 Caduceus.

The snake as a symbol for chaos is highly ambivalent. Just as the snake's venom provides both toxin and cure, here we see two intertwined snakes that form the healer's staff or Caduceus, ancient symbol for Western medicine. How ironic and fitting that another symbol of chaos as constrained by coupled dynamics should be recognized so long ago. How easily we ignore our ancient, intuitive wisdom, as Western medicine only now returns (e.g., Adler, 2007) to the importance of the emotional exchanges between doctor and patient so obvious in ancient and traditional culture.

Of course such intense and sudden moments of therapist insight also carry dangers of over-identification or becoming too involved emotionally. Further how do we know that such a moment is indeed a valid one, rather than springing creatively from our own desires and unconscious needs? With such intimate linkages between therapist and patient at multiple levels, many of which are not only unconscious but also inaccessible to consciousness, we must always be on guard to keep from exploiting patients in order to meet our own personal or theoretical ends. The same coupled dynamics that provide a potential handle for empathy also provide the potential mishandling of resonating issues. Real life may abhor a vacuum, but also loves a paradox. Paradox implies an unlikely marriage of opposites, and as the Chinese word for "crisis" and motto of crisis counseling suggests, every opportunity also carries its dangers. No matter how careful we are, such parallel processes are a natural part of deep clinical work. They inevitably emerge out of coupled dynamics occurring both at conscious and unconscious levels.

As the contemporary interpersonal school of psychoanalysis suggests, such occurrences need to be recognized and taken to a deeper level of understanding with patients, for too much personal identification during intersubjectivity always carries hidden potential for un-self-aware enactments. Even "sacred" moments in therapy must be explored thoroughly to safeguard against intuitive knowledge manifested as a form of resistance that closes off the work prematurely.

Within the intersubjective field when all goes well, from the very same core of vulnerability, aliveness and elation that new healing brings, emerges the continual growth afforded to us as therapists that keeps our work as fresh and alive as we feel. These moments of self-creation represent new levels of complexity self-organized at the edge of chaos, which in turn fuel our professional and personal creativity. Charlotte's case reveals clearly how out of coupled dynamics, the complexity of psychotherapy often is a two-way road towards mental health and transformation. For this, I remain continually grateful.

Healthy development as complexity

Charlotte's story may be regarded as a case of derailed development in conditions too close to equilibrium. In her early years, there was not enough attuned emotional exchange across fluid boundaries. Communications moved primarily in one direction. Charlotte's narcissistic mother had difficulty attending to Charlotte's inner experience, which left her struggling to attune to herself. Excessive rigidity in Charlotte's lack of emotional proprioception and expression was mirrored by excessive rigidity in Charlotte's body. As with her emotions, she depended too much on outer signals, as if needing to bump up against external limitations supplied by her body's physical frame in order to compensate for the deficit in registering internal pain.

When Charlotte first entered psychotherapy, her psychological rigidity was apparent in other ways as well. She maintained a rigid schedule, from which she rarely deviated. She formulated and rehearsed endless to-do lists. Although rarely actualized, Charlotte was rigidly gripped by low level fear – of arriving late, not completing tasks on time, feeling lost with unstructured time. Her continual, low-level anxiety tended to be Charlotte's primary driving motivation. Excessive rigidity was also evident in Charlotte's presenting complaint – the repetitive, undifferentiated nature of her inner experience, regardless of feedback derived from life history or present surrounds.

Charlotte's most recent round of psychotherapy moved her closer to the edge of chaos. In this realm of dynamic variability, there was enough structure and stability to support a firm sense of self, plus sufficient fluidity and freedom of movement for Charlotte to break through feelings of being isolated, stuck and uncreative. We see here how the edge of chaos exists as a dynamic state of tension between the extremes of rigid order and complete disorder. Here complexity emerges as a balance between opposing pulls of stability and change, constraint and release, inhibition and expression, negative and positive iterated feedback.

Within the intersubjective context of psychotherapy, Charlotte emerged with a more complex inner life than when she entered. Her later experience became more variegated in her capacity to hold a mixture of negative and positive feelings while staying fully engaged with self and other. Her experience of similarity and difference from the Other became less fantasy driven and more differentiated. And with the emergence of psychological boundaries, her pain lessened, though did not disappear, as she no longer needed to use her body as a primary signaling system with the world.

Within Charlotte's morphing image of the Wild Woman, we see the increase in complexity quite literally depicted. From the initial two-dimensional view of the cage, Charlotte's perspective eventually expanded to include a third dimension. Charlotte succeeded in breaking loose from the flatness of appearances to perceive a depth formerly invisible. Metaphorically to symbolize the emergence of this shift from her unconscious, the opening in her cage had to be in the back. Whereas we need only look down to get a conscious take on our front bodies, our back bodies remain forever invisible and tucked away from consciousness, unless we compensate with the help of a mirror outside. My increasingly transparent self became Charlotte's mirror, helping to reflect the missing portion omitted from her two dimensional awareness.

In complexity terms, I served as an expanded embedding space for new, higher dimensional psychological attractors to emerge. Within nonlinear science, an attractor's embedding space always needs to be one dimension higher than that of the attractor itself. Perhaps this is why we seek wise or enlightened others to surround ourselves with. When coupled dynamics arise, iterated feedback loops even at unconscious levels may serve to expand the dimensionality, or internal freedom, of consciousness. Here is variability at its highest form.

The image of Charlotte's cage gives a good feel for the clinical emergence of psychological complexity. Daniel Siegel (2007) uses the FACES acronym to identify certain properties – flexible, adaptive, coherent, energized, and stable. In self-referential fashion, the face of complexity is a fluid affair that depends intimately upon the lens and scale of observation chosen. Complexity at the level of brain physiology looks different from that of intrapsychic dynamics, which in turn looks different from that of social dynamics, even if all do share common features. The pursuit of complexity is an idiosyncratic, full body affair, unique to the physiology, explicit and implicit dynamics of the therapeutic couple. No formula exists for bringing an individual or system closer to the edge of chaos. The very same intervention that dislodges one individual away from equilibrium may drive another into dysregulated, disordered extremes.

Despite the dearth of formulas, the edge of chaos remains a useful heuristic for feeling our way towards mental health. Although there are as many ways to understand complexity as there are people interested in trying, this book aims to introduce ideas from contemporary science to inspire therapists to play and research these ideas creatively. However we get there, one hallmark of psychological complexity is *an enhanced capacity to differentiate as well as integrate ongoing experience emotionally, cognitively, and behaviorally*. This often results in the heightened sensibilities of feeling more alive, present, and creative, long recognized as a beneficial outcome of therapy. Notably, even though each person may follow a different clinical course in relation to order and disorder, on a higher level of analysis we are all headed in the same "meta-direction", toward a healthier balance between order and disorder at the edge of chaos.

In line with Daniel Siegal (1999), I suggest that mental health be defined as *the complex flow of mental and behavioral states self-organized at the edge of chaos*. The edge of chaos is a transitional zone located between poles of stagnant order at one extreme and utter disorder at the other. At the edge of chaos, there is variability and flexibility for adaptation and change, yet the capacity for great stability as well. This view addresses deficiencies of a negativistic definition of mental health by providing an affirmative framework for understanding health that guides clinical work toward more concrete, yet open, individualized goals, plus the presence of creativity and growth, rather than the absence of disease.

Science box 3.6 Healthy variability and differential diagnosis

Susan Mirow is the first person to use nonlinear methods of visual recurrence analysis, including short- and long-term changes in physiological signal, as correlates for psychological states, such as mood or more persistent patterns falling under the category of psychiatric diagnostic conditions. A unique feature of her methodology is to measure the ultraslow frequencies of the heart rate variability (HRV), which last from minutes to hours, corresponding to the slow time scales of mood states and psychiatric conditions.

Traditional medical HRV studies have used only the ratio of low to high frequency oscillations. They could watch pathological systems move towards health, but because their methods relied on averaged linear information alone, they lacked the specificity required for differential diagnosis. By contrast, Mirow's methods do not rely on averaging, but rather compute nonlinear mathematical functions that preserve signal variability throughout the course of study. Using up to three simultaneously collected physiological measures, Mirow can preserve the full specificity of physiological coordinated patterns to provide functional analysis for any psychiatric condition.

Figure 3.10 represents HRV data for a person with Dissociative Identity Disorder (DID; formerly Multiple Personality Disorder), taken before and after successful psychotherapy. A healthy person has both short-term and long-term (up to 24-hour) correlations in HRV, with those in the short term dependent upon activities within the 24-hour period. The box at the top shows HRV data from a person with DID, revealing many separated states. Each personality state in itself appears to have normal variability, as seen by the distinctive "baseball bat" distribution. But the short-term correlations in this visualization of DID remain disconnected from one another and from the long-term correlations that persist over 24 hours. The bottom box constitutes biological evidence for integration and emotional healing in this same individual several months into a course of psychotherapy treatment.

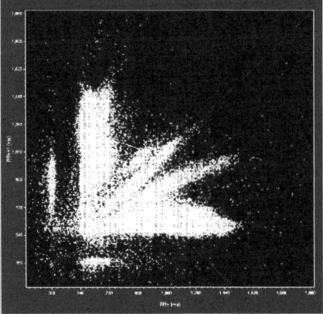

Figure 3.10 Heart rate variability in Dissociative Identity Disorder.

Courtesy of Susan Mirow, Department of Psychiatry, University of Utah

continued

If we consider the neurobiology of early fetal development, we understand why operations in the heart remain coupled with those in the brain. Initially the fertilized cell, or zygote, multiplies by period doubling, from one to two to four to eight cells, and so on, until it reaches the blastocyst stage, where inner cells form the embryo and outer cells form the membranes to nourish and protect the embryo. In the early weeks of development as the embryo elongates, the spinal cord, heart and brain all differentiate at the same time in coordination with each other, and they remain intimately connected throughout each individual's life.

Complexity at the edge of chaos affords a system ready access to the entire repertoire of all possible states – both positive and negative, expansive and contractive, joining and disrupting. Within a complexity vantage point, the focus is on working with the fullness of the whole, rather than on the reduction or elimination of unwanted parts. When people naively chase happiness, as if this can be achieved in the absence of negative states, ironically they often wind up among the most discontented of all. Within the proper context, there is a time and place for every mental state. Having ready access to any potential one, without undue constriction by rigid defenses, becomes the hallmark of variability so central to a formulation of mental health based on complexity. Within psychotherapy, complexity at the edge of chaos is most evident intersubjectively, in terms of multiply coupled dynamics at two levels:

- how the therapist joins with the patient, and
- the emotional, cognitive, and behavioral impact of this joining on both patient and therapist.

Within psychotherapy, as within development at large, how feedback is incorporated and used determines whether or not novelty will emerge as a nonlinear process at the edge of chaos. In the next example of a treatment failure, which happens occasionally to even the most seasoned therapist, we find an opposite set of circumstances to those described in the case of Charlotte. The therapist's difficulty entering into a more complex relationship with her client resulted in the client's fragmentation instead of growth. Unfortunately, when we fail to recognize and address unconscious levels of iterated feedback, sometimes results are disastrous.

The breakdown of complexity

The following presentation is slightly altered, including names, from a story that ran on June 15, 2002 on National Public Radio (NPR), on "This American Life," hosted by Ira Glass. The therapist, who I call Sage, was a counselor during the 1980s and early 1990s, when it was not only popular but also fashionable to use guided imagery to uncover repressed memories of child-hood sexual abuse. This story involves one of Sage's clients, a young woman whom I call Suzy.

When Suzy began psychotherapy, she appeared to have an intact personality born of a happy childhood. But early on in therapy, Sage introduced guided imagery techniques to facilitate their mutual exploration, and something shifted. Red flags began to emerge out of the material Suzie produced, which only increased over time. Sage grew continually on the alert, as she began to suspect Suzy was the victim of incest. Upon uncovering signs of early abuse, the therapist responded by using similar techniques to probe further. From implicit clues, this additional work resulted in more and more explicit images of sexual abuse by Suzy's father.

Sage had no reason to doubt the veracity of the process she was using. Suzy expressed appropriate affect upon uncovering evidence of early abuse. Meanwhile Sage's previous clinical training had emphasized the importance of always trusting client reports. Over the next several months, using similar methods, incident after incident of early abuse surfaced. During this period, Suzy's mental condition steadily worsened, as she suffered a stream of new symptoms. Additionally each recovered memory grew more bizarre than the last. Throughout, Sage remained convinced of the veracity of Suzy's reports. Because she retained such an unwavering commitment to her position, Sage misinterpreted Suzy's deterioration as a need for more uncovering. The therapist responded by revving up both the number of sessions and the frequency of recovery techniques used.

Despite Suzy's steady deterioration, Sage would not entertain the possibility that her clinical judgment was in error. Having encouraged her client to confront her alleged perpetrator, Suzy's father was publicly humiliated and professionally destroyed. As a result, Suzy's family, along with her psyche, became shattered and splintered. Meanwhile Sage began receiving pamphlets sent by other clients from the newly formed False Recovered Memory Syndrome Foundation. Despite all the signs of things falling apart rather than coming together, Sage still failed to seek professional consultation or reconsider the clinical path she had chosen.

Then one day an incident occurred that was so bizarre as to plant seeds of doubt within Sage's mind. Suzy "remembered" her mother aborting a fetus with a coat hanger, cooking it in oil, and forcing her daughter to eat pieces of its tiny body. Even at this point, Sage held firm to the certainty of her convictions, and responded by misinterpreting her own doubt as the problem. Sage continued to feel her client deserved to be trusted, no matter what. As a result, the therapist referred Suzy to a colleague who specialized in ritual Satanic abuse and Multiple Personality Disorder. Under the care of this new professional, Suzy continued to deteriorate until, of her own accord, she broke away from psychotherapy altogether. Only then did Suzy slowly begin to put her life and family back together.

Meanwhile Sage continued using similar techniques to "recover" memories in other clients, until several years later when finally she realized the error of her ways. This happened after Sage walked into a room filled with parents, all of whom had been accused of bizarre atrocities similar to ones Suzy had uncovered. Most of these accusations stemmed from children who had been in psychotherapy and exposed to similar techniques. Sage had finally attended a meeting of the False Recovered Memory Syndrome Foundation, when this light of new awareness dawned.

As painful as Sage's story is, upon perceiving what had really happened, this therapist was amazingly brave. She committed herself to whatever it took to correct the problem, which by then had reached epidemic national proportions. Sage even agreed to the NPR interview I had heard, despite its obvious humiliation. In poignant commentary, she described her own psychological naivety. Looking back, she understood the subtle, but pernicious feedback loops that had operated with clients. Sage's rigid convictions as a therapist fed the unconscious needs and fantasies of her clients, whose responses in turn fueled her own convictions further, all within a closed system of rigid certainty.

As the Uroboros swallows its own tail/tale, creative dynamics that arise from underlying chaos sometimes appear monstrous. As mentioned, iterative feedback loops born of deep intersubjectivity are unavoidable. They operate, for example, whenever a Jungian patient brings archetypal dreams into therapy suggestive of the collective unconscious, while Freudian patients bring different sorts more suggestive of sexual repression within the personal unconscious. In their most destructive capacity, positive feedback loops work much like a microphone picking up feedback from an amplifier. Tiny bits of noise become powerfully amplified, to the point of shattering speakers.

Unfortunately, such coupled dynamics sometimes can be more powerful than the underlying machinery supporting them. This subject is beautifully explored from a psychoanalytic perspective in the work of Wilfred Bion and Michael Eigen, and can be easily understood by physical analogy, when feedback resonance from high winds leads to the destruction of bridges by self-amplifying vibrations. A famous movie loop now showing in the Los Angeles Museum of Science reveals a suspension bridge in Portland, Oregon, whose structure was literally torn apart by winds. Other bridges in Europe have been torn apart by resonance from footsteps of a crowd of people.

Within psychotherapy, resonances amplified by positive feedback or dampened by negative feedback can be partly conscious, as occurred between Charlotte and myself, or they may be wholly unconscious, as occurred between Suzy and Sage. If their signs remain undetected, the very implicit nature of such resonances carries danger for enactments sometimes so powerful as to rend psychic structure apart. As therapists, we must be extremely careful not to let previous training, beliefs or theory stand in the way of perceiving and incorporating feedback at all levels, lest things get out of hand.

Enter culture and historicity

The NPR story reveals simultaneous iterated feedback loops at multiple levels of observation. One level involves interpersonal and intrapsychic dynamics as we have seen before in the cases of Sabina and Rita, where accurate therapist attunement served as a negative feedback loop to dampen, reduce and stabilize inner and outer disorder. By contrast, here in the case of Suzy, the lack of accurate attunement served as a positive feedback loop driving the system too far from equilibrium, where escalating dysregulated states and symptoms emerged to shatter structure rather than to build it, both internally and externally.

The story of Suzy likewise reveals feedback dynamics provided by other descriptive levels, including culture and social politics. Consider the historical context: in the early twentieth century, Freud had revised earlier ideas about the origins of psychopathology. Whereas he initially believed that symptoms arise primarily from early childhood trauma (the seduction theory), he later decided they originated out of repressed fantasies for forbidden, incestuous sexuality (the theory of infantile sexuality). Due to his own cultural and personal factors, Freud grew more interested in origins connected with intrapsychic fantasy rather than in interpersonal trauma.

Judith Herman's book *Trauma and recovery* (1997) describes well how trauma has been alternatively addressed and ignored within clinical theory and practice over history. From Freud's time until immediately before Sage began her marriage and family practice, reports by women of childhood sexual abuse were dismissed repeatedly as fantasy by mental health professionals. With feminism came the horrific discovery that sexual abuse was very real, under-reported, and under-treated. Between the 1970s and the early 1990s, more and more cases of repressed memories were uncovered. This corresponded with the height of feminism, plus high interest in developing alternative models of psychopathology to Freud's. Researchers and theoreticians sought approaches with aims to empower women and amplify their voices. No wonder Sage felt pressure to trust female client narratives no matter what. This message was absolutely integral to her clinical training.

Then during the 1990s, the pendulum began to swing the other way. Feminism had peaked, and the opposite possibility for false memories was discovered. Unfortunately, as happened with Suzy, apparent but false repressed memories were uncovered in treatment, often with sparsely trained people who walked in with biased assumptions or used leading methods. More and more countersuits in the courts have brought the problem to the public eye by people claiming to be falsely accused. Over time, the veracity of techniques like guided imagery and hypnosis for recovering veridical memories has fallen into question.

By telling this story, I do not mean to discount the reality that repressed memories exist for early trauma. A case presented in Chapter 8 involves the uncovering of a memory previously dissociated. Nor do I question whether therapists sometimes unwittingly plant seeds for false memories in vulnerable people. Instead I aim to reveal how complicated these issues can be, especially in patients that hunger for this type of solution. The notion of repressed memories can appeal as a simple answer to complex, inner turmoil, if it provides a concrete hook on which to pin painful, confusing experiences that otherwise can seem unreasonable or overly severe.

At times it is the longing for clarity itself that needs interpretation, especially when such desires serve as a defense against the muck of uncertainty. We might call this condition "pathological certainty" or "excessively linearity," a condition which, as illustrated here, is sometimes stimulated by surrounding culture. As therapists, we can sensitize ourselves to the complicated nature of these issues partly by recognizing forces that pressure us towards this kind of countertransference dynamic.

To me, the issue is not whether or not repressed memories or any particular clinical phenomenon exists. The problem comes when, either wittingly or unwittingly, therapists are overly influenced by pre-existing biases or beliefs, cultural trends or "political correctness" to the exclusion of personal and professional instinct carefully garnered in the moment. To preserve wholeness, we must guard against entering with pre-existing, certain beliefs. The case of Suzy warns against the dangers of a closed system that inappropriately and regressively leads a patient back to where the therapist already began.

Nonlinear science helps us to understand clinical causality in a fuller, more reciprocal, multidimensional way. We can now model recursive loops within the intersubjective web, where what we/our patients see and experience depends at least partly upon how we therapists look with/at our patients. The therapeutic bond is an inextricably entwined, coupled system, whose dynamics emerge out of the tangled hierarchy of feedback loops that extend both horizontally and vertically through neurobiological, social, cultural and historical levels. These open boundaries at all levels of observation serve both as a fertile place of creative change, as well as a dangerous place of patient/therapist enmeshment. By illustrating this complexity from a nonlinear perspective, I hope that as therapists we can better avoid these pitfalls of enactment, while capitalizing on the strengths and beauty of coupled, resonant dynamics.

Chapter 4

New metaphors arising

> When psychopathology is viewed from the clinical point of view the primary task is to find the narrative point of origin – invariably, the key metaphor(s).
>
> Daniel Stern

Within psychotherapy, complexity is revealed partly by the metaphors we choose. As Daniel Stern (1985) suggests, metaphor lurks at the narrative base of how we understand our selves, our patients and our work. The art and science of psychotherapy merge within its metaphors. Like liquid poetry that congeals into precise methods of inquiry, metaphors frame how we look with patients and ultimately what we find.

The word metaphor derives from the Latin word *metaphora*, meaning to "transfer" or "carry over." We use metaphor to transfer or carry over experience from one domain to another. Through metaphor, we understand "this" in terms of "that." Metaphors are not just the fluff of fancy speakers and poets, but a capacity deeply wired into our brains (Lakoff and Johnson, 1980, 1999; Modell, 2003). Metaphor is a primary cognitive tool by which we make sense of the world.

As infants developmentally we start with an embodied experience of the world; initially through gesture-play and later through the play of words, we bootleg this early experience into more abstract, symbolic forms. As its Latin derivation *metaphora* hints – we first must know concretely the meaning of "carrying over" an object from place to place, before we can understand this concept abstractly, as a movement in the mind. This developmental progression in the individual, from somatic, interpersonal and nonverbal origins, towards later conscious experience and verbal articulation, parallels evolutionary speculation that the human capacity for metaphor developed independently of language and probably earlier (Modell, 2003).

Psychoanalyst Arnold Modell suggests that through metaphor we transform unconscious into conscious experience plus a felt sense of meaning in life. I share this perspective, which I attempt amply to illustrate in this book.

Many of the cases, including that of Wayne next, begin with metaphors embodied as symptoms, that later progress to a more direct emotional and linguistic representation.

Modell's view of the unconscious presumes *potential meaning*, an assumption consistent with most psychoanalytic thinkers. Although cognitive neuropsychologists sometimes strip the unconscious of potential meaning, reserving this phrase more narrowly for procedural memory surrounding motor routines, recent interpersonal neurobiologists reverse this tendency. Allan Schore (1999, 2003a, 2003b), among others, proposes that implicit memory also stores sensory and emotional information during preverbal, right-brain to right-brain exchanges between caretakers and infants.

Derived initially from our most concrete interactions with others and the world, the body employs metaphor as a kind of "corporeal imagination," to use Cornelius Castoriadis' phrase, for transferring experience from inside to outside, past to present, one sensory mode to another. Within psychotherapy this preverbal aspect has been called the "unthought known" by Christopher Bollas (1987) and more recently "the unrepressed unconscious" by Mauro Mancia (2006). The internal cacophony formed during the first few years that does not include words and cannot be remembered, continues to tune the background and melody of experience thereafter. So deeply is this feeling-sense wired into the brain, that I believe it likely to be one origin of repetitive dreamscapes.

By fusing various perceptual, emotional, and cognitive capacities, metaphor-making becomes a primary way to construct meaning. Through metaphor, we interpret and transform experience; mark value; declare relationship; and hold mirrors up to our being, doing and moving in the world. By welding discrete experiences together, metaphor expresses a sense of continuity versus fragmentation of the self through time.

George Lakoff and Mark Johnson (1980, 1999) claim that all cognitive activity derives from a primary set of bodily metaphors. Consider, for example, the importance of verticality and balance in expressions like *things are looking up* or *what a put down*. A second important class of metaphors derives from the body as container for psyche, such as *her envy leaked out* or *he couldn't hold in his criticism*. Wilfred Bion (1962) conceptualized mutual affect regulation in metaphorical terms by viewing mother as *container*, infant as *contained*. This concept readily spills into psychotherapy, where therapists are challenged to hold and contain both their experience as well as that of patients.

Within psychotherapy, metaphors often arise spontaneously as images, body sensations, feelings, or impulses around which words are woven later, which happened repeatedly in the case of Charlotte in Chapter 3. Images of the stuck car and caged wild woman proved pivotal points of contact between mind, body and history. At the neurobiological level, by operating both at the explicit level of meaning-making and at implicit level of felt experience, metaphor-making helps therapists to capitalize on differentiation and integration of brain function. In this way, metaphors can be seen as central to Daniel Siegel's concept of "neural integration" (2007, 2008) including horizontally between the left and right hemispheres, as well as vertically between cortical and subcortical levels.

The best metaphors resonate deeply, helping to broaden awareness, precisely because they reach towards the whole. Metaphors exist in the fertile *space between* "this" and "that" – known and unknown, past and present, sameness and change, order and disorder, self and other. By evoking the unknown in service of what is partly known, metaphors ride at the edge of creative thought and change. Metaphors allow us to dive into the ambiguity, uncertainty, and paradox so characteristic of psychotherapy's intersubjective space. By adding new dimensions for holding and appreciating the ongoing experience of self, including self-through-the-eyes-of-other, metaphors help to increase internal complexity. The notion of increased complexity, which I sometimes call "complexifying," dovetails nicely with Siegel's emphasis on promoting integration of differentiated components, first introduced in *The mindful brain* (2007), and spelled out in great detail in *Mindsight* (Siegel, 2008).

This chapter explores metaphor as a primary means for maximizing complexity within psychotherapy. I first introduce the self-referential significance of metaphor, and then survey metaphors underlying the origins of psychoanalysis as a school of thought. Next I present clinical examples of idiosyncratic images arising from psychotherapy with two different men. The first case treats a literal circumstance metaphorically; the second reverses this process to flesh out the literal embodiment and meaning of a metaphorical image. These cases serve as a springboard to examine a central metaphor historically – of mind as mechanism – plus increasing recognition of memory as a dynamic, creative, and holistically embedded process.

Self-reference and metaphor

I now return to the importance of self-reference, a phrase introduced earlier. Contemporary science and mathematics, especially second-order cybernetics, suggest self-reference is a quality pervasive in all complex systems of observation. This means that any system of observation inevitably circles back recursively to implicate the observer, until the observer becomes inextricably entangled with the observed.

Metaphors are inherently self-referential, by pointing inwards to the self as the imaginative author of experience, at the very same time as pointing outwards to the world as a primary source of creative inspiration. By speaking from embodied experience, metaphors are grounded in the most foundational level of self. They continually pull the observer into the observed while implicating relational and embedded origins of experience, whether to self, world or other.

Metaphors are nonlinear because they do not just comprise a "line of reasoning." Instead they fan out in all directions; they are multi-tiered, spanning across various scales and levels of observation, some self-similar, some not. For all of these reasons, metaphors speak to and from the heart of the complexity within psychotherapy. Cases in this chapter demonstrate the nonlinear power of central metaphors partly through their self-referential significance and resonances (see Figure 4.1).

Because self-reference lies invisibly curled within all communications,

Figure 4.1 Self-reference in photography.

Courtesy of Georgianne Cowan
When photography was invented, some doubted its potential as art. This stemmed from naive assumptions that photographs capture only objective but not subjective reality. We deepen our appreciation of photography partly by attending to the observer's stance, including choices of subject and frame. With all art a vehicle for metaphorical expression, even photography is inherently self-referential. As you gaze at this photograph by Georgianne Cowan, feel your way into the self-referential quality of art by asking yourself not only "What does this image mean?" but also "What does this image suggest about the photographer?" You might be surprised by how readily an intuitive sense of the artist comes to you.

much like the extra dimensions posited by string theory, therapists must listen with multiple channels simultaneously. We are challenged to address not just linear narrative threads, but also nonlinear, recursive loops that self-referentially implicate the quality of the therapeutic relationship as a whole. No matter how distant from the room a session's content may seem, the self-referential resonance of all transactions obscures lines between the observed and observer at the edges.

For some therapists, due to theoretical orientation, personal bent, or the short-term nature of the work, the self-referential complexity of therapeutic communications can seem irrelevant. Whether these hidden resonances remain implicit or get extruded to their maximum reaches, the very existence of self-referential resonances blurs boundaries between the individuals, the nature and direction of their communications, and the relationship as a whole. These blurred boundaries render the issue, "Which cures – the intervention/interpretation or the relationship?" an outmoded product of reductionist thinking that posits a false dichotomy.

A major premise of this book, fleshed out here and more fully in Chapters 7, 8 and 9, is that our experience of self, world, and other is self-referentially entangled at the edges. In the tradition of Francisco Varela, Robert Rosen, George Spencer-Brown and others, I believe that *fundamental entanglement between observers and observed is the paradoxical foundation upon which all of creation, whether material or psychological, rests.* If true, this primal stew provides the raw material for an endless series of living metaphors to capture and congeal the dynamic flow of ongoing experience across fluid boundaries (see Figure 4.2).

Figure 4.2 Gaia

Courtesy of Georgianne Cowan

In many of Georgianne Cowan's photographs, self-reference lurks within images of women projected into nature. The effect has a reverential effect; the homage to Mother Nature creates true Gaia moments. Roger Bacon, renowned thirteenth-century scientist, also projected women into nature, but in a way more controversial according to contemporary feminine critique. Credited with the discovery of the scientific method, Bacon wrote of his intentions to "force nature to yield her secrets" (Jardine and Stewart, 1999). After interpreting Bacon's underlying motivation as rape, no wonder Western science is considered patriarchal, with its primary focus on understanding as a vehicle for control. In a book combining feminist thought with science, Linda Shepard (1993) suggests that chaos theory, with its emphasis on limits to certainty and predictability, has been suppressed for decades in Western culture precisely because it symbolizes the re-emergence of the feminine into science.

Figure 4.2

In the beginning

Daniel Stern places metaphor at the narrative point of origin for individuals. The same holds true for schools of theoretical thought, which distinguish themselves partly through their axiomatic metaphors, both explicit and implicit. In the history of clinical theory, central metaphors were derived from any and all sources. Creative inspiration was as likely to be drawn from mythological as from scientific sources. Jungian psychologists chart mythological waters to plunge deeply into the unconscious; intersubjectivists chart interrelational space to venture into "the analytic third;" neuropsychologists chart fMRIs (functional magnetic resonance imaging) to construct objective maps of subjective experience.

The conflation of science and art within and between different schools of thought has led our profession to identity confusion, not to mention debates still raging today over whether psychotherapy is really a hermeneutic art or an empirical science. Yet the realms of art and science may not be as distinctive as they appear at first blush.

Under the broad umbrella of nonlinear sciences, I believe the importance of distinguishing between science and art within psychology dissolves still further, especially when within mental health. Theoretically, many implications of nonlinear, holistic sciences address qualitative, unique aspects impossible to grasp within the narrower framework of linear science alone.

Science box 4.1 Even mathematics is metaphorical

Cognitive scientists George Lakoff and Rafael Núñez (2001) suggest that even the most rigorous and abstract level of inquiry – mathematics – rests upon metaphorical foundations derived from concrete experience. Numbers can be considered "objects in a set," "points on a line" or "units of measurement." Each view rests upon a completely separate metaphor whose entailments pave the way for different mathematical branches. Paradoxes can arise in mathematics when implications of these different metaphors contradict one another, such as the "true" nature of the infinitely small. The conflation of art and science within psychology may as much reflect the embodied, metaphorical nature of all human inquiry, as it suggests a young field still grasping for preliminary understanding (see Figure 4.3).

Figure 4.3 Stack of books.

Courtesy of Megan Williams

Like numbers, books can be considered in many ways. They can be treated metaphorically as objects to read, or physically as objects to stack on one's night table, or as in this piece of art by Megan Williams, they can be objects to skewer and stack with the firm commitment never to read. If you are an avid reader, notice whether this image gives you a physical sense of violation. That visceral sensibility is the body basis for aesthetic appreciation as well as clinical intuition.

Pragmatically at the critical intersection between mind, brain and world, the sources for our creative metaphors may be less significant than how these metaphors function, either to expand or contract consciousness. In this book I happily conflate science with art, concretely mixing images from both, while abstractly shuttling back and forth between different discursive realms.

Projection at the source

Science and mythology may seem different on the surface, with science designed to address the "real" and mythology designed to express the imaginary. Yet as forms of inquiry within the human mind, both spring from unconscious sources. Both are creative acts emerging from the ambiguous space between inner and outer. Both are born of fundamental uncertainty, sharing with psychotherapy an interest in the narrative origins of experience. Both begin with an act of projection.

Here is my meta-metaphor for similarities and differences in art versus science: each brings forth a picture from the imagination laid atop the world like a set of clothes. The clothes either suit Nature's contours well or they do not. When they fit Nature's exact dimensions, she keeps them; when they do not, Nature returns the items to the store. In the case of science, the wardrobe is precisely tailored, with a dialogue ensuing back and forth concerning qualities of fit. In the case of mythology, style, fashion, culture, and freedom of expression and movement are more important than customized fit.

For those of us spawned in Western culture, it is easy to recognize projection in mythology, especially when extreme cultural differences exist. Few of us readily embrace a description of the Earth's origins as excreted by an earthworm upon the back of a swimming tortoise, as the Santals of India do. Yet for those of us steeped in Western culture, it can be harder to recognize projection within science. Too easily we become enthralled and enmeshed with our own theories. According to Jungian analyst Marial-Louise von Franz (1972: 10), "As long as we feel subjectively that we are not talking about projections but about the true quality of the object – a special aspect of our Western mentality – then we call it the scientific truth." In the name of objective science, we easily mistake the finger for the moon, according to Alan Watts, or the map for the territory, according to Alfred Korzybski (1994).

We mis-take our models for reality partly because the two blend so recursively and self-referentially together. Consider the complex feedback loops of modern technology: imagination becomes embodied and harnessed to bring forth computers. Computers drive the imagination and even body, as with virtual reality and neurofeedback. This in turn leads to the next generation of technology. With computers now implanted in the brain, under the skin, and in various body cavities, inner and outer become even more recursively enfolded at their creative origins, an observation at the heart of science fiction like *Neuromancer* (Gibson, 1987), movies like *The Matrix* (1999), and social commentary like *How we became posthuman* (Hayles, 1999).

Freud's cornucopia

Long before computers were spawned, psychoanalysis was birthed towards the end of the nineteenth century. Freud, its metaphorical father, was an amazingly prodigious thinker who combined the clinical observation of patients with a host of metaphors derived from multiple sources, some artistic, some scientific. That Freud's discourses were filled with evocative images was one reason he received the Goethe Award for writing in 1930. His highly metaphorical style still ignites our zest for reading his work into the present day, even for many of us who have discarded the majority of his theories.

Within Freud's choice of the sexual instinct around which to construct a developmental theory, he fused scientific and mythological modes and metaphors. His drive theory rested upon the scientific foundations of a hydraulic understanding of tension build-up and release, modeled after the newest technology of his times, the steam engine. Sexual and aggressive impulses in the psyche were thought to build up internal tension that had to be released, either through direct expression or indirectly through cathexis and sublimation. Without tension release came danger of an explosion. Later Freud transferred his interest to mythology by selecting the tale of Oedipus to deliver his theory of psychosexual development. Psychology historian John Kerr (1993) believes this to be the flash point when Freud propelled himself to international fame. Chapter 5 revisits the myth of Oedipus in greater detail from the perspective of metaphor and nonlinear dynamics.

In constructing his theories, Freud drew upon the prevailing medical beliefs of the time. Trained in neurology, Freud was originally mentored by Jean Charcot, a French physician who proposed a disease-pathology model of development. The cultural context also influenced Freud's adoption of materialism and theory of epigenesis, by which he proposed a universal sequence for the unfolding of psychosexual development (Galatzer-Levy, 2004).

Modell (2003) points out the metaphorical quality of Freud's developmental theories through the example of cathexis. When describing how primitive, sexual impulses within the unconscious become *converted and represented* into higher-order, conscious thinking, Freud employs a political metaphor. Primitive instincts move *like ambassadors* from one realm, the unconscious, to another, conscious experience, as if to *bridge their separate territories.*

Here the political metaphor blends right into a topographical one. For many of us "depth psychologists," we rarely stop to consider the origin of this notion of *depth*. Long before Freud's time, we can detect ancient roots for this topography within Heraclitus: "You could not discover the limits of soul even if you travel by every path in order to do so; such is the depth of its meaning."

Freud's treatment of psychological depth emerged out of his lifelong fascination with archeology, evident in the original psychoanalytic lay of the land. Repressed instincts of the id are located underground, in an undifferentiated, unconscious reservoir of desire and impulse. The superego hovers over our shoulder, where it serves to praise and haunt us. The ego is grounded at the surface, navigating according to the reality principle in order to mediate between warring factions of desire and conscience.

Even contemporary practitioners who have discarded one-person, structural models of the psyche in favor of two-person intersubjective ones bear a residue of Freud's topography when *digging* into the psyche of another with hopes of *interpenetration*. Note the conservative, static quality to Freud's archeological metaphor. Implicitly, Freud's topography suggests that everything in the psyche already exists, simply waiting to be unearthed by the investigator, with minimal creativity or interaction effect by the observer (see Figure 4.4).

From Freud's time until the present, central psychoanalytic metaphors have evolved from static, neutral, objective observers towards dynamic, involved, co-creative participants. Contemporary New York analyst Benjamin Wolstein (1995; see Wilner, 1998) illuminated this trend by identifying five metaphors to describe the psychoanalyst's psyche:

- mirror
- blank screen
- neutral interpreter
- participant observer
- coparticipant therapist and patient.

More recently Daniel Stern (2004) introduced a unique topography for the patient/therapist dyad.

> During a shared feeling voyage (which is the moment of meeting), two people traverse together a feeling-landscape as it unfolds in real time. . . . During this several-second journey, the participants ride the crest of the present instant as it crosses the span of the present moment, from its horizon of the past to its horizon of the future. As they move, they pass through an emotional narrative landscape with its hills and valleys of vitality affects, along its river of intentionality (which runs throughout), and over its peak of dramatic crisis. It is a voyage taken as the present unfolds. A passing subjective landscape is created and makes up a world in a grain of sand.
>
> (Stern, 2004a: 172)

Figure 4.4 LACPA Convention cover, 2004.

The topographical metaphor is clear in this cover designed for the Los Angeles County Psychological Convention (LACPA). Notice how my puns emerge from a literal rendering of metaphorical ideas. While a fertile source of humor, in real life I sometimes have problems understanding dry humor due to my concrete tendencies.

By fusing a topographical metaphor with temporal dynamics during the present moment of psychotherapy, Stern addresses implicit, nonlinear realms hidden within embodied, relational experience. Fractal landscapes are implied in the final phrase from Blake's poem, "To See a World, Fragments from Auguries of Innocence." Because the very perception and construction of a fractal depend intimately and self-referentially upon the scale of the observer, we can sense the dynamic, interaction-dependent flavor of topographical metaphors borrowed from this area of contemporary science. I believe the beauty of nonlinear science is partly in its fluid capacity to provide "living metaphors" that emerge in the moment, naturalistically. This perspective accords with Fogel and Garvey's (2007) recent application of nonlinear dynamics towards "alive communications" within infant development.

I next concretize the complex role of metaphor during psychotherapy by presenting a case where therapeutic progress accompanied a more metaphorical understanding of a concrete experience. Through self-reference and a critical twist of perspective, sometimes what appears to be part of the external world shifts inwards, as outer and inner topographies reverse places.

The big shake-up

Wayne viewed his life as divided into two clear stages – *before* and *after*. During the *before* period, Wayne was a carefree guy who glided through life's vicissitudes easily and fearlessly. No major problems. No real upsets. His childhood was totally "normal." Wayne grew up in a restaurant owned by his parents. He went to college, met his current wife, got married, owned and sold various businesses. Now Wayne and his wife owned their own restaurant.

Before the change, life proceeded without a hitch. *After* the change, Wayne was a different person. For more than a decade, he had felt scared much of the time, especially if venturing farther from home. Wayne panicked easily when driving, particularly in traffic. He was scared of elevators where he tended to feel trapped. He feared crowds, imagining himself getting sick in public, needing help or even suffering an embarrassing death. Every morning Wayne spent considerable time and energy making elaborate plans to get where he needed to that day. He decided exactly what to bring, what might go wrong, and how to escape if necessary. By the point of seeking psychotherapy, Wayne's life had contracted to a tiny nucleus surrounding his home, the only place he felt safe.

What brought about this *before–after* change? About a decade earlier, Wayne was staying at a desert resort when a major earthquake hit at 4 a.m., measuring 6.7 on the Richter scale. Wayne and his wife were caught asleep, many storeys in the air. The hotel swayed wildly for over a minute. Wayne scrambled in the dark to dress and escape. The journey outside seemed like an eternity, as Wayne traveled an endless hallway to reach the exit stairs. From that moment on Wayne was scared. He had tried a few months of therapy shortly after the earthquake, got some immediate relief, but his symptoms never really left, only slowly, insidiously worsened with the passing years.

Hmmm, quite a dramatic story. Such a sharp split between before *and* after. *Something feels funny. Before feels too simple. Too perfect a childhood. Like Helene Deutsch's AS IF personality: no detail . . . no texture . . . no nuance. I'm suspicious. Wayne's too flat in the telling. I can't feel his life Before. While After feels too opposite and extreme. Too much texture. Too much emotion. Like some inner switch thrown. Where's the middle ground?*

Wayne clearly suffered from an uncomplicated form of Post-Traumatic Stress Disorder (PTSD). A number of effective approaches exist to address this disorder, including systematic desensitization and cognitive-behavioral therapy. I do not claim that the method I selected was any more or less appropriate than other possibilities. I tell this tale instead to illustrate how my technique emerged out of the whole of who I am in response to the whole of who I perceived Wayne to be. In this respect alone, my use of metaphor was the best method possible, as it arose uniquely from our intersubjective chemistry.

The clinical musings above reflect that my attention was caught by a lack of complexity within Wayne's account of life *before* the change. His narrative seemed too mechanical, too robotic, largely un-self-reflective and un-feeling. Wayne's parents, so adept at the restaurant business of serving others, had taught him the same. Wayne grew up eager to please others, to the point of thoroughly overlooking himself, except in the most superficial ways. Wayne tended to deal with his feelings by avoiding them, tuning instead into the needs of others. One indicator of Wayne's difficulty being with himself was that his television was continually turned on, 24 hours a day.

At the point of seeking psychotherapy with me, Wayne and his wife had a young daughter. The timing seemed significant. Instinctively as Wayne tuned into his daughter's feelings better than his own, he could sense how his narrow life restricted his daughter's budding awakenings. Wayne came to therapy in order to wake himself up and expand his horizons as much for his daughter as for himself.

During my work with Wayne I used the trigger for the PTSD episode – the earthquake – as our central metaphor. The earthquake was not only at the center of his narrative, but also served as a concrete symbol for the emotional *shake-up* he so desperately needed. Because Wayne had become rigidly habituated to what he later dubbed his "machine mode," he required something as huge as an earthquake to awaken his inner, relational self.

Whereas the earthquake seriously shook Wayne up in one way, I shook him up in another. I did this by pointing out repeatedly how little "sense" Wayne's current system of operation made. All of his complicated schemes were backfiring. The more he planned around his fears, the more scared he got. The more he wanted to expand his repertoire, the farther it contracted. The more preoccupied he became with finding safety, the less he succeeded in achieving it.

One day these observations culminated in the following observation:

"Wayne, your problem is one of confusing inside with outside. You think you're afraid of traffic, elevators, and crowds. It seems quite the opposite to me. It's not what surrounds you scaring you most; it's what's inside you. You're frightened of yourself – your own feelings, your inner life. You think you're afraid of dying. Again you've got it backwards – what terrifies you is really living, to feel what it is to live in the moment, with all the scary, unpredictable emotion this stirs. You think you're afraid of being alone. What frightens you most is *being*, period."

This intervention had been building for months, rising slowly from within the depths of my own unconscious. The formulation originated out of the grating of those before/after opposites like two tectonic plates. The tension grew and grew, until finally it erupted in an unpremeditated and spontaneous way into the shake-up of this interpretation.

Wayne resonated with my words, a slight tremble present in his voice as he simply replied, "You're right." From this point on a series of small changes began gently to rock Wayne's world as he more fully embraced the significance of the earthquake as metaphor. Wayne's therapy did not involve the miracle cure therapists sometimes assert surrounding a sudden and complete removal of traumatic symptoms. Instead Wayne continued to struggle with his moods.

As his panic lessened dramatically, to the point of nearly disappearing, Wayne grew more inclined towards intense crying jags instead. These episodes sometimes prevented him from leaving home, but usually were brief and followed by long periods of feeling relatively calm and competent. Although Wayne continued resisting being alone and yearned to slip back into "machine-mode," he countered these impulses by starting a self-reflection journal and reading a book on *Mindfulness* by Ellen Langer (1989). Wayne turned off the TV more often, moving from what object relational theorists might call a "paranoid schizoid" to a "depressive" position.

Within psychotherapy the earthquake metaphor was clearly self-referential. Not only did it refer to the outside world and real facts lodged in Wayne's history and memory, but also it captured an implicit dimension of our intersubjective work through embodying my ultimate intentions to shake up Wayne's maladaptive system of processing his ongoing experience. In this sense the metaphor functioned not only to reflect "what was" in Wayne's history but also to encapsulate my influence interpersonally by suggesting "what could be." In nonlinear terms this is much like two coupled oscillators, where one drives the other.

Wayne's inner shake-up helped to remove his focus from a scary world outside him to a scary world inside, grounding him more solidly within his internal experience. My purposeful conflation of inner/outer processes had two opposing effects. The bad news was it took away the one remaining source of safety for Wayne – his home. Now he was safe nowhere. The good news was that an internal focus on his feelings reduced Wayne's need to seek external safety, helping to soothe that out-of-control, panicky edge.

Wayne ceased to enact his fear, which had taken the form of running and moving away from whatever external objects his fear seized upon. Wayne grew more skilled in stilling himself so that he could face his feelings from the inside. As he did so, little by little Wayne expanded his external horizons. Courageously he began venturing farther from home, testing the limits of his previous comfort zone.

The earthquake metaphor also helped to in-form Wayne of the deep origins of his fear, not in the actual earthquake but in the period *before*, arising from Wayne's lack of attunement to himself. By not attending closely to his inner experience, there developed a dearth of self-interaction, or what I designate in Chapter 7 as self–self interactions. Wayne's disinclination towards self-reflection suggested the absence of recursively looping emotional energy.

Complexity and memory in present time

Wayne's shake-up in awareness represented an increase in complexity, involving both internal and external levels of experience. From rigidly held extremes of a carefree world *before*, where self-reflection was unnecessary, to a risk-laden pit of dangers *after*, where self-inhibition was the only choice, Wayne found more safety and freedom of movement in the middle, closer to the edge of chaos. Here Wayne became better attuned to the immediacy of his own emotional fluctuations. This helped him to contend with life's ultimate unpredictability while rolling with its emotional vicissitudes. Wayne reduced his need to anticipate every little bump in the road. As a result he better enjoyed the freedom and spontaneity of the moment, trusting himself to take more risks and handle whatever unexpectedly might arise. Now Wayne could wait for obstacles in the real world, instead of having to continually generate them in his imagination.

Interestingly Wayne's increase in complexity fed back retrospectively to influence his memory, so that his understanding of the precipitating trauma became more emotionally textured and differentiated. Originally when Wayne told the story of the earthquake, he had described being so scared that he had instantly felt trapped. In a panic he had flailed around in the dark, eventually following others until he stumbled upon the exit stairway at the far side of the building. When reviewing the event with me later, Wayne mentioned a new realization – his panicky feelings had caused him to overlook the *exit route that existed right next to his room.* With this more differentiated, integrated memory came a more embodied perception that Wayne had never really been trapped at all. All these years of fear had related more to a subjective feeling than to any objective condition. Being trapped was an illusion Wayne had created in his mind due to limitations within his perspective that prevented him from opening his eyes in the moment to see and utilize resources that surrounded him. How like Charlotte's release from her cage!

In Chapter 3 I discussed mental health in terms of the complex flow of mental and behavioral states self-organized at the edge of chaos. While no tight definition yet exists for psychological complexity, Wayne's increased capacity to remember details about his history appears evidence for heightened psychological complexity via increased neural integration (Siegel, 2007, 2008). Wayne's enhanced episodic memory also relates to attachment research (see Siegel, 1999) indicating that the best predictor of secure attachment in children is not the degree of trauma in their parents' history, but whether their parents can tell a coherent narrative about their own childhood. As Wayne felt more secure in his current life, his memory and narrative reflected greater coherence and security in his past.

Preliminary research (Tschacher et al., 1998) identifies factors related to increased complexity during psychotherapy. Over time degrees of freedom become more constrained during therapeutic exchanges, taken as evidence for increased coupling between therapist and patient. This kind of higher order coupling born of recursive feedback loops occurred in therapy with Wayne. His earthquake story evoked an unconscious rumble in me, which slowly rose to consciousness through a series of observations. Finally it erupted within a single powerful intervention that triggered a continual series of aftershocks in Wayne. Our mutual influence on one another indicated fewer degrees of freedom in the therapist–patient system. Meanwhile the earthquake metaphor became increasingly harnessed into a particular direction, towards therapeutic change.

Wayne's shift in memory reveals the value of returning to the past during psychotherapy, not so much to drum up ancient discontents as to consolidate present therapeutic gains. To return to memories of the event and later to his early childhood helped Wayne better to understand how his symptoms derived insidiously and invisibly from a hidden, underground fault that took over forty years to erupt.

In our psychotherapy as a whole, Wayne's early relationship to his parents took a back seat to his current relationship to the world. Even though Wayne's healing occurred within the intersubjective context of our therapeutic relationship, this aspect of therapy remained implicitly curled within self-referential resonances of the earthquake metaphor. The feel of psychotherapy differed greatly from the case of Jim described next, where the intersubjective field was much more consciously in focus.

The complexity of metaphors

As different schools of therapy cluster around different central metaphors, they naturally select one aspect of wholeness, sometimes at the expense of others. Contemporary psychodynamic theory focuses primarily on the self–other, intersubjective matrix. Cognitive-behavioral therapy focuses primarily on the self–world relationship outside of the therapeutic alliance. Meanwhile Jungian therapy focuses largely on self–self revelations emerging from the wisdom of dream symbolism and deep introspection.

Each school of thought employs a unique set of congealed metaphors to direct the therapeutic investigation. Every avenue of exploration precludes others in the process. Out of this recognition Wilner (1998) and Wolstein (1995) warn against therapists beginning with reified metaphors, such as *analyst as mirror*, that serve primarily to bolster defensive operations or unduly constrain authentic encounters between therapist and patient (see Figure 4.5).

The framework of nonlinear science can help avoid unnecessary narrowing born of reified metaphors. Nonlinear dynamics may be a living metaphor both fluid and specific enough to move along with experience, shaping it in an organic, self-organizing manner without extruding it too far though a rigid template. Note psychiatrist/psychoanalyst Grant Brenner's use of metaphor as he muses on the potential for nonlinear dynamics to move closer to lived experience (personal communication, March 4, 2006):

> I feel that immediate experience is at the boundary of the self experience as it comes into being; the closer we get to that singularity the closer we come to dissolution and at the same time to a genuine sense of self as individual. It is like trying to go into a fountain though, against the pressure, and never being able to get there; a reverse black hole of sorts, but one which can go back and forth from spewing out to sucking in, in many dimensions.
>
> However, immediate experience is like melted wax in that once it comes out it begins to harden and cool. As it cools it becomes more and more rigid, from association, to loose metaphor, to solid metaphor, to theory, and so on. Culture is divided as to where people tend to reside in relation to immediate experience, depending on what kind of anxiety they are most comfortable with, perhaps . . . Wolstein wonders if a metaphor exists which can move with experience, and so do I. Can such a metaphor be constructed or as I suspect, must it create itself as highly flexible to approach the unique, unpredictable dynamics that emerge out of the present moment?

To operate as experience-near as possible within this zone of living metaphor, I believe a truly complex picture of the psyche necessarily includes awareness

Figure 4.5 After Holbein.

The mirror has frequently served as metaphor for an ideal therapeutic relationship. The mirror implies clear sight plus an objective, undistorted reflection of patient dynamics. Yet no matter how uncontaminated the therapeutic feedback may be, in the sense of freedom from ghosts haunting the therapist from the past, due to self-reference, even mirrors sometimes make unexpected contributions.

of three separate, but intertwined types of relationships: self–self, self–other, self–world. Each becomes relevant for different patients at different moments during therapy. As therapists, I believe we expand our clinical repertoire by including metaphors that implicate all three relational areas. Such an expanded view in the context of the unity between all areas of science as well as other ways of knowing is a central aspect to interpersonal neurobiology. By including all levels of interface between self, world and other we can employ both axiomatic and spontaneous metaphors that emerge dynamically out of the therapeutic process itself in order to highlight problematic areas in response to patient particulars. I expand upon this way of parsing out psychological complexity in the Chapters 7, 8 and 9.

Mind as mechanism

Along with evidence for his increased psychological complexity, we can analyze Wayne's shift in memory in terms of the creative, continually responsive nature of memory itself. Contemporary nonlinear research (e.g., Freeman, 1991) reveals memory as a dynamic function of present circumstances, including physiology, rather than as a fixed snapshot of past events. I reached the same conclusion in Chapter 3 in the case of Suzy, whose false memories of childhood and sexual abuse appeared largely a function of set and setting, including biases driven implicitly and explicitly by the professional culture.

Many previous notions about memory within psychological theory have been static, often presuming the veridical or accurate inner representations of outer events. Here the notion of representation is less political and more technological, deriving from a larger class of mind-as-mechanism metaphors. This kind of metaphor is deeply entrenched in our culture's thinking, evident in assertions like, *she has a photographic memory*.

There is a long, time-honored history of using machine metaphors to broaden our understanding of the human mind (see Draaisma, 1995/2000). Dating back to ancient Greece and *Theaetitus*, Plato compared memory to a seal in a wax tablet. Both are "impressionable," one figuratively, the other literally preserving impressions over time to accumulate and transmit culture. Socrates conceptualized the wax tablet as a gift of Mnemosyne, mother of the Muses (compare mnemonic devices as memory aids). Whereas Plato used mythology to play with these images, Aristotle gave them more a literal meaning by stressing physiological aspects of memory traces. Over the centuries the image of static representations has remained similar, although the nature of the writing surface has varied. Whether involving wax tablets, codex, parchment or paper, figures such as Cicero, Thomas Aquinas, and Augustine all used notions of "imprinting" and "impression" to describe the retention of memory.

Freud likewise drew inspiration from the latest writing gadget – the "Mystic Writing-Pad" – a toy that still exists nowadays. The device has three layers: a celluloid sheet covered wax paper, with both atop a soft underbelly of wax. A pointed object leaves an impression. The clear paper can be lifted to erase the upper layer, while invisible hints are left in the soft underside. The mystic writing-pad inspired Freud to speculate about separate layers in the physiology of memory, anticipating current neurological distinctions between short- and long-term divisions.

Many major revolutions in the history of psychology trace back to mechanistic metaphors. The older discipline of behaviorism attempted to bypass consciousness altogether by banishing it to the invisible, irrelevant category of a "black box." The black box metaphor was based on input–output connections from a telephone switchboard model. Then the twentieth century invention of the great computing machine ushered in the modern cognitivist revolution that still continues (e.g., Gardner, 1985; Penrose, 1989). The computer provided new, concrete methods of investigation, as well as an abstract source for theorizing how the mind "operates" on the contents of consciousness. The cognitivist revolution likened the psyche to information processing by a computer.

Modern thinkers, like Margaret Boden (1992), boldly claim that this association solves Descartes' old metaphysical quandary of the relationship between body and mind by separating information processing into two levels. One level involves the "hardware" – the body and physiological underpinnings, such as brain chemistry and neuronal circuits known as "wetware." The second level involves the "software" – the mind, including its symbolic levels of operation and representation. More recently an article about "Morphware" appeared in *Scientific American* (Koch, 2005), proposing a more dynamically complex hardware able to reconfigure itself on the fly to meet different task needs.

Freud's idea about layers of memory perseveres, even though our senses do not record like a mystic-pad with traces literally impressed upon the brain. Yet even "wrong" metaphors are partially right. Traces of earlier experience do exist more abstractly within the interconnectivity of neurological pathways. Whereas older metaphors derived from the phonograph helped us to understand analog processes that exist in neurochemistry, the compact disc helps to model the all-or-nothing, digital quality of electrical signals. Another recent invention, the hologram, furthers our thinking by capturing the parallel, distributed and projective qualities of memory (see Levenson, 1976; Pribram et al., 1974; Wilbur, 1982).

Whereas mechanical models of memory imply static recording of past events, as mentioned previously, the dynamic, present-centered quality of memory is revealed by more recent, nonlinear research of Walter Freeman (1991; Skarda and Freeman, 1987). Freeman used computers and EEG recordings to record patterns of neuronal firing in the olfactory bulb of rabbits exposed to different smells. When rabbits were exposed to different smells, Freeman noticed that the background pattern of chaos gave way to more ordered, lower dimensional attractors associated with each smell. When Freeman presented the same odors in different orders, he discovered something truly remarkable – when a rabbit was re-exposed to the same smell, the physiological underpinnings proved completely different from the first exposure. Most significantly this effect occurred only when smells were associated with particular consequences.

This research suggests that the dynamic quality of memory requires stimuli to *carry meaning*. Freeman (1995, 1999a, 1999b) believes that meaning can be understood neurobiologically when the brain imagines intentional behaviors directed towards future goals and then changes itself in line with the sensory consequences of those behaviors. Modell (2003: 19) cites Freeman's research in his own attempt to formulate a neurobiology of meaning, succinctly stating that "Meaning is achieved through action in the world, and in turn, the self is altered by that action." By including the imagination in its processing, memory is as much a forward-looking as it is a backwards-reaching affair. The creative function of memory, as illustrated by its underlying neurophysiology, is also endorsed by contemporary constructivist thinking.

Science box 4.2 The nonlinear brain

During the 1980s and spearheaded by the groundbreaking work of Walter Freeman, neuroscientists believed they had found low-dimensional chaos in the brain, serving as the background for more ordered perception. Seeing this as an elegant explanation for how the brain waits in readiness and quickly mobilizes, scientists sought chaotic attractors within messy EEG data. We now know that the brain is better characterized as high-dimensional, constrained noise, rather than as low-dimensional deterministic chaos.

The human brain is essentially nonlinear, which leads to several important generalizations. At the cellular level, the neurological underpinnings of the brain are ever unique, even when manifest behavior or experiential states appear similar. Due to sensitive dependence plus critical developmental windows, tiny neurological differences early in life can amplify into huge effects or irreversible deficits later on.

When investigating the relationship between structure and function in the brain, caution must be exercised against using brain imaging in overly linear or reductionistic ways. A one-to-one relationship never holds between a single part of the brain and particular functions. The brain always operates holistically; its coupled operations often link near and distant areas. For a given task, even where neurons do not fire, neurotransmitters do not release, and signs of metabolic activity are not present, the silent portions of the brain contribute just as significantly as do the more active areas.

The next case illustrates Modell's insight that metaphor links unconscious autobiographical memory with conscious experience. During psychotherapy with Jim, the past became embodied within the present through Jim's creative imagination in the form of a spontaneous image. By merging current symptoms with early childhood origins, the metaphor brought past into the present, as well as present into the future by presaging the solution Jim eventually found. Through metaphor, with the whole in sight, new in-sight and novel sources for inner complexity became possible.

Fathers and suns

Jim sought psychotherapy because he had a deep, dark sense that something was wrong. Pleasant and highly ambitious, in his mid-twenties, Jim set high standards for himself and worked hard to live up to them. In fact most of the time, no matter what else he was doing, even during recreational activities, Jim worked really hard. He had trouble having fun or playing, ever responding to the joyless, plodding, pressured voice inside, relentlessly driving him (see Figure 4.6).

Jim had a vision. If he could only get far enough down the road to success, he would be rewarded with the thing he wanted more than anything. This reward was something Jim had sought since childhood, the one thing that kept eluding him – happiness. Jim could visualize exactly how the process would work. He would rise up the corporate ladder to accumulate power and wealth. These acquisitions would prove irresistible magnets for attractive women. After earning the girl and finding romance, ultimately love was destined to bring Jim the happiness he perpetually sought.

According to this linear formula, happiness would be the automatic outcome of hard work. The system worked well in theory, but something kept going awry in practice. Jim had been at his plan for quite a while. He had climbed up the corporate ladder several rungs. He had had girlfriends. Yet Jim's advances only seemed to bring him further from the happiness he sought, rather than closer. What was wrong?

Consciously Jim did not understand his problem, yet unconsciously he was wiser than he knew. One day during session he produced a poignant metaphor for his condition, characterized by a most peculiar topology. Instead of a bright sun shining on his inner landscape, Jim envisioned a black hole in the middle of his event horizon. In physics, black holes are points of singularity where gravity collapses and ordinary laws of nature break down. Everything within a radius defined by the event horizon gets sucked into the black hole forever. In real life black holes are invisible. This is because even informational signals associated with light get sucked inside. By contrast Jim's black hole was very visible, appearing as a big black sun, an image that carried multiple connotations – sexual, womblike, excretory, and so on. No matter what happened, no matter how hard Jim tried, no matter what corrective actions he

Figure 4.6 Belt tightening.

Courtesy of Megan Williams/Collection of Jon Lee

  We tighten our belts literally in order to hold up our pants. When we tighten our belts metaphorically, we buckle down to endure hardship. It is one thing to tighten our belts when times get tough; it is quite another to become compulsive about the matter, and recursively wrap our belts so many times around our torsos that our freedom to breathe and move become entirely constricted.

took, the result was always the same – everything got sucked down into the black hole. This repetitive process was like a law of nature – all light shall turn to darkness; all vestiges of hope must disappear. Nothing could alter such an all-encompassing force.

  Wow, what a powerful image. What a gaping hole sucking in all life and light . . . right at the center . . . smack at the core. Where does this force come from? What are its origins? Nothing apparent at the surface . . . no big traumas . . . no hurts . . . no disappointments . . . no failures. What is so powerful underneath as to collapse all light and hope?

Together as Jim and I sleuthed out the deep meaning of his image, an interesting pattern emerged regarding Jim's work history. At several different jobs, under completely different circumstances, the same interpersonal dynamics kept emerging. All of Jim's attention and energy would eventually become focused upon a single individual, usually a man. Superficially, the two would get along; underneath, struggles would erupt. To Jim, this person held all the power and kept using it unfairly to thwart his ambition and advancement. Jim's current boss was a good example – he adored Jim's bright ideas, yet continually absorbed them into his own narcissistic agenda, without credit. Immediately Jim and I recognized how his boss represented the black hole sucking away all independent sources of light and aliveness.

Okay, this fits. But there must be more. Still too superficial. Why does the same scenario happen over and over? The same dynamic at all jobs? This is a symptom, not the origin. Different people, different reasons, same effect. Something deeper . . . something at the core . . . something else driving the repetition.

There is a saying among Interpersonal Relation circles that "Whatever is dissociated gets enacted." As we continued to stalk the mythic origins of Jim's mysterious black hole, intuitively I sensed something deeply dissociated in his continual enactment related to unvoiced yearnings. My hunch alluded to the repetition – in the sense of asking again and again – underlying the repetition compulsion.

One day I casually observed to Jim, "Funny how that black hole is right at the center. It's risen up in place of the sun. Why is there no sun?"

"No sun. No sun. No sun." Over and over, Jim repeated the phrase.

Then he said, "You know, that's just how I felt at home – like there was no son (sic!)."

Jim was onto something. The homonym between sun and son gave a clue to the metaphorical origins we sought. The time arrived to shed some light on Jim's childhood. He was an only child, his father unusually old when Jim was born. Dad was a heavy smoker, continuing his habit despite chronic lung problems that extended back to before Jim could remember. Jim was about 10 years old when dad developed emphysema. His father was in and out of hospitals with medical flare-ups that appeared and disappeared unexpectedly. These continual episodes forced all family plans to revolve around dad's health. Whether the family went on this trip or that one depended completely on dad's physical condition. What was worse, dad was morbidly preoccupied with his own death. Every vacation was potentially his last, something he seemed compelled to vocalize.

There it was, right at Jim's emotional center. A complete nonevent of dad's impending death hung in the air like a black hole. With this at the intersubjective core, there was no safe space for a son as a separate being, no room for any shining dreams or rising agency of his own. No wonder boss after boss seemed to eclipse Jim's bright future. No wonder happiness kept eluding Jim, lurking somewhere far off within a fictitious future. Even with all obvious barricades to Jim's advance removed, it did not matter. Now Jim's black hole was as much inside him as it was in his outside conditions.

Jim and I had reached the emotional, narrative origins of his black hole. So now what? What is the solution to this problem as now posed? Here I offer a method of letting metaphor speak from a place of wholeness, first to flesh out the problem of felt experience more fully, then to let solutions arise more spontaneously. This method fits into an explicit framework for therapist training developed by psychologist Richard Kopp in *Metaphor therapy* (1995). According to Kopp's protocol, patients first produce metaphors to represent their problems; then they are encouraged to consciously manipulate these images to find solutions.

The approach I have found helpful is similar although less systematized, more emergent and self-organizing. The direction a metaphor takes is dictated by its own inherent dynamics. With Jim, the image of the black hole initially represented external relations with bosses and his father. Later the same image served to forge another level of depth of self–self relations with himself. Here is what eventually emerged from further exploration of the sun/son homonym: Jim's parents loved him dearly, responding to him emotionally in "good enough" fashion. The problem arose from Jim's ambivalent attachment to his father. Out of love, Jim retained a close connection. Out of guilt, Jim subsumed all his own needs, wants and feelings to the black hole of his father's impending death. Out of anger, Jim turned all his needs and feelings inwards, imploding his own capacity for pleasure and happiness.

In this way, love, anger and guilt were so thoroughly mixed together as to form another black hole, this one wholly within. We can see multiple scales of the black hole image, which represented both Jim's merged external relations with his father as well as his undifferentiated internal relations with himself. This multi-tiered understanding laid out the emotional territory for the next phase of therapy. Jim had to sort through these various strands of feelings to express his love for his father in a less self-sacrificial way. Only by distinguishing his own needs from those of his father could he reclaim his right to be/ have a son/sun. As Jim worked through these deeply personal issues, slowly but surely, Jim found glimmers of satisfaction in outer, daily life. At his job the situation with his power-hungry boss resolved suddenly in an unexpected way. When his boss left to take another job Jim was promoted to the top rung, where he has functioned as an uneclipsed star ever since.

Concurrent with these changes, one day Jim announced he had been thinking about the black hole and had noticed a difference. While still there, the
black hole was now "decentered," in that it no longer occupied the center of
his universe. The black hole was off to the left, left somewhere in the past. At
the center where the black hole used to be had risen a little bitty sun. Over
time Jim used this new version diagnostically to report his mood variations.
When he felt particularly good the black hole was almost out of sight and the
sun larger. When his mood was darker the black hole migrated towards the
center, carrying the ever-present potential to eclipse the neophyte sun.

In this clever way Jim's image represented the whole – his early childhood
relations with dad, his current relations with bosses, his ongoing emotional
relations with self. The metaphor became not only diagnostic but also prognostic, moving from static to dynamic, as Jim's psyche became more complex
and fluid, relationships more securely attached. Wholeness is evident within
the spontaneous shift, where a solution had been implicitly enfolded within
the problem space itself. Jim's increasingly flexible perspective was also symbolized in the movement of the black hole from the center of his experience.

With the appearance of the sun emerged a new, brighter dimension. Jim's
expanded illumination of self and other represented an enhanced ability both
to differentiate and integrate the original, tangled knot of emotion into a
more complex inner organization. As Jim attained inner separation from his
father, he was free to offer positive feelings of aliveness to the relationship
in place of negative, self-sacrificial ones. These changes also reflected themselves during psychotherapy in lighter moments that became more frequent.
Jim even began to laugh at my jokes.

Loss of complexity in depression

A nonlinear perspective reminds us that all remains in flux. Within the psyche, through unconscious potentiality, the past carries meaning into the
future with a dynamic quality even reflected at the neurobiological root,
through changing physiological underpinnings evoked by current sensation
and memory. We cannot undo, change or remove any part of the past. All we
can do is to render the present more complex by adding new dimensions to
current experience. This idea is illustrated beautifully by Jim's decentered
black hole. Even though the black hole remained in the sky, it lost its power to
define Jim's whole/hole existence.

In this final section I explore the significance of this image further, by
tunneling into the black hole broadly as a metaphor for psychotherapy
with depression. Jim's imagery is highly suggestive. Although decentered,
the black hole remained, lurking on the horizon. This concurs with the
neurophysiology of depression. Once the potential to fall into depression is

expressed, the neural circuitry remains, even if never used again. To decenter the black hole is to open up the future without having to undo the past.

Once depression no longer occupies the center of experience, where it inevitably becomes entwined with one's identity, other experiences help to render a person's emotional repertoire more complex. The more time spent in positive moments, the greater the potential for a future life more filled with light and joy. Certainly these musings fit with a cognitive-behavioral perspective, where the construction of new thoughts and corresponding actions in the world carries hopes of corresponding new feelings. These ideas are also consistent with positive psychology's focus on gratitude and the tracking of positive events.

When someone is chronically or characterologically depressed, to spend excessive time in psychotherapy exploring how black feelings today link with traumas in the past may function to reinforce the current episode. Consider Hebb's rule for the neurophysiology of state-dependent memory: neurons that fire together wire together. To continually revisit bad feelings today as they link up with bad feelings in the past is to add new, intersubjective loops to old, depressive circuitry. Many people in the contemporary trauma field reach similar conclusions. For example, people interested in Eye Movement Desensitization and Reprocessing (EMDR) frequently employ positive, skill, resource and ego-building techniques. EMDR is an information processing model of therapy that posits trauma-related symptoms to arise when events are inadequately processed in memory.

This said, going over the same material over and over again can be useful for increasing complexity, changing narratives, reworking traumatic memory or recontextualizing old memories. These opposite results especially seem to hold when self–self relations are underdeveloped, with memories that are especially fuzzy, or when current functioning is not highly impaired. It remains an open empirical question as to when such repetition is beneficial during psychotherapy and when it worsens things. Even in light of such research, clinicians still must feel their way into patient particulars, partly by drawing upon experience-near metaphors.

This chapter presents metaphor as a central vehicle within psychotherapy to find meaning through reflecting upon past and present circumstances, and driving an ever-evolving future. Viewed from a nonlinear perspective we therapists seek bifurcations that signal change from old attractor patterns into new ones. To find the central metaphor is to locate a potential control parameter for driving change, whether implicitly or explicitly. Originating metaphors are significant neurobiologically, by representing the intersection of image, sensation, emotion, thought and impulse, all central to the creation of meaning. In the case of Wayne, the central metaphor was supplied externally by a major life crisis. With Jim, as with Charlotte in Chapter 3, metaphors emerged spontaneously within psychotherapy. In all three cases, at first the image represented the problem as an impasse. Later, along with the evolving psychotherapeutic dyad, the image morphed dynamically to represent new solutions and emergent shifts towards greater complexity, both at inner and outer levels.

Chapter 5 revisits the myth of Oedipus as the originating myth of psychoanalysis. Viewed through nonlinear lenses, I revisit Oedipus' past in hopes of changing our future. By tinkering with our collective memory of this story I strive to nudge clinical psychology a step further in its natural path towards increased complexity.

Chapter 5

Riddle of the Sphinx revisited

Only when seeing is no-seeing is there real seeing.

Zen koan from D.T. Suzuki

Within psychotherapy metaphor sings at the creative heart of personal narrative. Metaphor also establishes whole schools of psychological thought. Freud embraced the sexual instinct as the originating metaphor for his psychosexual theory of development. By contrast, Fritz Perls, founder of the Gestalt school of psychotherapy, rebelled against Freud partly by choosing a different bodily function – the hunger instinct. In *Ego, hunger, and aggression* (1969), Perls likened mental absorption of the world to stages of food consumption, his language fitting: Perls *chewed* on psychoanalytic theory; in response to its *undigested* morsels, he *cooked up* a set of *oral* defenses. Among these, introjection meant to *swallow* information *whole*, as when reporters *gulp down* bits of news, only to *spit them back up* again in the form of articles.

At the level of metaphor the work of Fritz dovetailed nicely with his European counterpart, Melanie Klein. Klein rebelled against Freud by attending to pre-Oedipal stages of emotional development. Like Perls, Klein's neo-analytic, British Object Relations school highlighted the hunger instinct, but more relationally, within the mother–infant bond. Kleinians observe how patients seek mental nourishment from therapists, as if infants nursing at the breast.

Psychoanalytic and Gestalt therapies vary considerably, both in theory and practice. Yet underneath each converges upon a concrete human function treated symbolically, as a method to heighten patient awareness. Whereas psychoanalytic techniques feed patients' interpretations in order to make the unconscious more conscious, Gestalt therapists design experiments to render split off aspects of the personality more digestible (see Perls, 1969; Polster and Polster, 1973).

In Chapter 4 I introduced metaphor as a primary tool for increasing internal complexity. Metaphor is hardwired into the brain to make sense of the world, often by fusing image, feeling and word into felt understanding. In this chapter I suggest that the progression from concrete to symbolic meta-phorical expression is one important, if not universal, developmental path to internal complexity.

With the hunger instinct as a central metaphor, this chapter begins with the clinical tale of Linda to illustrate this progression during psychotherapy. As Linda worked through early trauma, she moved from unconscious levels of enactment and body symptoms towards an increased capacity to hold and process emotion more consciously and verbally. Following this case material, I introduce the role of paradox in the emergence of complexity by revisiting the myth of Oedipus through contemporary lenses. The Sphinx's riddle appears as a paradox of self-reference that points inwards, towards the self. By drawing implicitly upon his traumatic origins to understand the riddle self-referentially, Oedipus solved the riddle by shifting from a literal interpretation of "morning," "midday," and "night" to a more metaphorical understanding regarding stages of human life.

This contemporary neurobiological reading presents the path to inner complexity as metaphorically paved with paradox. I suggest that paradoxes of self-reference serve both as the bane of the psyche's existence, as well as its salvation. This central proposition, in line with Ghent's (1992) thinking in "Paradox and process," plus Beisser's (1971) "paradoxical theory of change," sets the stage for later chapters introducing fractals as metaphors for the complex, twisted geometries of intersubjective and interobjective space.

Therapeutic food for thought

When Linda first appeared for help, I knew my plate was full. Still in therapy with another therapist, despite years of working together, Linda now felt stuck and frustrated by the lack of progress. At the time she was taking lots of psychotropic medication, suffering many side effects, and deriving no clear benefits from her daily cocktail. Linda endured long periods of hopeless, wordless withdrawal, both from husband and her previous therapist, lasting for weeks, punctuated by fits of rage.

Treatment impasses or failures hold special interest for me, as if a puzzle that has eluded others, now assigned to me to solve. Whenever possible, I confer with previous therapists in search of clues to avoid similar pitfalls. I find it helpful to capitalize on their perception of what happened – especially what went wrong. Linda's previous therapist described their work as trauma-related, centering upon Linda's history of severe sexual and physical abuse. This woman cared deeply for her client, feeling she had taken Linda as far as she could, and had little sense of any missing ingredients. After many years working together, she sent Linda on with many blessings.

From the beginning, I instinctively took a different tack. I focused less on the details of Linda's history and more on the texture of our present relationship. My cue came from those long spaces punctuating Linda's previous work, with its disjointed rhythm of engagement and disengagement. I wondered what drove Linda away from contact. There appeared a clear attachment problem. I grew determined to tune in into a different scale of therapeutic complexity by turning away from facts and focusing on emergent dynamics at the micro level of minute-to-minute process in the room.

I paid close attention to the therapeutic dyad as a coupled system characterized by tiny, emotional exchanges, both at implicit and explicit levels, continually crossing the open boundaries between us. I focused intensely on nuances of Linda's internal experience, helping her to verbalize these. I was a highly active participant, an interpreter of Linda's unconscious, helping her to find meaning and make sense of otherwise mute symptoms and blind impulses.

Initially my approach felt alien to Linda. Yet it also delighted and relieved her from the start. No one had ever tuned in this way before. No one had ever talked to Linda about her experience of the present moment. Linda confessed feeling as soothed by the sound of my voice as by the words I used. The melody felt like a feeding to her; and the more Linda felt fed, the more this highlighted what she had unwittingly been starving for – a way to illuminate subterranean emotional waves of approach and retreat based on fear, desire, hope, abandonment and disgust.

Within this present-centered focus, it took months to piece together Linda's history from the bits of information that dribbled in through context. Linda grew up in the South in a trailer park, and was emotionally and physically abused by a mother who was unpredictable and erratic. From day to day Linda did not know whether she would awaken to a smiling mom making pancakes or a rage-aholic about to batter her child instead. Linda was molested by a grandfather when quite young, and then later lost her virginity to rape by a high school classmate.

Linda took all these events into stride, including the rape. Surrounded by inappropriate sex from the beginning, Linda was determined to normalize her own sex life. Linda determined not to be like her mother, whose open refusals to sexually service her husband led to violence and drove her father to other women. More often than not, Linda was dragged along to these "secret" trysts by her father and asked to "wait outside" where she could hear everything.

Linda was the oldest of three. From as early as she could remember, Linda felt more grown-up and wise than either parent. She protected her siblings by throwing herself in the middle of her parents' conflicts. She learned how to cook, clean and babysit when only a few years old. Linda was a hard worker, always taking multiple jobs. She did whatever was necessary to escape her current plight. Given her maturity, why was she so often confused by life? Most of the time, Linda was too busy to worry about this, being too caught up in survival mode, pushing hard through adversity.

When just a young child, Linda found safety by dissociating from her body and separating from her feelings, a style in place since age 5. At this turning point, her father beat her senseless with a belt. Linda relied on her thinking instead. She used logic to combat and compensate for the violence around her. Linda also had a long history of medical symptoms. Her success dissociating from her feelings appeared to take its toll by driving distress into her body. Both medically and personally Linda's history was filled with drama. As a teenager she ran away with a carnival. Then she became an exotic dancer. Slowly in response to her own contempt towards abusive boyfriends, Linda deepened her involvement in the dark underbelly of sex, first as a call girl, later as a dominatrix, all the while priding herself on talents for sexual performance and enjoyment.

Then in her mid-twenties Linda met Bill. He was neither abusive nor irresponsible. For many years, Linda could not believe Bill was for real. She was angry, not ready, "over it," and tested him like crazy. But Bill hung in there, so faithful, so sweet. Nothing like those other guys. Then when Linda suffered physical symptoms surrounding her "female parts" and saw that Bill continued to stick by her side, she began to trust him as the first kind, gentle man she had known. Eventually they married. Soon after, following a stream of doctors unable to help, Linda found a female gynecologist she also trusted. The doctor performed surgery, which finally healed her longstanding, severe and painful case of endometriosis. With a healthier body, and from the more solid relational platform of a female caretaker, Linda was now ready to deal with her emotions.

Here was the attachment picture, as I conceptualized it. During the early years, Linda fed on rage. With her parents primarily attached through anger and all the violence of her childhood, not only was there a model for being angry, but there was always an enemy to fight, a negative influence to push away from. Now for the first time, Linda was in an odd position – she was surrounded by support, with no obvious enemy in sight. She could mobilize in service of her own needs, wants and feelings.

But initially Linda was at a loss. Given all the safety and support, why did she struggle so? Why was she eating herself up alive? Her experience made no sense to her logical mind. Linda felt crazy and confused by her own illogic. During this transition period, Linda relied heavily on my capacities to digest her experience, feeding it back in bits, as if a mother bird. As Linda weaned off the strong psychotropic medications, repeatedly I interpreted the chaos of her emotions counter-intuitively as progress. What was dissociated before was now breaking through, affording us both opportunities to "feast" on and metabolize Linda's ongoing experience together.

As therapy progressed, the metaphor of mental digestion became more explicit. Linda's increasing trust in my ability to interpret her "psycho"-logic, helped her to do the same. What began as bodily impulses to push away from therapy or go unconscious by sleeping much of the day slowly gave way to words that expressed Linda's violent struggles with her own emotions. But the metaphor went beyond this symbolic level to capture a process quite literal.

Linda's digestive system got increasingly pulled into the middle of our work. First came a slow, steady weight gain, despite no apparent change in her eating habits. Linda developed a body armor sending a double message. It permitted us the work of identifying dangerous emotions, while cautioning and cushioning Linda from these very risks. Even beyond, Linda developed a body symptom specific to digestion – severe constipation. Linda's bouts of constipation directly corresponded to therapeutic material hard to digest. Appropriately she sought medical help to rule out physical problems. She then got some assistance through colonics, while slowly relaxing into my symbolic interpretations, aimed at coaxing "her system" along.

Here is one example of a constipation bout that accompanied Linda's painful decision whether or not to attend the birth of her sister's first child. Linda's true feelings – that she did not want to go – were difficult to swallow. Within the safety of therapy and her own marriage, and upon relaxing into these "irresponsible" feelings, Linda's colon followed suit. Soon after, another bout accompanied the trauma of successfully getting pregnant, only to lose her own baby to miscarriage within the same week.

Understandably this course of events was also extremely difficult to digest. By using metaphor to concretize Linda's struggles with emotional digestion plus her perception of feelings as interpersonally dangerous, we reached deep into the bowels of her dissociation. Food metaphors became an explicit vehicle to address implicit, unconscious processes. The language of mental metabolism helped to illuminate Linda's struggles to process emotions on multiple levels.

As Linda gained the capacity to use words to work through feelings, relations with her husband bettered. Linda had fewer rages and periods of withdrawal. Their communication improved. Meanwhile Linda began to tolerate the intensity of psychotherapy without having to stop up the process by disappearing or disengaging, descending into sleep, or other enactments of danger and desire to go unconscious. Linda gained confidence in the wisdom of her emotions. She chose the path of articulating and trusting her experience while seeking guidance from within, no matter how illogical or indigestible her experience might initially seem.

Toxic nourishment

One day Linda had imagined her inner struggles as a "stand off" between internal players. In one corner stood Linda's Body, ready to do battle; in the opposing, diagonal corner stood Thinking and Emotions together. Are Thinking and Emotions connected or not, she wondered? Together we examined the answer implied by the structure of her image: Linda's feelings and thinking aspects were both disconnected and connected to her body through the "fight." Just as Linda placed her own body between her parents where it served both to connect and separate their violent struggles, so Linda's body stood between her thinking and feeling sides, keeping them apart while bringing them together through inner, self-similar enactments.

In the tradition of Klein, contemporary psychoanalyst Mike Eigen (1999) uses the hunger instinct as a central metaphor by proposing the poignant concept of *toxic nourishment* to capture dynamics such as Linda's. This paradoxical phrase underscores a tragic condition that happens all too often to abuse victims. Whether the violence is physical or mental, intended or not, these children subsequently have trouble distinguishing interpersonal toxins from nourishment. Even worse, they become so adept at extracting nourishment from the very toxins themselves, that a toxic environment remains critical to their continued emotional survival. Such children can wind up so ill equipped to handle interpersonal nourishment as to tragically perish from hunger in a room full of food.

In related books, *Toxic nourishment* (1999) and *Damaged bonds* (2001), Eigen presents case after case of this paradoxical sort. Then in a crescendo of self-disclosure, Eigen reveals how self-referential and embodied his ideas truly are. In *Toxic nourishment*, he describes how his intimate relationships with women fed off his own tortured psyche:

> I was the red thread that ran through my life. What was bothering me was my pain, the pain of being alive. Sex soothed it; work soothed it; triumph soothed it. But it continues, a background throb, building like a toothache that leaves room for little else. Is that why I am a therapist? Spending my life doing root-canal work on other people's souls? While my own ache needs the most work of all?

> (Eigen, 1999: 213)

In *Damaged bonds*, Eigen furthers his story, voicing suspicions of becoming an analyst in order to bring back to life his younger brother who had been killed by a truck at age 11. Years after the tragedy, perhaps in response to guilt and pain, Eigen became so intensely attached to his first analyst that his life contracted rather than expanded with psychotherapy. Worrying that Eigen had "no life," first the therapist reduced his weekly number of sessions, and then he abandoned the therapy altogether. When Eigen's analyst's own life fell apart and the man moved from New York City, Eigen was left with an acute feeling of ruptured bonds. Hate was mixed with love for his analyst, just as it had been with his father, for promises not kept.

> My analysis was repeating wounds of my life, broken promises, broken hearts, broken connections. As deep as I could go, the wound was there. It seemed that it had been there before time. And now time intensified it.
> (Eigen, 2001: 161)

Eigen's story epitomizes the paradox of so many people – how what makes us most alive and connected also renders us most vulnerable and fragile. Eigen's perspective was deeply inspired by another brilliant psychoanalyst, Wilfred Bion, who reputedly was so paralyzed by early trauma as to lack spontaneous response to young children. Bion's ability to articulate the silence under the scream resonates with Eigen's exquisite, metaphorical accounts of his own and his patients' hidden agonies.

Self-referential theories

In his doctoral thesis Robert Stolorow (see Atwood and Stolorow, 1979/ 1993), one of the original proponents of insubjectivity theory, examined the personal histories of Freud, Jung, Adler, and Rank. When it comes to psychological theory, Stolorow discovered just how thoroughly "the observer is the observed." Stolorow documented ways in which the theories of each giant emanated uniquely and specifically out of their personal histories and worldviews. Although Stolorow never used the term "self-reference," he elegantly postulated the self-referential significance of inner resonances during innovation in creative giants.

Clearly we can see how this occurred for Eigen. I believe this kind of self-reference holds at the smaller scale, of day-to-day creativity evinced by help-givers during psychotherapy. As therapists, we gravitate towards ideas about psychotherapy that speak to us, that address our embodied, human experience, what has triggered personal healing in the past. That our thoughts and theories about psychotherapy are self-referentially meaningful is consistent with research from developmental neurobiology (e.g., Schore, 1999, 2003a, 2003b) suggesting that left-brain, cognitive development comes subsequent to and rests upon right-brain relational/emotional foundations. This notion of self-referential resonances between theory and embodied experience also coincides with Hirsch's (2003) interesting speculations about meta-theory, or analytic stance, in therapists as countertransference.

Generally when therapists harbor similar plights to their patients, understanding and empathy can be compounded, even if the path towards change is confounded. The next several sections examine self-reference within the Oedipus story, where self-referential paradox forms a hall of mirrors reflecting the convoluted path into impasse, plus the way out again.

An uber-myth

Within the history of clinical theory, if one myth rises above all others, it is the story of Oedipus. This tale has been analyzed over the millennia by many esteemed thinkers. Some such as Lacan, Lévi-Strauss, and Ricoeur, have understood the myth intrapsychically as an individual quest for personal origins or identity. Others such as Aristotle, Socrates, and Nietzsche have used sociopolitical and cultural lenses to analyze its meaning to society. Restrictions against infanticide, patricide and incest helped to establish the modern day state, serving as social glue binding individuals into larger collective units, while protecting society's youngest, most vulnerable members.

Among all who have endeavored to analyze the Oedipus myth, Freud was perhaps the most influential. At the inception of psychoanalysis, Freud fused this myth with his psychosexual theory of development. That this tragic hero killed his father and then married and seduced his mother became immortalized thereafter during psychotherapy as the "Oedipus Complex." In the century since Freud, the significance of the Oedipus myth to the psychological community has largely fallen by the wayside. Feminists critique Freud's use of myth to highlight the male psyche, deemed irrelevant to women. Others condemn its cultural biases, deemed irrelevant to non-Western societies. Both lines of criticism call into question the myth's universality. The final blow of irrelevance comes from a contemporary psychoanalytic focus on here-and-now, intersubjective dynamics between patient and therapist. Individualized attention to unique inner worlds and interpersonal chemistry renders Freud's very search for universal trends "experience-far" and obsolete.

My goal here is to reignite interest in the broad significance of the Oedipus myth based on neurobiological developmental principles, while preserving the unique, idiosyncratic path of each individual and course of therapy. But first to refresh the reader's memory comes a brief recounting of the Oedipus tale in its entirety, as it dates back to Greek antiquity.

Oedipus' tragic plight

King Laius of Thebes was married to Queen Jocasta, but the marriage was barren. Feeling desperate to conceive an heir, King Laius consulted the oracle of Apollo at Delphi, a common practice in those days, not unlike visiting a therapist or psychic. The oracle relayed an utterly shocking prophecy: the couple should remain childless, because any offspring of the union would grow up to murder his father and marry his mother.

Laius took the oracle's warning seriously and immediately ordered Jocasta confined to a small palace room and placed under strict prohibitions against sleeping with him. But Jocasta was not to be stopped – she conceived a plot to intoxicate and fornicate with her husband that worked, and a son was born. Now feeling even more desperate to prevent the oracle's fulfillment, Laius ordered his son's ankles pinned together. The boy was to be left upon a mountain slope to die, but a shepherd heard the child's cries, took pity and rescued him.

The child was delivered to King Polybus of Corinth, who promptly adopted the boy as if his own. Due to his pierced feet, the child was named "Oedipus," which translates in English to mean either "swollen foot" or "know-where." Indeed Oedipus implicitly "knows where" he came from due to his "swollen foot." I will return to the self-referential significance of Oedipus' name later in my analysis.

As Oedipus grew, he overheard rumors that King Polybus was not his real father. Eager to know his true heritage, Oedipus followed in the footsteps of his biological father to visit the same oracle at Delphi. Much to his horror, Oedipus received a similar prophecy: he was bound to murder his father and marry his mother. Just like his biological father, Oedipus attempted to avoid this fate.

Still believing Polybus to be his real father, Oedipus decided not to return home. Instead he took the road from Delphi to Thebes, rather than to Corinth.

Unwittingly at the narrow crossroads of three paths separating and connecting the cities of Delphi, Corinth, and Thebes, Oedipus met his true father. King Laius ordered the boy out of the way to let royalty pass. Oedipus responded that he himself was a royal prince with no betters. Laius ordered his charioteer to advance and struck Oedipus with his goad. Oedipus became enraged and grabbed the goad from Laius' hand in order to strike back. As the horses reared, Laius was thrown to the ground and instantly killed. In this manner Oedipus fulfilled the first part of the prophecy.

Upon Laius' death, suddenly there appeared the figure of the Sphinx, perched high upon the mountain pass leading to Thebes. This lithe monster possessed the body of a dog, the claws of a lion, the tail of a dragon, the wings of a bird and the breasts and head of a woman (Figure 5.1).

The Sphinx began to ravage Thebes, strangling trade, causing the treasury's depletion by stopping every mountain traveler attempting to enter the city to ask a riddle: "What goes on four feet in the morning, two at midday and three in the evening?"

The Sphinx either ate or hurled to the death anyone unable to answer her riddle correctly, and until the arrival of Oedipus, the puzzle remained

Figure 5.1 Sphinx.

The Sphinx is a metaphorical creature, with a body like a dog, claws like a lion, a tail like a dragon, wings like a bird and breasts and a head like a woman. By juxtaposing similarities with differences, metaphors, literally translated as "carry over," carry us towards greater complexity from known into unknown realms. In this whimsical creature it is easy to see the Sphinx as a partly humanized derivation of the ancient dragon, ancient symbol for chaos. Like other classical Greek sun-hero myths, Oedipus must defeat the dragon in order to survive, again revealing the highly polarized relationship between chaos and order so characteristic of Western culture.

unsolved. Upon facing the Sphinx, Oedipus responded correctly: "It is man who crawls on four legs in the morning, stands on two in midday and leans on a cane as a third in the twilight of life."

Incensed at being outwitted, the Sphinx suffered her own punishment, by casting herself to death upon the rocks far below. Thebes was freed. As a reward for saving the city, Oedipus was offered its throne plus the hand of the widow, Jocasta. Still unaware of his true origins, Oedipus accepted both honors to rule Thebes and marry his mother, with whom he multiplied fruitfully. In this manner Oedipus fulfilled the second part of the oracle.

Soon afterwards Thebes became stricken with a horrible plague and famine that rendered the city barren. Eager to end the affliction, Oedipus once again consulted the oracle and was told that the murderer of Laius must be found. Wanting only what was best for the city, Oedipus relentlessly pursued the truth. He declared that whenever the murderer was found, the offender would be banished forever from Thebes.

Oedipus called in the blind prophet Tiresias for help, but Tiresias refused to tell what he knew. Oedipus' wife/mother Jocasta divined the truth and responded by committing suicide by hanging herself. When Oedipus discovered the horrific truth – the one he sought was none other than himself – he too was unable to bear what he saw. He tore a brooch off Jocasta's hanging body to blind himself.

Then Oedipus faced the punishment he had meted out to Laius' murderer and was led into exile by his sister/daughter Antigone. Over the years to come, through his extensive wanderings, Oedipus became wise. In the end he died in peace in Colonus near Athens, amidst great respect from his countrymen, even with the blessings of the Gods. In one more self-referential twist of fate, Colonus became an oracular spot.

New twists to an old myth

To Freud the tale of Oedipus was interpreted literally to depict *real* sexual and aggressive impulses towards *real* parents. Repressed impulses to overcome and kill one's father and sleep with one's mother permeated the unconscious wilds of the *id*. With forbidden impulses unable to pass through the "repression barrier" erected by the superego, the ego's job was to steer the psyche clear of these warring factions. Neurotic symptoms formed out of the tension between these conscious and unconscious factors, including conflicting needs both for repression and expression.

Among the many kinds of anxiety Freud highlighted, one was castration anxiety – the fear that incestuous desire for one's mother would be discovered by the father and punished with castration. Both desire for the mother and fear of castration were sources of murderous impulses towards the father. Working through these feelings and symptoms helped lift the repression barrier to gain insight into the unconscious origins of the conflict. Meanwhile society, with all its discontents, must be protected from the potentially destructive id of its individuals.

In contrast to Freud, Carl Jung and his followers interpreted the Oedipus myth far less literally. Jung took a symbolic approach that applied to the broader class of all hero myths. In hero mythology (see Neumann, 1954/ 1993), to murder the father generally and the King in particular can symbolize separation from an external source of authority in order to come into the self as an internal source of guidance and wisdom. Fear of infanticide or being murdered by the King amounts to castration anxiety that symbolizes the terror of not acquiring one's own authority because one never killed the father. In hero mythology to defeat the Sphinx is a civilized form of conquering chaos, more primitively incarnated as a dragon or personified as the Terrible Mother. In her worst incarnation, the Terrible Mother appears as the Vagina Dentata, or toothed vagina, another allusion to castration anxiety in the form of emasculation (Figure 5.2).

Once the Terrible Mother is vanquished, her other sides may be harvested. To have incest and fertilize the mother symbolically can represent overcoming

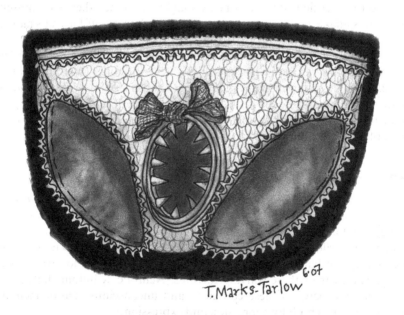

Figure 5.2 Vagina Dentata.

The mythology of the Vagina Dentata, or toothed vagina, lives on today, popularized in Dominatrix wardrobe items such as this one. The Vagina Dentata is also the subject of Mitchell Lichtenstein's horror movie called *Teeth* (2007). As described by *Wired* blog network (December 5, 2006) this movie concerns a mutant girl named Dawn who "discovers that she's well-defended 'down there' after she was nearly raped."

fear of the feminine and her dark chaotic womb in order to tap into riches of the unconscious and bring new life to the psyche. This psychological picture reveals how the Sphinx and incest fit together – the hero kills the Mother's terrible, female side in order to liberate her fruitful and bountiful aspect. For Jung, to truly individuate is to rule the kingdom of our own psyche, by overthrowing the father's masculine influence of power, the ultimate external authority, while fertilizing and pillaging the mother's feminine territory deep within the unconscious (see Figure 5.3).

Following in Stolorow's footsteps, when this segment of the early history of psychoanalysis is viewed self-referentially, the stories of Freud and Jung take on an ironic twist reaching mythic proportions. Here is my own version of their self-referential enactments, slightly mythologized.

Figure 5.3 Spelunker.

Courtesy of Megan Williams/Collection of the Duke University Art Museum
   Megan Williams' painting is a rather literal depiction of man harvesting the fruit of women's loins. Notice the vast artistic space created in the expanse between concrete and symbolic understandings.

Jung, the Swiss psychologist Freud mentored, had been earmarked as the "royal son," the "crown prince" slated to inherit Freud's psychoanalytic empire (see Jung and Jaffe, 1961/1989; Kerr, 1993; Monte and Sollod, 2003). The early intimacy and intellectual passion between these two men gave way to great bitterness and struggle surrounding Jung's creative and spiritual ideas. In his autobiography, Jung described Freud as imploring:

> My dear Jung, promise me never to abandon the sexual theory. This is the most essential thing of all. You see, we must make a dogma of it, an unshakable bulwark . . . against the black tide of mud . . . of occultism.
>
> (Jung and Jaffe, 1961/1989: 150)

But Jung was not to be stopped from his heresy. To Jung, Freud's topography of the psyche mapped only the most superficial level, the "personal unconscious," which contained personal memories and impulses towards specific people. Partly on the basis of a dream, Jung excavated another, even deeper, stratum he called the "collective unconscious." This level possessed a transpersonal flavor, containing archetypal patterns common to peoples of all cultures and ages.

Every therapist knows the futility of psychoanalyzing oneself. Perhaps because he was the first psychoanalyst with no one available to assist his self-reflection, Freud was destined unconsciously to re-enact the Oedipus struggle, rather than to observe, analyze and control his own aggressive impulses. By reacting as if there was room only for what Jung called the "personal unconscious" within the psyche's subterranean zone, Freud responded to Jung as if to a son attempting to murder his symbolic father. This dynamic was complicated by yet another, even more concrete, level of enactment: both men reputedly competed over the loyalties of the same woman, initially Jung's patient and lover, later Freud's confidante, Sabina Spielrein (Kerr, 1995).

In these ways Freud and Jung acted out the classic Oedipal myth at multiple levels, with Jung displacing Freud both professionally (vanquishing the King) and sexually (stealing the Queen). When the conflict could no longer be contained or resolved, an explosion ensued. As a result, the relationship between Freud and Jung became permanently severed. Jung suffered what some believe a psychotic break (see Hayman, 2001) and others have termed a "creative illness" (see Ellenberger, 1981).

By breaking with Freud and finding his way through his psychosis, Jung enacted the myth symbolically. Jung killed the King and overcame the Terrible Mother to harvest her fearful symbolism for his own creative development, both in theory and body. Jung descended into nightmare regions of his own unconscious from which he recovered to establish the field of depth psychology. Ironically as mirror images of one another, Freud and Jung both arrived at their ideas partly self-referentially, by living them out.

Riddle as paradox

When taken literally, the riddle of the Sphinx is a paradox that appears to contradict all known laws of science. No creature on earth changes its form of locomotion so radically in the course of a day, not even the well-studied slime mold. While not a formal, mathematical paradox, the Sphinx's riddle is reminiscent of the type of ordinary paradox that befalls science continually. Here paradox is more loosely conceptualized as a set of facts that flies in the face of known scientific theory.

The word "paradox" is a synthesis of two Greek words: *para*, which translates as "beyond," and *doxos*, which translates as "belief." The *Random House Dictionary* defines paradox as "any person, thing, or situation exhibiting an apparently contradictory nature." According to Kuhn (1962) science advances erratically in fits and starts, as resolution of ordinary contradiction leads to paradigm shifts offering ever wider, more inclusive contexts in which to incorporate previously discrepant facts.

Beyond this ordinary type scientific paradox, the Sphinx's riddle is also in essence a paradox of self-reference, because its solution "man" (or more gender neutrally "human") requires deep understanding of human nature, including knowledge of self. In order to know what crawls on four legs in the morning, walks on two in midday and hobbles on three in the evening, Oedipus must understand the entire developmental life cycle. He must be intimately familiar with the dependency of infancy, the glory of maturity and the waning powers of old age.

To approach the riddle without self-reference is to look outwards, which here leads only to contradiction with all known facts of Nature. To approach the riddle with self-reference is to turn inwards, where Oedipus was uniquely positioned to apply the riddle to himself. Almost killed by his father at birth and still crippled, he harbored implicit, vestigial memories of death in life. His limp and cane whispered of a helpless past and shattered future.

Self-referentially, Oedipus' own life trajectory showed the same three parts as the Sphinx's riddle. Through the kindness of others, Oedipus survived the helpless dependency of infancy. In his prime, he was more than able to stand on his own two feet; clever enough to slay the proverbial monster; strong enough to kill a king; and potent enough marry a queen and multiply fruitfully. As foretold by oracle, Oedipus' waning powers in old age were in sight as in-sight. His kingdom and wife would be lost, while he hobbled around blindly, leaning on his cane and the goodness of others, primarily his daughter/sister, Antigone.

Within the self-referential resonances between the three-part structure of the Sphinx's riddle and Oedipus' personal life history, lie multiple levels of self-similar pattern. The three-step process describes the march of human-kind developmentally, both in body and mind, as well as the fate of Oedipus specifically. The namesake and body memories of Oedipus connect him with chance and destiny, past and future, infancy and old age.

Recall the name Oedipus means both "swollen foot" and "know-where." Oedipus "knew-where" he came from implicitly in his body due to "swollen feet," even while remaining ignorant of traumatic origins explicitly in his mind. Feder (1974/1988) analyzed the Oedipus myth in terms of the clinical reality of adoption trauma. Like many adopted children, Oedipus was relentlessly driven to seek his own origins in order to "know where" he came from both genetically and socially. Here we see the impact of early physical abuse – attempted infanticide – on the neurobiology of different memory systems. In early infant development, *implicit memory* is the first kind to develop (e.g., Rothschild, 2000; Siegel, 2001), helping to tune ongoing perception and emotional self-regulation in the nonverbal context of relationships with others. In this way contingent versus non-contingent responses of caretakers become hardwired into the brain and body via particular neural pathways. Alluded to by others previously (e.g., Ornstein, 1972) and still controversial, Allan Schore (2001) proposes that implicit memory exists within the right, nonverbal, hemisphere of the human cerebral cortex to constitute the biological substrate for Freud's unconscious instincts and memories.

Whatever the neurobiological underpinnings, Oedipus' implicit memory of his early abandonment and abuse became the invisible thread providing deep continuity despite abrupt life changes. Implicit memory unconsciously pointed to the perpetrator of Oedipus' early abuse despite his conscious ignorance. Evidence now arises for the direct transmission of implicit emotion-related information between subjects via amygdala activation in rats (Knapska et al., 2006). Due to its embodied origins, implicit memory also offered a clue to Oedipus regarding the commonality beneath the apparent disparity in the Sphinx's three-part riddle. Structurally, to solve the riddle was equivalent to Oedipus' self-referential quest for explicit memory of his own origins.

My interpretation of the Oedipus myth dovetails with that of anthropologist Claude Lévi-Strauss (1977), who examined similarities and differences between myths from divergent cultures all over the world. In myth after myth Lévi-Strauss noticed one commonality – the near universal human concern with the search for origins. Out of a spiritual search and quest for the meaning of existence, each of the world's cultures looks to its creation myths for origins and answers. Just as Oedipus' search for his own origins led him self-referentially to find and solve the Sphinx's riddle, Bion (1983: 46) also had a self-referential take on the Sphinx's riddle as "man's curiosity turned upon himself." By understanding the Oedipus story broadly in terms of the self-conscious examination of the personality by the personality, Bion understood the Oedipus myth to illuminate ancient origins of psychoanalytic investigation. Rather than to view the story as Freud did, as illustrating the universal origins of intrapsychic repression, Bion focused more on the universal human curiosity to know one's self and origins fully. Bion's interpretation amounted to Oedipus' drive to make the unconscious conscious, regardless of how horrific self-knowledge might be.

Metaphorical thinking and cognitive development

To solve both riddles – that of the Sphinx and that of his own origins – Oedipus needed to sink beneath the concrete level of appearances. On the surface, Oedipus lived relatively happily but in ignorance, as children and innocents reputedly do. Ignorance sometimes may be bliss, but it is not necessarily maturity. The Sphinx's riddle enabled maturity, by serving as a self-referential mirror reflecting and later enabling the integration of implicit with explicit memory (see Siegel, 1999, 2001, 2003, 2007, 2008; Siegel and Hartzell, 2003). By successfully answering the riddle, Oedipus could bridge the earlier, developmental territory of the "right mind" with the evolutionarily and developmentally later "left brain" (see Schore, 2001). In the process Oedipus matured on many levels. He addressed castration fears by conquering the Terrible Mother after defeating the Terrible Father. And even more significantly, Oedipus leaped from concrete to metaphorical thinking. By understanding "morning," "midday" and "evening" as stages of life, Oedipus demonstrated creativity and cognitive flexibility characteristic of internal complexity. After previously suggested metaphor as the foundation for all abstract thinking, Lakoff and Johnson (1999) later argued for metaphor as the method by which implicit memory becomes hard-wired into the brain as the cognitive unconscious.

The leap from concrete to metaphorical thinking can also be understood in light of Piaget's developmental epistemology (e.g., Flavell, 1963). Overall Piaget's theory remains one of the most important and universal accounts of intellectual development to date (see Sternberg, 1990), though details are still disputed. Using careful observation and empirical studies, Piaget mapped the shift from a sensorimotor period of infancy, through pre- and concrete operations of early childhood, into formal operations of later childhood characterizing the adult, "mature" mind. To Piaget, the hallmark of maturity involves freedom from the particulars of concrete situations, granting cognitive flexibility needed both for abstract and for metaphorical thinking.

Finally the leap from concrete to metaphorical thinking dovetails with the dynamic systems approach to the development of cognition by Thelen and Smith (1994). Combining neural organization with developmental observations, these researchers deviated from the traditional reductionist, computational metaphor of cognitive development holding sway for decades. Thelen and Smith (1994) investigated the origins and complexities of human cognitive development dynamically, in terms of holistic, self-organizing, nonlinear, hierarchically arranged, embodied processes. While appearing to carry a structure, these researchers declared cognition an emergent function that arises out of the ongoing and continual fusion of perception and action accompanying minute-to-minute interactions and transactions with the world.

A cybernetics view

A central theme of this chapter is how self-reference lends cognitive complexity to perceive, formulate metaphorically and solve life's important riddles. To understand more about self-reference as a critical ingredient, here I wish to introduce some principles from the contemporary field of cybernetics, the study of information sciences, where the human psyche can be modeled as a complex, recursive system of feedback loops.

From a computational perspective, present behavior depends sensitively upon the past at multiple, intertwined levels of brain, emotion, cognition and body. Self-reference arises in this complex system of open yet closed loops, when through acts of self-awareness, human consciousness attempts to step outside of itself, in order to examine its own origins, yet is ultimately unable to do so. Instead the mind examines the mind examining itself, caught in its own recursive looping.

Within cybernetics, there exist a number of different types of abstract machines, each possessing certain computational powers. One objective of the science itself is to identify particular strengths plus limitations of each type of abstract machine. To assess computational power, a central ingredient is the degree to which any given system recursively retains access to its own memory for past action.

Within computational science power is often ranked according to "Chomsky's hierarchy." At the bottom of the hierarchy lies the "Finite State Automaton," a machine that possesses only *implicit* memory for its current state. This automaton operates automatically, in line with current input, without access to its own past. In the middle of computational power lies the "Push-Down Automaton," a machine that possesses *explicit* memory. This machine possesses memory, but only temporary access to the recent past, not its entire history. At the top of Chomsky's hierarchy lies the "Universal Turing Machine." This computational machine possesses the most powerful memory of all, full self-reference, that is unrestricted, permanent and explicit memory for all past states.

Cyberneticist and comparative culture theorist Ron Eglash (1999) provides a text metaphor to contrast these differences. The least powerful machine, the Finite State Automaton, is like a person who accomplishes all tasks instinctively without the use of any books. In the middle the Push-Down Automaton resembles a person limited by books that are removed once read. At the top the Universal Turing Machine is like a person who collects and retains access to any book ever read, in any order.

Translated into psychotherapy, the least powerful machine, the Finite State Automaton, is like a patient operating on impulse, according to fantasy, flight, fight and freeze impulses of subcortical systems. In the middle the Push-Down Automaton resembles a patient starting to engage higher cortical areas, by beginning to use past experience as a guide. Yet the person is still too caught in the present, and the result is more repetition than growth. At the top the Universal Turing Machine is like a patient possessing the complete capacity to capitalize on past experience in order to change the present. But take note – the type of memory necessary for this kind of computational power is implicit, unconscious memory as an embodied affair, not explicit conscious memory for episodic events.

Remembering to forget

The power of the Universal Turing Machine comes from its capacity to recognize all computable functions. Once complete memory for past actions is attained, there is a critical shift in computational power – the point where full self-reference is achieved. With full self-reference comes the capacity of a system to analyze its own programs. Is this not a rather technical way of describing self-awareness? In delineating features of the Universal Turing Machine, Eglash noted that its power lies in its *ability not to have to* know how many transformations or applications of an algorithm a system will need ahead of time, before the program can be terminated.

To me, something profound if not paradoxical exists in this formulation. *Full computational (read: cognitive) power in the present moment equates to full access to the past plus complete uncertainty about how the future may relate to the past.* While an ideal impossible to attain in the flesh, this formulation dovetails beautifully with previous speculations about inner complexity. Psychological complexity is achieved once people are securely enough attached to the memory of their own histories to fully relax into the present moment, without having to predict, know or control what the future will bring.

Perhaps this quality of full self-reference is what leads in parents to secure attachment within their children (see Siegel, 1999; Siegel and Hartzell, 2003). Complete access to the past (in so far as is consciously possible), leading to a coherent narrative, allows full comfort and presence in the moment, all necessities for attuned responding to children. The ability to respond flexibly without having to know or rigidly control the future signals a maximally open future for children optimally who are divorced from the baggage of their parents' past.

Taken together this provides an excellent characterization of psychological complexity. An ideal combination of stability related to the past lends maximal openness, flexibility, and creativity for flow in the present, all tools to handle the future. This cybernetic model suggests that clear and ready access to a coherent narrative about the past, plus full, openness to the present moment without having to know the future constitute the most powerful cognitive and emotional stance.

This characterization of full self-reference is consistent with the "warrior's stance" in the various marshal arts. A true warrior has his training so embodied under the belt, so to speak, as to be present in the moment and ready for anything. A true warrior waits calm and alert in a non-reactive stance, not needing to waste cognitive power on speculation, worry or calculations about what's to come, simply standing ready to deal with the future once it arrives in embodied form.

This combination of elements that characterize self-reference also brings us full circle back to uncertainty. Developmentally, we begin with implicit uncertainty born of "ignorance," where our collective instincts led within ancients to the creation of mythology and cosmologies. Over time, humankind travels the path of certain knowledge, only to arrive at a different kind of uncertainty, one more explicit within the modern sciences and mathematics of chaos theory, stochastical analyses, and various forms of indeterminancy. As discussed, many spiritual disciplines cultivate this very same paradoxical state of uncertainty, so empty yet full: devoid of specific agendas for the future, but fully able to capitalize on the past.

And so the myth of Oedipus reveals this paradoxical wisdom – it is often our very attempts to predict the future, whether through oracle or other means, that get us most into trouble. Both Oedipus and his father before him hastened if not brought on their fates through their very efforts to avoid them, a topic taken up again in the chapter to come. As therapists, if we try too hard to get ahead of ourselves or of the process in which we are immersed, we derail the very thing that we seek. Either we step out of the moment to miss its full complexity or we become calculating and prescriptive and so lose the mutuality of co-creation. In the Oedipus myth, we see how implicit memory helps us to know in ways that cannot be made conscious until the time is right, if at all, much like a premature peek at a soufflé can collapse it.

The Universal Turing Machine tells us how full self-reference involves trusting the process – once we achieve full access to our past, we achieve the inner power and cognitive flexibility *not to have to know* our future, which will unfold according to its own intrinsic space and time, often revealing self-similar pattern in the process.

A final case below illustrates this clinical leap into the unknown through therapy that turns upon the pivot of self-referential paradox. Using my own patient pseudonym, I adapt the following case from New York psychoanalyst, Stephen Kurtz's *The art of unknowing* (1989) in order to show how a well-placed metaphor can mystify, clarify and ultimately complexify consciousness all at once.

The success of failure

From the first moment a new patient called June floated into Kurtz's office, she sang a sensuous, sad song about giving more to men the more they take.

The psychoanalyst immediately sensed the script for their respective roles: June would be the star and he her "enraptured audience." As the months passed, the two played their parts gloriously, with results nothing short of spectacular. Under the proud mirror of Kurtz's therapeutic gaze, June magically transformed. She came out of her pent-up, private suffering and shot up as a highly visible star as an instant success in the music world.

Through the process, June moved from victim to victimizer. She morphed from downtrodden damsel to bloodthirsty vampire. She grew larger than life and entered the public limelight by sucking the lifeblood out of the adoring fans surrounding her. But whether in fairytale or life, mood or stock market, we all know that what goes up must come down. Sensational inflations tend to be followed by messy deflations. And true to these natural oscillations, June's career collapsed just as suddenly as it rose.

Just at that vulnerable moment when June was most shattered, while teetering under the pressures of her manic-depressive-like, either/or, worldview of has-been-success/now-am-failure, Kurtz made a pivotal intervention. Overlooking a vague premonition that he was about to do something wrong, not by violating a therapeutic rule so much as in stirring up emotional trouble in the transference/countertransference relations between them, Kurtz felt compelled to follow through on his clinical intuition.

What the psychoanalyst did was simple – he quoted a line from a Bob Dylan's song, *Love minus zero*: "There's no success like failure, and failure's no success at all."

Kurtz cited no obvious, immediate effects of this intervention. Yet in looking back the remark seemed like a torpedo carrying deep, subterranean impact. June's unconscious responded to Kurtz's strange comment by producing and delivering the following dream, exploding with significance.

Set within a "new-wave" nightclub called the "False Dawn," June's dream depicted to her left, a monumental gray boulder carved like a skull. The gaping mouth obviously led to Hell. To her right was a marble pyramid that towered skywards. The pyramid cradled a throne occupied by a luminous Presence. June was filled with marvel as she gazed upon this magnificent Being who returned her loving gaze in kind. The two remained locked in mutual adoration until it was time to walk away. Although June heard the warning, "Do not look back!" like Ruth in the Bible, she could not help herself. She turned to behold a horrifying sight. The two faces – the beauty beyond description and death's daunting visage – were now merging grotesquely into one.

While telling her psychoanalyst of the dream, June doubled over in agony as if physically tormented. Kurtz noticed that for the first time he was no longer magnetically drawn into June's suffering. Instead of his previous state of high sensitivity, he felt an emotional distance. It was as if implicitly he somehow grasped the necessity and larger value of this less empathic state of affairs.

In the months to come Kurtz maintained his newfound stance. Meanwhile the insight dawned that "in making that paradoxical statement I had taken up a position outside the symbiosis and declared my separateness." Kurtz recognized his betrayal of June with his comment. He had broken her illusion of "two-in-oneness." Kurtz also recognized that his betrayal was also the very power of his intervention. Through the success/failure of betrayal, Kurtz helped to usher June into her next phase of individuation. Although abuse always involves betrayal, betrayal is not always abuse, as reflected in Richard Gartner's insightful book *Betrayed as boys* (2001).

There is deep resonance between Kurtz's intervention and the riddle of the Sphinx. Both represent paradoxes. Both provide multiple scales of observation. Both are self-referential mirrors as applicable to their makers as to their solvers. Both reveal critical phase transitions characterized by sensitive dependence on initial conditions. Here at the edge of chaos, tiny events allowed new self-organization to spontaneously fold. In both new order and complexity emerged at these critical bifurcations, or pivot points that serve as self-referential hinges by which a "hero/heroine" tragically and triumphantly swings towards greater, albeit more painful, self-awareness. Finally in both Kurtz's intervention and the Riddle of the Sphinx, paradox is the source both of confusion as well as its resolution.

Kurtz's intervention was paradoxical by muddying the distinction between two apparently opposite states: success and failure. On the surface Kurtz commented on the bittersweet flavor of success/failure in June's career. Underneath, his comment shot to the heart of June's narcissistic pathology. Within her self-image, deep wounds cut too sharp a line between feeling good and feeling horrific. June's internal world had been too simply and primitively split into good and bad objects. Too much defensive energy had been invested in keeping these facets apart.

In response to Kurtz's perplexing comment June's dream suggested the painful, horrifying, yet liberating capacity to blend good and bad into one. Ironically this internal blending of "two-into-oneness" served to cleave the previous state of "one-into-twoness" externally. Through her physical writhing, June grieved not only the loss of success in the music world, but also that of her childlike, symbiotic ideal that carried the impossible promise of unlimited success without a touch of failure. In her dream, by looking back, June opened up her future. Her loss of innocence unfurled possibilities for a more balanced, integrated, self-reflective and relational life.

We can see that Kurtz's intervention was not only paradoxical, but also self-referential. The psychoanalyst simultaneously described June's subterranean, state of affairs as well as the intersubjective state of the case. Intersubjectively Kurtz's deep emotional involvement with June plus their mutual enactment of her narcissistic dynamics reflected blurry lines between self/other as well as the success/failure of treatment. By referring self-referentially to his own complex, entangled boundaries with his patient,

Kurtz alluded to the need for bittersweet, paradoxical reversals in how success/failure is considered within treatment.

As with Oedipus, by explicitly calling to consciousness what had previously only been implicitly enacted, everything shifted. Within the newly formed alchemical vessel of Kurtz's emotional separateness, June gained the opportunity for in-sight, in-cite, ex-cite, re-cite, re-sight. Her psyche, now more complex, revealed increasing order and fewer degrees of freedom to indicate greater integration and cohesion. The case of June hints at the importance of paradoxes of self-reference in everyday life, a theme explored more fully in Chapter 6.

Riddle as mirror

> Paradox . . . does more justice to the unknowable than clarity can do, for uniformity of meaning robs the mystery of its darkness and sets it up as something to be known. . . . The paradox therefore reflects a higher level of intellect and, by not forcibly representing the unknowable as known, gives a more faithful picture of the real state of affairs.
>
> Carl Jung (from "Transformation Symbolism in the Mass," Psychology and Religion, CW, par. 417)

As the Sphinx held a mirror up to Oedipus, so the myth of Oedipus holds a mirror up to us all as witnesses. Deep within Oedipus' search for origins lurks our own search. Oedipus' plight resonates with our own struggles. Our hearts soar as Oedipus solves the Sphinx's riddle, only to sink as the tragedy of his success propels him out of the frying pan into the fire. And like Oedipus we grasp upon metaphor to make meaning of life's cruelties. Ultimately we all face the cosmic irony of hastening our own fates through our very efforts to escape them, rendering our psyches more complex in the process, not by eliminating conflict, but by enfolding it within.

When self-reflecting as a psychotherapist, I perceive myself as a rabid Meaning Monger with a secret agenda – to embrace all of life self-referentially. *Everything is a symbol for itself*, said the late poet Allen Ginsberg. In order to make meaning, even out of the seemingly inconceivable, I help patients to select metaphors that unhinge outward experiences from their concrete context, in order to point them inward towards internal space. If we cannot stop or escape our struggles, at least we can find solace in their symbolic significance. If we are lucky, perhaps we can hone our psyches on life's sharp edges.

During its search for meaning, throughout the Oedipus tale dynamic tension builds between poles of knowing and not-knowing. Oedipus started out naive to his condition – not knowing who he was or where he came from. By contrast, as witnesses we start out knowing who Oedipus really was but blissfully unaware of the truth in ourselves. By the end of the tale the situation reverses. Oedipus has solved all three riddles – of the Sphinx, of Laius' murder, of his own origins – while ironically we participant/observers are left not-knowing. Instead we harbor a gnawing feeling of uncertainty, as if another riddle has invisibly materialized, as if we face the Sphinx herself, whose enigma must be solved upon threat of our own dis-solution.

In this vague struggle, the heightened sense of uncertainty serves as a higher plane from which to gain perspective for our inward search. The same process lies at the heart of psychoanalytic inquiry. There the search for origins need not focus historically, narratively, or even verbally, pertaining as much to the feeling level of the "unrepressed unconscious," to those wordless hungers and yearnings regarding the origins of our nonverbal experience unfolding within each moment. Our ability to stick with uncertainty, doubt, ambiguity and discomfort such as is opened up by the Oedipus story, creates an expanded inner space from which higher-dimensional insights eventually can crystallize. Goldstein (1997, 2007) and Masterpasqua and Perna (1997) typify a new breed of thinkers linking the traditional method of free association to the emergence of self-organization within contemporary nonlinear science. They speculate that free association is one means by which new order can emerge from internal chaotic bases (see Figure 6.1).

On the neurobiological front, it is the right hemisphere that processes negative emotions. During psychoanalytic inquiry our tolerance of vague, negativity in titrated doses, such as that evoked by second-hand accounts, in combination with the freedom of unstructured reverie may open up access to the unconscious origins of all verbal and nonverbal experience within the right-hemisphere (see Schore, 2001). Such speculation dovetails with the central role that contemporary Interpersonalists postulate mild to moderate anxiety to play, both in analysts and patients alike, during psychoanalytic defense and its penetration.

Within the philosophical realm of logic, conditions of complete certainty coincide with Aristotle's either/or thinking. Aristotle's Law of the Excluded Middle, for example, delegates all propositions into one of two baskets – truth or falsity. This is the logic of the left-brain, useful for analyzing situations, picking apart problems, or laying out plans of action. But such thinking does not always compute in real life. The closed logic of the left-brain serves us little in the face of incomplete information, on the precipice of deep change, or when we must put our lives back together after a crisis.

A major aim of this book is to illuminate the nonlinear psycho-logic of mixed motivations and emotions at the heart of the psyche. Within the realm of psycho-logic, the line between true and false may be fuzzy with ambiguity or sharp with contradiction. This chapter explores these concepts further by applying the myth of Oedipus as a mirror of everyday life, where ordinary self-referential riddles serve to stump and amuse us in contrast to Oedipus' rather extraordinary ones.

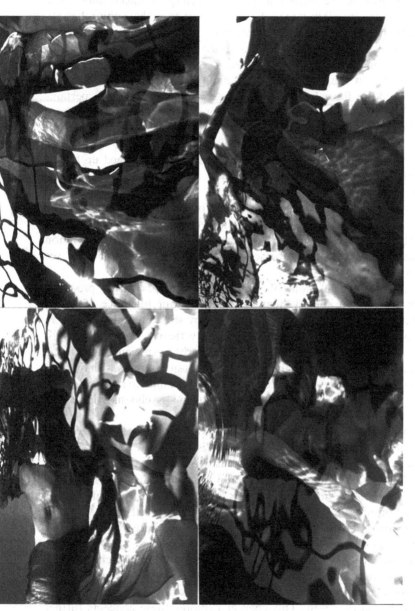

Figure 6.1 Ambiguity in photography.

Courtesy of Georgianne Cowan

Uncertainty in the form of ambiguity plays an important role within free association during psychotherapy. The same is true when viewing certain types of photography. Crisp, narrative images tend to evoke pinpoint descriptions, along with clear emotion and convergent thought. By contrast, photographs such as this by Georgianne Cowan move the mind in the opposite direction by opening up wide interior expanses. If you let yourself drift in response to your own inner promptings, where does this image take you?

Because self-referential search involves ambiguity that inevitably leads to contradiction, this chapter suggests that the very fabric of the psyche is knitted together by the chaos of paradox, which forms the inevitable knots of inner and outer conflict plus sure-fire methods towards their resolution and release. I introduce fuzzy logic as a right-brain alternative to left-brain either/or logic. Then I review the inevitability of paradox, both in states of psychological health as well as illness.

I present a dream during psychotherapy wherein self-referential paradox constitutes a deep layer of struggle between conscious desire and unconscious need. Next I contrast two very different psychological conditions where paradoxes of self-reference appear – Borderline Personality Disorder and the psychology of genius. My point is to show the pervasiveness of paradox, both in the healthy as well as unhealthy psyche. I assert that the primary difference between the two lies in our degree of flexibility and openness to embracing this state of affairs. Finally I link the inevitable, even desirable, nature of paradox to African Trickster stories as well as to Buddhist koans in order to demonstrate paradox as a teaching tool. In culturally distinct traditions self-contradiction goes beyond strife and pathology to signal the edge of chaos as fertile ground for creativity and higher consciousness.

Both/and logic

Within the big picture of life-in-context the operation of nonlinear, psycho-logic is more pertinent than the sterile, laboratory conditions necessary for traditional logic. Psycho-logic beats to a different drum than Aristotle's. Much like African drums differ from ordinary Western use of percussive rhythm, psycho-logic is more textured and nuanced, as it stretches beyond the two values of true and false often to become multi-valenced.

One example of a multi-valenced system is fuzzy logic (e.g., Kosko, 1994; McNeill and Freiberger, 1993), which presents truth on a continuum. Its degrees can be quantified as percentages, applying to qualitative propositions like "She is quite tall" or "He is an artist." Neurobiological evidence mounts for the operation of fuzzy logic not just in the mind, but also in the brain. A group of neurobiologists (Kulish et al., 2006) conducted fractal analyses of EEGs in order to compare underlying differences between "yes" versus "no" responses. In contrast to crisp differences between "yes" and "no" on the surface, at the level of the physiological substrate there is evidence for information overlap, leading the authors to speculate that the brain uses fuzzy logic during its ordinary operations.

Nathaniel Hellerstein (1997) offers another approach to multi-valence logic, using a four-value system he calls "diamond," due to the diamond shape of its corners – true, false, true-false, and false-true. The latter two terms represent different kinds of uncertainty, with the true-false term portraying

Science box 6.1 Fuzzy logic

Fuzzy logic was invented in 1964 by Lotfi Zadeh, an American professor at Berkeley, California. Whereas conventional logic divides the world into only two categories – black and white – fuzzy logic quantifies shades of gray, which can empower computers to process more qualitatively, like people. Zadeh foresaw the value of his system for creating "smart" technology, like washing machines that dispense detergent based on how dirty the clothes are plus how full the load. Zadeh met with great resistance and prejudice when he tried to sell his ideas to American academics or companies (see McNeill and Freiberger, 1993). By contrast, because the Japanese are culturally more comfortable with ambiguity and the role of chaos within order, they took to fuzzy logic immediately. Now, decades later, they are way ahead of Americans in fashioning "smart" cars and other machines that think for themselves.

Figure 6.2 illustrates a fuzzy logic cube. The corners are anchored by the clear bivalent sets of true or false of traditional logic. Inside the cube lie multivalent or fuzzy sets that express

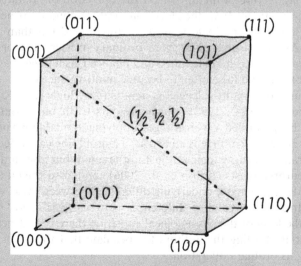

Figure 6.2 Fuzzy logic cube.
Adapted from Kosko, 1994

degrees of truth. The middle of the cube enjoys the completely ambiguous position of being just as true as it is false. Due to the potential to capture complex, subtle and qualitative thought, as well as to model recursive feedback loops that often arise between people, fuzzy logic is an important tool to understand.

an *underdetermined* condition of ambiguity, and the false-true term conveying an *overdetermined* condition of contradiction.

I propose that all open inquiry, whether scientific or subjective, ultimately becomes self-referential as it stretches dialectically between these two poles of uncertainty. At one end, the unknown is rooted in not enough information; at the other end, the unknown extends to internal struggle surrounding inherent contradiction in what is known. The continuum between these two kinds of uncertainty serves as a kind of growth-promoting attractor that self-organizes higher levels of complexity in the form of the spontaneous emergence of novelty and creativity. Pressure from the underdetermined, ambiguous end of the pole is an underlying parameter that "drives" the psyche towards the other, over-determined end that constitutes paradox plus the drive towards its resolution.

We understand this state of affairs intuitively when we catch ourselves reeling between poles of not-knowing exactly what is wrong or how to define the problem, to not-knowing what to do with what we eventually uncover/discover/create or how to solve the conflicts and ambivalences unleashed. This energy bound in this conflict might even drive the paranoid system of tension release within problem detection.

The psycho-logic of paradox

In the search for meaning, with ambiguity forming one pole and contradiction the other, let us turn to the centrality of paradoxes of self-reference. If taken too seriously such paradoxes appear crazy making. When held more lightly these paradoxes reveal the deep, universal logic of illogic that forms the fundamental structure of the universe, both inside and outside us. Inherent contradiction, borne of self-reference, reveals both the struggles to which we are all subjected, internally and externally, as well as the limits to which we can know our selves and these struggles intellectually.

To review, an act of self-reference is one that points to the self. The neurobiology of perception includes proprioception or interoception, which links egocentric awareness of the self at an unconscious, body level, to allocentric perception of a world "out there" (see Austin, 2006). At conscious levels, even to use the word "I" is to point to the self.

Whether consciously or not, every act of self-reflection is also self-referential. At another descriptive level, the entire enterprise of psychology, both academic and applied, is the self-referential study of the psyche gazing upon itself. Interestingly psychology often ignores this aspect of itself, and sometimes must rely upon the broader lens of another field – such as art or the anthropological (see Molino, 2004) – to remind us. Whether explicitly or implicitly, when we grope to understand our selves, our very symbol-making capabilities themselves partially refer back to our origins in consciousness as symbol-makers.

The poetry of Walt Whitman suggests the creative potential for self-referential paradox. Whether cause for celebration or frustration, we are fated to contradict ourselves over and over. Psychologically, contradiction can occur through the expression, suppression, or repression of opposite emotions,

---

Science box 6.2 Self-reference in art

As is often the case, major discoveries in science are often preceded or accompanied by artistic renderings, often at implicit levels by artists. Consider how paradoxes of self-reference appear in the work of two different artists. In the left frame of Figure 6.3 is the author's rendition of Maurice Escher's famous drawing, *The Art Gallery*. An observer looks at a picture of a gallery that includes the observer himself. We can notice the perspective is continuous, as it wraps around from outside towards inside the observer. Yet a point of discontinuity remains in the form of a blank spot in the center. The blank spot indicates a singularity forming where all order breaks down and the image dissolves recursively into internal contradiction.

The right-hand frame was inspired by a David Hockney drawing that appeared in a short-lived, Los Angeles based magazine *MAIN* (Vol. 2, no. 6, December–February 1987–88). Here self-reference takes a different form, appearing as a canvas within a canvas, which implies a more discontinuous relationship between external observation and the embedded nature of the self who does the observing. Almost the way a different picture can emerge with the next blink of the eye, this representation is discrete, displaying crisp edges between embedded levels.

Figure 6.3 Self-reference in art.

like love/hate, tension/relaxation, compassion/contempt, or feelings that change over time. Contradiction can occur though acts of self-reflection whose degree of truth or falsity becomes self-referentially mired in paradox.

When lies tell the truth

Some say that the job of psychoanalysis is to make the unconscious conscious, though there is increasing awareness that huge expanses of the unconscious can never be made conscious. Other therapists tackle a similar feat, for example, when confronting the denial of addiction. Patients are busy trying to convince themselves/us they do not have a problem and are not hurting themselves. Meanwhile we feel differently, striving to help our clients reveal this fundamental truth to themselves. For deep change to occur versus superficial conformity to authority, the confrontation of addiction becomes an attempt to make the unconscious more conscious, particularly in light of contemporary neurobiological speculation (Erdelyi, 2006) that repression is not always unconscious but exists on a continuum from conscious to unconscious processes. Yet often from the patient' perspective, this therapeutic endeavor may appear more like a power struggle/dynamic about whose view of reality will prevail.

From a depth perspective, therapists often help patients to unravel layer after layer of self-referential commentary, in an effort to separate conscious/unconscious assertions versus denials about the self. Self-referential commentary can be explicit, involving words we say and hear in our heads. We might argue with ourselves, cheerlead, criticize, self-sooth, blame or condemn. Buddhists call this incessant verbiage "monkey chatter." Self-referential commentary can also be implicit, extending into wordless domains of contradictory conscious or unconscious feeling. There are many sources for implicit commentary. Some arise through wordless engagement with the non-verbal, right hemisphere of the brain. Much emerges preverbally, before we have words to refer to the self, when we float, bask, swim or drown within intersubjective waters related to how we see others seeing, feeling, and treating us. Finally implicit commentary can arise as a dissociated response to trauma too horrific to put into words – *the silence under the scream* that Bion so eloquently asserted.

Whether explicit or implicit, internal commentary tells the truth about who we consider our selves to be. But few people are simple enough to be characterized by single lines of linear truth. The internal story about how we feel about ourselves tends to be much more complex than this. Complications often arise when self-referential commentary serves more a defensive than expressive function, so that we tell our selves lies to protect the self from unwanted truths. This can become a hall of mirrors when trying to pick apart which part of the self is lying to which other part (see Figure 6.4).

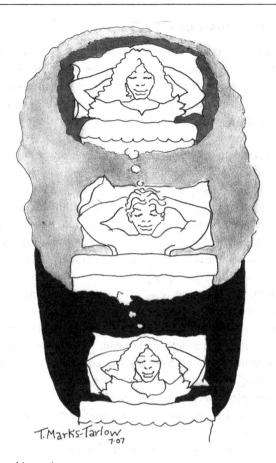

Figure 6.4 Fractal iteration.

After Sempré, in the *New Yorker Magazine*, 1985
    We are so accustomed to recursive loops in social awareness that we hardly stop to consider their complexity. This cartoon, illustrating a girl dreaming about a boy who is dreaming of her, shows the natural entanglement between self and other during self-referential musings.

    As we sink to the core of our selves and our patients, we seek the depth where body, emotion, and belief originate on a moment-to-moment basis. At this core, self-referential commentary is ever in motion in the form of micro-emotions, which often display exceedingly complicated, recursive twists. As new truths emerge from moment to moment, metaphors become alive to capture the ever-shifting nature both of internal and external representation. At the very core of this process lies a paradoxical dimension where truth lurks in lies while lies hide out in truth.

Sometimes up equals down

With this paradoxical state of affairs in mind, let us turn to the topsy-turvy dream of Smitty, a young man in his early thirties who entered psychotherapy with the highest of hopes. Smitty wanted to write a best seller. He longed to become rich and famous. This way, he would gain respect and admiration from friends and strangers alike. Only then would he prove truly worthy of a fabulous woman's love.

A year into psychotherapy, Smitty's high aspirations still had failed to lift, inspire and motivate him. In fact they seemed to do quite the opposite, weighing him down instead. Smitty struggled to produce anything creative at all. He was too busy procrastinating. He would spend hours lying on the couch, fantasizing endlessly about what he could and should be doing, plus where it could and would be taking him. His seductive dreams inevitably were followed by vicious attacks on himself for failing to produce. Exhausted by all this unharnessed mental effort, Smitty would solve his dilemma by falling asleep in order to escape the whole struggle, at least for the moment.

One day while snoozing on the couch, an important dream caught up with him. Smitty was scaling a high wall rapidly, anxiously trying to reach the top before his competitor to the right succeeded. The two peaked/peeked simultaneously. Then Smitty climbed over the top to enter the other side – quite telling that in telling and naming the dream he called "the Afterlife." In this seemingly spiritual place everyone appeared "above" the body and its worldly concerns. No one had to eat or consume anything. There were no names. There were no laws.

In this land where no one had to eat, the setting was a supermarket. As Smitty entered the store, he noticed plastic zombies roaming everywhere. Amidst the bananas loomed huge cannabis joints. Smitty inadvertently offered marijuana to a woman who later revealed herself to be a recovered drug addict in "real" life. Eventually Smitty wound up in a room with a man who sported a five-foot penis (compare the story of Ananse ahead) and clearly enjoyed his situation, as he carried on a ménage-à-trois with two gorgeous women. In response to these visions Smitty jerked himself awake. As I listened to Smitty's "spiritually high" interpretation of his dream, I noticed a vague feeling of horror building inside me.

Oh my God! Why's he calling this a spiritual place? Too weird . . . like a carnival trick or an inverted mirror. The scene sounds more like a den of iniquity to me . . . like the underworld . . . the night of the living dead. My skin is crawling.

As Smitty associated to various elements in the dream, its "subverted" quality became apparent to him as well, as together we pieced together an interpretation. Competitively scaling the wall of ego towards inflated visions of success had the opposite effect of bringing Smitty down, of deflating him into lower depths of the underworld, where he was flooded by unexamined impulses of the id. What at first appeared to be a morally high place, an enlightened land of lightened load, turned out to be an immoral state of heightened self-indulgence, a place of rampant sex, drugs and darkness. What at first seemed "above the law" was instead below, chaotic and lawless. Here, despite good intentions of giving to an Other, Smitty did harm instead, by threatening to rob an ex-addict of her newly earned sobriety. What initially appeared a land of blissful relationship later seemed a Hellish place devoid of authentic human contact.

Smitty's dream was highly paradoxical. In this custom-made Heaven, people were stripped of all individuality. In a place where no one ate, food abounded. While all desires could be sated, no one had any appetite for nourishment. All needs were passively taken care of without any pro-active need to find satisfaction. During his search for Heaven, Smitty put himself through Hell, much like the ancient Greek figure, Tantalus, source of the word "to tantalize." Like Sisyphus, Tantalus was punished for his sin of stealing ambrosia from the Gods by being sent to an underground region of eternal punishment. Here he lay in a puddle that dried up every time he reached for water under a tree that also dangled fruit just out of reach, tantalizingly close. Like Tantalus, Smitty's dream reflected his desire to reap reward by stealing it, without submitting himself to the hard work of earning the fruits of his labors (Figure 6.5).

To psychologist James Hillman, author of *The dream and the underworld* (1979) all nocturnal reverie connects us to the underworld. In the Greek imagination Hades was conceived not metaphorically as a symbolic realm, but concretely as a real place. Invisible to mortals one traveled to Hades by crossing the River Styx, at risk of no return. During the Alexandrian age, the Netherworld lost its concrete localization on Earth above to become geographically transposed to an underside below, on an invisible lower horizon or hemisphere.

The ancient Egyptians carried to extremes this perspective of a reversed world below our feet. Everything about how we move, act and think was flipped. The dead walked upside down. With heads down and feet up, logic stood on its head. Meanwhile digestion went in reverse, with excrement arriving in the mouth. What looked like "shit" during the daytime became "soul food" when inverted. Jung also wrote about the primitive quality of the unconscious in terms of identity of opposites, *coincidentia oppositorum*, where opposites in a pair are brought together with no distinctions between them. Good equals bad, right equals wrong, up equals down.

Much like the success of June's failure, Smitty's dream embodied the

Figure 6.5 Tantalus' agony.

In Smitty's dream and life, he dealt continually with the pleasure and pain of temptation. Nowhere is the agony of the dilemma better captured than in the myth of Tantulus, where in punishment for his sins, the hero winds up forever in view of "tantalizing" fruits that hang just out of reach. Smitty's dilemma stemmed from reaching towards the fruits of his labors in fantasy without harnessing this vision through the discipline and the patience required to do the labor. A similar dilemma arises in addiction, where people reach for the fruits of pleasure that ultimately hang beyond their grasp, as tolerance, withdrawal and increasingly difficult life circumstances foil all attempts to feel good.

paradox of core conflict. Smitty's urge for inflation and heartthrob became a bittersweet recipe for deflation and heartache. The dream's message was clear: Smitty's drive was too harsh, producing needs too consuming, dominating and ruthless. Smitty's highly competitive nature left no room for his own aliveness, for his goodness, for an ethical heart.

In response to Smitty's lofty ego, his conscious wishes to attain new heights and reap great things in life, Smitty's unconscious responded with a vision of waste, self-indulgence, and moral degradation. What seemed good for the ego proved devastating to the soul. Or to invoke a different therapeutic paradigm, whatever becomes dissociated, winds up enacted. That which remains outside of full awareness sometimes gets expressed in repetitive behaviors or decisions that are self-destructive, until the individual becomes aware enough to choose a different course.

Smitty's dream served as a warning, a sign he was harming himself through the ruthlessness of desire combined with failure to admit and address his true needs. The dream suggested a more balanced approach to life. The dream was a gift serving to illustrate the source of Smitty's creative block, the side of his unconscious that refused to participate with his conscious agenda under such one-sided conditions. Within psychotherapy, we worked with this dream along with several others to define a more wholly gratifying inner path that included goals more in accordance with Smitty's innermost self. While he still has not written that best-selling novel, Smitty has become a self-supporting journalist, roaming the world to balance inner with outer needs for truth-telling, drama and adventure.

To be and not to be

Within the clinical setting of our offices, therapists can experience paradox as a hopeless morass, especially when there is danger of falling into those contradictions that surround the edges of the self/world/other. For therapists this often happens when working with people suffering from Borderline Personality Disorder, which usually results from early severe or persistent trauma.

A modern condition, less prevalent if existing at all, before the current disintegration of traditional family, church, and other authoritative institutions, people with Borderline Personality Disorder characterologically lack a firm sense of self. With psychological boundaries that are ever in flux, often chaotically so, these individuals tend to form highly unstable, dramatic relationships, as they vacillate between unintegrated extremes of love and hate, fusion and isolation, caretaking and abandonment.

Whereas people characterized by Narcissistic Personality Disorder often deny the presence of an "Other" in search of self, those with Borderline Personality Disorder tend to bounce reactively off the selves of the Other, inadvertently affirming the existence of other while denying that of self. Unconsciously this can lead into the murkiest, darkest, most vulnerable waters of relationships. As a beginning therapist, I recall the case of a 10-year-old child, a borderline personality in the making. Fraught with childhood diabetes, she already struggled with the contradiction of painful shots given to her daily in the name of caretaking. What is more, her mother became convinced that the child was psychic in the worst way possible, perceiving the girl like the Devil, able to tune in and hurt her mother exactly where she was most vulnerable.

If only this irritating grain of truth – that attuned sensitivity is the blessed job of all children – could have been better converted into pearls of wisdom. Much like the early, primitive stages of childhood, individuals suffering from Borderline Personality Disorder unerringly choose the least safe waters in which to test the trustworthiness of others in order to establish the safety of finding themselves-in-others. The enactment of such tests can make psycho-therapy with borderline personalities incredibly tough. This work is not for everybody, as it requires the greatest strength of character exactly where we feel least equipped and most weak.

From the perspective of self-reference, the borderline personality may be conceptualized as a self actively and chronically denying he or she possesses a self. While every person suffers from occasional feelings of invisibility, worthlessness, or the self-annihilating impact of shame, those with borderline personalities use this form of self-interaction on a regular basis. As a chronic trait, rather than an occasional state, this is reminiscent of Hamlet's famous,

A Fool and His Scepter's Scepter

Figure 6.6 A Fool and his scepter's scepter.

The paradoxical idea of the Wise Fool achieved full articulation during the Renaissance. The superiority of the instinctive, intuitive and irrational is the essence of the Fool's wisdom. The concept sometimes arises from nostalgia for a simpler life, appearing whenever reason has been able to question itself or acknowledge that the heart has its reasons that reason does not know.

often parodied query, "To be or not to be, that is the question." The question, by its very existence, paradoxically begs the question at the precise moment of inquiry.

In *The fool and his scepter*, psychologist and scholar William Willeford (1969) cleverly equates Hamlet's impossible question to the intellectual equivalent of a clown trying to take a step with one foot while standing on it with the other (see Figure 6.6). This way of getting bogged down is the opposite of raising ourselves up by the bootstraps – an equally impossible feat more akin to magic than buffoonery (Figure 6.7).

Figure 6.7 Raising ourselves by the bootstraps.

In so far as we must bootleg the meaning of new experience out of the stew of old experience, emotional and cognitive development is a bit like raising our selves up by the bootstraps or pulling our selves up by the suspenders. While the challenge may not seem problematic on the surface, this drawing illustrates how inherently contradictory it can be both to ground ourselves in true experience while raising our selves up towards our dreams and aspirations.

Science box 6.3 Iterating paradox by computer

Classical Aristotelian logic requires that all assertions are either true or false. The liar, "This sentence is false," is a paradox of self-reference that is true if it is false, and false it if is true. Philosopher Patrick Grim and his colleagues (Grim et al., 1998) use fuzzy logic along with the computer to iterate and so visualize the complex semantics of paradox. Recall that fuzzy logic is an infinitely valenced system of logic, with false equal to 0, true equal to 1, and all other degrees of truth somewhere between.

The simple liar is expressed as the fuzzy logic equation: $x_{n+1} = 1 - Abs(0 - x_n)$ that is iterated on the computer, as always by recycling the output from each round as the starting position for the next one. In this simplest case, we see in Figure 6.8 an a periodic attractor that oscillates between 1 and 0. Ordinarily, logic is considered to exist outside of time. Yet some believe this method of iterating the liar actually solves it. Just as a light switch contains opposite states that cannot coexist, i.e., the light cannot be on and off at the same time, by placing the liar in time, true and false become non-overlapping states that oscillate such that they no longer appear contradictory.

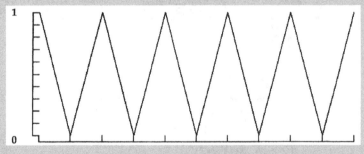

Figure 6.8 The simple liar.

Courtesy of Patrick Grim, Group for Logic and Formal Semantics, Department of Philosophy, SUNY at Stony Brook

Because a person with Borderline Personality Disorder possesses a self that actively denies he or she possesses a self, the effect is the ontological or psychological equivalent of the Liar, the oldest, most celebrated paradox of reference in existence that dates back to Greek antiquity: a Cretan, who is a known liar, says that all Cretans are liars. If what the Cretan says is true, then according to what he says, he must be telling a lie. But if what the Cretan says is false, then he is not lying at all and must be telling the truth. Historically, the Liar was the first paradox of self-reference to enter the Western mind, where it has taunted, teased and troubled our collective consciousness for millennia.

In self-similar fashion, astronomy professor, John Barrow (1999) offers a variety of meanings for "paradox" which appear contradictory. These include:

Something that appears contradictory, but is, in fact, true;
Something that appears true, but is, in fact, contradictory;

My favorite definition comes from Nicholas Falletta (1990):

A paradox is truth standing on its head to attract attention.

Sounds like the borderline condition to me: instead of *cogito ergo sum*, "I think therefore I am," it is "I am not therefore I am." More poetically, recall e.e. cummings, that only the truest things are always true because they cannot be true, or the wisdom reflected in the Tao Te Ching: "The way that can be named is not the true way."

As therapists dealing with such patients, inevitably we get sucked into a whirlpool of confusion surrounding this morass of boundaries. In chapters to come, I emphasize the beautiful fractal order within such chaotic messes. In this chapter I simply wish to underscore the existence of paradox clinically, as in the following case illustration.

Damned if you do . . .

Becky developed Borderline Personality Disorder out of the all-too-ordinary paradox of a sensitive girl challenged to grow up in response to a physically abusive father and an emotionally restrictive mother. Becky's father dished out abuse in the name of caretaking, while her mother denied the reality of Becky's emotional reactions. No wonder Becky harbored such terrifying and dangerous feelings of rage and shame at the core.

In our nearly two decades of psychotherapy together Becky and I often quarreled. Inevitably this quarrel wound up centering on control struggles surrounding, "Who's right?" The more I tried to avoid this struggle the more I involuntarily sunk into it. When stuck within this highly unpleasant condition I frequently queried and quarreled internally.

Is she right that I'm to blame for what she feels – that in my subtle choice of words I'm blaming her, standing in denial of my true motivation and evading responsibility for hurting her feelings? Or am I right that I'm not interested in motives of control or shaming, or invested in blame as a concept? But if I'm right, then she's right, because she also accuses me of wanting to be right at her expense.

"Your choice, but remember: You're damned if you do, damned if you don't..."

Figure 6.9 Damned if you do . . .

A classic catch-22. A no-exit, damned if you do, damned if you don't situation (see Figure 6.9). This evokes the self-referential knots of schizophrenics, so poignantly captured by the poetry of R.D. Laing (1970) in his classic book, *Knots*. Consider Laing's opening stanza:

> They are playing a game. They are playing at not playing a game.
> If I show them I see they are, I shall break the rules and they will
> punish me. I must play their game, of not seeing I see the game.
> (Laing, 1970: 1)

In psychological circles this is called a "double-bind." The great psychologist and anthropologist Gregory Bateson (1972) believed double-binds are so

Science box 6.4 The mote in math's eye

In the history of mathematics, paradoxes of self-reference became increasingly bothersome to mathematicians. At first, in the form of the Liar, paradoxes entered collective consciousness as vague, almost humorous annoyances. Over time more than one philosopher was known to commit suicide over them. More recently, the logicians Whitehead and Russell (1910/1927), authors of the *Principia mathematica*, tried to construct all of mathematics upon the foundation of logic, dismissing these paradoxes as mere linguistic tricks. But this trick did not work.

In the 1930s a brilliant mathematician named Kurt Gödel dealt the final blow to the mighty Fortress of Truth as a purely logical, internally consistent, either/or affair. Gödel invented a system of numbering that translated any mathematical statement into a number. Gödel's system included meta-mathematical statements, or higher order, self-referential statements that could be made about mathematical statements. Gödel used his numbering system to show conclusively that no logical system can prove its own logical consistency.

All systems of enough complexity to be interesting are either incomplete, by containing true self-referential statements that cannot be proved within the system, or they are inconsistent, leading to self-destruction via internal contradiction. The implications are profound. Contradiction is inherent in all complex systems of formal analysis and description. This challenges the assumption that Nature is rational or can be fully apprehended through rational means.

Enter the importance of the irrational to psychology. Nonsense is literally built into the very fabric of our means for making sense. Every system for asserting truth, whether mathematical, logical, or psycho-logical, is either hopelessly ambiguous and incomplete, or includes an assertion of its own falsity. Like the Indian God Shiva, every creation of consciousness contains seeds for its own destruction. The contradictory nature of deep truth is more fundamental than our search for "clean" absolute truth.

crazy-making when in parents, as to trigger episodes of schizophrenia in vulnerable children. Schizophrenia is a form of psychosis characterized by an even more severe dissolution of self, including auditory or visual hallucinations that completely blur lines between internal and external reality.

As every first-year clinical psychology student learns, Bateson's classic example of a double-bind is the mother who says explicitly in words, "Come closer, I love you," while gesturing implicitly with her stiffened body, "Go away, I hate you." We now know from contemporary neurobiology that this kind of double-bind represents implicit, right-brain elements of emotional and body-based expression in opposition to more explicit, left-brained, intellectually and logic-driven interests.

Bateson's theory that double-binds lead to schizophrenia has not been proven, although efforts currently exist to revive the theory in light of nonlinear dynamical thinking (see Koopmans, 2001). My suspicion is that doublebinds in parents are just as likely to result from schizophrenia as to cause it, though perhaps they trigger dissociation and trauma characteristic of Post-Traumatic Stress Disorder and Borderline Personality Disorder.

What strikes me about Bateson's theory is that it posits paradox as a source of madness. This reminds me of Western science swimming frantically to stay afloat amidst ancient seas of chaos, avoiding the murky depths, where mythological monsters resonate with deeply engrained, primordial fears of the illogical. Bateson's suggestion that paradox is crazy-making is preceded by a rich heritage.

With such biases running through, if not defining, Western civilization, no wonder Bateson conceived double-binds as crazy making. Yet in many non-Western cultures, inherent contradiction, ambiguity and paradox are woven positively into the fabric of myth, often embodied in the figure of the Trickster. Meanwhile in a host of mystical traditions, not to mention Smitty's dream, paradox also serves a higher function – to spark spiritual openings. To set the stage for exploring both these genres the next section reveals how, in everyday life, not all paradoxes of self-reference are tragic; nor are they necessarily pathological.

The genius fool

In contrast to Becky here is a paradox of a different, self-referential color, one manifested in a personality type perhaps polar opposite to the Borderline Personality Disorder just described. It is both my privilege and pleasure to present a personal Feynman story, based on my own friendship with the man. First, a little background.

Richard Feynman was a brilliant, Nobel prize-winning physicist, inventor of a new field called quantum electrodynamics. Some say Feynman was the most intelligent man on Earth following Albert Einstein, with whom he overlapped for a short period at Princeton. Dick Feynman was the "bad boy" of physics – a practical jokester who liked to sneak into places incognito. He was a real life Trickster who loved to shed his civilized skin and play Congo drums in dark, musty clubs. Like his African, Trickster counterpart, Ananse, Feynman swayed to the rhythms, as if turning cartwheels and baying at the moon, all the while thumbing his nose at authorities.

How could mythology not spring up around a man who regularly invented his own foreign languages in order to trick others into pretending they understood his gibberish? One infamous prank occurred when Feynman was at Los Alamos while working on the creation and testing of the first atomic bomb. After repeatedly complaining about the lax security at the labs and still getting no response, Feynman took matters into his own hands, by picking the locks himself and breaking into the deepest security areas in order to drive his point home that this problem existed. Ironically to this day, security issues persist at Los Alamos. The problem has progressed from the "concrete" space of real locks on physical doors to the "virtual" space of top-secret computerized data. Between July 2004 and January 2005, the labs were all but closed due to the seeming disappearance of tapes classified as secret. This infuriated many of the 14,000 employees, especially upon learning that the Cosmic Trickster was at work in the end, when the report of the missing tapes turned out to be a clerical error.

A striking feature of Feynman was his contempt for publicity of any sort. He was quite irreverent upon winning the Nobel Prize in physics. His father was a salesman of military uniforms, and Feynman came to mistrust formal ceremonies and accolades of any sort. A famous photo of the Nobel ceremony reveals Feynman standing next to Swedish royalty, a cigarette dangling precariously from his mouth. Quite regularly the physicist refused to appear on late night talk shows, sign autographs, or permit gawking fans in his presence.

Once *Los Angeles Times* correspondent Al Martinez spied Feynman at a Cal Tech Halloween party dressed as Moses. Following the event, Martinez speculated in his column that perhaps Feynman really *is* God. Clearly the physicist's contempt for publicity fueled the hundreds of stories now in circulation (cf., Feynman and Sykes, 1995; Feynman et al., 1997), each immortalizing some antic or aspect of his unusual character. With this introduction, here is my Feynman story.

I befriended Dick Feynman during the last five or six years of his life when we met weekly at drawing sessions sponsored by a sculptor and mutual friend named Tom Van Sant (see Figure 6.10). A few of us stayed ritually after these sessions to share a hot tub and conversation under the stars. Recognizing this once-in-a-lifetime opportunity to pick the brain of a genius, immediately after meeting Feynman, I furiously began reading up on science, which is how my interest in nonlinear dynamics began.

Figure 6.10 Dick Feynman drawing.

This drawing, a Feynman original, is one of the few he ever signed or gave away. I have altered it here digitally by compressing it and heightening the contrast. Dick preferred to draw the faces of models rather than their whole torsos. He confessed to me in private that his love for his first wife, Arline, was so great that he continually sought shadows of her features in the face of every woman he drew. The story of Feynman's first marriage was an amazing love story, as the young man stuck by Arline throughout her diagnosis of and deterioration from tuberculosis. Feynman brought her to Los Alamos while working on the atomic bomb project. They were married only shortly before Arline died.

Every time I would read something of interest, I turned to Feynman to ask him the hardest questions I could imagine.

- Can time go backwards?
- Are the laws of physics everywhere the same in the universe?
- Do universal laws evolve over time?

I was hungry to know everything. One day late in the mid-1980s, I came across a new branch of mathematics called fractal geometry. Instantly and intuitively my imagination went wild. I feasted on what I read, finding fractals deeply significant in ways I could feel but not yet articulate. After such a strong gut reaction, I eagerly ran to my intellectual hero.

"Don't you think fractals are profound?" I asked Feynman one night. A number of other people were present. Before Feynman could answer my question, someone else asked, "What's a fractal?"

Ever so patiently I waited, while Feynman gave a state-of-the-art, textbook description of fractals. He described them as mathematical objects able to model highly complex aspects of nature like coastlines and clouds. Feynman explained that these objects possess the surprising quality of fractional dimensionality, which means that they are neither one-, two-, nor three-dimensional objects, but something in between. Feynman also noted that fractals are scale-invariant, which means that their patterns repeat across different measures of space and time. Finally Feynman proclaimed fractals to possess the quality of self-similarity, a newly discovered symmetry in nature by which parts of fractal objects resemble the pattern of the whole.

After Feynman finished his rather technical description, again I repeated my question, "So Dick, don't you think fractals are profound?" What he answered will be etched in my mind for the rest of my life. To my utter surprise Feynman turned towards me and replied quite simply,

"I don't know. I don't really understand them."

My initial response was shock. Here was Dick Feynman, an absolutely brilliant man who, after just flashing his intellectual prowess, was now asserting his lack of understanding. This made no sense at all. The event kept simmering in my mind, over and over. Then one day, I suddenly understood the deep psycho-logic of the matter. How like Socrates was Feynman! The Delphic oracle asserted that Socrates was the wisest man of all. Why? Because he was the one who knew that he did not know anything.

More recently I have come to realize that this incident with Dick Feynman was my first encounter with a paradox of self-reference in everyday life. Here is how I now see the matter. Within his own psyche Feynman's creativity was balanced precariously on a tightrope that stretched dialectically between two poles – one of ignorance (not meant pejoratively, but only descriptively as not knowing), the other of knowledge. By proclaiming his uncertain understanding of fractals, Feynman's intellect remained open to curiosity, novelty, and discovery. The trickster in Feynman kept pushing back the boundaries of the unknown by admitting his lack of understanding in the midst of the purported known. No wonder Feynman perpetually saw the world through fresh eyes.

What should we make of Dick Feynman's perplexing self-assertion of not understanding? Was the man stating the truth or telling a lie about his own mental faculties? Clinically we might speculate that this Nobel-winning physicist had low self-esteem and was unable to recognize his genius so obvious to everyone else. After all I personally witnessed him more than once rudely dismiss any and everyone, including celebrities like Peter Falk, who approached him during drawing class with fawning or reverence. (By the way, ironically at least one of Falk's movie roles is self-referential – *Wings of Desire* – by portraying Falk's own passion to draw.)

Alternatively we could speculate that Feynman's self-assertion of not knowing was actually the truth. His genius was evident precisely because he used a whole different scale to measure what it meant to understand something fully. One legacy he left behind was to redefine freshman physics. This he did by tossing aside all previous assumptions about how this subject should be taught. In true trickster fashion, Feynman turned all tradition on its head to design a course that started at the end and ended at the beginning of what had been taught before. Perhaps Feynman changed the whole frame for scientific investigation precisely by claiming his own lack of understanding, reordering the search for truth itself, and so redefining meaning at the most fundamental level.

Was Feynman a genius or an ignoramus? I personally subscribe to the both/and paradoxical view – that Feynman simultaneously told a lie as well as the truth about his own mental capabilities. I do not claim this from a stance of psychological relativism. I am not saying this was his truth, but not mine. Rather I offer a paradoxical stance of truth and falsity merged as one. I offer paradox as the royal road to inner complexity, because I believe that at many, if not all levels of understanding, the universe hinges upon such contradictory underpinnings. Of course even this assertion of paradox at the core of everything is subject to its own self-referential contradiction/annihilation. Perhaps Freud's "royal road" is more moderately conceptualized as the Buddhist "middle path" in deference to Oscar Wilde's humor (and my own personal mantra): Everything in moderation, including moderation.

The fluid psyche

I would like to compare the two examples of everyday paradoxes of self-reference just described. On the one hand we have Feynman's extraordinary openness, emanating from thinking he did not understand what others claimed to know. On the other hand stood the hermetically sealed world of the borderline personality into which no new information, or Otherness, could enter. This rigid stance emanated partly from my patient thinking she knew the one thing she could not possibly know – the truth about my interior world.

In Chapter 5 I approached the issue of mental openness computationally, through abstract Turing machines, including the ultimate power not to have to know. In this chapter my Feynman story serves as a real life demonstration of this kind of openness plus its association with brilliance. Whereas Feynman was an open-minded Trickster willing to contradict himself, my patient was

Science box 6.5 Complex semantics of paradox

In contrast to the simple liar, the chaotic liar takes advantage of the infinite possibilities of fuzzy logic. The chaotic liar asserts, "This statement is as true as it is estimated to be false." With fuzzy logic this translates mathematically to:

$$x_{n+1} = 1 - \text{Abs}((1 - x_n) - x_n).$$

Figure 6.11 is called a progressive web diagram based on an initial value of 0.314. In contrast to the predictable periodicity of the simple liar, the chaotic liar displays an irregular, non-repeating pattern characteristic of sensitive dependence on initial conditions. As with any chaotic system, within certain critical parameter zones, the tiniest deviation in initial value can lead to huge differences in the diagram's trajectories.

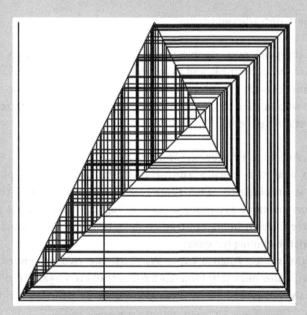

Figure 6.11 The chaotic liar.

Courtesy of Patrick Grim, Group for Logic and Formal Semantics, Department of Philosophy, SUNY at Stony Brook

more closed-minded and unwilling to be contradicted by anyone, especially me. The difference between the two makes all the difference, to quote Gregory Bateson. Through his willingness to contradict himself, Feynman retained a highly flexible mind much as the African Trickster figure Ananse does, as described in the section to come. In loving to be contradicted, Ananse deals openly and directly with the complexities of sorting truth from lies.

Hate-to-be-Contradicted

In West African mythology, there is a collection of Ashanti Trickster stories about the spider Ananse, a figure transformed into "Aunt Nancy" in African American folklore. Among these West African myths is found the tale of a man named Hate-to-be-Contradicted. His story as drawn from Pelton (1989) follows.

Being rather peevish if not downright antisocial, Hate-to-be-Contradicted lived alone on a small settlement. One day Antelope came to visit. Together the two sat under a palm tree. Antelope commented on some ripe palm nuts that fell.

Hate-to-be-Contradicted replied:

> "When the palm nuts ripen I cut them down three bunches at a time. I boil them to extract oil, and then take it to Akase to buy an old woman. When she comes, she gives birth to my grandmother, who bears my mother, who in turn bears me. When my mother gives birth to me, I am already standing there."

Incredulous, Antelope exclaimed, "You're lying."

Unable to bear the social affront, Hate-to-be-Contradicted picked up a stick and beat Antelope to death. Over time other animals came to visit. On each occasion the same sequence occurred. Together the two sat under the same palm tree. Upon being contradicted, Hate-to-be-Contradicted ended each social visit by killing his guest.

One day the spider Ananse came. As usual the two sat under the tree. After ripened palm nuts fell, Hate-to-be-Contradicted again told his story. But being a sly Trickster, Ananse's response differed from that of the other animals:

> "What you say is true. Perhaps it'd interest you that I have okras on my farm. When they ripen I join together seventy-seven hooked poles. But even this is not long enough. So I lie on my back and use my penis to pluck them."

Hate-to-be-Contradicted responded, "I understand. I'd like to see this. I shall come tomorrow."

Before Hate-to-be-Contradicted arrived, Ananse instructed his children to put off the expected visitor, "Tell him that yesterday my penis broke in seven places. I took it to a blacksmith for repair, but he didn't finish in time."

When Hate-to-be-Contradicted arrived, he asked for Ananse. As instructed, Ananse's children told their tall tale. But Hate-to-be-Contradicted would not be deterred, next inquiring after Ananse's wife.

The eldest child replied, "Yesterday mother went to the stream. Her water pot would have fallen, had she not caught it in time. But she didn't quite finish. So today she returned to do so."

Finally Ananse arrived. He served a small fish and some hot peppers to his guest. Hate-to-be-Contradicted's mouth caught on fire. In response to his request for water one of Ananse's shrewd sons replied,

> "We have three different kinds of water. That of my father is on top. That of my mother's co-wife is in the middle. That of my own mother is at the bottom. I must take care to draw only the water of my mother, so I won't cause a dispute."

Upon hearing this Hate-to-be-Contradicted boiled with anger, "You lie, you little brat!"

At once Ananse ordered Hate-to-be-Contradicted beaten to death. When asked what he did to deserve such a harsh fate, Ananse replied, "You hate to be contradicted and yet have contradicted someone else. That is what."

After Hate-to-be-Contradicted was dead, Ananse cut up his flesh into little pieces and scattered them all about. That, say the Ashanti, is the story of how contradiction came to spread among the people.

Pelton (1989) interpreted this tale as a contest between liars designed to explore the warped relationship between truth and falsehood, possibility and impossibility (see Figure 6.12). Hate-to-be-Contradicted was a sterile figure who lived in isolation and turned away from the biological necessity of social discourse. He rejected, even killed, those who made friendly overtures. Ananse was the opposite – he loved to contradict because he loved to relate to others. He embraced Otherness in social intercourse in all its dense, complex messiness.

Ananse embodied paradox by serving as a medium of coherence and incoherence. He destroyed the enemy of contradiction, by tricking him into contradicting someone else's self-contradiction. Yet by doing so, Ananse did not destroy contradiction, but instead brought it into the very bosom of

Figure 6.12 The Trickster.

Trickster figures are found in myths and folk tales in cultures throughout the world. Everywhere they symbolize forces of chaos shaking up the natural order, sometimes without design, sometimes through calculated efforts (e.g., Combs and Holland, 1990; Pelton, 1989; Willeford, 1969). Most trickster figures are highly ambivalent symbols, possessing both positive and negative aspects, with constructive and destructive results. Ron Eglash (1999) details how various African Tricksters embody ideas and even mathematics related to chaos and fractals. Within the Judeo-Christian tradition of Western culture, the Lucifer, Satan and the Devil are contemporary highly polarized, Trickster figures, symbolic of the evil of chaos as derived from ancient dragon origins.

humankind. In the process Ananse flipped ordinary rules of discourse upside down.

As half spider, half man, Ananse broke through boundaries that separate nature from culture. He was a true borderline figure in the positive sense who used outrageous lawlessness to perpetually transform the social order of humankind. Ananse rejected that which is static or sterile while embracing disorder and chaos, in the end triggering a bifurcation out of which emerged more complex order.

Much like my borderline personality patient, Hate-to-be-Contradicted lived in a hermetically sealed box where he harbored a core of rage surrounding his need to be right and maintain control over others. Abhorring ambiguity, he could not tolerate the differences, multiple perspectives or multiverses that true Otherness represents. His life, devoid of creative chaos, however well defined, was socially isolated and creatively barren. By contrast Ananse countered the rigidity of Hate-to-be-Contradicted's overly ordered system, not by fighting it directly, as the other animals did, who were bound to lose and so die. Rather Ananse acted in an attuned way instead, by embracing Hate-to-be-Contradicted's system and responding to it recursively and self-referentially, by taking it to such extremes as to nudge towards destroying itself. Through paradox Ananse introduced a higher level of chaos to soften disruption, transforming it from a potentially destructive into a creative force.

According to Pelton (1989), Ananse possessed a "double doubleness." He loved-to-contradict and by contradicting the contradictor, he negated negation. In this way Ananse opened his arms to a dynamic, dialectic process aimed not towards synthesis, but towards forever juggling thesis and antithesis. The story of Hate-to-be-Contradicted suggested that openness to everything, no matter how chaotic or contradictory, is the key to healthy life.

This philosophy dovetails beautifully with contemporary dialectical behavioral therapy, the treatment of choice as articulated by Marsha Linehan in *Cognitive-behavioral treatment of Borderline Personality Disorder* (1993). In her early work with highly suicidal, borderline patients Linehan noticed herself utilizing double-bind statements typical of the Bateson project (see Watzlawick, 1978). She also encouraged the acceptance of feelings rather than their change, in the tradition of Zen Buddhism, as a paradoxical strategy of change. Linehan chucked cognitive therapy's traditional emphasis on rationality as the criterion for healthy thought, attending to the value of intuitive and nonrational thought characterizing what I call *psycho-logic*.

As Linehan developed her new therapy, here is the central metaphor that emerged when describing the dialectics of working with severely disturbed, chronically suicidal patients.

> It is as if the patient and I are on opposite ends of a teeter-totter; we are connected to each other by the board, trying to balance it so that we can get to the middle together and climb up to a higher level, so to speak. This higher level, representing growth and development, can be thought of as a synthesis of the preceding level. Then the process begins again. . . . The difficulty in treating a suicidal borderline patient is that instead of on a teeter-totter, we are actually balanced on a bamboo pole perched precariously on a high wire stretched over the Grand Canyon.
>
> (Linehan, 1993: 30)

Like Ananse who fluidly incorporates Hate-to-be-Contradicted's brittle either/or system of logic, Linehan's image fluidly and relationally enfolds the borderline's dilemma, however dangerous and precarious this may sometimes feel. Upon breaking through the excessive order and rigidity of the borderline's cognitive either/or system, like Ananse we can spread contradiction through the land as fertile seeds to capitalize on the creative potential available at the edge of chaos.

Ron Eglash (1999) suggests African Trickster stories utilize self-reference and paradox broadly to create, resolve, as well as perpetuate mystery and uncertainty. Here is another popular Ananse story recounted in Eglash's book, *African fractals* (1999).

Among the Nupe of Nigeria the story is told of a hunter who tripped over a skull while hunting game. He exclaimed in befuddlement,

"What is this? How did it get here?"

"Talking brought me here," replied the skull.

The hunter was amazed. He returned to his village where he gushed about what he had found. Eventually the king heard of the wonder, demanding that the hunter take him to the skull. Together they returned to the bush where the skull sat. Naturally the king wanted to hear the skull's message, but when the hunter repeated the question, "How did you get here?" the skull said nothing.

The king became angry, accused the hunter of deception and ordered the poor man's head cut off on the spot. After the royal party left, the skull spoke aloud asking the hunter, "What is this? How did you get here?"

The head replied, "Talking brought me here!"

Like the myth of Oedipus this story both presents mystery and solves it simultaneously, partly by issuing a warning against trying to solve, count on or repeat mysteries (see Figure 6.13). Among primitive cultures as well as among Western mythology, including stories told by chaos scientists, there appears universal recognition that ambiguity, uncertainty and contradiction must prevail in order to preserve openness and novelty in the universe. Paradoxes of self-reference help us to celebrate mystery, whether appearing in the form of ancient mythology, mathematical logic, or psycho-logic. They warn us of the dangers of trying to convert everything unconscious into consciousness. The process of revealing and re-veiling these mysteries helps us to render consciousness more complex while increasing self-awareness, no matter how painful the process.

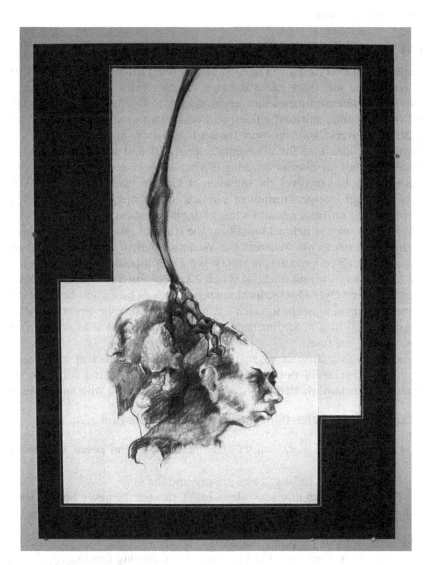

Figure 6.13 Suppression.

Courtesy of Myrna Katz

Myrna Katz was born in South Africa where she lived until 1972, when she immigrated to the United States. This drawing, *Suppression*, was inspired by her experience under apartheid. Symbols of bone represent structure. The bony hand pushes down hardest on the head in front, which is most outspoken and most contained. The middle head, which knows much but says little, is less contained. The head in the background or shadow of the others knows much but turns a blind eye, saying nothing. No hand pushes down on this third head, which remains uncontained. Both Katz's drawing about apartheid in South Africa and the Ananse story from Nigeria illustrate risks and consequences of speaking out and of not speaking out. Each stems from a different cultural heritage and historical period, yet their common sensibilities feel haunting.

The sound of one hand clapping

As proof that everything changes, while "Nothing's new under the sun," let us review the idea that paradox helps to complexify consciousness as it derives from ancient times. From Jewish mystics to Buddhist priests, throughout the millennia, spiritual guides worldwide have used paradox to understand the universe and transport the soul. In Hindu mythology the veil of Maya is the idea that the fragmented, separated and transitory nature of existence is but an illusion masking eternal oneness and wholeness underneath. Pantheism involves the presence of God in material reality, a kind of paradoxical interpenetration of physical and nonphysical realities. This portrait of the universe resembles that of Jewish mystics.

Mysticism may be defined broadly as the study of propositions equivalent to their own negations. Whereas the Western point of view holds that the class of all such propositions is empty, the Eastern point of view holds that this class is empty if and only if it is not. As a less abstract example, a mystic friend, Stephen Oyer-Owens, speaks experientially of being/non-being as well as living/dying as a means to reach a complex inner state he terms, "hyperdimensionality." In a hyperdimensional zone, opposites, such as good/evil or man/woman, are fused.

Such thoughts strongly resonate with the Kleinian idea of going from the paranoid-schizoid position, where things are black and white, to the depressive position where the patient learns to tolerate/live with ambivalence.

Paradox also breathes through the following spiritual aphorisms:

> God is day and night, winter and summer, war and peace, satiety and hunger.
> The way up and the way down are one and the same.
> Those who insistently seek pleasure for themselves never find it, while those who help others find pleasure invariably locate it themselves.

How fitting to this chapter's theme and Smitty's dream, that the bad-boy of physics, Dick Feynman, liked to quote the following frontispiece from a Buddhist temple in Honolulu, "To every man is given the key to the gates of heaven; the same key opens the gates of hell."

Finally in Zen Buddhism paradox is purposefully applied to religious students in the form of koans. This systematic method towards higher consciousness employs impossible queries, such as "What is the sound of one hand clapping?" or "What was the sight of your face before you were born?" Riddles like these date back to the sixth-century Chinese patriarch Hui-neng, toying with physical and temporal dimensions of existence, much like the Ananse tales did.

Koans serve as a kind of "holy folly." They remind us how like the Fool we are, as we inevitably stand on the borders of consciousness, where the most important truths always extend beyond reach. Koans jar consciousness partly by short-circuiting the logical side of the mind to pry open the imagination and broaden the spirit. They make our relationship to the "beyond" more immediate than it was so that enlightenment is possible.

Koans capture universal truth that transcends cultural lines. The following koan, epigraph of this chapter was paraphrased from D.T. Suzuki's classic, *Zen koan as a means of attaining enlightenment* (1994). The message applies as readily to the blinded Oedipus from Greek myth as it does to modern Buddhist students.

> *Only when seeing is no-seeing is there real seeing.*

Another koan, also drawn from Suzuki (1994: 93), resonates with self-referential interpenetration of inside and outside described by fractal boundaries in Chapter 8.

A monk asked Li-Shan: All things return to emptiness, but where does Emptiness return?
Li-Shan: The mouth is unable to locate it.
Monk: Why not?
Li-Shan: Because of the oneness of inside and outside.

Our ability to face, hold, contain, resolve and straddle, not just to remove or ignore paradox is not only the stuff of madness, but also the fodder for creative intuition in search of harmony and wholeness. Whether in domains of mythology, art, psychology, science or spirituality, paradox reveals the fractal seams between levels, much as it coaxes us to transcend current limitations, rendering the psyche more complex by prying open new dimensions.

This book began with chaos, in the form of fundamental uncertainty built into the dynamics of deep transformation. I defined mental health as inner complexity that emerges at the edge of chaos, between extremes of excessive order and utter disorder. As with Oedipus, self-knowledge, differentiation and integration characteristic of inner complexity often arise out of introspection. I asserted that any system of inquiry or logic inevitably leads either to incompleteness or self-referential paradox. In the psyche, much like science, internal contradiction, whether in the form of opposite yearnings, feelings, tuggings or beliefs, proves fertile, albeit it painful, ground for change in the form of its own re-solution.

Chapter 7

The fractal psyche

If you like fractals, it is because you are made of them. If you can't stand fractals, it's because you can't stand yourself. It happens.
Homer Smith, Computer Engineer, Art Matrix

Even more basic than whether we like ourselves is that we are able to recognize our selves at all. When emotionally healthy, we often take for granted continuity in our basic sense of self and other. Yet beneath day-to-day stability there exists great flux. From the quantum mechanics collapsing each waveform, to the molecules that continually replace themselves in our bodies, to the neurochemistry of rapidly shifting brain states, at the material level of existence everything changes. So what constitutes identity?

Within clinical theory the nature of self is well under focus. Interpersonalists have covered the topic since Harry Stack Sullivan, identifying dialectics between the singular, unitary self versus the multiple, socially constructed selves that Sullivan favored. Entire contemporary psychoanalytic movements have crystallized around concerns with how identity forms and functions. Self-psychologists like Heinz Kohut study how we experience others either as part of our fundamental selves or as separate. Object relationists like Otto Kernberg analyze how the self emerges out of early childhood relationships that become internalized. Meanwhile postmodernists assert that no essential self exists at all, but only multiple, sometimes competing dispositions, and Craig Piers (2005) sees nonlinear dynamics as resolving the dilemma between the mind's multiplicity and continuity.

Within each perspective, the self seeks the nature of self, and so points self-referentially (see Stern, 2004b) towards paradoxes related to how identity can change even while remaining relatively stable. Ancients were well aware of the paradoxical quality of the self. By declaring the impossibility of stepping into the same river twice, Heraclitus illuminated how nouns and names can crystallize dynamic processes into static entities. The Hindu concept of *Maya* underscores the illusory nature of fixed categories of perception. The Buddhist notion of *emptiness* asserts that nothing exists independently from anything else, resulting in utter entanglement between observers and observed. It is this entanglement that causes confusion between our finger and the moon towards which it points.

All of these world-views suggest that our "ordinary" experience of things, either as unchanging or as fully separated, is false – lies we tell ourselves to support the truth of existence. James Austin (2006), a neurologist and long-time Zen Buddhist meditator, endorses a similar view, providing evidence that egocentric (or self-referential) neural pathways may drop out during deep states of enlightenment, to leave experience primarily a function of allocentric (or world-centered) pathways.

Fractals shed important light on deep mysteries such as these because fractals embody the essence of how identity forms in nature. Being multidimensional objects with detail on multiple levels, fractals illuminate how different aspects of the self can emerge at different times, across different situations (Marks-Tarlow, 1999, 2002, 2004). Fractal properties of self-similarity, scale-invariance and power laws help us to understand how identity can be preserved across scale, ranging from extremely fast moving, micro, neurobiological levels that unconsciously support the hardware of self, to minute-to-minute interactions that tune our brains and minds on an ongoing way, to slow moving large-scale events comprising episodic memory and slowest of all – our sense of self across a lifetime.

Along with their tremendous aesthetic appeal, both in art (Richards, 2001) and as art (e.g., Taylor, 2003; Taylor et al., 1999), complexities related to the paradoxes of identity are why fractals have always seemed so profound to me. Recall my Feynman story from Chapter 6. I rushed to confirm my immediate, felt reaction to fractals. Instead of addressing my question, Feynman claimed not to understand fractals. From this experience, I sensed the centrality of paradox to core identity, but had not yet worked out the mystery of fractals as central to paradox itself.

It has taken me over 20 years to flesh out an intuitive understanding of fractals. Over time and with lots of exposure and great determination, my knowledge has deepened. My sensibilities are now less abstract, more embodied, and acutely self-referential. Especially in my office, I understand fractals relationally through living out self-similar patterns. I cannot help but notice when a patient "pulls" at me on multiple scales, as when a passive individual wants me to organize them on many levels: from topics during a session, to courses for a school semester, to fantasies and career plans for a lifetime. It is through repeated clinical experience that I find fractals and their paradoxes at the heart of identity and its struggles.

Inner complexity

Chapters 7, 8 and 9 represent my initial attempts to flesh out clinical concepts related to fractals plus their value as a potential therapeutic tool. To introduce fractals both as model and metaphor, first I wish to revisit the issue of psychological complexity. Previous chapters have treated this issue in terms of edge of chaos dynamics, where the psyche dances between poles of stagnant order and complete disorder. This formulation equates psychological health with complex functioning primarily *within* the psyche of individuals. A purely intrapsychic view runs the danger of invoking Cartesian dualism. To locate healthy psychological functioning inside of people's heads draws upon the metaphor of psyche as *container*, as if lined by smooth, fixed boundaries that cleanly separate inner, subjective from outer, objective realms (see Damasio, 1994).

Along with much of contemporary science, including neuroscience, fractal geometry inspires a whole different picture than splitting body from mind, isolating self from other, or wrenching inner from outer processes. Fractal edges are neither fixed nor smooth, but instead are rough and bumpy, with detail on multiple scales. Even more defiantly, fractal edges entangle inner with outer space, as they move dynamically with the perspective of the observer. Along with serving as a vessel to enclose, fractal edges function paradoxically as portals to open. The simultaneously opened yet closed nature of fractal boundaries makes it impossible to cleanly separate brain from mind, mind from body, or body from world. Emotionally, this corresponds with the intersubjective capacity to experience the other as one's self or to experience oneself as autonomously functioning, despite being embedded in the physical environment or even while resonating deeply implicitly, behaviorally, if not explicitly with another person.

In a fractal model, psychological boundaries are dynamic zones of transaction across various states, dimensions, and scales of existence. Fractal boundaries are semi-permeable and infinitely deep, at least in theory and on an endlessly iterating computer (Mandelbrot, 1977; Peitgen, 1986; Schroeder, 1991). Fractals reside in the eye of the beholder, being of variable length depending upon the resolution used. In this way, fractals can model vibrant relationships where there is always more to discover the closer one looks.

In order to set the stage for these fractal explorations, I wish to divide psychological complexity into three main areas: self–self relations, self–other relations, and self–world relations. Each area involves self-similar pattern emergent across open boundaries separating and connecting inner and outer processes. For each area, fractal patterns represent self-organizing processes that crystallize into structure. Within each area, self-organized patterns emerge out of continual feedback loops, both at conscious and unconscious levels, involving physiological, emotional and relational exchanges. Finally fractal patterns self-organize out of properties of the whole that in turn constrain, shape and perpetuate the existence and interrelationships among the parts.

Within my typology for psychological complexity, self–self relations carve out the subjective space of introspection, equating to Siegel's (2007, 2008) notions of reflexivity and attunement to self, self–other relations articulate a language of intersubjectivity, while self–world relations tread into territory I call "interobjectivity." Moghaddan (2003) introduces the term interobjectivity to reconcile social reality as shared between and within cultures. I use the term to indicate objective reality as intersubjectively defined. This usage resembles the idea of "consensual validation" offered by early Interpersonalists and relates to social constructivism popular among postmodernists. Yet, as discussed in Chapter 9, the notion of interobjectivity contributes to psychoanalysis by avoiding endlessly regressing subjectivities, as well as anchoring relativist and constructivist arguments in an external reality, no matter how objectively ungraspable. The notion of interobjectivity provides a material foundation for considering interpersonal neurobiology, brain function more broadly, and mind/body issues specifically. According to this dialectical or "multi-lectical" position, the objective is both privileged and not privileged simultaneously.

How these three areas of self–self relations, self–other relations, and self–world relations pertain to fractals occupies the subject of a chapter each. This chapter examines introspective relationships, or how the psyche sees itself, by tackling the fractal geometry of identity. Chapter 8 covers intersubjective space, or how self and Other co-create one another, by exploring the fractal geometry of psychological boundaries. Chapter 9 extends fractals into interobjective space where self-similar strands of experience weave patterns of destiny.

The current chapter subdivides into two main sections. Section I fleshes out the fractal notion of self-similarity, by focusing on qualitative nature of fractal pattern. I begin clinically with a patient I call Sue by illustrating how the perception of self-similarity across nested scales enriched her psychotherapy. The case illuminates how the same core dynamics reflected across multiple, simultaneous levels of observation and description – from a therapeutic moment of meeting, through dynamics of a dream from the night before, to larger existential struggles surrounding a current phase of life.

From this case I springboard to the geometry of fractal construction. By applying the same algorithm repeatedly to a seed shape, something initially vague and unformed retains its central identity while growing more complex with each iteration in time. Because fractals arise wherever nature self-organizes, they are ideal for modeling natural complexity, including within psychotherapy. I explain why fractal growth by accretion is best conceptualized as a developmental, process-structure where form and function are intertwined. I then demonstrate how fractal deletion models erosion of structure, useful for understanding the impact of toxic relationships.

Fractals possess self-referential symmetry central to identity formation across nature at large. When a fractal is "flipped" across space or time, the pattern of the whole remains recursively embedded in self-similar parts, and so its essential core remains intact. These concepts serve both as metaphor and model for the psychological self, helping to address the dialectic between unique versus multiplicity of self, between process and structure, and between conscious, explicit aspects of self and unconscious, implicit ones.

Fractal consciousness may represent the essence of therapeutic intuition by which we implicitly sense the fine texture of experience during clinical inter-actions, and link these "now" moments to larger events and conceptualiza-tions. Fractal consciousness is also useful for patients as an explicit tool for self-exploration. Section I concludes by illustrating the value of introducing fractals directly to patients. Fractal metaphors are warm, fuzzy and organic, helping people to gain self-trust, patience and a feeling of control over unseen, unknown, even unknowable internal frontiers. While this statement might be considered controversial, if viewed in terms of values to be uni-versally applied towards patients, it is neither my intention broadly to coddle patients nor to feed them false feelings of control. As always, appropriate therapist interventions must be assessed within the full complexity unique to each patient within each dyad and therapeutic moment.

SECTION I: SELF-SIMILAR DYNAMICS IN PSYCHOTHERAPY

When Sue began psychotherapy, she was a timid, middle-aged housewife long-ing to enter professional life now that her child had grown and her nest was empty. At first glance I actively admired and appreciated Sue's carefully coiffed, auburn hair and the delicately chiseled features of her face. I was struck by her unusual beauty and how put-together she appeared.

This woman looks perfect!! That tiny nose, those sensuous lips, that pointed chin . . . all so delicate . . . so vulnerable . . . like china. Maybe she could shatter. Yet something else . . . some kind of strength . . . an inner force . . . capable of withstand-ing great pressure. Clearly this face has seen hard times! Those features have endured! This perfection almost seems outside time and space.

As quickly as I noticed Sue's beauty I lost track of it during the nitty-gritty of our first conversation. I learned that no part of Sue's life had been easy. She wore her history like an albatross, her suffering draped around her neck in beads of sweat. Over and over Sue had played the silent, teeth-gritting hero-ine, the resigned martyr. Throughout childhood she suffered poverty. During school years struggles focusing her attention caused her to abandon her intel-lect in favor of her good nature and good looks instead. Shortly after squeak-ing through high school, Sue snagged a charismatic, hunk of a young man. Their passionate romance led to a quick marriage proposal. But their relationship proved short-lived. After Sue got pregnant, her handsome husband aban-doned ship, fleeing from the day-to-day responsibilities of the baby on board.

Over the years Sue addressed the problem of her finances by taking multiple menial jobs. She charmed employers with her conscientious, impeccable work habits and her beautiful baby. Usually Sue brought her infant daughter to work, but even with this convenient arrangement she nearly went under emotionally as she struggled to make it financially and wring money from the stone of a dead-beat dad. But as Sue sat in my office, all this lay behind. Her baby was grown and pursuing the college degree Sue never had. The time was ripe for Sue to concentrate solely on herself. Tired of too many struggles in life, Sue perceived psychotherapy as a path towards relief.

Invisible light

One day several months into our work together, Sue forgot to turn on the red light in my waiting room to signal her presence in my inner office. Previously Sue had always been punctual. When running late she had always called ahead, even for delays of only a minute or two. Ten minutes into the hour something nudged me to open my door. When I did so, I was little surprised to find Sue sitting dreamily on the loveseat.

Sue began our session with an unrelated nicety, while I silently deliberated whether or not to bring up her omission. On the one hand Sue was incredibly sensitive and invested in her perfect appearance. To discuss her "mistake" was to risk offense by calling attention to an imperfection. On the other hand this same sensitivity meant Sue was quite psychologically minded. Despite insecurities about her intelligence, Sue always took pleasure in my observations about her, even subtle ones. During the split-second of internal debate that manifests as instantaneous clinical intuition, I decided without deciding to risk the exploration, and inquired in a slightly joking manner, "Struggling with some visibility issues today, are we?"

A tiny startle ran through Sue, as if her body resonated to something her mind had not yet articulated as she replied obliquely that while waiting for me to open the door, she had not noticed time passing or even my late retrieval of her. Rather she had fallen into a reverie over her dream from the night before.

In the dream, Sue was frantically trying to get the attention of her boss. She had just spent hours poring over the business books when she noticed a critical flaw. The flaw was so tiny as to be easily overlooked, probably the reason it had not been detected before, despite many employees with access to the data. Yet the flaw was important and serious enough to threaten the continued operations of the business. Through the glass wall that enclosed the area in which she worked, Sue could see her boss. Despite appearing to turn towards her, the man looked right through her. As he ignored her frantic arm gestures, Sue's anxiety mounted. Finally she seized the phone to reach him. Over and over Sue got a busy signal. Her numerous futile attempts left Sue feeling confused and uncertain. Meanwhile behind her Sue heard the ticks of a grandfather clock, striking loud enough to feel like an assault.

As we explored Sue's dream, she uncovered deeply rooted fears surrounding tiny cracks hidden under the surface of her impeccable appearance and flawless performance. Previously and very consciously, Sue had felt relief that these flaws lay so well hidden from others. Currently her unconscious was delivering a different message. Sue's dream suggested that the very invisibility of her concerns was a source of great anxiety. At some deep level, where Sue had previously been invisible to herself, Sue could now recognize how endangered she felt by her own flaws, to the point where the very continuation of her own enterprise, both personal and professional, was in question.

Looking at the dream in combination with the waiting room omission, Sue and I carried the dream's meaning a step further. With Sue's child gone and her caretaker role all but eliminated, Sue's primary identity was now threatened. She felt invisible and wondered if she could be seen as vital to anyone, including me and of course, her own self. The allusion to the grandfather clock hinted of ancestral issues related to the passing of time. Memories of Sue's grandfather had been cut short painfully when he was killed in the Korean War. Memories of her father faded after his early death. The ticking clock harkened backwards towards multiple generations of invisible relatives, as well as forward to the urgency of addressing Sue's visibility/vitality problems before too much more time elapsed.

We can now examine how Sue's core issues reflected themselves in self-similar fashion across multiple, recursively embedded levels of observation:

- Sue became invisible and isolated from me during a "present moment" of psychotherapy, as Daniel Stern might put it.
- Sue felt disconnected and invisible from others most important to her, including her grandfather, father, former husband, and child now absent from home.
- Sue was cut-off from her deepest fears, invisible to her own potential as a full human being who deserved attention and merit.

No wonder I had quickly forgotten my first impressions of Sue's stirring beauty that so quickly had vanished from my own consciousness. Almost immediately and implicitly, on a tiny scale, I too had been drawn into Sue's invisibility issues. By contrast, how beautiful and highly visible the fractal pattern now appeared, as it emerged from Sue's enactment in my office in combination with her dream. How meaningful Sue's tiny implicit signals felt today.

Ironically when Sue forgot to turn on the light, unconsciously she isolated herself in lone reverie at the very moment consciously she was quite eager to share her inner world with me. Ironically the dream roused the very anxieties that ultimately, our mutual embodiment and joint interpretation helped to quell. Together by carefully scrutinizing and linking Sue's failure to turn on my light with all its self-similar strands of pattern, Sue could find emotional rebalance. She later reported that our discussion about her omission in my waiting room and its connection to her dream and life themes proved quite valuable. She exited the session feeling fully attended to, from the tiniest scale of a minute to the grandest scale of multiple generations enfolded within a lifetime. Sue felt understood at levels she had not previously noticed in herself. By forgetting an outer light, Sue turned on an inner one to guide her way.

Self-similar dynamics and the psyche

I chose the clinical vignette of Sue in order to demonstrate the value of fractal consciousness. To perceive self-similar dynamics is to cut beneath the surface of outer events while getting to the self-similar quality of core dynamics. Core dynamics are where we recognize our selves largely through the embodied experience of repetitive perception-feeling-thought-action cycles. These ongoing cycles of transaction constitute the psyche-as-process whose emergent structure, however cohesive or fragmented, is fractal. The psyche as process extends from the fast-moving neurobiological level of implicit, nonconscious processes to slower moving emotional and cognitive processes accessible to conscious awareness.

Self-similarity becomes one way multiple descriptive levels and time scales are linked and crosscut. Perhaps its fractal structure explains why Freud chose an onion to represent the psyche, a good physical representation of endless layers of recursively embedded cycles of self-in-interaction with others and the world. Ultimately the onion is a smelly, if not disgusting, metaphor, whose essence is fractal (Figure 7.1).

Fractal pattern is both transcendent and immanent. The pattern is transcendent – some may call this archetypal – by existing in a purely abstract realm outside of any particular scale of time and space. Simultaneously fractal pattern is immanent, by manifesting concretely within each scale. Temporal and event dynamics range from the tiny scale of minute-to-minute events to larger-scale life circumstances that might extend over months, years, decades, and even generations. The ability to weave together multiple time and event scales into a coherent picture of self, no matter how fragmented

Figure 7.1 A-pealing onion.

Composed of circles within circles, the layers of the onion are a self-similar representation of the whole at ever smaller scales. Jung recognized the circle as a longtime symbol for the psyche. Jungians also embrace a self-similar image of the little circle of the self within the larger circle of the Self as a spiritual representation of the personal unconscious within the collective unconscious sometimes understood as God. This drawing, completed during a summer in the early 1970s of "playing" at being an artist at Rhode Island School of Design, has hung in my office since the inception of private practice. Not only does it capture "the whole" of my professional aspirations and struggles regarding art versus psychology, but also it captures my interest in fractals more than a decade before I became conscious of them.

the self it depicts, can be useful to patients, partly by having an integrative effect. Because fractals abound in nature, we have an intuitive feel for the complexity of their self-similar patterns. There is data showing aesthetic preferences for fractal-like visual and auditory patterns (Richards, 2001; Spehar et al., 2003).

Science box 7.1 Fractal aesthetics

Consider the photo collage in Figure 7.2 and choose the one pattern most pleasing and a second pattern least pleasing to your eye. Why did you make your choices? Each collage element is composed out of the same pieces of a series of nested dolls. That children all over the world love nested dolls is one sign of a fractal aesthetic. Research by Ruth Richards (2001) indicates that when given the choice to look at a fractal image versus a non-fractal one, people prefer fractals. To find out if you have a fractal

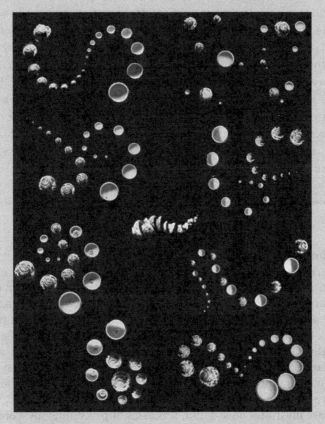

Figure 7.2 Pattern preferences.

Collage photography elements courtesy of Sarah Seyler

continued

aesthetic, review the color section towards the back of the book, devoted to fractal art to see if you find yourself captivated by their aesthetic appeal.

During the nineteenth century, an American mathematician named George Birkhoff formulated a "theory of aesthetic value" (see Schroeder, 1991). Birkhoff claimed that works of art are most pleasing and interesting when they are not too regular and predictable, nor too surprising and off the beaten trail. Birkhoff's theory proved strangely self-referential. This was the discoverer of a torus attractor known as Birkhoff's bagel, which is intermediate in complexity between regular and predictable point and cycle attractors and irregular, unpredictable chaotic attractors.

Manfred Schroeder (1991) has translated Birkhoff's theory of aesthetic value into the mathematical language of power spectra. Expressed this way, Schroeder suggests aesthetics should fall into the spectrum of pink noise. Indeed, a Bach concerto and music in general fall into the category of pink noise, which as we have seen with the heart rate variability data, enjoy a power law (f^{-1}) mid-way in complexity between white noise (f^0) and brown noise (f^{-2}).

Sue's willingness to explore the larger inner meaning of a tiny event – forgetting to turn on my light – occurred not because she thought the event was significant in and of itself, but because Sue resonated with the fractal picture of the whole. When the therapist–patient system is critically poised at the edge of chaos, there can be a cascade of meaning from tiny events up through huge ones. In this way fractal consciousness can help therapists to find significance within a grain of sand without making mountains out of molehills. Self-similar resonance could be the formal mechanism by which symbolism becomes meaningful. The emphasis is not on the event itself, but on how the event serves to reveal the larger fractal pattern of the whole.

Sue's case illustrates how, within processes of psychotherapy, core dynamics readily stir up the stew of self-referential patterns. Self-reference occurs as the patient's deepest issues get "acted in," or revealed within the intersubjective entanglement between patient and therapist. Sue's internal issues regarding invisibility crossed the threshold into my office quite literally, first implicitly when my initial impressions of her beauty were rendered invisible and then explicitly when she forgot to turn on my light and so rendered her self invisible. At this point the issue became self-referentially embodied within our relationship, rendered "alive" between us on a full scale.

Sue's omission in my waiting room represented a tiny unconscious "slip" whose significance many a less sensitive patient would easily dismiss. That Sue retained interest in examining this event without defensiveness showed how trust and safety had built between us. Our therapeutic collaboration had reached the edge of chaos. At this critical edge between unbridled disorder and stagnant stability, a tiny event sometimes carries as much power to trigger a cascade of change as does a large one.

Self-referential embodiments within this clinical tale relate to Freud's concept of transference. Yet self-reference is not just a one-way perceptual projection. Self-reference involves outer world embodiment or enactment inseparable from inner world perception. This view implicates the body implicit in Damasio's (1994) description of "somatic markers". In clinical settings the therapist also works by somatic markers (Schore, 1997), and can be as fully implicated in the action as the patient.

The case of Sue, like others within this book, displays the classic form of self-similarity during psychotherapy, when the form of a session self-referentially mirrors its own content. I resume discussion of such entangled intersubjective dynamics in Chapter 8. In this chapter my goal is more to underscore the fractal essence of psychological pattern as transacted repeatedly and recursively in self-similar form, across multiple time and event scales.

Self-similarity as process-structure coiled in a snail's shell

A central theme of this book is how change self-organizes out of the dynamic quality of the psyche. In nature everything – even mountains – keeps moving, albeit on very long time scales. Because the range of our perception is attuned to our survival needs, this dynamic quality of mountains or galaxies is not always easily discernible by our senses alone. One advantage to the new sciences includes metaphors that recognize the dynamic nature of everything as it continually moves in space and time, however slowly.

In nature, fractals are less static things than dynamic process-structures whose pattern emerges *as time becomes etched into space in the form of fractal structure (or space becomes etched into time in the form of power laws)*. The former is evident in the example of wrinkles on an old person's face. The branching pattern of ever-smaller fissures within fissures is both a physical fractal as well as a visual record of the person's emotional history. The case of wrinkles on an elder's face involves the erosion of skin over time. Shortly I introduce a fractal deletion algorithm for modeling the deterioration of structure over time, critical within clinical theory for understanding the destructive impact of toxic relationships. The flip side involves the growth of structure, instead of erosion, which I illustrate concretely now with the example of a snail's shell.

Snails in our gardens appear fixed in form, but this is an illusion occurring because the time scale of their growth is too long to be perceived by the naked eye. Like the self, snail shells are dynamic process-structures that grow continually over time by processes of accretion through iteration.

Self-similar pattern emerges as the same internal operation is carried out over and over, and one cycle become the starting point for the next, a process resembling how our underlying DNA gets translated into protein structure. In the case of the snail, because the same underlying algorithm governs shell's growth at every size scale, *a constant, self-similar relationship exists between the old and new parts* of the shell.

The snail's logarithmic pattern is governed by the mathematics of the Fibonacci numbers. Heralded over the millennia for its magical and mystical properties, the Fibonacci series and Golden Mean describe the mathematics for the arc of the Nautilus shell, the seed pattern of sunflowers, and leaf distribution of many green stems.

Science box 7.2 Fibonacci numbers

The Fibonacci series, known since antiquity, takes the form of 0, 1, 1, 2, 3, 5, 8, 13, 21 ... This sequence of numbers resembles my description of the physical shell's growth, in that both retain a constant relationship between the old and new parts. In the Fibonacci series, each new number is obtained by adding the previous two numbers together: $0 + 1 = 1, 1 + 1 = 2, 2 + 1 = 3, 3 + 2 = 5$, and so on. The series displays self-similar pattern, as each successive number preserves the same relationship between old and new parts. Increased precision and articulation of detail is evident over time, as the ratio between successive numbers gets closer and closer to the famous Golden Mean -1.618033. For instance, the ratio for the fifth Fibonacci term is 1.6666666; at the fifteenth term, the ratio is 1.618037. Because it is an irrational number, it never becomes precisely or finally articulated, but is instead a dynamic relationship between successive numbers. As the Fibonacci sequence expands, the ratio gets more fully formulated.

These mathematics, inspiring thinkers since antiquity, also have been incorporated into pieces of ancient art and architecture. The Fibonacci pattern, ubiquitous in nature's growth (see Figure 7.3), also describes the internal proportionality of the human body, e.g., the ratio of bone length like finger bones to the next longer finger bones, longest hand bones to forearm bones, forearm bones to upper arm bones. Moving up the scale into social complexity, the Fibonacci numbers permeate cultural trends.

For example, towards the beginning of the twentieth century R.N. Elliott (2005) perceived the Fibonacci numbers within cycles of bear and bull trends on the stock market. He also noticed similar numbers in the valuation of other fluctuating commodities, such as the price of gold, bonds, etc. Believing he had discovered the secret of the universe, Elliott detected the near universal appearance of self-similar principals in natural

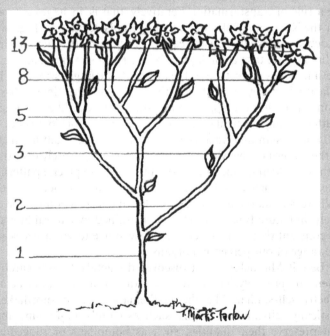

Figure 7.3 Phylotaxis.

continued

rhythms long before fractals were discovered, predating Mandelbrot's (Mandelbrot and Hudson, 2004) observations of the stock market as fractal by three-quarters of a century. Such self-similar patterns demonstrate lawfulness to often invisible seams of connection between physiological, psychological, social, cultural and historical levels. Linking physical to social phenomena, this lawfulness extends from micro to macro size and time scales, representing strong evidence against relativist/perspectivist views where "anything goes."

Fractal growth algorithms

Upon seeing self-similarity operate in the growth of a snail's shell, we turn to how self-similar principles operate formally within fractal construction. There are several ways to make a fractal. One involves taking a seed shape and then applying a rule of transformation iteratively, that is, in stages over and over. Consider the Koch snowflake, one of many kinds of fractals (Figure 7.4).

The Koch snowflake demonstrates *perfect* self-similarity across various size scales. That is, if we take a small piece of the Koch snowflake and magnify it, the pattern matches perfectly and linearly with the larger size scale. In nature self-similarity is rarely perfect like this. Most of the time, self-similarity appears in forms that are approximate and statistical, like a real snowflake where pattern at any particular scale resembles the whole, but is not identical with it. By understanding fractals as process-structures built up in stages, we see how the pattern of the whole emerges ever more precisely over time.

As with the golden mean, so with fractals – a more precise pattern emerges over time, as experience and history get etched into structure at ever-finer scales. Whereas in mathematics fractal pattern construction can be extended indefinitely, in nature fractal growth is constrained by natural limits, such as Planck's constant that typically enfold between five to seven size scales, similar to the range of our perceptual organs.

When Benoit Mandelbrot first discovered fractals, he was careful not to define them too precisely. There are many ways to understand fractals. Some are perfectly self-similar, like the mathematical Koch snowflake. Others are statistically self-similar fractals, such as clouds, mountains and shorelines that preserve their qualities, such as bumpiness or ruggedness, only approximately from scale to scale. Mountains and shorelines are also physical fractals, whose self-similarity is visually evident (Figures 7.5a, 7.5b, 7.5c and 7.5d).

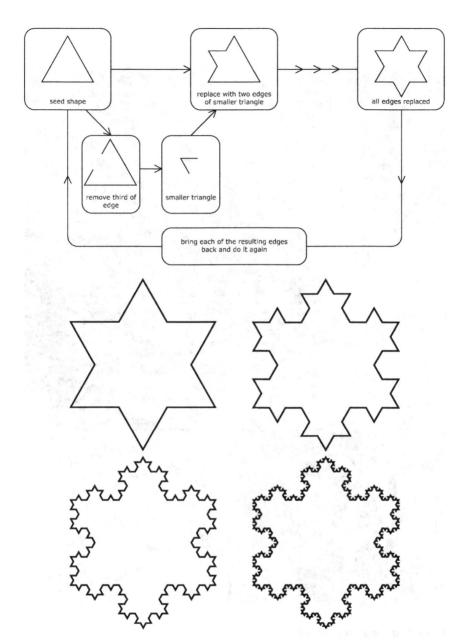

Figure 7.4 Geometric iteration: building a Koch snowflake.

Courtesy of Nicolas Desprez

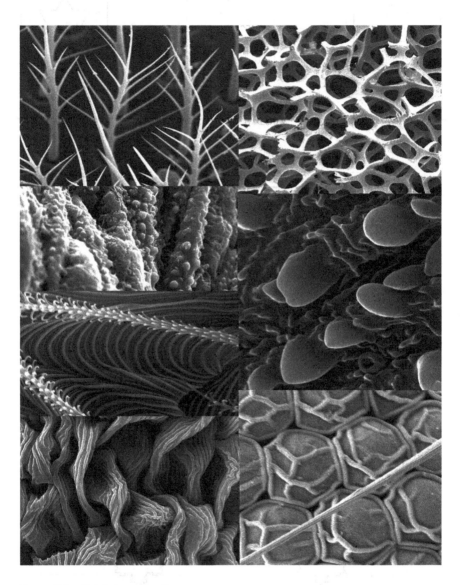

Figure 7.5a Gaia's fractal veil.

Figure 7.5b   Continued

Figure 7.5c

Figure 7.5d

Science box 7.3 The power of power laws

Power laws quantify fluctuations from regularity found in complex systems that possess multiple scales of observation. When power laws operate, fluctuations are self-similar across size and/or time scale, where patterns statistically relate across all scales. In the case of the heart, this means if we were to sample variability across three different time intervals, for example one-second, one-minute, and ten minutes, the degree of fluctuation would hold statistically constant across all three intervals.

Bruce West (2006), who champions a complexity approach to modern medicine, believes Western physicians made a fundamental error by accepting Gaussian statistics instead of recognizing the importance of power laws. In the normal, bell-shaped distributions of Gaussian statistics, most of the values cluster around the center point, or mean, while outliers distributed within the tails carry little power to define the curve broadly. This is why mean or average values carry such weight. The bell curve presumes linearity, meaning independence of underlying factors. This leads to a related assumption that the larger the population size sampled, the smaller the variance and the closer to the "true" mean the data will asymptotically approach.

West argues that inverse power laws more appropriately describe most distributions found in nature, including characterizing healthy physiological functioning within the human body. The shape of a power law superficially resembles that of a bell curve, although the hump is flatter. Power laws are the signature of nonlinear, self-organizing forces in nature (see Bak, 1996; Leibovitch, 1998; West, 1990, 2006). They reflect the asymmetrical pull of interdependent elements, such that their power is in the tails, not in the middle of the curve. This led West (2007) to give a talk entitled, "The average person is truly exceptional.

When a power law operates, a few people set the trends, while many people follow. Everyone is truly unique, because the more people you sample, the more the variance diverges to approach infinity. For a clinician where the extremes often prove the defining moment, this kind of nonlinear distribution better captures the role of unique and unusual events to shape systems under observation.

Temporal fractals exist as well, like 1/f intermittent noises in nature. Here self-similar pattern extends across time scales, occurring in the form of power laws that characterize many natural frequencies; 1/f noisy bursts can be found in neurons (Lowen and Teich, 1993), chaotic patterns of emotional fluctuation (Gottschalk et al., 1995; Hannah, 1990), as well as noise patterns in cognitive emissions (Gilden, 2001). Along with characterizing many natural rhythms, power laws characterize the frequency spectrum of most music (Schroeder, 1991).

Having modeled growth by accretion within the Koch snowflake, I turn to how fractals can model the erosion of structure. An example of fractal iteration involving the deletion or degradation of structure is the Sierpinski pyramid. To create this kind of fractal, we start with a triangle, just as in the Koch snowflake. Instead of replacing each side with additional structure, remove the middle third with each stage of iteration. It does not take many stages to leave a very holey structure (Figure 7.6).

Developmentally we might speculate that key interactions during early experience-dependent maturation and transformational times of successful psychotherapy are associated with structure building processes well modeled by fractal growth through accretion. On the other hand, toxic interactions, either during early development or destructive psychotherapy, could be characterized by structure degrading processes instead. A fractal model such as the Sierpinski pyramid can help us to understand why certain people, especially those with character disorders, have a complex feel to them, yet lack the kind of substance associated with edge of chaos dynamics and mental health (Figure 7.7).

Fractal metaphors

I now offer two examples of fractal metaphors given directly to patients to aid with introspection. Note one technical challenge to working with nonlinear dynamics: often we must educate the patient in nonlinear metaphor.

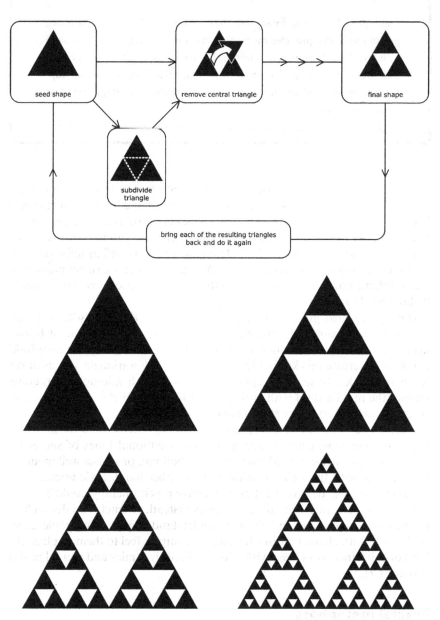

Figure 7.6 Stages of the Sierpinski triangle.

Courtesy of Nicolas Desprez

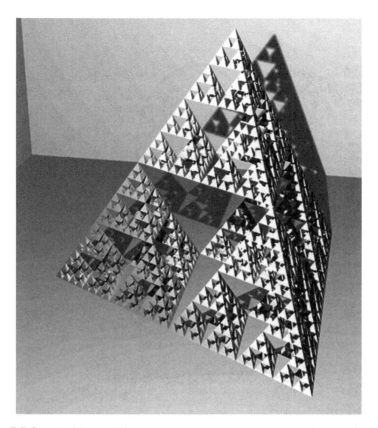

Figure 7.7 Sierpinski pyramid.

Here is the Sierpinski triangle rendered as a series of pyramids within pyramids as it exists within three-dimensional space. One remarkable feature about this object is that despite its clear extension through three-dimensional space, its formal fractal dimension is exactly two, as if this were a flat object. What a well-suited physical metaphor for the kind of "holey" psychic structure that lend people who lack depth a "flat," superficial presentation.

While comfortable for therapists accustomed to making educational interventions, such as cognitive-behavioral therapy, such an active, directive stance might be less comfortable within some analytic circles. The option exists to wait for people to get the idea about nonlinear dynamics on their own from other sources, for instance reading a *New York Times* article about fractals in the art of Jackson Pollock. However, given that the patient does take on the therapist's theoretical metaphors anyway, whether implicitly or explicitly, we might as well acknowledge this level of coupled dynamics consciously, which opens the door to using it responsibly (see Figure 7.8).

Figure 7.8 Humpty Dumpty.

As therapists, we need not feel too guilty about introducing new ideas to patients, because they are probably not so new after all. Fractal sensibilities lurk in the oddest places, including old nursery rhymes and folktales. Ever wonder why "All the King's horses and all the King's men couldn't put Humpty together again"? One reason might be the fractal shape of an eggshell crack. In stress fractures and other erosion patterns, self-similar fissures within fissures exist on multiple scales, from macroscopic to microscopic levels, rendering the crack infinitely long for all practical purposes.

Puck's plunge

Puck had never been in therapy before. A frenetically paced doctor and compulsive exerciser, this young man in his early thirties loved to use action as a defense against emotion. Puck took pride in his efficiency and the degree to which his life was packed. Puck was a multi-tasker, with every minute slotted into one or more activities or adventures.

As a kid, Puck was groomed by a narcissistic mother to perform and treat the whole world as a stage. Continuing this pattern as an adult, Puck was superficially attuned to appearances, incredibly image-conscious, and reluctant to commit to any strong stance that might cause conflict. Puck practiced a zero tolerance policy – he possessed zero tolerance for negative affect. He was an absolute whiz at rationalizing, justifying, denying and intellectualizing away any semblance of trouble or pain. When Puck entered therapy there was no crisis precipitating his call. He described a vague sense something was wrong, yet could not quite determine what it was.

As a physician, naturally Puck leaned heavily on his rationality, carrying a medical model of treatment, a model some therapists know all too well.

1   Patient details symptoms.
2   Doctor diagnoses problem.
3   Doctor prescribes treatment.
4   Patient follows prescription in step-by-step fashion.

Given this highly linear model plus tremendous internal pressure for relief and instant change, initially Puck could not relax into psychotherapy. He was fidgety. He talked a mile a minute, flying from subject to subject. Puck carried tremendous anxiety surrounding his inner dictate to present each issue once and only once. Together doctor and patient were supposed to be efficient by applying the medical model. Each problem needed immediate and efficient resolution, in order to move on to the next. To Puck, to bring up the same topic twice was tantamount to failing at psychotherapy. Over a lifetime characterized by limitless potential and glittering achievement, failing was not part of this man's emotional vocabulary.

To prepare Puck for the kind of depth work in which I specialize, first I had to address his model of treatment. I began by suggesting that Puck's internal world looked less like a doctor's chart and more like a fractal. In a fractal model, the psyche is co-created through the relationship between self and other, observer and observed; it is infinitely deep and beautifully complex. Because of self-similarity, Puck might begin anywhere, for any little snippet his mind caught carried endless potential to take our explorations to the heart of matters. Puck could discuss the tiniest detail of life forever, and there would still be endless frontiers left for self-exploration and novel discovery. Despite returning to the same topics over and over, the repetition would never be exactly the same.

As a scientist Puck was familiar with fractals. He instantly understood the significance of the metaphor. I was deeply moved to witness how impactful Puck's fractal understanding was on his emerging abilities to gain insights into his life. Puck irreversibly relaxed into the process of psychotherapy. Five years later, as his life and relationships considerably deepened, Puck was still taking pleasure in self-exploration. I return to more specifics of Puck's case in Chapter 9. Here I wish to underscore how a fractal metaphor helped prepare Puck for deep exploration, with visions of an infinitely deep and rich psyche prompting him to lay aside initial fears about being flat, empty, boring or a poor performer.

A fractal metaphor shares commonalities with the early psychoanalytic metaphor of consciousness as "the tip of the iceberg." Both convey a feeling of depth and underground connectedness to unseen aspects of the psyche. They convey a similar sense, yet important differences exist between the twentieth century Cartesian iceberg metaphor and twenty-first-century non-linear one. The iceberg is cold and forbidding, limited and bounded, although unwieldy, implying the danger of *Titanic* crashes, while a fractal has the feel of endless detail, finer and finer rendering with ongoing exploration, dizzying complexity and creativity. An iceberg exists independent of the observer, while a fractal image, partly through its quality of self-reference, implies the necessity of observation for its very existence. This can render an encounter with our selves more natural and more desirable.

A fractal metaphor has an organic, neutral feel, while handing control for the exploration of self back to the self. Due to the inherently appealing aesthetics of fractals, the frontier may go beyond neutral to a positive feel, characterized by endless frontiers of visible and invisible beauty, plus unexpected joys of self-discovery. Even when the iterative process of self-examination brings negative emotions, there is still beauty possible in the mere existence of fractal pattern. The back of the book includes a section on fractal art to bring home this point.

Perhaps giving Puck a fractal pill to swallow merely represented an act of compliance. Or perhaps it was more like a Trojan horse that started out linear and had its effect once swallowed. With multiple factors all pointing in the same direction, as Freud noted, the outcome of every case is over-determined. While other aspects of this case, such as qualities of our therapeutic relationship both implicit and explicit were helpful, I nonetheless believe in the tremendous value of prescribing fractal metaphors to patients.

Infinity in a nutshell

When I first started psychotherapy, I expected to come for a few sessions – at most, a few months. It has been years, and the work appears to go on forever. . . . Am I going to be in your office for life? There is always something new to process; the same issues keep returning. How does anyone ever finish up psychotherapy?!

Many long-term patients make declarations to this effect. Such utterances may drip with dread if therapy tends to bring confrontation and pain, or dangle with desire if support and soothing are more in the forefront. I often view such declarations as the hallmark of the middle, working-through phase of therapy. For a second example of the utility of a fractal metaphor, consider the case of Jimbo.

I introduced fractals after nearly six years of intensive work. Initially Jimbo had been sent to therapy by a disgruntled, on-and-off girlfriend, who had grown tired of his sweet promises and sickly deceits. Jimbo was a charming sex addict, who was ever-hungry for another encounter, perpetually "on the hunt." He spent hours concocting fantasies, with elaborate courtship rituals to seduce women. He would say or do anything to "catch his prey," and then carefully "collect material" for later masturbation, only to recover before beginning the next cycle of seduction and departure.

Jimbo regularly lied and cheated. He was unconcerned about his own lack of integrity and tended not to make commitments, even to himself. This style reflected itself both in his personal and professional life, or lack thereof. In business, Jimbo would fantasize endlessly about schemes, scams and shortcuts – anything to close the "big deal" that would set him up for life. Meanwhile Jimbo lived hand to mouth. By the time he entered treatment, he had grown tired of being a perpetual man-child, endlessly spinning his wheels to get nowhere.

Jimbo felt an instant connection with me, which allowed him to field my harsh confrontations. Never having talked about this aspect of himself to anyone before and greatly concerned about how I viewed him, Jimbo responded to our therapy immediately by giving up his addictive sexual behavior. He stopped lying, cheating, running around, retreating into fantasy and avoiding hard work, eventually marrying the woman who sent him to treatment. He has been able to remain faithful, and meanwhile tucked a chunk of money in the bank, after finally closing one of his deals. As Jimbo dealt with his addictions, the more money Jimbo earned, the less materialistic he became. He increasingly chose inner development over outer.

Of course this fairytale sounding process took lots of hard work and side-trips, which this oversimplified description necessarily skips over. But somewhere around the time he was to marry, Jimbo hit an impasse. In contrast to the never-never fantasyland of problems disappearing forever, Jimbo kept re-encountering the same problems again and again. Especially surrounding his marriage proposal, engagement and wedding, as well as at other significant intimacy markers, sexual temptation flared unexpectedly, taunting Jimbo like the specter of the Devil.

Luckily by this point, Jimbo's denial had been fatally pierced. Whereas Jim had begun treatment dismissing the sexual significance of a lap dance, he eventually recognized that even a tiny smile could count as a dangerous sexual encounter. Jimbo now smelled sex all around. How depressing! How deflating! No matter how "good" his behavior, if temptation was always to return, what is the point?

Rather than to delight in the opening up of his sensibilities and his own capacities to perceive subtle nuance, Jimbo hit a wall of discouragement and disappointment in reaction to new frontiers of urge and temptation. Jimbo expressed the fear that no matter how far he had come or how far he might go from here, he would never be ready to graduate from psychotherapy.

In response to this bump in the road, my own internal reverie landed on the fractal quality of scale-invariance, discussed more fully in the section to come. Going with my own creative process, I directly introduced the notion of the psyche as fractal. Jimbo had never heard of fractals before, but was extremely sensually oriented and could visualize the metaphor quite easily. The image became a vehicle for Jimbo to understand how at the core, he remains the same person essentially, still struggling with familiar issues and impulses, yet by dealing with different and tinier scales of himself, Jimbo had also changed completely. The metaphor underscored the dynamic, creative aspect to self-reflection, as the fractal psyche travels to ever-finer scales of observation, from relatively primitive to more refined level.

The fractal image helped Jimbo to recover his faith and to restore direction, momentum and meaning to his inner work. It allowed him to see that as we evolve to higher dimensions of self-awareness, we do so in wholeness, while bringing all of our selves with us. We endlessly return to the same patterns, but only because we need never leave any pieces behind. There is the difference that matters to see these patterns in a self-similar way. To watch fractal patterns manifest at increasingly subtle, more sophisticated ways is a beautiful, moving portrait of self-as-it-constitutes-and-is-constituted-by-world.

This fractal intervention ushered in the last stage of Jimbo's treatment. Finally he could freely celebrate his newfound mastery within the full glory of his limitations. Jimbo went from naivety to wisdom in recognizing how paradoxical the fruition of self can be: only by leaving our selves do we create the opportunity of finding our selves through observation, yet we can only come home within our selves by never leaving at all.

During this final stage of treatment, Jimbo replaced unreasonable expectation for complete symptom disappearance with a more realistic vision of "endless frontiers," albeit on smaller scales of observation. Within his newly awakened spirituality, fractals were one way to re-commit to the "path" in place of the "prize."

Jimbo became excited about the fractal metaphor. He was so moved by its power, he suggested I write a self-help book about the fractal psyche. Jimbo shared his fantasy of me on Oprah with him as my poster-boy, together introducing the public to the magic of fractals. Although Oprah still awaits our arrival, the self-referential irony gives me a chuckle. Out of the co-creation of self that accompanied Jimbo's transformation, in writing this book and these words, I live out his fantasy along with my own.

In the description above there is easily the feeling of this clinical material being "too good to be true." The question could arise if my own enthusiasm and faith was analyzed in the course of sharing these metaphors with patients. As always, it is never a single ingredient that is curative but always a multiplicity of factors not easily pulled apart. In this particular case much of the hard work surrounded uncovering early and repeated sexual abuse by a babysitter who sensationalized Jimbo's sexuality by asking him to "play his penis like a guitar" while riding his rocking horse wildly into self-stimulation. Jimbo had always been proud of these events, never considering them as abuse, but over time he began to understand how powerfully and pervasively they had sexualized nearly every moment of his life. Jimbo's case did not turn on a fractal metaphor, although it did help to demarcate a bifurcation, or change point in therapy from middle to final stages of the work.

When it comes to a complete course of depth psychotherapy, I consider it a privilege whenever the outer bounds can be defined organically, that is from the inside out. This is ever more satisfying than having my therapeutic frame dictated by external factors like financial limitations, third parties or unforeseen circumstances, such as job transfers. To move gracefully from those middle stages of immersion, from a total sense of not-knowing, to final stages of recognition that it is time to terminate is sheer pleasure. It is also to understand how psychological boundaries form autonomous wholes, even as they remain open and incomplete. And I believe that it is here that deep clinical wisdom abounds.

Psychotherapy as a developmental sequence

The clinical vignettes in Section I implicated issues of scale and temporal dynamics. Upon conceptualizing his psyche as infinitely deep, with endless scales possible for self-exploration, Puck could plunge whole-heartedly into the open-ended exploration necessary for depth psychotherapy.

At the other end of therapy's temporal frame, in order to break through remnants of his denial, Jimbo needed the deflation of understanding that the fractal essence of his identity will never disappear. No matter how much Jimbo improved, no matter how much progress he made tackling his shadow and resolving core conflicts, he would always face possible recurrences of his addiction and related struggles on different scales, especially at key times of transition. Yet this recurrence does not necessarily imply a lack of progress, especially if the size scale shrinks to levels that render the dynamics perceptually invisible, for example as occurs with a dry drunk.

An advantage to a nonlinear dynamics perspective is increased sensitivity to issues related to time and sequence. Psychoanalysts have known from the start that "timing is everything," at least when it comes to making an interpretation. The same holds more broadly. As therapists, we can gauge progress as much by how patients cycle into and out of symptoms, e.g., shorter sequences, smoother transitions, as by whether symptoms completely disappear or not. Because the *transition between states* is where the action is from a neurobiological perspective, attention here helps us to most readily detect change, while calling attention to these subtle shifts in dynamics can feed back in recursively to help drive future change.

SECTION II: SCALE-INVARIANT DYNAMICS IN PSYCHOTHERAPY

In Section II, I introduce a property related to self-similarity called scale-invariance. This feature of fractals highlights temporal, size, event and other descriptive scale related elements of fractal pattern. To get an intuitive feel for scale-invariance within self–self relations, I first present a dream from my own childhood whose central symbol manifested on three separate size scales. Then I demonstrate another way to generate fractals mathematically on the computer by iterating a simple formula on the complex number plane. Within the Mandelbrot set, we encounter the original and most inclusive fractal of all. Never-ending fractal images help us get a feel for the property of scale-invariance plus one key paradox of fractals – how *more* information and *greater* detail become available the *smaller* the size scale.

Awareness of scale-related dynamics is a highly useful clinical tool rarely, if ever before, discussed. I believe many empathic failures involve scale mismatches in need of reparation by re-attuning to scale or rescaling. Such sensitivity can help us to understand how psychological structure can build intersubjectively from tiny events within coupled systems as well as to reveal new aspects of age-old, clinical problems, such as perfectionism and addiction.

To sleep, perchance to dream

Towards the beginning of this chapter, I selected the clinical vignette of Sue partly to illustrate how dreams emerge from the unconscious. Dreams serve as powerful mirrors of the psyche precisely through their fractal potential to point towards the whole. When examining a dream we can use our conscious powers of observation to bring to light self-similar patterns reflected by the dream structure. Each time we revisit a dream, it is like another iteration of self–self relations. The observer is inextricably linked to the observed while both discovering and creating dream structure through the very looking.

Over history dreams have enjoyed a full range of interpretations. Ancients honored them for their power to prognosticate disease and foreshadow important events in history. Freud declared dreams the "royal road to the unconscious." In the history of science numerous discoveries have been attributed to dreams. One example is the benzene ring in chemistry, emerging out of Fredrich Kekulé's dream image of a ring of snakes, each biting another's tail. A second example of discovery through dreams is the notion of the collective unconscious in psychology, which emerged out of Carl Jung's nighttime reverie of discovering a subterranean floor in his house filled with bones of ancient ancestors (see Jung and Jaffe, 1961/1989).

Just as dreams have been revered, they have also been maligned and dismissed as meaningless. For example the contemporary scientist Francis Crick, co-discoverer of the DNA helix, declared dreams mere epiphenomena of random neuronal firings in the brain. Yet we know from chaos theory that even seemingly random events at the surface often carry deep fractal order within the structure of underlying strange attractors. Ben Goertzel (1997) reconciles Crick's claims with nonlinear science in order to integrate a theory of meaning with the neurophysiology of dreams.

At Harvard University, neuroscientist Carl Anderson and colleagues (1998) studied neuronal firing patterns during REM (rapid eye movement) sleep in fetal sheep. Anderson detected fractal pattern at the neurophysiological level, in the form of $1/f$ power law distributions. As discussed, when power laws operate, self-similar fluctuations become evident on multiple time scales, here detected within the random surface pattern of neural firings. From this data Anderson and colleagues speculated that dreams serve to integrate various levels of functioning, ranging from the neurophysiological underpinnings right up to the level of consciousness and behavior (Anderson and Mandell, 1996).

Few psychotherapists need scientific proof for the meaningfulness of dreams. Most of us understand from experience the power of a tiny dream fragment to magnify the whole of the psyche. Intuitively we see how dreams display formal fractal structure that is observer dependent. In other words the revelation of a dream intimately depends upon how the dreamer handles the dream.

Dream work is a perfect example of iteration within self–self relations of conscious awareness. We have a dream that emerges into consciousness from the unconscious by feeling real in our bodies and emotions. We then revisit the dream at a later time and so recycle it back into consciousness. Out of this recursive iteration new patterns emerge in the form of more effective self-understanding. The more often we return to a dream the more likely we will find new meanings to broaden our self-knowledge.

Here is an early dream from my own childhood used to illustrate the role that scale and iteration can play in developing fractal consciousness. Whereas all dreams carry the theoretical potential to represent the whole of the psyche, this dream is striking in its literal depiction of a fractal.

Liberty in hand

In my dream I'm sitting in the dark, on my bed in South Orange, New Jersey, surveying the sea of lights and treetops outside my window, as I love to do before going to sleep. Suddenly above all else towers the silhouette of the Statue of Liberty, appearing as a giant figure in the distance, as she rapidly pursues me. Terrified, I place all my stuffed animals along my windowsill in a frantic effort to protect myself. After lining all the animals up, I dive under the covers.

In the morning I awaken to the sound of the front doorbell. Alone in the house I go downstairs to answer the door. But when I look outside, no one is there. Instead, sitting atop the stone bench stoop to the left is a miniature replica of the Statue of Liberty. Filled with delight I scoop her up and bring her into the house, shutting the door behind me.

This is one of the few dreams I recall from childhood. I have returned to its scary but beloved images repeatedly at various stages of my life. Within my personal psychotherapy and during clinical training, I have enlisted various therapist and supervisors, approaching the dream from multiple perspectives and theoretical orientations.

The more I have turned this dream over in my psyche, the more new dimensions and facets of understanding reveal themselves to me. I have seen conflicts with my mother; fear of my femininity; narcissistic issues, including anxiety about being crushed under the enormity of important others; terror surrounding my personal liberty and creative freedom. With each new iteration comes a new shade of meaning.

Symbolically, within the very structure of this dream, a fractal appeared as a gift from my unconscious long before my conscious mind knew what they were. I had this dream in the 1960s, well before fractals were discovered, presaging my current intellectual and therapeutic interests. Throughout history there are numerous famous stories of dreams serving diagnostic, prognostic, inspirational and even precognitive purposes (e.g., Van de Castle, 1994). Perhaps the seeming magic occurs less out of foresight and more out of archetypal resonance with the whole of the self, that transcendent place where past, present and future converge (see Figure 7.9).

Dreams emerge in the space between conscious and unconscious aspects, reflecting not just who we are in a present moment, but also what we might become in the future, in places where being shades into becoming, the individual into the collectivity. Successful dream work carries the fractal

Liberty
in
Hand

T. Marks-Tarlow 7/01

Figure 7.9 Liberty in hand.

Here is my rendition of the central fractal image of my dream. I have entitled this piece "Liberty in hand," because as an artist and psychologist I am highly aware of the importance of the hand, both literally and symbolically. I believe my dream concerned my doubts and insecurities about handling my lot in life. I view the last scene of scooping up the miniature statue in my arms as an active moving towards, a way I was working through the issues. Along with the central fractal image presaging my own interest in fractals well before their discovery, this drawing also contains an eerie foreshadowing. Notice the date: July, 2001. Never in my life had I drawn a city skyline before. It shakes me a bit to have captured the twin towers only two months before their destruction.

feeling of detecting the whole of our selves in the pieces of nightly reverie. Thorough dream work can demonstrate how creative pattern formation during successive iterations of consciousness constitutes the essence of effective introspection.

When iterations of consciousness are less successful in building psychological structure we might call this "thought-looping." As the mind returns to the same end-states again and again, new patterns of meaning fail to emerge and the products of self-reflection cannot be harnessed into more effective inner-world–outer-world relations. If thought-looping occurs repeatedly, iteration in consciousness can become the defining feature of neurotic, self-absorption.

Neurologically, thought-looping ties into obsessive thinking plus the absence of complexity when functions of the left verbal hemisphere become dissociated from those of the more insightful, relational, body-based, right hemisphere. This lack of complexity reveals the danger of intellectual or interpretive analysis alone without experiential, right-brain techniques for dream analysis, like Gestalt enactments or James Hillman's dictate to let the dream image "speak for itself."

Scale-invariance and bounded infinity

In my dream the central symbol of the Statue of Liberty appeared explicitly at two size scales – giant and miniature. She also appeared implicitly on the third scale of her real life manifestation in New York City, an exciting but scary place for me to visit from my sheltered, suburban, New Jersey home. I believe that the property of scale suggested by fractal phenomena has much to offer clinical observation. Whereas self-similarity calls attention to qualitative aspects of fractal pattern, scale-invariance points to the importance of quantitative features related to scaling. One of the most significant contributions fractal geometry makes to psychology is the promise of more precisely aligning quantitative with qualitative aspects of experience.

In my dream scale reveals much about my internal conflicts as a child. The initial large-scale appearance of the Statue of Liberty suggested anxiety-provoking internal struggles that felt larger than life and too much to handle. Lining up my stuffed animals and then plunging myself under the covers, where I could no longer see what was happening, was a concrete enactment of my tendencies to use lines of reason (intellectualization) plus ducking and sleeping (denial) as central defenses. In the morning Liberty's reappearance in static and miniature form suggested eventual mastery of this central conflict, by my ability to titrate my fear and happily assimilate her form on a manageable scale into my psyche at ground/grounded level.

Scale-invariance reveals how the pattern of the whole remains unchanged despite shifts in size or time scales. As we shall see in "The Buddha bug", if we look at a mathematical fractal underneath a microscope, the pattern will appear quite similar regardless of how much we zoom in on it or pull back. Likewise if we examine a moving fractal it will appear similar if we speed up or slow down the film. Within music, self-similarity can lead to paradoxes of sound where jumping up an octave can have the effect of sounding lower (e.g., Schroeder, 1991). Anderson and Mandell (1996) suggest that scale-invariance links neuronal with global brain and subjective events, with our capacity to jump from one time scale to another accounting for shifts in the perception of time.

Scale-invariance lends a set of paradoxical qualities to fractals: the pattern of the whole appears on all scales and so transcends any particular scale. Yet at the same time what we actually see depends acutely upon the scale we use to observe it. In this way, fractal pattern manifests concretely on every scale in space or time, as well as transcends any particular scale in space or time. When we look at a fractal branching tree in nature, the pattern both permeates the specific scales as well as exists outside of them. When reflecting on this feature of fractals, we can directly experience the sacred (transcendent) in the profane (immanent).

The Buddha bug

To further explore the importance of scale concretely, let us examine another way to create a fractal. Recall that when we made a Koch snowflake and Sierpinski pyramid, we used geometric iteration by starting with a seed shape

Science box 7.4 Iteration on the complex number plane

The Mandelbrot set, appearing as the central image in Figure 7.10, consists of a very simple nonlinear equation ($z \rightarrow x^2 + c$) iterated for every point on the complex number plane, now rendered as a dynamic zone of re-entry. The complex number plane consists of two axes – a horizontal axis for the real numbers (rational plus irrational numbers) plus a vertical axis for the imaginary numbers (based on i or the square root of -1).

After the same formula is applied over and over, the results are color-coded. The area outside the fractal is chaotic, with numerical sequences that gallop away unpredictably towards infinity, at one speed or another. When translated visually, this chaos can be indicated by color or black and white gradations. Different colors are determined by different speeds of escape towards infinity.

continued

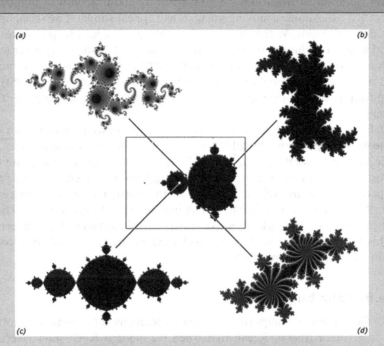

Figure 7.10 Mandelbrot set and some Julias.

Courtesy of Nicolas Desprez

This is evident in the first few images of the color section at the end of Chapter 9, though in Figure 7.10, the chaotic area is rendered as white.

By contrast, the territory inside the fractal is ordered. Its iterative progression of numbers is stable, settling down eventually to one or more fixed-point attractors, visually rendered as the solid black area that occupies the middle of the figure, as is the case in Figure 7.10. The fractal itself constitutes the complex edge between these two realms of chaos and order. Here, in the delicate interface between unbounded and bounded zones, the fractal neither flies out of control, nor comes to rest. Instead, at this edge of chaos, the fractal self-organizes into an infinitely deep border that moves dynamically with the scale and perspective of the observer.

There is only one Mandelbrot set, and it is the most complicated mathematical object known, because it contains all other
fractals. Each point on the set corresponds to a different fractal,
known as a Julia set. Figure 7.10 gives us a feel for the incredible
complexity of the Mandelbrot set, by illustrating four different
Julia sets with lines pointing to their location.

and following a geometric rule for its construction. Each subsequent iteration
either added or subtracted structure to arrive at greater complexity. This
time we begin by using a mathematical formula that is iterated mathematically rather than geometrically, and rendered visually on the computer.

To iterate using the computer, we examine the granddaddy of all fractals,
the Mandelbrot set. Named after Benoit Mandelbrot, who coined the term
fractal in 1975, the Mandelbrot set, which consists of a simple formula iterated on the complex plane, is the most complicated mathematical object
known to humankind, and contains all other fractals. Many nicknames for
the Mandelbrot set exist, including the Abominable Snowman or the Warted
Arthropod. Personally, in hushed, reverential tones, I have always thought of
the Mandelbrot set as the Buddha bug.

The Mandelbrot set is infinitely deep. In theory, this process continues
indefinitely because calculations of fractal dimensionality presume infinite

**Science box 7.5 Complexity at the edge of
the Mandelbrot**

We get a feel for the incredible complexity residing at the edge
of the Mandelbrot set when we examine a computer-generated
image that reverses the usual coloration. By highlighting the
inside rather than outside of the set, Figure 7.11 lets us see the
progression from linear order to chaotic disorder.

At the very center of the Mandelbrot set, iterating the equation leads to one stable solution, indicated visually by a single
white stalk. As we move towards the set's edges, a series of
period doublings occurs: first there are two stalks, then four, then

continued

Figure 7.11 Reverse depiction of the Mandelbrot set.

Adapted from Briggs, 1992

eight, then sixteen, and so on. This process continues until order gives way to chaos right at the edge of the Mandelbrot.

This period doubling follows a bifurcation progression known as the Feigenbaum universal. In the 1970s Mitchell Feigenbaum, a pioneer in the mathematics of chaos, discovered a constant in nature, 4.6692016 . . ., that describes how some different systems in nature follow the identical progression from order into chaos (see Gleick, 1987). From dripping faucets, to fluctuations in animal populations, electrical signals in circuits, lasers, and various chemical reactions, the scaling details are identical in every case, independent of system details or composition.

feedback loops. In practice, iteration continues until either there is a stable endpoint or an artificial cut-off giving a clear indication of where the equation is headed. This fractal is nonlinear, because its miniature representations of the whole approximate without duplicating the pattern of the whole perfectly or predictably. The incredible complexity of the Mandelbrot set highlights a critical insight derived from nonlinear science – it does not take complex parts or even a complex formula to wind up with a complex form. Iteration of simple parts and a simple formula *over time* does the trick. In this way, over the course of evolution, time plus iteration leads naturally to greater complexity in a way perfectly compatible with entropy, or the second law of thermodynamics.

Iteration of the mathematical formula is the technical part of producing a computer-generated fractal. By contrast, how the fractal is colored is an aesthetic decision. There is no right or wrong way to color a fractal (see Figure 7.12). Each choice (perhaps like each possible psychoanalytic interpretation) highlights a different fractal quality. Here we see the melding of science and art possible within contemporary science. Consider the process of creating a fractal something like a Rorschach test in motion: iteration symbolizes objective reality testing, while infinite possibilities for its coloration represent the endless range of subjectivities possible.

Bounded infinity

When rendering a technical fractal like the Mandelbrot set where scientists use the computer like a microscope to zoom in on fractal edges, we see how fractal pattern is both scale dependent and scale independent. This is demonstrated in Figure 7.13. As the computer operates on tinier and tinier size scales and detail, self-similar representations of the whole unpredictably loom. Whether or not the Buddha bug is detectable, each scale reveals unique pattern.

Because this zooming in could continue indefinitely, with the computer unearthing ever new fractal landscapes, iteration of the Mandelbrot set reveals a fractal property I call "bounded infinity." Although theoretically, scientists could iterate a fractal forever, practical limitations limit the process. Meanwhile every pattern is distinct and constitutes a visually bounded area. The nonlinear unfolding of the Mandelbrot serves as a beautiful metaphor for the continuity yet uniqueness of self from moment to moment (see Piers, 2005).

This property of bounded infinity touches upon another paradox of the nonlinear kind mentioned earlier: the tinier the area under investigation, the more there is to see. This lack of final resolution to fractal pattern iterated on the computer may sound like Merlin's mythological bag of magical tricks or the bottomless fountain of youth. But to me it also sounds a lot like the psyche: the more we gaze inward the more there is to see. The infinite depth

Figure 7.12 Different Mandelbrot color schemes.

Courtesy of Nicolas Desprez

In this composite figure, the same area of the Mandelbrot set is colored with two different schemes. Much like various schemes of coloration highlight different formal properties of the Mandelbrot set, different emotional properties in a therapist will serve to highlight different structural features of their patients. Just as the final fractal portrait balances and blends objective and subjective elements, so too do inner and outer worlds blend during the integrative work of psychotherapy.

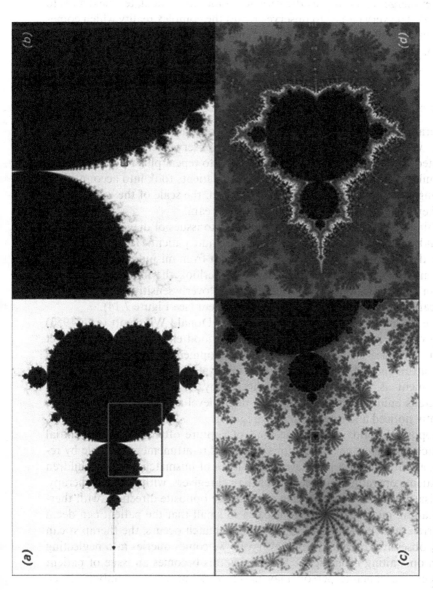

Figure 7.13 Mandelbrot set zoom.

Courtesy of Nicolas Desprez

Because the Mandelbrot set represents the iteration of a nonlinear equation on the complex plane, self-similarity is not exact as it was for the Koch snowflake and Serpienski triangle. Instead, self-similar repetitions bear an approximate resemblance to the whole, much like children tend to resemble their parents.

within, including endlessly recurrent self-similar process-structure, only stops if we stop looking.

In both fractal inspection and personal introspection, the observed and the observer merge seamlessly, as the very act of looking articulates the details to be found. The very choice to observe creates the complex reality which comes into being as a result of the act of observing; likewise, the conscious choice to avoid or defer observation, or unwitting omission of observation, leads to a different, less complex and less changing reality.

Empathy and scale-matching

As therapists the notion of scale helps us to consider the importance of coarse- versus fine-grained scales of clinical observation. In the two cases presented at the end of Section I, the impulse to repeat plus reappearance of self-similar dynamics was discouraging until patients took into account their changing scale. In my Statue of Liberty dream, the scale of the central symbol is key to interpreting the meaning of the dream.

Within clinical practice scaling also relates to issues of diagnosis, observation and attuned contact between therapist and patient. Therapeutically I believe that empathic failures sometimes result from misjudgments or misattunements involving scale. Therapists can overlook the importance of tiny scales in patient awareness, frequently labeled "overly sensitive" by parents or other caregivers, to constitute lack of attunement (see Figure 7.14).

There is clinical line of thought, voiced by Donald Winnicott (e.g., 1953) among others, related to the notion of the "good enough" but not perfect mother. The idea is that psychological development proceeds not through perfect attunement, but via tiny ruptures in the attachment bond during early development as well as during psychotherapy. The theory goes that new structure is built out of repair of these micro-level ruptures as they are subsequently noticed and addressed by caregivers.

I propose that this therapeutic kind of rupture often involves an initial mismatch of attentional scale with subsequent re-attunement possible by re-scaling attention to resonant levels. One form of mismatch involves children and patients operating on tinier scales than caregivers, within psychotherapy. But misattunements can also take place in the opposite direction, with therapists taking interest in events on scales so small that the patient can deem them irrelevant. When this kind of scale mismatch occurs, the therapist can appear obsessive to patients. Not everyone welcomes queries into neglecting to turn on waiting room lights. Sometimes this becomes an issue of patient character – a concrete person may never work on such a symbolic level. Sometimes this is an issue of patient readiness – at one stage in therapy, the meaning of such an omission might induce a passing chuckle; at another state, closer to the self-organized critical edge of chaos, the very same event could trigger an avalanche of change as it did for Sue. Sometimes patient

Figure 7.14 Baby Bud.

Sometimes juxtaposing different scales has a positive impact, if it sensitively high-lights the distance between two people. Other times juxtaposing different scales carries destructive potential, if one or the other feels discounted, invalidated, or even annihilated. This drawing illustrates that attention to scale does not always require scale matching. What is most important is attuned awareness to the impact of issues related to scale.

disinterest in where the therapist focuses may appear initially as empathic failure, but later as resistance surrounding topics of central import. At times the patient may suffer from alexythymia and lack the capacity to feel feelings surrounding such tiny events. As always each instance within each case must be explored uniquely to tease apart such factors.

I believe scale-matching between therapist and patient may prove an important part of empathy. The degree to which scale-matching leads to resonant, intersubjective dynamics may be critical to feeling understood is an empirical issue in need of further investigation. This conjecture certainly appears consistent within attachment theory with the emphasis on the importance of micro-level dynamics between mother and child, but awaits further investigation.

Learning to work "from inside out" is sometimes a matter of scale. To teach patients how to pay attention to the subtle landscape of tiny feelings can be intrinsic in right-brain processing and necessary to understanding events symbolically. To process something symbolically often involves a change in scale through rendering a small event to mythic proportions.

Attention to scale may prove important to understanding certain psychopathological dimensions, especially as they play themselves out in patient experience and relationships. Diagnostic categories, such as obsessive thinking, perfectionism, or distorted body image, can be understood as problems in scale, for example excessive attention to tiny scale levels while missing the larger perspective. Such an approach might help to inspire new treatment strategies.

Our field is only in the initial stages of recognizing the importance of scale-related dynamics to clinical work. I believe this issue will prove fruitful for future clinical harvesting. The notion of scale-dependent and scale-independent dynamics appears a central aspect of fractal consciousness. This chapter offers a beginning exploration of the value of fractal consciousness for introspection and self-regulation. I hint at possible implications for conceptualization and treatment in hopes others will flesh out concepts in greater detail.

Chapter 8

The fractal geometry of intersubjectivity

Jack sees
　　Jill can't see Jill can't see
and that
　　Jill can't see
　　　　Jack can see and
　　　　　　see he sees
what Jill can't see she can't.
　　　　R.D. Laing, from *Knots*

Many contemporary therapists have shifted from one-person to two-person psychologies. Allan Schore (1997, 2003b) illustrates this difference visually by placing a portrait of Freud alongside Mary Cassatt's painting, *Baby's First Caress*. Freud's picture reveals the "icon of a monad, a single unit; an adult, conscious, reflective mind attempting to understand the realm of the dynamic unconscious that forms in early childhood; a man's face gazing inward; a representation for a paternal-oedipal psychology" (2003b: 3). By contrast Cassatt's work, also gracing the cover of Daniel Stern's landmark book, *The interpersonal world of the infant* (1985), symbolizes "a dyad, two interlocking units; gazes between two faces, one of an adult female, the other of an infant, a representation of a maternal-preoedipal psychology" (Schore, 2003b: 3).

From a one-person perspective, psychological boundaries appear straight-forward. The therapist's eye forms a clean mirror separating patients' inner from outer processes, subjective fantasy from objective truth. The move to a two-person perspective causes everything to shift, with the matter of psychological boundaries becoming especially complicated. The interlocking gaze between mother and baby functions like two mirrors facing one another, displaying the infinite recursion of two worlds, each endlessly reflected in and of the other.

The transition from one- to two-person theories calls for a new language of intersubjectivity flexible enough to contain feedback loops and recursive elements, including the paradoxical entwinement of self and other. Chapter 7 introduced a fractal metaphor to illustrate the complexity of repetitive dynamics and core patterns within the individual psyche. This chapter expands these ideas by using fractals to contextualize the psyche within a rich and generative relational field.

George Atwood and Robert Stolorow (1984) defined intersubjectivity within psychoanalysis as the intersection of two subjectivities – that of patient and that of therapist – each carrying a differently organized subjective world. One revolutionary implication of this perspective for the science of psychoanalysis is that observers became formally indistinct from the observed. After declaring the observational stance of psychoanalysis to be always *within* the intersubjective field, no wonder Stolorow's group highlighted introspection and empathy as primary tools for therapeutic observation and intervention. While introspection and empathy are important to any effective psychotherapist's repertoire, they are not the only means to formulate a language of intersubjectivity.

At the material level, advances in EEGs, fMRIs, and other brain-related technologies reveal the underlying neurophysiology supporting experience-dependent maturation. Researchers in interpersonal neurobiology implicate body-to-body, brain-to-brain communication. To draw upon nonlinear dynamics broadens the language and methodology of intersubjectivity even further beyond exclusively subjective and phenomenological terms. To conceive of intertwined subjectivities in terms of coupled dynamical systems implicates affective, energetic, and informational exchanges at multiple, simultaneous levels of observation and description. We can track conscious, explicit processes as well as unconscious, implicit ones. We can capture the full complexity of brains, minds and bodies in the relational dance, each stepping on different time scales, according to different rhythms, underlying parameters and intrinsic dynamics.

Science box 8.1 Material aspects of the intersubjective field

While brain and body elements at first appear external to the intersubjective field, they are not, due to open boundaries that separate and connect mind and brain, mind and body. Therapists know and work with these open boundaries intuitively by understanding how drugs, hormones, exercise and even food choices can affect how we feel, perceive and ultimately relate to others.

This book emphasizes how open boundaries between observer and observed apply not only to subjective ties between self and other, but also include the material level of existence by embracing boundaries between mind and body, as well as between self and environment/world.

Nonlinear science facilitates the inclusion of third-person, observational methods to clarify, supplement and contextualize first-person, intersubjective experience (see Varela and Shear, 1999). Whether tracking the brain in action or physiological correlates of key therapeutic processes and moments, new technologies enhance awareness of micro- and macro-scale brain and body elements that accompany conscious experience. This is especially useful for tracking tiny-scale motion of face and body accompanying right-brain, body-based, implicit, emotional exchanges. By aligning multiple observational levels, psychotherapists can more easily fold the material aspect of the work back into the therapeutic dialogue without worrying about stepping out of the intersubjective field.

One reason early intersubjectivitists concentrated primarily on conscious subjective levels is because the psyche all too easily *appears* to function autonomously, apart from the brain and body, by virtue of its emergent dynamics. Nonlinear science reveals that when complexity emerges at global, higher levels, the workings of lower level constituents and hierarchies are often rendered invisible. Yet we must not forget that the psyche remains embedded within a larger context of continual exchange of information, matter and energy across open biological, social, cultural, and historical boundaries.

This chapter covers complexity within self–other relations by exploring the clinical utility of fractals for reconceptualizing psychological boundaries. Along with Philip Bromberg (1998, 2006) among others, I view intersubjectivity as pattern that forms uniquely *in the space between* self and other. This pattern is both emergent and self-organizing, offering a degree of complexity not present at the level of constituent people. Because fractals often reside in *the space between* objects, processes and levels, this chapter illustrates the clinical utility of fractals to model emotional dynamics, such as projective identification, where what is inside versus outside one person versus another becomes unclear, and patterns appear to arise in the intersubjective space created by two interlocking psyches.

As usual I begin with a clinical illustration, the case of Mae, chosen specifically for core dynamics that "leaked" across open therapeutic boundaries to become enacted within the therapeutic alliance. Mae's early trauma led to her inner dissociation between good and evil. Self-similar repetition of this trauma within the therapeutic alliance brought hopes for new levels of integration within Mae. By making these dynamics relationally alive, they could be consciously and conscientiously examined in doses small enough to be tolerated and affect inner repair.

Through conceiving fractal borders between self and other clinically, I demonstrate how dissociation easily translates into projective identification, as split-off, "unwanted" pieces of self become projected onto the other. When post-traumatic symptoms are present, "loose" boundaries between self and other sometimes appear as the pathological outcome of derailed attachment. Yet open boundaries and projective identification do not only indicate pathological condition. In this chapter I also show how self-similar operations of projective identification characterize normal, adaptive development.

From these two examples of self-similar entanglements arising in the space between self and other, I turn next to the mathematics of fractal dimensionality. I illustrate how fractals exist in the space between ordinary Euclidean dimensions. I then explain another feature of their complexity – how their very construction and even perception are observer-dependent.

The chapter ends with the bootstrapping problem identified by psychoanalyst Stephen Mitchell (1997). Bootstrapping occurs when intrapsychic processes cross over interpersonal thresholds, and therapists become "caught" in the very dynamics they are supposed to step outside of and analyze objectively. Within psychotherapy, this impossible demand leads to the hopeless-seeming paradox of needing to step outside of one's self in order to effect a cure, an issue also tackled by Donnel Stern (2004b). To resolve this paradox of self-reference, I offer an interobjective level, where fractal boundaries between self and world help to ground the intersubjective thicket and avoid the endless recursion of becoming lost inside the mutual gaze.

Going to extremes

From the beginning working with Mae filled me with extremes of horror and marvel. Mae's parents lived in China until each immigrated separately to America during early adulthood. Mae's mother was an unwanted baby girl, whose own mother had hurled her to the floor upon birth. Passed among distant relatives, Mae's mother never felt wanted or loved. So much early abuse and neglect perpetrated against this woman had infused her with an erratic, explosive temper. At times Mae's mother would bang her little girl's head against the bathtub or drag her sister by the hair across the apartment. Unwittingly Mae's mother also carried misogynist seeds implanted within her into the next generation. She readily mistreated her two girls, while not once laying a violent finger on her youngest, a baby boy.

Family rumor had it that Mae's father was sold as a sex slave around age 8. Although managing to escape, the boy suffered a bike accident in which he landed on the front of his head. Mae talked about her father as if he were an animal leading a simple life centered on insatiable appetites for sex, fight, and food. From Mae's description, I speculated that her father's accident caused severe neurological damage to his prefrontal lobes, including executive functions involved in higher judgment and impulse control. Mae's mother was raped on their first date, with sexual violence continuing throughout the marriage. In the apartment pornography was strewn everywhere. The degree of neglect and squalor is apparent from Mae's recollection of hiding under the bed after neighbors had called 911 to quell a parental fight. A policeman walking through the door involuntarily exclaimed, "What a shit-hole!"

Mae was sexually molested by her father, which occurred at least twice around age 6. She remembered her father playing with her nipples, but did not perceive this as sexual abuse until her first boyfriend repeated the act during sexual petting. In her early twenties, that re-enactment brought out Mae's distress, causing her to seek psychotherapy. In the aftermath of so much early abuse and neglect, Mae struggled with compulsive eating and a host of physical problems, including fibromyalgia, endometriosis, and restless leg syndrome, for which she was taking L-Dopa medication. She remained in psychotherapy for about six months, until she became discouraged. Mae left believing her therapist had condemned her to the possibility only for adjustment and not full recovery.

This tenacious young lady rebounded by burying herself in college studies and attending medical school to become a surgeon. She also converted to Catholicism, where she found great solace in the strict doctrines and regular Church attendance. Mae stopped having premarital sex, a great relief, given that sexual activity had always felt "dirty." Mae had a history of compulsive masturbation beginning at age 11. She recalled a poignant moment as a teenager while babysitting, when she felt the clear potential to become a sexual molester herself. A little boy accidentally brushed against her groin. Mae felt a flash of temptation to pull him closer to masturbate herself, and resisted the temptation "but for the grace of God."

Now Mae was engaged to Shep, a Caucasian doctor much nicer than her first boyfriend. During their several year relationship Mae had become increasingly verbally and physically abusive to Shep. More and more she exploded with "episodes" she likened to epileptic fits, where she swore, taunted, hit, threatened and once even pulled out a knife to threaten him. Mae sought psychotherapy with me to interrupt the intergenerational pattern of abuse. Determined to make a good marriage, she expressed initial hopes of erasing all the bad from childhood. Mae's goal was to excise her trauma, as well as to undo and eventually redo her history. Mae had bucolic visions of living peacefully with her brother, sister, and parents, not in violence, but in love and mutual kindness.

Whoa! I've never seen anything like this! What an amazing contrast! Such exquisitely high functioning next to such primitive emotionality inside this competent doctor. Just look at that street kid from the inner city hood. So close to the surface. Wants to shake her fists. Yet such naïve hopes . . . such compassion for her abusive father . . . such a pure ideal to wipe out the bad, while preserving the good.

Over the next several sessions, months and years, I continually experienced reverberations of the "shock" at these contrasts within Mae's psyche and functioning. My awareness of the extremities of my own emotions provided a self-similar, titrated glimpse of Mae's own un-integrated extremes, providing good preparation for what was to come, and attesting to Bromberg's assertion (1998, 2006) of the utility of attending to such self-states.

During our fifth session Mae and I discussed a circulation problem in her leg that continued to elude the understanding of traditional Western doctors. The only thing relieving Mae's symptom even temporarily was a hip-opener, yoga pose called Virasana (Sanskrit for "Hero's Pose"). With 30 years of yoga practice under my belt plus an intense interest in the mind/body interface, I could intuit the meaning of Mae's symptom. I suggested that perhaps Mae's legs were still trying to carry her away from the extensive abuse, through symptoms of going numb plus the "running" of her restless leg. Adopting the posture of a hero gave Mae the strength and courage to still herself. Mae was nodding as I spoke, accepting my interpretation readily, as she sensed a fit with implicit processes within her body.

Mae appeared the following session clutching a piece of paper. As she walked into my office, she handed me the paper and asked me to read it to myself, because she could not speak the words. As I read silently, my entire being filled with horror. Apparently a new memory had surfaced in Mae between last session and this week's, consisting of Mae's father bouncing his young daughter on his lap. As he did so, he manipulated her genitals with his hand. Mae struggled to leave, but her father refused to let go. He pinned his young daughter down with strong arms, and as the sexual touching continued, Mae studied the look of utter determination on her father's face. Only upon bringing his daughter to climax, when her body slackened, did he release his daughter from his grip.

Mae clearly saw the pain written all over my face as I read her words. We discussed the sequence of events that had just led to the resurfacing of this memory. A female friend of Mae's had mentioned the word "orgasm," and Mae remembered a moment of physically recoiling at the word. Later at home, as Mae worked on a crossword puzzle, the image of her father from childhood spontaneously arose. Minutes later, Mae's fiancé entered her apartment. One glance at Mae's face and her furious scribbling movements alerted Shep that something was amiss. When Shep asked Mae what was wrong, she continued to work on the puzzle without once looking up. From somewhere deep inside her, strange and unfamiliar noises came out in low pitch, scream-like sounds. In a voice utterly unfamiliar to Mae, choppy words flew out of her mouth like bullets to spit out the hateful image.

As we talked about the incident, I quickly realized that nowhere inside of Mae did she want to believe her memory was real. No sooner had we discussed the episode, than Mae begged me to declare it all a product of an overly fertile imagination.

I'm aching with your pain . . . wish I could support your wishes, but I can't. The event is too embodied . . . your body is screaming what your mind has little capacity to believe. Your legs want to run. Your words come from a place beyond your control. All the while, your heart dedicates itself to preserving your father's innocence. As I experience this tragic split, my own gut yells out, "This feels all too real."

We could speculate that by accepting my interpretation about the comforts of Hero's Pose, Mae's symptoms themselves changed, as if she took something of me into her that served as a detoxified re-enactment of earlier boundary violations, leading to what happened next. While the content of my interpretation contributed to Mae's recall, simultaneously I suspect there was also a nonverbal enactment to our own interaction. In a way we could say I too was "touching her down there," not for the same reasons and clearly with a different intent of my own. The violation and penetration was similar but different enough from what happened with her father. The event occurred on a much smaller, titrated scale, allowing Mae's mind to re-create this memory within a new context.

Will the real devil stand up

For Mae the aspect that was too real to bear/bare concerned the problem of evil. When Mae had remembered the nipple fondling alone, she could imagine that her father acted out of the animalistic simplicity of his own damaged mind. If he did not know what he was doing, then maybe he did not realize he was hurting his daughter. Maybe he even acted out of love. However this new memory of being touched "down there" blew apart that whole construction. The actions of Mae's father were too sexually explicit to sustain her former belief. The revised version was too painful, too incongruent for Mae to assimilate and integrate. As Mae understood it, such acts could only be perpetrated out of evil. As therapists we can envision the behavior of Mae's father a bit differently. Through a more clinical lens, the abuse appears to be a dissociative re-enactment of Mae's father's own early trauma, however evil or driven out of his own acknowledged pleasure.

In the following months, as Mae and I dipped in and out of the memory and incident, she experienced some relief from chronic anxiety. Once in the middle of the night, Mae left a panicked question on my machine, "Can this 'thing' with my father ever go away?" Indicating a moment when Mae was not sure she had the resources to handle her dysregulated emotion, our work felt like a continual tooling and refueling of Mae's resources to address her difficulty accepting what she remembered and felt. Our sessions jumped around erratically, touching various topics including intense discussions about race, class, and abusive friends. Meanwhile eating-wise, Mae "fell off the food wagon." Then a series of violent explosions erupted towards Shep, plus a dream that her abuse of Shep was "all her own fault."

After asserting that she could never bring up this memory of early sexual abuse to her parents, fearing that it would "kill them," one day Mae spontaneously told her mother about the incident of sexual abuse she remembered. Having waited until the expression itself carried meaning, and without poignant need for a particular response, Mae was greatly surprised that her mother received the communication with some empathy and regret. This contributed greatly to Mae's increasing empowerment in speaking out. It also fortified her strength to differentiate her desire to move towards health in contrast with her family's continued pathological enactments.

In counterpoint to moments of intense emotionality, our sessions often waxed "clinical," as we delved into the neurobiology of trauma-driven symptoms. I highlighted the nature of dissociation within Mae's continued difficulty regulating emotions of fear and vulnerability that so quickly switched into bursts of anger and violence. Her outbursts were so subcortically driven that Mae felt she had no control over them and strained even to remember the events surrounding these explosions at all. Mae took well to this level of analysis, which was consistent with her surgical career choice. These discussions helped her develop a witnessing consciousness while decreasing shame, partly by normalizing Mae's strong emotions and violent outbursts.

Then one day for the first time, Mae did not show up to therapy. When I reached her by phone she confessed profound fears to face me. After running out of Paxil, she had masturbated for the first time in years while suffering withdrawal symptoms from the drug. Mae felt she had committed a mortal sin. Furthermore because I am Jewish, she feared I would not be able to understand the nature of her sin. I would respond by trying to take away Mae's beliefs, perhaps stealing something from her as her father had. Mae was also frightened that talking about this would trigger my anger concerning her doubts about the utility of our continued psychotherapy.

Our even-paced telephone conversation helped to relieve Mae, and because it had gone well, she agreed to return the following week. On that day, much to her surprise, Mae did not find it so hard to face me. During our session Mae was shocked to learn that her chronic, low-level "dirty" feelings around sex were not something everyone else felt, but were yet another post-traumatic symptom. Mae expressed both relief and hope for her future.

Two weeks later Mae missed another session. Again wanting to terminate therapy, she agreed to return for only one last meeting. That session proved to be one of the most extraordinary encounters of my life. Mae was open and frank about a new set of horrors. She felt the Devil was leading her down a dangerous path of temptation through our psychotherapy. My comfort and clinical attitude towards her masturbation was wrong. She now felt compelled to seek help in a different form. She strongly believed she either needed to visit a priest-therapist or someone else more like herself, who viewed masturbation as a sin and who, like her, perceived evil literally and concretely in the form of the Devil. The immediate trigger for Mae's crisis in faith had been a book she recently read about possession. One of the cases documented involved a therapist who was an atheist. Under the Devil's spell, the therapist denied the existence of evil, partly by treating the presence of the Devil more symbolically than concretely.

Oh my God. I can't believe this is happening. Feels like a dream. Maybe a movie. I feel so removed from Mae's world, yet so connected to her. So much sympathy for her plight. Of course she's confused. Of course our differences seem threatening. Maybe she's right. Maybe she does need a priest or a therapist who is more like her. What a strange contrast – I'm clear as a bell, yet filled with doubt. Have to hang in there until we figure the right course of action out.

Carefully Mae and I examined the nature of her promptings to leave therapy with me. Partly she yearned for guidance. Mostly she was gripped by fear that the Devil was leading her astray. But when it came down to terminating, Mae confessed that she did not really want to leave, especially when she considered how well understood, helped, and freed from previous symptoms she felt.

Next we talked about how the Devil operates (medical pun intended). Mae explained that the Devil does not want people to feel helped. Instead he instills doubt and fear in order to draw people away from the light of God. This was an eye-opening moment for us both. Upon hearing her own words, Mae suddenly experienced a change of heart. The Devil was not tempting her with the sinful, forbidden fruits of therapy. Quite the opposite – the Devil was tempting her away from an important source of solace and healing.

In a flood of relief, Mae recognized the necessity of continuing our work together. If there was anything about how I participated with Mae that allowed her to recognize this, I suspect it was my willingness to thoroughly entertain doubts along with her, so that the solution to the cultural "problem" of our psychotherapy became a shared affair. My "relenting" stance (see Hesse and Main, 2006) helped reverse any previous penetrations and opened up some space for Mae to come forward with her own new interpretation. By not starting out "aggressively" with an agenda towards which I was determined to move Mae, the "eye opening" instant came spontaneously for both of us from Mae, an intersubjective moment of mutual surprise.

Several months later Mae got married. After a preliminary discussion about the religious feelings of sex in marriage as sacred, Mae surprised herself by consummating her marriage with untainted feelings about sex, although later sexual issues did creep back into the relationship. Mae has continued to struggle with rage and violent outbursts towards a co-worker as well as her husband, whom she was later to stab in the face. This severe violence was followed by Mae rediscovering her passions for writing poetry, including a poem about "the beast" inside her, clawing at its cage for blood.

Clearly the work with Mae is ongoing. I admire her bravery to stick with it, especially given huge cultural expanses plus attention to inner work with the potential to rupture other long-term relationships tied by unhealthy bonds. Needless to say the rapid switches, progress and regressions with Mae continue to scare and delight me.

Fractional dimensionality

Before analyzing this case in terms of fractal boundaries, let us examine the formal quality of fractional dimensionality where, as mathematically defined, fractals reside in the infinitely complex space *between ordinary Euclidean dimensions*. Many of us remember Euclidean geometry from school, where we learned how regular shapes like points, lines, planes and solids, combine to form various angles and objects. We studied the Platonic solids, those regular polyhedra with angles and lines all equal in size, as the building blocks of nature.

Science box 8.2 Dimensionality

The dimensionality of a system relates to its freedom of movement. A point moves nowhere, and so is zero-dimensional. A line follows a single axis of movement (e.g., north–south) and so is one-dimensional. A plane adds a second, independent axis of movement (e.g., east–west) and so is two-dimensional. A solid expands its axes of motion into three directions of ordinary space by adding the up-down direction.

It takes two points to make a line, two lines to make a plane, and two planes to make a solid. To conceive of a four-dimensional space–time matrix, simply imagine two three-dimensional objects interacting across time. Perhaps like Feynman's (1949) quantum account of positrons as electrons moving backwards in time, our minds also enjoy the extra flexibility to move forward and backward in time. No wonder some have touted imagination as the fourth dimension.

As simple as these shapes are, their geometry is still abstract. No one has directly experienced a zero-dimensional point, a perfect sphere, or even a truly one-dimensional line. Perhaps the reason why these shapes are more prevalent in math books than in nature is because Euclidean geometry itself is linear. By contrast most of nature is nonlinear, including the curved form of non-Euclidean mathematics used to model Einstein's space-time equations. Perfectly straight lines rarely appear in nature, an observation that led nonlinear scientist Dick Bird (2003) to quip that the straight line is "one of humankind's most complex advances." By contrast, "real" lines in nature, like lightning or shorelines, tend to wander in self-similar form across two-dimensional planes or to branch over three-dimensional surfaces.

Whether involving points, lines or planes, this spreading out *between ordinary dimensions* constitutes the essence of fractal dimensionality. A fractal can be understood as a lower dimensional object that occupies a higher dimensional space. For example, a cloud is a cluster of zero dimensional points that spreads into three-dimensional space; a coastline is a one-dimensional line that squiggles around a two-dimensional plane; a mountain range is a two-dimensional surface draped over a three-dimensional foundation.

Science box 8.3 Measuring fractal dimension

Just as the nonlinear realm includes the linear realm, so too is fractal dimension inclusive of ordinary Euclidean dimension. To

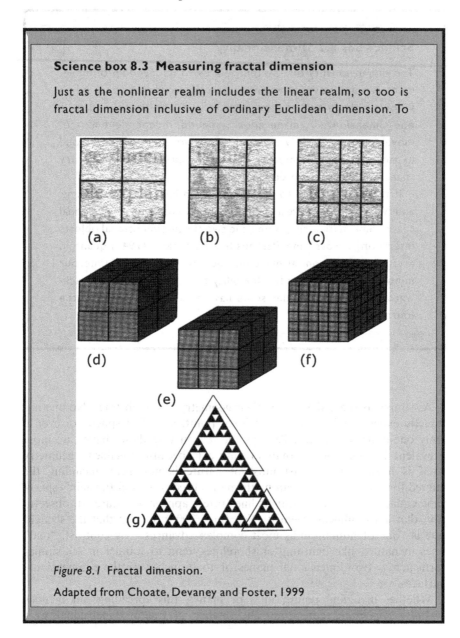

Figure 8.1 Fractal dimension.

Adapted from Choate, Devaney and Foster, 1999

understand this, let us examine the fractal dimension of a square and a cube. Both are fractal because they can be broken down into self-similar pieces.

Figure 8.1 presents three squares, each preserving the same overall size. In (a), the original has sides two times longer than any of its four pieces ($4 = 2^2$). In (b), the original has sides three times longer than any of its nine pieces ($9 = 3^2$). In (c), the original has sides four times longer than any of its sixteen sides ($16 = 4^2$). In the general case, a square has sides n times longer than any of its m^2 pieces.

number of pieces = (magnification factor)^2

Similar reasoning holds for the cube. In (d), the original has sides two times longer than any of its eight cubes ($8 = 2^3$). In (e), the original has sides three times longer than any of its twenty-seven cubes ($27 = 3^3$). In (f), the original has sides six times longer than any of its two hundred and sixteen cubes ($216 = 6^3$). In the general case, a cube has sides n times longer than any of its m^3 pieces.

number of pieces = (magnification factor)^3

With m as the magnification factor, a square can be broken into m^2 self-similar pieces, while a cube can be broken into m^3 self-similar pieces. For both, the exponent of m shows the dimension of the object. The broad formula is:

$$n = m^d$$

where n = number of self-similar pieces

m = magnification factor
d = dimension

Now let us apply the formula to an object with fractional dimensionality, the Sierpinski triangle (g). This figure can be broken down into three pieces ($n = 3$), each of which can be magnified by a factor of 2 ($m = 2$) to yield the whole figure.

continued

Since $n = m^d$, then $3 = 2^d$

To calculate d, we take the log of both sides:

$$\log 3 = \log (2^d)$$

which translates into:

$$\log 3 = d \log 2$$

and then:

$$d = \log^3/\log^2$$

The fractal dimension of the Sierpinski triangle is approximately 1.585

The general formula for fractal dimension is:

$$\text{dimension} = \log(\text{number of pieces})/\log(\text{magnification factor})$$

$$d = \log n/\log m$$

Understood broadly, fractal dimension measures the rate by which more information becomes available as the size of our measuring device shrinks.

Quaternions are three-dimensional objects that dance across four-dimensional space (Figure 8.2). Some believe that quaternions and other hyper-complex shapes provide clues to the internal landscape of higher dimensional thought (see Mindell, 2000; Wolf, 1994).

When it comes to a technical understanding of fractals, the number before the decimal point is the ordinary Euclidean dimension or "static" anchor point, while the fraction after the decimal point delineates its dynamic aspect – how much of a higher dimension this lower dimensional system occupies. The more twisted, folded or convoluted the pattern, the higher the fractional dimensionality. Think of a child's meandering scribble – the more of the page taken up by the wild scrawl, the higher its fractal dimensionality. Coastlines

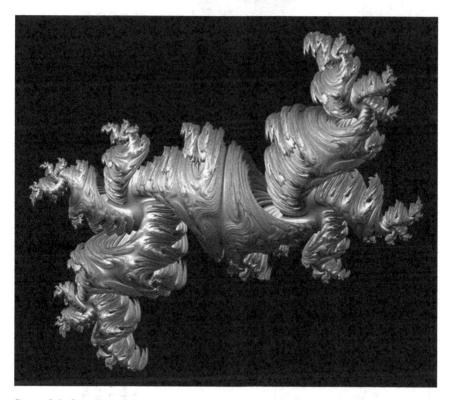

Figure 8.2 Quaternion.

Courtesy of Nicolas Desprez
   A quaternion is a fractal rendition of a four-dimensional object, here viewed as a three-dimensional slice. Quaternions are computed by iterating the Mandelbrot set on the hyper-complex plane, which contains one real and two imaginary axes. The first time they were visualized, it took days to render the image by computer. Along with static images such as this, it is also possible to have a more dynamic view of a quaternion, either by watching its shape morph as it rotates through three-dimensional space or by flying around and through a quaternion on film. This wild ride, akin to Alice's trip down the rabbit hole, may indeed relate to archetypal shapes of the imagination.

are also like squiggles that range between dimensions of 1.05 for relatively smooth ones, like South Africa, to 1.52 for very craggy ones, like Norway (Taylor, 2006) (see Figure 8.3).

The eye of the beholder

Fractals are entirely observer-dependent shapes, because the exact shape seen is completely relative to the size and quality of the measuring device (see

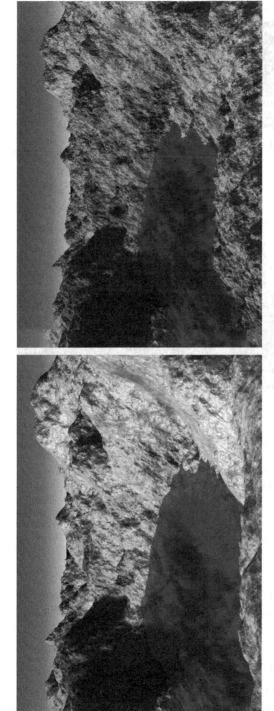

Figure 8.3 Fractal mountains.

Courtesy of Nicolas Desprez

It becomes difficult to doubt that fractals are the geometry of nature when we see fractal renderings of landscapes such as this one that seem so perfectly to capture nature's features as to appear more like a photograph than a mathematically generated computer image. This diptych reveals the very same landscape rendered with higher versus lower fractal dimensionality. The smoother figure on the left has a dimension of 2.38 versus the rougher landscape on the right with a fractal dimension of 2.50. In both cases, the number 2 before the decimal represents the topological or Euclidean dimension of the object, while the fraction after the decimal captures the fractal complexity of the object.

Science box 8.4 Infinity in a nutshell

Ordinarily when we think about measuring something, we expect to capture the object of interest fully with our numbers. When asked the dimensions of a table top, we pull out our rulers, assuming that the smaller the calibration we use, the more precise our measurement will be. We presume this because we are used to non-fractal objects with fixed shapes and sizes.

As Figure 8.4 illustrates, fractals do not work like this. Their shape is observer-dependent and their size irresolvable in any

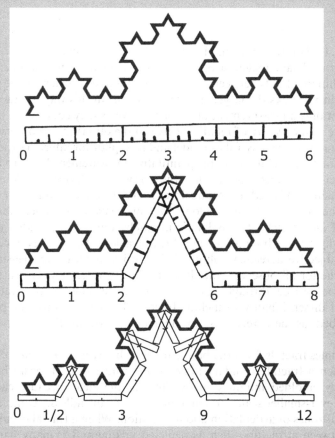

Figure 8.4 Paradoxical rulers.

Adapted from Eglash, 1999

continued

absolute sense. If we use three different-sized rulers to measure the very same Koch curve, we wind up with three entirely different measurements. The smaller the ruler, the larger the results. This happens because tiny rulers are better suited to weave in and out of the curve's intricacies. As our rulers shrink, rather than achieving converging results and reduced measurement error, we obtain wildly diverging results, that race towards infinity as our rulers contract towards zero.

Figure 8.4). For this reason, the notion of fractal dimensionality reveals some extraordinary magic in ordinary objects surrounding the unexpected relationship that holds between observer and observed. Generally the smaller the measuring sticks the larger the measurement. In this way fractal dimension is not only a measurement of *quantity* as we usually conceive it, but also a measure of the *quality* of relations between the observer and observed. No wonder fractals are so useful as model and metaphor for internal experience.

With fractals, sticking only to quantitative measurement leads to a paradox, precisely because the smaller our measuring device, the longer the measurement. This led to Mandelbrot's (1977) famous question, "How long is the coast of Britain?" along with his remarkable conclusion – the length of *any* stretch of coastline is infinitely long. This paradox demonstrates why fractal boundaries are "irresolvable." We can never converge on any objective agreement about their precise quantitative measurement that is true for all observers on all scales. But as often happens in science, paradox is averted through new discovery. By expanding the traditional notion of dimensionality to include fractional dimensionality, the paradox is absorbed as new relations are redefined between the observer and observed.

Sometimes fractals form the boundary zone between two basins of attraction. When a fractal boundary appears, the whole of each basin becomes recursively enfolded infinitely many times at the edge. Because each side recurs at ever-smaller scales, fractal boundaries form endlessly complex, self-referential zones of articulation and negotiation. When a fractal occupies the space between attractors, such as depicted in Figure 8.5, many paradoxes arise. The boundary comprises a defined area, yet is infinitely deep. By including everything surrounding it, the boundary is both inside and outside the attractors it divides, serving to separate and connect at the very same time.

Science box 8.5 Fractal boundaries

Sometimes fractals comprise the complex boundary zone between two or more attractor basins. This is illustrated in Figure 8.5, which is a computer-generated image of Newton's method of approximation, as it leads from different starting points to possible solutions. In this case, the equation illustrated is $x^4 - 1 = 0$, which has four clear answers, indicated by dark points inside differently shaded basins of attraction. Although the eventual solutions are clear, the transitions to each are very complicated. When a fractal boundary is present, the whole of each system or attractor is represented at the boundary zone as

Figure 8.5 Newton's method of approximation.
Adapted from Gleick, 1987

continued

an endless series of ever-smaller recursions. At a fractal boundary, between any two points exists an infinite number of other
points.

Psychologically I am reminded of Narcissus trying to pierce the
boundary of his own reflection: the closer he got to his image in
the water, the further he was from his real self. By studying fractal
borders and features like fractional dimensionality, we heighten
our intuition for the complexity of psychological boundaries,
which seem to exist and not to exist at the same time. When a
fractal boundary is present, at every scale of observation, this
boundary both separates and connects two complex systems,
forever destined to remain distinct while remaining paradoxically
entwined.

Interestingly, Newton's method of approximation itself
involves mathematical intuition, those "gut feelings" arising from
implicit knowledge that emerges from the unconscious, or bottom up, a kind of knowing without knowing how we know.
Neurobiological evidence (e.g., Volz and von Cramon, 2006)
points to the importance of right-brain, emotion-related, limbic
structures, including the medial frontal cortex, the amygdala
complex and anterior claustrum, for intuitive reasoning executed
amidst a high degree of uncertainty. Given that intuitive reasoning relies heavily on the holistic, integrative, massively parallel
style of the right-brain (e.g., Grabner et al., 2007), perhaps this
image clues us into the kinds of fractal boundaries an intuitive
understanding of the world regularly involves.

We can easily translate this image to a psychological situation. Simply
imagine an obsessive-compulsive person trying to use logic to make an emotional decision, such as which flavor of ice cream to select at the store. Trying
to decide between strawberry, vanilla, mint chocolate chip, and bubblegum,
the person will jump from one to the next randomly, getting lost in the spaces
between them, within fractal boundaries that separate while connecting each
attractor basin. Images drawn from nonlinear science can help us better to
understand why thought needs to be integrated with emotion, the left-brain
with the right, in order to avoid endless thought-looping if attempting to use
only linear logic when making decisions such as this.

Who holds the evil?

With these new concepts in hand, now we are ready to conceive of coupled dynamics within the intersubjective field in terms of fractal borders. In returning to the case of Mae, rather than picturing four colored basins representing possible flavors of ice cream, imagine only two basins of attraction, one shaded black and the other white in order to represent good and evil. Once again porous fractal boundaries both separate and connect these two basins permeating multiple intrapsychic, interpersonal and even cultural descriptive levels of observation (see Figure 8.6).

With this concrete image in mind, let us try to form an intersubjective picture of what happened in psychotherapy. Mae could not tolerate the recognition of evil within her father. So she relocated the conflict first within herself,

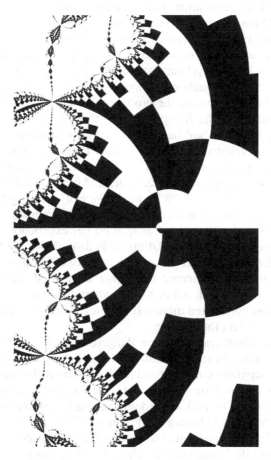

Figure 8.6 Binary decomposition for Newton's method.

Adapted from Peitgen, 1986

through her concerns about masturbation, which she perceived as evil, and then into me, for my comfort in supporting Mae's evil behavior.

From a dynamical systems perspective we can see self-similar repetitions of the original abuse within coupled operations of our psyches working together, albeit it largely at unconscious levels. The multiple enactments between Mae and myself reveal how open, fractal boundaries surrounding core dynamics can so easily and self-referentially spill across the intersubjective space between therapist and patient.

The internal boundary, between good/evil, impermeability/untouchability, permeability/vulnerability, so clear-cut in the beginning, became increasingly mixed up and violated by me as therapist at multiple levels, both implicitly and explicitly. When I touched her "down there" with my interpretation, the violation – in the form of interpenetration between good and evil, black and white – first triggered inner trauma and then crossed an outer boundary to translate into transference/countertransference enactments between us.

Within the safety of our therapeutic alliance echoes of early trauma transformed Mae's internal split into an external struggle between us. This repetition, related to what psychoanalyst Edgar Levenson calls "isomorphic enactment," proved a double-edged sword. Self-similar themes carried the threat of dissolution alongside the promise for healing. My relenting, in the form of compassion for the disruption in our therapy, was a role reversal that probably helped Mae to find her own penetrating insights. As Mae healed from the split that erupted between us – where I/therapy appeared evil versus a priest/religion appearing good – at a small scale, Mae integrated what she needed to heal similar splits on larger scales and other descriptive levels.

The trauma-based issue of "Who holds the evil" was too hot to handle. When she first entered psychotherapy Mae had not repressed the memory of her father's sexual abuse, so much as split off her experience of her father's evil plus her own rage at the violation. This distinction points towards an important difference between repression and dissociation as defenses/processes. Internally Mae preserved her father as a good, sick, simple soul who knew not what he did. All of Mae's parental rage was reserved for her mother, who Mae considered more responsible for her sins of failing to leave her husband or protect the children.

Over time psychotherapy became dangerous to Mae's internal world, threatening to break down her dissociative barriers by which good and evil had been kept separate. On a cultural level, this could threaten harmony in the household, a condition so central to the Chinese psyche, reflected by Mae's early fantasies of undoing/redoing the past. Emotional and cultural issues distilled together to form a single core conflict – whether I/therapy was good or evil. Part of Mae wanted to protect the split inside by thrusting the issue outside and declaring me evil. Then she could flee from self-reflection and the difficult emotional struggle of integrating her incongruent images and emotions. By declaring our work evil, Mae could eject the part of her father she wanted to deny – the same part of herself she struggled with actively when abusing Shep or justifying her right to do so.

Here is the core paradox of self-reference: if Mae succeeded in splitting off the evil and injecting it into me or into our therapy, ironically she would have embodied the very evil she sought to avoid. The Devil would have acted through her unconsciously to ensure that the multigenerational pattern of abuse begetting abuse perpetuated. Fortunately Mae had come too far along to succumb to such temptation. By choosing to stay, Mae allowed her psyche to grow more complex. She understood implicitly that the evil in her father had begot the evil in herself, which now threatened to demonize her very healing – the work of the Devil indeed!

We can see how a fractal interpretation of this case provides an expanded context for "radical" ideas presented by Object Relations/Kleinian thinking, such as projective identification, now almost universally recognized as body-to-body communication that arises through physiological coupling. Fractals help to concretize the transpersonal dimension to intersubjectivity, which changes the whole quality of transference/countertransference phenomena.

The nonlinear account of self-similar enactments also fits nicely with how Schore (2002) conceptualizes dissociation and elegantly links such dynamics to the neurobiology of resonant, subcortically linked, right-brain to right-brain processes. Such intersubjective processes also tie in fundamentally with Borderline Personality Disorder, as well as its spectrum recently identified (Meares et al., 1999) linking Borderline Personality Disorder with dissociative phenomena like post-traumatic symptoms that stem from early relational traumata.

Who holds the anger?

As Mae and I enacted the age-old struggle between good and evil, we descended into ambiguous fractal boundaries that separate and connect the edges of opposite people and poles. The profound wisdom of this becomes evident in the Chinese yin/yang symbol, where seeds of each pole lie buried in the center of the other. When conceptualizing projective identification using a fractal model, as when conceptualizing it from the neurobiological perspective of body-to-body, implicit communication, it is unnecessary to resort to voodoo, or magical processes by which someone puts something in someone else in order to understand how emotions and other states "jump" from one person to another.

In the case of Mae, projective identification manifested as a symptom of attachment gone awry due to trauma. Because of early neglect and abuse, Mae could not stay connected to her mother and father without internally separating and splitting off the bad from the good. Now I wish to illustrate how similar enactments often occur naturally during the course of normal development by describing next an incident when my daughter was 5 years old. By so doing I hope to illustrate the expressive, rather than defensive, function of projective identification as it spills across open, fractal boundaries, plus how such processes contribute to the emergence of internal complexity.

Darby is a charming little girl, but an emotionally volatile one: when she is good, she is very, very good; and when she is bad, she is horrid. This trivial but revealing episode occurred as Darby was awakening to social consciousness, and grew unbearably upset at any hint of disapproval, plus enraged whenever either parent set an unwanted limit (see Figure 8.7).

Having clearly inherited the sweet-tooth gene from her mother, one day Darby wanted ice cream in the afternoon.

"No ice cream before dinner, please," I replied.

"You hate me!" Darby quipped.

Figure 8.7 Darby's fractal drawing.

Courtesy of Darby Tarlow

It fascinates me that these fractal-like drawings were created by my daughter, Darby Tarlow, during the same developmental period as the ice-cream incident reported here. How did Darby chance upon self-similar form in her imagination? I do not recall talking to my young child about my work or interest in fractals at that age. When reflecting upon this issue with developmental psychologists and other parents since, I have come to believe that fractal creations displaying scale-invariance and self-similar shapes within shapes may be a developmental stage of art many if not most children go through. If empirical investigation were to bear this out, this would be not unlike the tadpole stick figure – of a circle for a head atop a line for a body – that children tend to pass through when first representing people (e.g., Gardner, 1982).

What? I hate her?! How preposterous. Clearly right now it is Darby who hates me, not vice versa.

My instinct shouted that Darby had it all backwards. In her efforts to discriminate/not discriminate self from other across emotionally merged lines, our perspectives were opposite. In the battle of *Who holds the anger?* from my corner, my daughter held anger projected onto me. Yet as our discussion continued, I could feel my face going flush. Why was I getting so physiologically aroused? From Darby's corner of the relationship arena, no wonder I appeared the angry one. After all why was mom's face now so red? Why was her voice becoming high pitched? And the clincher – why would anyone purposely deny a little girl such pleasure?

Who was right? Who was wrong? A fractal model of open boundaries between self and other, self and world, suggests that both of us were right, and both of us were wrong. If I had insisted on being right and tried to enforce what I "knew" was the truth – that Darby and not I was the angry one – I would have discounted my daughter's experience and invalidated her perspective. Yet going the opposite way and "giving in," either by maintaining peace at any cost or by collapsing into Darby's success at riling me, would have invalidated my own perspective. Full complexity and mutuality required something different from these either/or possibilities.

Here was what I said: "Darby, I'm sorry you can't have ice cream now. I know this upsets you. It must be hard to imagine that I could say 'no' without hating you." A little later, I added:

> "You're such a good kid, and maybe you're afraid to upset me with your upset. But I want you to know that it's okay if you feel angry when I make the decision to take care of your body instead of giving in to what your mind wants instead."

Certainly these complicated formulations strain the brain of a 5-year-old. But if the neurobiologists are right, it is the emotional exchange that counts, because it is the melody that comes through more than the words. Whatever the reason, this exchange worked to hold the ambiguity and diffuse the intense emotions of the moment. Although I am not always so lucky, I believe part of the trick when dealing with emotional development in my daughter is to acknowledge open, fractal boundaries that complicate and render intriguing all intersubjective edges. As with Mae, I knew my daughter enough to know I did not know the ultimate truth about "who was right." Like with Mae, I could accept Darby's projection. I could respect the potential truth-value of her assertion of hate, without impulsively and defensively yelling, "No Darby, *I* don't hate *you*. It's *you* who hate *me* right now!"

Science box 8.6 Semantics of interpersonal paradox

In the classical interpersonal version of the liar, Socrates asserts, "Plato speaks falsely," while Plato counters, "Socrates speaks truly." Translated into a chaotic version that allows some infinite-valued variations, we arrive at the following two assertions:

> x: x is as true as y,
> y: y is as true as x is false.

These assertions are translated as follows:

$$x_{n+1} = 1 - \text{Abs}(y_n - x_n)$$
$$y_{n+1} = 1 - \text{Abs}((1 - x_n) - y_n)$$

Figure 8.8 Chaotic dualist.

Courtesy of Patrick Grim, Group for Logic and Formal Semantics, Department of Philosophy, SUNY at Stony Brook

When Patrick Grim and colleagues (1998) iterate these equations on the computer, fractal images appear when escape time diagrams are colored according to how long it takes various pairs of points to cross certain thresholds. The delicate fractal figure was produced by plotting only those points at which the number of iterations required to reach a chosen threshold *changed*, underscoring once again the importance of attending to transition zones (see Figure 8.8).

As therapists we continually assess the truth value of our patients' semantic declarations about themselves, while they do the same towards us. Faced with a stream of self-referential declarations, we continually host gut feelings regarding how honest people seem to be versus how invested in building false defenses against facing and experiencing their inner truths. The use of computers and fuzzy logic helps concretely to reveal the fractal boundaries that arise out of complex feedback loops between self and other.

By remaining mindful (see Siegel, 2007, 2008) and resisting what Siegel and Hartzell (2003) call "the low road," this exchange did not escalate into control struggles or degenerate into humiliation tactics. Meanwhile as my daughter grows more internally complex, she becomes more adept at emotional talk, plus differentiating and recognizing her own subtle feelings. She also grows more skilled at articulating feelings in a way that enables her to remain relationally engaged. As Darby grows more self-reflective, I find these double-bind scenarios to decrease in frequency. Yet I secretly/not-so-secretly admit that I found this event, however tiny, to be scary. The clinician in me whispers warnings of Darby's future potential for borderline pathology. Yet the crone responds with soothing reminders of the inevitable fractal edges that continue to plague and taunt us all.

Selves in the space between

This description of fuzzy, fractal boundaries during normal development reveals intersubjective patterns emerging in *the space between* self and other. This idea is not new and was elegantly articulated by British Object Relations psychoanalyst, D.W. Winnicott (1971). One of Winnicott's most important contributions to psychoanalysis was the notion of the transitional object. The transitional object is baby's first possession, such as a blanket or teddy bear that occupies the fertile space between mother and baby. Winnicott recognized the paradoxical nature of the transitional object that serves both to connect and separate baby from mother.

The transitional object is partly discovered and partly created. Being neither wholly of the one nor of the other, it partakes of both. For Winnicott, out of the nebulous *space between* comes the creative emergence not only of the transitional object, but also of all symbol and play, and more broadly still, of culture at large. Winnicott came to his ideas about transitional objects after returning again and again to a line by the Indian poet Tagore: "On the seashore of endless worlds, children play."

Born in 1861 in Bengal, Tagore was the first Asian to win the Nobel Prize for literature. Like a grain of sand that eventually produced a pearl, this inspirational fragment entered Winnicott's psyche, with wave after wave of meaning washing over him through time. At first the poem represented the endless intercourse between man and woman, with the child emerging from their union. Then in a later iteration of meaning, the sea symbolized the mother's body and the land her ego, with the baby spewed upon the land like Jonah from the whale. Finally out of a long, chaotic state of not-knowing, the notion of "transitional object" crystallized in Winnicott's mind.

Stuart Pizer (1998), an East Coast pioneer applying nonlinear dynamics to psychoanalysis, noted that Winnicott's creativity emerged through contemplating a classic fractal image – the shoreline as a liminal zone. Because fractals also inhabit the "space between" traditional, Euclidean dimensions, their borders provide endlessly fertile, endlessly deep frontiers. Symbolically in the fertile zone between consciousness and unconsciousness, complexity arises in the form of bits of dreams and creativity dredged up from the depths. As Science box 8.7 suggests, there are both literal as well as symbolic aspects to fractals occupying the spaces between.

Science box 8.7 Fractal physiology

There are several reasons why nature abhors a vacuum but adores a fractal. The redundancy of structure enhances durability and flexibility in the case of injury. Also given maximal surface area exposed within minimal space, fractals maximize packing potential. We see this especially in the extraordinary length of the lungs, whose 600 million alveoli occupy an area of 100 meters squared, the approximate equivalent to the surface area of a football field. While the length of the small intestine is only about 20 feet, classically folded into the abdominal cavity, its surface area is truly fractal, occupying 2000 meters squared, with all its folds, villi, and microvilli.

Just as mathematical fractals occupy the space between Euclidean dimensions, fractal physiology occupies the space between various organs, physiological systems, and levels of operation within our bodies and brains (e.g., Iannaccone and Khokha, 1996; Leibovitch, 1998; West, 1990, 2006; West and Deering, 1995). From micro through macro dynamics, from physical through mental operations, fractals both separate and connect levels in order to communicate, transport, and transform energy, matter and information across open boundaries. The lungs cross the inside/outside boundary, bringing oxygen in while expelling carbon dioxide out; the arteries and veins circulate blood and nutrients throughout the body; the intestines extract nutrients from food while transporting waste outside; while the brain is our executive center for communication, transportation, navigation and broadly modulating relations between internal and external worlds.

Within the brain, not only are the branching patterns of axons and dendrites fractal, but so too are the ion channels by which chemicals pass across cell boundaries. Bieberich (2002) speculates that fractally configured neural nets promote feed forward dynamics necessary for rapid recognition. Ben Goertzel (1993) uses branching fractal networks to model the mid-level the role of consciousness in perceptual-motor loops. We also find a central role for fractals within the psychophysics of how physical stimuli in the environment get converted into mental sensations and perceptions. Many senses, including sight and hearing, follow power law distributions in the transduction from physical to psychological signals (e.g., Kvalseth, 1992).

Pictured in Figure 8.9 is the placenta where baby is nourished within mother's womb. Here we literally can visualize

continued

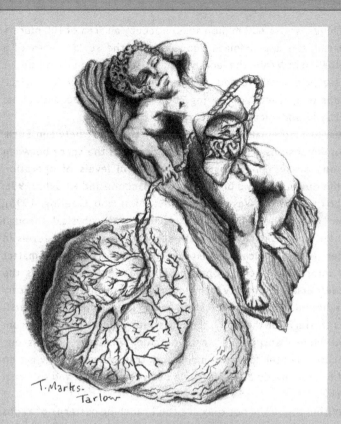

Figure 8.9 Fully formed fetus with umbilical cord and placenta.

After a woodcut by Adriaan van den Spiegel, 1578–1625, found in United States National Library of Medicine.

transitional space in the form of the fractal branches that serve both to separate and connect baby to mother. Here we can readily imagine how the very same fractal structure is both intrapersonal and interpersonal in nature. The placenta enables the transportation of matter, energy and information across open boundaries. More and more evidence accumulates that emotional shaping as well as trauma begin in the womb, as sensory feedback loops begin and hormones connected with mother's emotional state permeate this sensitive boundary.

Parallel processing and bootstrapping problems

As we have seen, when fractal boundaries exit, the whole of each side becomes enfolded again and again at the edges, providing a zone both of separation and connection between. The deeper we go, the smaller the scale, and the subtler the boundary. A fractal model of psychological boundaries helps to preserve the natural complexity of everyday life.

Within fractal boundaries, we can also see their self-referential, self-similar symmetry. Many of the cases in this book reveal fractal boundaries in the form of self-referential dynamics. Before discussing the bootstrapping problem specifically, here is a short quip to illustrate fractal boundaries in the form of self-similar, self-referential, parallel processing. Several years ago an American adolescent lived in Singapore with his parents. The teenager committed a crime almost unheard of in that country by spraying graffiti in a public place. The punishment was stiff – a public caning. Despite protest and negotiation attempts by the US government, the caning occurred anyway.

The incident caused a stir in the United States, with some people expressing outrage, others cheering. During the aftermath a US Senator introduced a bill in congress authorizing caning as legal punishment for graffiti. The response? One day, the astonished Senator arrived to find his office covered with graffiti tauntingly inscribed, "Spank me!" From one perspective there was a linear, causal chain of events leading from the spray painting in Singapore to the spray painting in the Senator's office. From a dynamical systems perspective the two events emerged in a synchronous manner, much like the resonant extreme self-states of Mae and myself.

Clinical supervisors frequently talk to supervisees about parallel processing when the process of a session mirrors the very content under discussion. Quite often, yet a third level of complexity comes into view via self-similar resonances within the supervision relationship. Rather than attend to the content of a session, psychoanalyst Edgar Levenson (1983) sought an underlying structure by suggesting we interpret not the content of patient's presentations, but rather our own "awareness of patterning." Levenson compared the manifest, unmistakable patterns underlying experience to repeated motifs in a patchwork quilt forming "harmonic variations on the same theme."

> [A]ny small piece of the clinical material contains the total configuration. Both past and future. Thus the patient's opening comment in the waiting room or coming in the door or as he sits in the chair, will establish the leitmotif that runs through the entire session, picks up the last session, and will very likely continue on into the next session. Any 10 minutes of a taped session can be explicated to an entire analysis. Any dream of a patient contains implicit in it – literally, enfolded in it – the entire story of the patient's neurotic difficulties
>
> (Levenson, 1983: 19–20)

Despite no explicit mention of fractals Levenson's description clearly captures fractal boundaries between self, other and world. By positing an underlying structure to experience discernible objectively, from the outside, Levenson attempted to circumvent a critical problem – "Who holds the truth?" (as objectively defined) – presented by most two-person theories honoring the simultaneous presence of different subjectivities.

As mentioned previously, it is also commonly said that in classical psychoanalytic thinking the first dream of the treatment will portend how the treatment goes. If we go a step further, the general belief that this is so may become a self-fulfilling prophecy, if the privileged observer creates the Truth he or she expects. In similar fashion the two-person model may do just the same thing, although presumably creating a different, better, or at least more contextually adaptive, congruent, and resonant reality. This forms the crux of the social constructivist critique of Stern's interpersonal infant – that it unwittingly gives people what they want – a purportedly universal developmental and linguistic theory which is nonetheless an artifact of the context, created out of a circular process of what seems self-evident.

This problem of "Who holds the truth?" is masked in a one-person theory. Even with the subjectivity of the patient of primary interest, that of the analyst is the ultimate arbiter of reality. The enterprise of self-psychology, typically a one-person affair (though I have also heard rumor of it characterized as a one and a half person affair) may be understood as follows. The analyst reconstructs the patient's construction of the analyst's internal world, by suspending her own subjectivity in order to empathize with the patient's point of view.

A two-person theory carries no recourse in the rational authority of the analyst. The therapist is always within both the patient's and his own system of observation, and so cannot step outside to obtain a truly "objective" point of view. These problems within most two-person psychologies led the late Interpersonalist Stephen Mitchell (1997) to identify two major issues. Without possibilities for objective truth, the analyst becomes vulnerable to mistaking his own experience or perspective for realty itself. Mitchell described this problem to involve a contradiction between veridicality and perspectivism.

Mitchell's second issue – that of bootstrapping – also arises out of the same entangled dynamics derived from a two-person theory. Any interpretation delivered by a therapist, no matter how true, will not necessarily serve to illuminate a patient. Nor does it automatically ensure patient change. This is because any interpretation will always be received from within the very dynamics the therapist attempts to portray. Mitchell (1997) describes this bootstrapping problem as the *heart* of every psychoanalysis:

> The analyst makes an interpretation about the way in which the patient eroticizes interactions, and the patient experiences the interpretation itself as a seduction. The analyst makes an interpretation about the way in which the patient transforms every interaction into a battle, and the

patient experiences the interpretation itself as a power operation. Or . . .
the analyst makes an interpretation about the patient's masochism, and
the patient experiences the interpretation as a put-down to be agreed to
and feel humiliated by.

(Mitchell, 1997: 45)

The problem is even worse, when it extends to countertransferential dynamics
plaguing the therapist.

Generally speaking, the analyst, despite his best intentions, is likely to
become entangled in the very same web he is trying to get the patient to
explore. So the analyst making an interpretation of the patient's tendency to erotize interactions is likely to be speaking from an eroticized
countertransferential position in his own experience. The analyst making
an interpretation of the patient's tendency to transform all encounters
into battles is likely to be feeling embattled himself and trying to use
interpretations as a potent weapon in his arsenal. And the analyst making an interpretation about the patient's masochism is likely himself to
have felt victimized by the patient's long-suffering misery and is speaking
in a voice laced with exasperation. Thus, the analyst's experience is likely
to be infused with the very same affects, dynamics, and conflicts he is
trying to help the patient understand.

(Mitchell, 1997: 46)

Clearly these patient–therapist dynamics speak of intersubjectivity as
self-similar resonances between minds and bodies, sometimes consciously,
often unconsciously. A model of fractal boundaries between self and other
suggests the normalcy of such resonances. *The work exists at the boundary
precisely because the boundary reflects the whole of both.* Levenson's appeal to
the formal structure of experience hints at fractal boundaries, as they lace not
only self–self and self–other relations, but also self–world relationships. This
lends hopes for an objective level, however intersubjectively defined. To point
towards the fractal nature of inner/outer boundaries, I end this chapter with
yet another variation on some earlier themes. "Who holds the evil?" which
then morphed into "Who holds the anger?" now appearing as "Who holds
the truth?"

Who holds the truth?

For millennia philosophical arguments have attempted to differentiate inner
from outer worlds. Such differences pervade not only the nature of religion,
but also basic schools of psychological thought. Whether projective
identification exists as described by object relations theory hinges on whether
one believes that emotions can be materially transmitted from person to

person. Similarly stances therapists take on the mind–body controversy, for instance whether biochemical problems cause psychological problems, or whether psychological problems cause biochemical changes, define their school of psychological thought depending partly on purely philosophical issues.

In one corner of the philosophical battle stands the objective materialist who aims to reduce all subjectivity to the material stuff of objective existence. In the other corner stands the monistic idealist who strives to do quite the opposite: to elevate all the lowly stuff of material reality up to invisible levels of consciousness and spirit. These two camps, with the mind–body dualists both there and not there, have been duking it out for millennia.

The basic philosophical positions remain similar, although clothed differently in different ages. Materialists these days often dress as radical positivists who explain the emergence of mind in epiphenomenal terms, as a function of bottom-up, self-organizational, neural processes in the brain. Contemporary idealists tend to draw inspiration from current-day physics, where consciousness is postulated as primary and originary, driving the top-down collapse of the quantum wave-function into the single, material reality evident in everyday observation.

Which position is right? Can our advances in science or consciousness help us to answer this question definitively? Personally I do not think so. I believe we are doomed to reside in the fertile uncertainty of this unanswerable question. To me what seems more significant than the "right" answer is the irreconcilability of the controversy, despite ever-increasing scientific evidence weighing towards both sides. From my perspective the controversy itself is evidence of fractal boundaries forever entangling inner with outer, subjective with objective levels, reminiscent of dialectical constructivism (e.g., Hoffman, 1998) as well as Hindu philosophy.

Möbius strips and Klein bottles

Perhaps both positions are right in a paradoxical entanglement of possible imaginings. My own philosophical stance is informed by what psychologist Steven Rosen (1994) dubs "nondualist dualism." Here the two sides of the coin, inside and outside, function as an Uroboros, the snake eating its own tail, to remain both two and one at once (see Marks-Tarlow et al., 2002). This position is modeled mathematically by a Möbius Band with a twist: like a fractal object or a Rössler attractor, the Möbius Band sits between dimensions, hovering in the space between one and two dimensions (Figure 8.10). Here this topological oddity functions as if it possesses two edges and two sides, but really has only one of each.

Moving up into higher dimensional space, Rosen models the same "inbetweenness" by a Klein bottle that perches on the edges of dimensions three and four (Figure 8.11). Although appearing to contain both an inside and

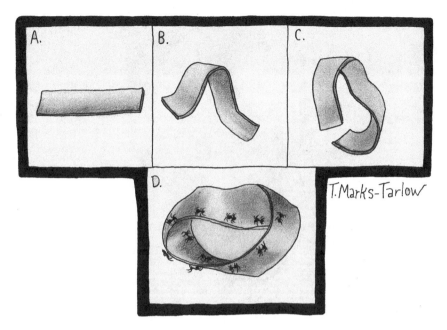

Figure 8.10 Möbius Band.

In order to make a Möbius Band, cut out a long strip of paper, give it a half twist and then tape or glue the ends together. To see how the strip is an interdimensional object with only one side and one edge, try drawing a line along one side of the strip to see what happens. Some surprising features of this strange mathematical object inspired the following limerick:

> A mathematician confided
> That a Möbius Band is one-sided,
> And you'll get quite a laugh,
> If you cut one in half,
> For it stays in one piece when divided.

outside, like the psyche, this boundary-less process mercilessly leaks its insides into its outsides forever.

The bad news about psychological boundaries modeled by fractal boundaries is that they are hopelessly fuzzy. They are intrinsically irresolvable. All the logic in the world can do nothing to untangle this messy complexity. The good news about psychological boundaries as modeled by fractal boundaries, is that they are hopelessly fuzzy. They are intrinsically irresolvable. And all the logic in the world can do nothing to untangle this messy complexity.

Due to fractal boundaries we may all carry the potential to look paranoid, psychotic or to act like borderline personalities under the right conditions. In the end, this does not matter. If we simply surrender to the inherent messiness and complexity of ordinary psychological life, we will find the openness and

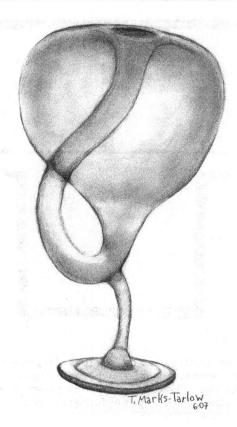

Figure 8.11 Klein bottle

infinite potential for aliveness, creativity, inner complexity and higher consciousness. Whether between self and self, self and other, or self and world, the subject of the final chapter, fractal boundaries are filled with beautiful, recursive patterns that help to reveal and "re-veil" the mystery and wonder of life.

Chapter 9

Whole in the part

> Nature uses only the longest threads to weave her patterns, so each small piece of her fabric reveals the organization of the entire tapestry.
>
> Richard Feynman

> To study Buddhism is to study the self; to study the self is to forget the self; to forget the self is to be awakened to all things.
>
> Eihei Dogen, thirteenth-century Japanese Zen Master

What is the ultimate goal of psychotherapy? One could say *greater* self-awareness, allowing more conscious decisions regarding life's direction. One could also say *reduced* self-consciousness, allowing fuller participation in life's flow. According to the ancient wisdom expressed in the second epigraph above, these two aims are not as contradictory as they might seem. To come into our selves most fully is also to release our isolation from all things. When considering the "big picture," this spiritual perspective of open borders between self and world dovetails nicely with models derived from contemporary science. Both posit selves paradoxically entwined with the universe as a whole.

Chapter 8 explored the intersubjectivity of open, fractal boundaries in the co-creation of self and other. Within our entangled relations, we glimpse the interobjective realm as coupled emotional flows become interchangeable with the material level of brain and body. This chapter moves more fully into self/world relations, my third dimension of psychological complexity.

At the interface between inner and outer realms of experience, between subjective and objective levels, between consciousness and matter, once again we find paradoxical entwinement well modeled by fractal borders. Within psychotherapy, self–world borders become foreground when we gaze into the crystal ball of our lives in search of meaning. To find self-similarity in patterns of destiny is to dance at edges of nature and nurture, chance and inheritance, conscious and unconscious aspects of life.

As I sit with patients, the experience feels deepest when what is objectively outside the psyche seems to blur with what is subjectively inside. At this bifurcation in awareness, the relationship between inner and outer realms can appear to flip. When outer events reflect inner, psychological structure, fractal patterns in destiny can serve as a mirror to the psyche. By operating at these edges, psychotherapy can attain the sacred feeling of working at the very origins of experience. When we become privy to the dynamic *zone between* material and spiritual realms, occasionally we are graced with the profound experience of witnessing self and universe in co-creation.

In introducing contemporary science to the public (Briggs and Peat, 1989, 2000), psychologist John Briggs and physicist David Peat referred to chaos as the "science of wholeness." In earlier chapters I discussed how wholes are irreducible to their parts within highly chaotic realms, how more complex wholes self-organize spontaneously and unexpectedly from underlying parts; and how fractal algorithms distribute patterns of the whole among the parts. The wholeness of fractal patterns is also evident in yet another nickname for the Mandelbrot set: "God's fingerprints."

A concern with wholeness not only permeates contemporary science but also the enterprise of psychotherapy. Many people who seek emotional guidance do not feel whole inside. They struggle to put together the pieces of their selves and lives, traumatized by a myriad of fragmenting forces in society. Many have gotten caught in mental health systems that inadvertently reduce people to symptoms or diagnoses. By drawing upon nonlinear paradigm for tools and by seeking strategies at the interface between science, psychology, art and spirituality, we therapists can counteract some of these destructive forces. We can use holistic methods to focus upon whole people embedded within whole contexts.

In this final chapter my aim is to focus fractal lenses on the big picture by using the metaphor of the whole-in-the-part to address patterns of fate. Section I begins with the clinical tale of Puck, who succeeds in breaking through a personal impasse by embracing faith in the fundamental interconnection between inner and outer realms. Puck's plight reveals how synchronicity can link subjective experience with objective events through self-similar patterning, and how in the process, nature reveals her longest threads. I then present acausal connection as the scientific underpinnings for synchronicity, helping to anchor the awe of the spiritual level with a foundation of physical understanding. When acausal connection operates, seemingly unrelated events become linked through their interrelationship to the whole. Because the whole history of a nonlinear system is embedded within each moment, one instant in time is enough to reconstruct the pattern of the whole. In this chapter I demonstrate a final method of fractal construction. Based on random iteration, this method most clearly reveals the holistic quality of the underlying pattern. For no matter how the winds of chance may blow on a nonlinear system, the same fractal attractor inevitably emerges out of chaotic trajectories.

Section II wraps up the book by reviewing its major themes as reflected in the myth of Psyche, origins of the words "psyche" as well as "psychology." I give the myth a nonlinear twist by reinterpreting Psyche's central challenge as the universal human struggle to grope for light and love in a nonlinear world filled with chaos and uncertainty. Despite unforeseeable occurrences that bring despair, Psyche's fate reveals fractal patterns of the whole that animate the tiniest of scales, down to the very ants, reeds and even towers that surround her. In the end, even in Psyche's darkest moments, life is infused with meaning that invisibly connects the smallest of mundane details with the grandest spirit of the whole.

The story of Psyche and Eros is a tale of love, separation and reconnection at higher levels of complexity. In the realm of spirit from which love emerges, what appears disconnected at first is often united through hidden channels in the end. The myth of Psyche and Eros is a tale of nonlinear couplings – between man/woman, male/female, conscious/unconscious, explicit/implicit, active/intuitive, and at its neurobiological depths, between cortical and sub-cortical levels, as well as left and right cerebral hemispheres. Viewed in this way, the myth self-referentially describes the interface between matter and spirit required for positive emotions and the very experience of love itself.

Given open fractal boundaries and interconnection to all things, the myth of Psyche teaches us ultimately to trust in self-organizing forces as they unfold naturally, according to the underlying order of the whole. Whether during clinical reflection or self-reflection, using intuition to feel our way towards the whole broadly quenches our natural curiosity about how spirit animates matter in matters of ordinary life. Whether as therapists we seek historical, intergenerational or present-centered patterns of destiny, or as people trying to navigate through life more broadly, to find the whole in the part is to detect the magical enactment of psyche-in-the-world.

SECTION I: FATE'S FRACTAL FINGERPRINTS

We first encountered Puck in Chapter 7 as a physician trying to apply a medical model to problems of the psyche. When Puck's strategy backfired, it left him feeling frustrated, impatient and discouraged, until a fractal metaphor helped him relax into the ongoing process of psychotherapy. As Puck slowed his pace and became less resistant to self-exploration, he grew more curious about his inner boundlessness, including the impact of his early history.

From the early days of childhood Puck had dedicated his life to pleasing and performing for others, especially his mother. This was true externally: he played violin beautifully, spoke flawless Italian, excelled as a childhood athlete, and since the age of 5 relentlessly pursued his dream to become a physician. Puck's performance was also an internal affair: he skillfully manipulated his own experience, sometimes with mind-altering substances, sometimes without. Puck easily produced positive emotions to enhance his pleasure and increase his approval by others, while eliminating negative emotions that caused pain or sparked conflict. His style called to mind Helene Deutsch's (1942) "as if" personality, Winnicott's (1960) notion of the "false self," or in more contemporary parlance a weak form of dissociation.

Puck initially sought psychotherapy out of a vague sense that something was wrong. Internal and external pressures were nagging at him. Puck had a girlfriend who desperately wanted him to marry her, but Puck could not commit. He was a rising star professionally, but likewise had not committed himself in his heart to being a doctor. Despite lots of acquaintances Puck was acutely lonely when he slowed his frenetic pace enough to consider his internal world. On the outside Puck's life looked perfect; everything was in order. On the inside the pieces of his existence did not cohere into a whole.

What a character! So funny, so charming, so sensitive. The guy reads my face like a book ... maybe a comic book ... look at him going for those laughs ... going for approval ... responding so thoughtfully to my every word. An ideal patient! Yet something's missing. No real contact. No sense of deep, emotional truth. Something feels slippery like water ... he's seeping through the spaces between.

When Puck first came to see me, he was dating Penelope whom he had known since childhood. She was extremely wealthy, generous to a fault and wildly in love with him. Using her family jet, she would fly Puck to private islands for his birthday. They had lots of fun together, as they lived the good life. They even enjoyed the blessings of Puck's picky mother.

With so much going for their friendship, Puck figured he would try shifting the friendship to a romance, but the experiment was not going so well. Puck felt no passion for Penelope. Hard as he tried to wield his internal magic he could not muster up this elusive emotion, as if now immune to his own magic. Having entered his thirties and watching others settling down and into themselves, Puck had shifted from believing his own story to questioning it.

With fear of repetition safely behind him in therapy, Puck began discussing his dilemma with Penelope relentlessly. He really liked his long-time friend, was wildly attracted to everything that surrounded a life and future with her; he even loved her. Deep in his heart Puck was not *in love* with Penelope; and yet he could not stop his clutching. Puck was deathly afraid to let go. He valued the friendship too much. He loved what he got out of Penelope. He did not want to risk losing anything. Having never truly loved a woman before, Puck tried to convince himself that what they had together was as good as it gets. Yet deep down inside, Puck could not make peace with himself. Despite living the good life, he felt miserable and stuck.

Oooo . . . this is a hard one. I remember well the devastation such a shift takes. What a narcissistic blow to learn we can't force fit life into fantasy. No amount of will power will do. Only humility and surrender helps us to find the ideal within the real. But how can I tell him his heart needs to break at least a little for it to truly crack open? The guy needs lots of space. He really didn't know his heart at first. Now he does. He's caught hold of his inner truth. But will he listen? Especially when it whispers messages he doesn't want to hear. Some marry without love and get away with it. Not this guy. Too deeply divided . . . too much inner betrayal. . . . Too much going through the motions. . . . Needs love to find wholeness. How frustrating to see someone look into the mirror of his own soul and refuse to pay attention. I can't do any more than I am. Or can I? Just sit tight. Cultivate the very patience Puck lacks. Trust his fate will unfold in due course . . .

After nearly a year of talking about his dilemma, Puck still felt paralyzed. He was unable to move toward Penelope with a marriage proposal or away from her with a break-up. What would motivate him to let go and face the unknown when the known felt so sweet? I am reminded of the urban myth about the monkey who reaches into a jar for sweets. Entranced by what he sees, the monkey grabs for them all but winds up with none, out of the unwillingness to release his fist and free his hand. During our sessions Puck intellectually acknowledged his need to take risks and trust himself and the universe enough to release Penelope. Yet Puck remained divided. He could not find what it took to embody this inner knowledge into the whole of his being.

One day after months of internal preparation, after flipping the subject around from every angle, suddenly a bifurcation occurred and everything changed. Puck found his internal warrior and mustered up the courage to abide by the truth in his heart. This happened when he chanced upon the book, *There are no accidents: Synchronicity and the stories of our lives*, by Robert Hopcke (1998). Puck read that everything happens for a reason – even tiny chance events relate intimately to inner psychological needs. This perspective deeply comforted Puck, finally giving him the reassurance he needed to leap into the void without guarantees. Despite fears of never meeting a suitable lover, despite dread of losing his best friend, Puck broke up with Penelope. He released the woman to whom he had clung not for passion but for certainty. After years of maintaining stagnant, unhealthy conditions of excessive order, Puck surrendered to the disruptive forces of the great unknown.

Upon finding the inner flexibility to face a creative edge, what happened next surprised us both. A week or so later Puck brought in a dream. He and Penelope were in a Chinese restaurant. As they ate, a one-eyed monster attacked Puck in the throat and leg. The session was spent mulling over the dream's significance. I interpreted the monster to symbolize the short-sightedness of Puck's baser instincts. One-eyed monsters lack the complexity and depth perception of binocular vision. One eye on a head also connotes a penis plus the primal violence possible when the other eye is closed off and the Other is rendered flat and objectified.

By clutching onto Penelope, Puck was using fear and greed to try to feed his spirit. Despite his good intentions Puck did harm and violence both to himself and to Penelope by forcing the fit. By disregarding the objective implications carried by his subjective truth, Puck had spawned a monster. He was out of integrity – doing the wrong thing for the wrong reasons. By clinging to Penelope with only parts of himself at the expense of the whole, this monster had caused inner paralysis and fragmentation. No wonder the monster attacked Puck's throat. Puck pretended to have a meaningful relationship, yet his communication was off as he lied to himself and to Penelope. No wonder the monster attacked Puck's leg. He had been going through the motions, a condition that rendered him emotionally and relationally immobile. Puck could only move on when he was ready to address his higher needs for love and passion surrounding the inner quest for wholeness. Although Puck found my interpretation painful, it was oddly reaffirming.

Several days later Puck answered a telephone call from a stranger. The woman had mistakenly received his order for Chinese take-out food. Puck talked to her a long time. They arranged to meet. Upon hanging up Puck felt deeply excited. The event seemed like kismet that, in combination with his dream, felt like synchronistic signs he had made the right decision. Puck fantasized this to be the woman of his dreams, the one he was always meant to meet, the reward for his painful break-up. Had he not just read that there are no coincidences in life? Had the book not said that synchronicity increases during times of transition, especially the more we tune into it?

When Puck met Sophia both were primed to be pricked by Eros's arrow; and Puck fell in love for the first time. Yet out of danger in perceiving this more as a fairytale than a clinical one, let me cut to the chase. While Sophia did bring love to Puck, ultimately she proved less the woman of his dreams and more the succubus of his nightmares.

Initially attracted to Sophia for her spunk and independence, by the end of their relationship Puck's view had flipped. Sophia was leaning and pulling on him so thoroughly in every way, especially financially, that Puck felt used and resentful. He lacked the sense of true partnership. But given his recent experience, Puck had learned his lesson well and more easily attended to his heart to face his fate. One look at the full picture was all Puck needed to break up with Sophia.

Ironically the next twist of Puck's fate did have an almost fairytale ending.

Having experienced his core issues from both sides, Puck was now ready to find peace/piece and wholeness. The next woman he dated, Donna, proved the one he would marry. Puck met Donna equally by chance at a business-related social event, yet this time little magic surrounded their entwinement. Instead lots of hard work went into open feeling expression, difficult communication and honest negotiation. This relationship was less fantasy-driven and more realistic. Once in a while things were sublime, but much more often they were messy.

Self-similar threads of fate

By disregarding the whole of his self, by disrespecting what Puck knew in his heart to be "right," by refusing to embody the pain of self-knowledge, Puck's life had been out of integrity. This condition blocked the natural unfolding of his fate. Perhaps Puck was angry at my interpretation of his dream, for piercing the veneer of his integrity. Perhaps Puck needed to play out another round of force fitting fantasy into reality: after integrating those split off parts, Puck could then experience the drama from the perspective of the Other. Or perhaps he was still attached to taking the leap and eating his cake too. Whatever the many reasons, with Sophia, Puck had entered a phase transition zone of moving both forwards and backwards at once, of tasting future possibilities even as he revisited past patterns, all mixed chaotically together.

The core fractal pattern also was reflected within the transference/countertransference dynamics between patient and therapist. Despite my outward patience and acceptance of Puck's impasse, inwardly Puck felt the pressure of my unarticulated identification with him. When younger I too had sported a style of trying to force fit square pegs into round lovers. Although my inner feelings and judgments remained unexpressed, Puck undoubtedly sensed my stance, always reading my face like a book to intuit what he imagined I believed was right for him deep down inside.

This implicit circuit of emotional exchange constructed a self-similar, self-referential impasse within the transference/countertransference relationship. Not only did the unspoken pressure from me mirror that from Penelope, but it also mirrored the pressure freely expressed from Puck's mother for her son to be and act in certain ways. And here existed the bootstrapping element of this case: if Puck "gave in" to his sense of my sense, he would give up his autonomy, his independence, his very control over the direction of his life under the guise of taking it. But if Puck did not give into me and remained with Penelope, his mother would win. There was no way for me/us to step out of the dynamics that enfolded us both.

Within this therapeutic impasse we can see the self-similar pattern of the whole. Every repetition that was enacted brought dangers of falling backwards along with opportunities to move forwards through the emergence of something new. When Puck found Hopcke's book on synchronicity, he stumbled upon a unique, unexpected solution to all impasses at once. He could heed the book's words instead of mine, thus resolving the central paradox by expressing both independence and surrender at the same time. Relationally Puck's choice to leave Penelope and risk his mother's disappointment represented a more complex solution than previously had been possible.

Intrapsychically a belief in synchronicity helped Puck to face the chaos of the unknown by trusting in invisible threads connecting worlds unseen. The notion of synchronicity allowed this young man to hold onto his magic while embracing the risks inherent when trusting in a higher, more inward, spiritual path. Upon letting go at multiple levels, all inner and outer blocks fell away. Puck's fate was freed to continue its natural unfolding. More integrated and whole inside, Puck could better regulate the ambivalence inevitable in all real relationships. He no longer felt compelled to run towards fantasy in search of a more perfect Other.

Synchronicity played a central role in Puck's inner and outer marriages, themes that foreshadow synchronistic events in Psyche's search for wholeness through love and marriage with Eros. Puck's synchronicity proved somewhat perverse, though ultimately not too cruel. The Chinese restaurant dream clearly mirrored both past and future relationships with Penelope and Sophia. While seizing upon his chance encounter with Sophia as a sign of true love, Sophia did not prove the perfect match he had envisioned. Ironically she embodied the very shadow side of himself he was trying to eliminate rather than to integrate by leaving Penelope.

Puck's plight reveals the dangers of grabbing too hard upon synchronistic signs in search of certain meaning. Despite self-similar pattern, when it comes to the future, no surefire way exists to conquer the great unknown. While Puck's dream did not carry the exact meaning he anticipated, in yet another cosmic irony and self-similar riff on the Chinese restaurant theme, Donna, the woman Puck ultimately married, proved of Asian descent.

Puck's story reveals the self-referential flavor of the search for cohesion and wholeness – the more we seek to put the pieces of our selves and lives together, the more we find the peace to do so. Similarly the more we seek meaning and synchronicity in what befalls us, the easier it is to find/create this condition as a context for change. From a constructivist point of view we see how perceptions and expectations help to fuse imagination into the reality we come to inhabit, like a self-fulfilling prophecy or hermeneutic circle, although its eternal return will never be precisely as we envision.

Synchronicity

The book Puck read concerned synchronicity (Hopcke, 1998), a term coined by Carl Jung to describe meaningful coincidence. Where we might expect a random sequence, synchronicity instead indicates meaningful pattern. Jung (1973) believed synchronicity occurs when a complex is activated and material in the unconscious is blocked from conscious awareness. Because of this block, rather than to experience something internally within our own psyches, the material is forced out into the world and then backwards into consciousness through physical rather than emotional channels. How like the colloquialism, "those who forget history are doomed to repeat it," or its clinical counterpart, "whatever is dissociated becomes enacted." Certainly this was the case for Puck, who literally and figuratively needed a cascade of synchronicities to break his impasse and continue unfolding his fate.

I follow in the footsteps of Allan Combs (Combs and Holland, 1990) to examine synchronicity through the lenses of contemporary nonlinear science. Whereas intersubjectivity is born of open boundaries between self and other, interobjectivity is born of open boundaries between self and world. In the latter case, fractal boundaries arise from structural coupling between self and environment when self-similar patterns become evident at the interface between subjective and objective levels.

Solid state physics was the first arena for discovering self-similar patterns in time in the form of long-range intercorrelations during chaotic phase transitions from one state to another. Per Bak (1996) brought this insight from microscopic to macroscopic levels when he perceived the unity in nature between physical and temporal fractals. I suggest synchronicity is a form of temporal fractal most likely to occur during chaotic phase transitions in life. If so, no wonder that full crisis plus surrender to the unknown can move us into fractal boundary zones, allowing new portals to open us into and out of old dilemmas.

God's threads

When synchronicity occurs, there is self-similar patterning in time, such that fractal fingerprints of fate point towards a single unifying attractor. Call it God, Tao, nondual reality, universal consciousness or any other nom du jour, synchronicities are evident when the whole of things permeates the parts.

In *Heaven's fractal net* (2004) William Jackson, a professor of religious studies catalogues the abundance of self-similar iconography in the humanities throughout the millennia, especially related to aesthetic, spiritual and religious matters (see Figure 9.1).

One look at our temples, churches, houses, landscaping and urban planning reveals an abundance of fractal patterns at the intersections between inner and outer worlds, mundane and profound (see Figures 9.2a and b).

In the case of fractal patterns in art and artifacts we comfortably envision open boundaries from imagination to reality. When the direction of influence is reversed – from the outside world back towards our inner worlds, we are

Figure 9.1 Self-similar Buddhas.

Within much religious iconography self-similar patterns abound. In the Hindu system of Karma the whole of our karmic history is wrapped into each individual's lifetime. At the core of the Hebrew Cabala, each of ten sephirots, or world spheres, contains all others. In this drawing, each Buddha differs slightly from the others, yet contains approximately the same elements. This is much like medita-tion. With each moment or sitting recursively enfolded into the last, each "now" involves many of the same elements – stillness, emptying the mind of chatter, inward attention, diffuse or honed focus – yet remains thoroughly unique.

less comfortable. Yet the nonlinear model being developed here suggests cir-cular feedback and causality lead to the co-creation both of inner and outer worlds.

To Jung synchronicity was evidence for the *Unus Munde* – the one world connecting mind and matter – with meaning serving as the thread between. Modern day spiritual guru Deepak Chopra (1995) presents "the Wizard's Way" as an opposing but related stance. Rather than the result of blocked

Science box 9.1 Fractal architecture

Self-similar features are highly common in all sorts of architecture. Consider how the doors and windows of many houses, as well as the sand castle depicted in Figure 9.2a, mirror large-scale features of the whole. Rudolph Arnheim (1977), an authority on the psychological interpretation of the visual arts, speculated that architectural repetition is a way to ease transitions into buildings. As people get close to the entryway and lose the larger perspective, the mimicry of large-scale features on smaller scales allows preservation of the whole.

T. Marks-Tarlow 5-07

Figure 9.2a Sand castle.

continued

Fractals are especially common in religious architecture, such as Hindu pagodas, Gothic churches, or Buddhist stupas. Within architecture, the term "gnomon" refers to the self-similar accretion of structure. Sometimes this accretion follows proportions of the golden mean or a logarithmic spiral. Fractals are popular within religious architecture because they hint at infinite processes within finite space. By creating an ongoing sequence, where the whole is maintained in the parts every step of the way, a finite structure can build bridges towards the infinite.

That fractals are commonly found in transition zones may be another reason for their popularity within architecture around the world. Human shelter represents a transition zone between outside and inside conditions, a fact clearly evident in the ancient American Indian adobe structures pictured in Figure 9.2b.

Figure 9.2b Anasazi Cliff Palace in Mesa Verde, New Mexico.

consciousness, Chopra celebrates synchronicity as a kind of hyper-consciousness. He views synchronistic events as the manifestation of our spiritual intentions in the universe. Synchronicity occurs when we both seek and catch glimpses of the fundamental interconnectedness between mind and matter during higher rather than lower states of blocked consciousness.

Religion often embraces a fractal vision of the whole in the part. Consider the expression "the one in the many" to signify one God interpenetrating the diverse aspects of Creation. The whole in the part is central to the mystic's attempt to throw off the shackles of the ego with its limited perception. To attain the highest possible consciousness means to experience directly the underlying whole, the oneness of undifferentiated awareness. Mystics evolve forward by dissolving conscious ego to return back to the unconscious. Mystics differ from psychotics by bringing full awareness along. Many peoples of traditional and Oriental cultures paint a portrait of underlying interconnectedness down to the tiniest or most random seeming event. By infusing each moment with divine presence, inspiration or intervention, chance itself becomes animated with the invisible workings of God.

My own belief in synchronicity represents for me the ideal blend of scientific with spiritual and professional sides. I see synchronicity as evidence for invisible channels of spiritual connection deep under life's material surface, with self-similar flows governed by hidden attractors. By my account synchronicity represents self-referential symmetry occurring when spirit manifests physically such that outer events become animated with inner meaning.

Within psychotherapy I believe the presence of synchronicity can signal the impending emergence of change. Even though we can never interpret the future meaning of a present event with certainty, this does not mean we should not try to understand the symbolic significance of outer and not just inner levels, albeit with doubt and humility. As a therapist I find it invaluable to stay open to synchronistic happenings, especially when people ripe for change find themselves hovering at edges of chaos.

Even as I marvel at synchronistic events within my patients' lives and sometimes within therapy itself, I also recognize the dangers of "reading" too much into such signs. To perceive outer events as inseparable from inner processes, not only touches upon magical realms of interconnectedness, but also provides a good working description for the schizophrenic process. The fine line that separates the two is apparent by the resemblance of Puck's plight to the main character in Kurt Vonnegut's (1973) novel, *Breakfast of champions*. During a psychotic break the protagonist turns into a psychopathic killer after chancing upon a science fiction book written as if from God to the reader. When the book proclaims the reader as the only real person on Earth, with everything and everyone else merely a machine put on earth to test him, the anti-hero feels freed up to murder without consequence.

The danger of confusing synchronistic with psychotic signs underscores the presence of open, fractal borders that both connect and separate inner from outer worlds. Fuzzy borders between these realms highlight the importance of intersubjectively groping towards the objective. Only by joining hands with others in order to grope for truth and beauty from a group perspective can we hope to preserve full complexity of the whole.

Acausal connection

The fractal idea of the whole in the part is one scientific approach to synchronicity at the "joints" between mind and matter. Whether a branch in the road, a node of destiny, or a chance encounter, many encounters at the crossroads reveal self-similar pattern underneath. Recall that fractal boundaries occur when multiple basins of attraction are governed by the same underlying attractor. This notion of one underlying attractor governing the whole in each part of the universe seems to fit well with notions about indeterminate quantum waves and ideas about equipotentiality, but tends to wreak havoc on linear conceptions of cause and effect, which dictate that one event will lead to the next, which leads to another, and so forth.

When the pattern of the whole is present in its parts, we must embrace more complex models of causality and relatedness, including the notion of acausal connection. With acausal connection, the "glue" between parts is not based on a linear or temporal chain of events. Because fractal patterns exist outside of any particular time or size scale, fractal elements connect with one another instead through their self-similar symmetry. In the case of fractals, acausal connection preserves fundamental identity of the underlying wholeness as it permeates fractal parts. When acausal connection takes the form of synchronicity, the identity of the whole serves to unify inner and outer worlds, spirit and matter. When two seemingly unconnected things happen simultaneously, they can be acausally connected to one another through hidden self-similar channels of meaning.

The whole in the parts of a nonlinear time series

Whereas in linear systems, we detect the whole additively *as the sum* of the parts, in chaotic systems we detect the whole nonreductively *within* the parts themselves. This is illustrated by a prosaic but extremely well studied nonlinear system – a leaky faucet (e.g., Crutchfield et al., 1986; Williams, 1997).

How does the whole lurk in the part of a leaky faucet? There is complete interdependence of all elements in the underlying nonlinear system. Because each element is connected not just to every other element, but also to the whole, no matter which part of the time series data we use, we will continue to arrive at the same underlying attractor. Theoretically we could detect and flesh out the underlying attractor from sampling a single instant in time. This works because *the entire history of a highly nonlinear system is fully embedded within each time point.*

Science box 9.2 Attractor reconstruction from time series

An irregularly dripping faucet is a good example of a simple, chaotic system. To reconstruct the underlying attractor, first we place a microphone under the faucet to measure the time intervals *between successive drops*, yielding a stream of numerical data points. Next we figure out the embedding space for the attractor that corresponds to the number of dimensions needed to fully capture its trajectory. In the case of our one-dimensional faucet drips, we need a two-dimensional embedding space. In the case of two-dimensional data, such as a flat sheet of paper crumpled into a ball, we would need a three-dimensional embedding space to map out its self-similar crinkles. Generally the embedding space is one dimension higher than the attractor being plotted.

Given that we need two dimensions for our phase space, we create pairs of numbers to plot. We do this by placing our original data stream side-by-side with an identical stream, as displaced by a single point in time.

Time measured between successive drops: 1.3, 1.5, 1.8, 1.6, 1.7 . . .

T	T+1	Plotted pairs
1.3	1.5	1.3, 1.5
1.5	1.8	1.5, 1.8
1.8	1.6	1.8, 1.6
1.6	1.7	1.6, 1.7
1.7	. . .	1.7, . . .

Then we plot all of the number pairs on the x- and y-axes of a Cartesian graph. In the case of our leaky faucet, underlying order takes the form of the Hénon attractor pictured in Figure 2.11c. To detect the fractal structure of a strange attractor, we take its cross-section, called a Poincaré cut. The cut is one dimension less than phase space. In this case, our knife is one-dimensional, resulting in self-similar arrays of points known as Cantor dust.

Given that we are complex nonlinear creatures, perhaps the same holds for people. Perhaps the whole of our histories and broad outlines for our futures lies embedded within each present moment of existence. If so then self-similar patterns would be especially detectable during highly emotional times of transition, when even more than usual we operate in highly nonlinear states. One interesting way to conceptualize psychotherapy is as a higher dimensional embedding space for patients to perceive the underlying attractors of their lives. The juxtaposition of their eyes with our own helps our patients to displace the patterns of their lives just enough in time to reveal the underlying fractal structure. Like a Poincaré cut, our sessions represent a fixed lower-dimensional slice through life's ordinary flows. Perhaps the (em)bedding space of psychotherapy provide a new intersubjective metaphor for the old psychoanalytic couch.

Divining the whole in the part

With the entire history of a chaotic system embedded within each point in time we can better understand the method behind the madness of the I Ching, plus a host of other ancient divination techniques, such as the reading of tea leaves, remnant ashes, and eviscerated animal intestines. Each of these methods employs a fractal object. Each employs the fractal logic of the whole in the parts, independent of particular time or size scales. Seeing through fractal lenses helps to render such techniques less magical, flaky, new age-y and inaccessible.

To me it makes sense, not only in a spiritual meaning of the word, but also in an emotional and even logical one, that the significant events of our lives continually reflect the whole of our existence. If self-similar symmetry creeps into the joints of seemingly random events, then divination becomes less a matter of reading the future and more the ability to remain present with the full complexity available during each moment. By remaining fully present, by opening all of our senses to a right-brain, holistic style of intuitive processing, we are better able to detect invisible, acausal patterns of the whole as iterated within scale-invariant parts.

Earlier in this book I made the claim that nonlinearity is the norm while linearity is a tiny, mostly human-made, pocket of the universe. Here I would like to make an equally bold assertion – that acausal connection is the norm and linear cause-and-effect relations are the exception. If so then synchronicity may be more widespread than is realized. Perhaps within our primarily left-brain logic-driven culture, linearity is easier to see, both being objectively more noticeable and emotionally more acceptable to the vast majority of people.

If acausal connection is the norm then everything is fundamentally linked at fractal seams; and nothing is random. Fractal borders would then provide a mirror for wholeness that lies embedded in the space between coincidences, those accidents of fate or chance encounters, to shed light on the tangled territory between mind and matter, where each is co-created through and by the other.

This vision of synchronicity as it pervades human destiny dovetails nicely with the Hindu conception of Karma. According to this philosophy the entire history of not just this life, but also every other previous lifetime is enfolded within each person. Through intergenerational, recursive feedback each manifest being continually recycles spiritually, materializing into new forms as dictated by the consequences of all actions and encounters during previous existences. This system is based on acausal connection that renders meaning to every meeting large and small, including with animals. With each reiteration comes a new chance to change things just a bit and thus make progress based on the learning garnered from past lives.

On a different scale within psychotherapy, the system of Karma resembles how enactments in the present moment can lead to embodied change. Via the awareness of new experience, dissociated elements from the past can be integrated and reclaimed. Within psychotherapy broadly, I restate my belief that our power to assist the fullest and deepest levels of patient transformation can be facilitated through fractal consciousness. Fractal consciousness offers an embedding space in which to seek patterns of the whole however they may be detected within the parts and pieces of patients' lives.

To attend to fractal occurrences within the interobjective field of therapy means to remain alert to "synchronistic portals" that appear in patients' lives, whether inside or outside of the therapeutic room. The old saying, "When the student is ready the teacher will come," pertains as much to life lessons as to people. To pay attention to self-similar resonances within patterns of fate deepens our ability to listen with the third ear. This kind of right-brain processing brings the world back into our clinical musings, going underneath emotional exchanges at the intersubjective level into even more subtler energetic exchanges, at the origins of where spirit merges into matter and e-merges back out again.

Is anything truly random?

A full fractal vision of life filled with chance events, random occurrences and fearful unpredictability is also a vision of life meaningfully ordered. Although chaos theory dictates that the specific events in our lives remain fundamentally unpredictable, the possibility of fractal borders between inner and outer worlds suggests that nothing is truly random. Especially when looking back, despite the occurrence of so many chance events, we can usually detect underlying attractors in the form of self-similar pattern from the start.

This idea of self-similar pattern from conception resembles Cabalistic thinking as well as Hillman's (1996) "acorn theory" that the soul has shape prior to conception, much like an oak tree lies implicitly curled within each acorn. Within my own life, I find evidence for fractal patterns of fate detectable all the way back to conception. As a young child I learned that my literal conception was a "mistake," with my late August birthday the result of a wild Christmas party my parents attended. I also learned that my mother seriously contemplated aborting before consciously and conscientiously deciding to bring me into this world.

In self-similar fashion and at many levels throughout life, I have gravitated towards the edges of things. I have expressed this physically, as a rock climber clinging to tiny edges, literally hovering between life and death. I have expressed this emotionally, through early issues surrounding visibility/invisibility as a young child born to parents twelve and fifteen years after my brother and sister. I have expressed this intellectually as a rebel drawn to the edges of my discipline, including my current interest in nonlinear dynamics and fractal geometry.

If character is destiny, then fate appears as a fractal residue of self-similar pattern that is bound to emerge, no matter what chance brings our way. Before turning to the myth of Psyche, in one final technical flurry, I give a last mathematical demonstration of how self-similar pattern clearly and inevitably emerges beneath random-seeming occurrences.

The Chaos Game

Please try the following pencil and paper game (see Figure 9.3).

1　Draw a triangle with sides of equal lengths.
2　Label the three vertices, or tips, A, B, and C.
　　Make the game more psychologically interesting by giving your player human form and labeling each vertex with feared and/or desired fates, e.g., heaven, hell, purgatory; wisdom, foolishness, ignorance; a lottery win, the poor house, sound economic planning.
3　Invent a three-sided die and label each side A, B, or C. Label three cards and shuffle them randomly; alternatively use a six sided-die by marking each two sides with the same letter.
4　Pick an arbitrary point within the triangle as your starting place; throw the die to begin.
5　Use the letter indicated – A, B, or C – to determine which vertex you head towards and mark the point *halfway* between your current position and that vertex.
6　With this point as your new starting place, repeat the procedure, continuing again and again.

Suppose you kept playing until you plotted a million points, and so abandoned your fate to the winds of chance, that is, let the die arbitrarily select your direction and destination. What do you guess will happen? Will you ever

The Chaos Game

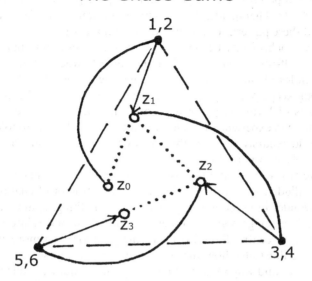

Figure 9.3 Chaos game.

Start at Z_0. Roll 2, plot Z_1. Roll 3, plot Z_2. Roll 6, plot Z_3. Keep going . . .

arrive at the final destination of any vertex? How do you envision the eventual pattern of dots to appear – random or ordered?

When initially posed with the Chaos Game, invented by mathematician Michael Barnsley, I sensed it was impossible to reach any vertex. I also understood my player would never step outside the invisible bounds of the triangular playing field. Beyond these two intuitions, the rest of what happened surprised me thoroughly, given that I pictured an eventual mess of disconnected dots. Instead the result is quite orderly. In fact, no matter how you throw the die, given enough iterations of the game, the result is always the same. What emerges is a highly patterned, infinitely deep fractal we encountered earlier – the Sierpinski triangle pictured in Figure 7.6.

By now, I hope I have driven home the point that there is more than one way to arrive at a fractal. We can start concretely with a triangle and remove its middle fourth over and over for successively smaller triangles. We can begin abstractly with a mathematical formula iterated on a computer. Or we can proceed randomly, as illustrated here, according to an algorithm whose precise implementation is determined by chance. Each method brings us to a self-similar fractal endpoint.

No wonder a rich entrepreneur can lose all of his money only to earn it right back again. No wonder an abused woman can find her way blindfolded into another abusive relationship. If patterns of fate are indeed fractal, then we continually walk down seemingly random paths only to arrive at the same highly ordered pattern. This appears so *even if the pattern becomes apparent only in hindsight*. Therapeutically contemporary nonlinear science helps us to understand these patterns of fate in a dispassionate way.

Similarly synchronicity becomes evidence for acausality in nature, for her tendency to self-organize using self-similar threads, where wholes continually fill in the holes of our experience. Just like the Mandelbrot set, where the Buddha bug keeps popping up in unexpected places, in a synchronistic universe islands of local order are interconnected beneath broad seas of disorder. As human experience stretches out into the world only to fold in again, events enfold recursively upon themselves to reveal self-similar pattern at multiple levels of organization.

If character is destiny and luck is the residue of design, then perhaps both aphorisms allude to fate as the ordered, fractal attractor of chaotically lived lives. No wonder in psychotherapy as we examine things again and again in greater detail, as we gain greater understanding of our selves interfacing with the universe, the central fractal pattern emerges more and more clearly. The Chaos Game illustrates how the pattern in our lives arises out of random steps of chance and why we must play the game for quite a while in order to visualize the underlying order that was always there and will be always there. The Chaos Game lends a clue as to why wisdom "knows so little" and takes so long to develop: the underlying fractal order of things – that place where the spirit of the whole injects itself into the parts of existence – can be visualized only in hindsight, after a sufficient base of experience collects.

Let me add one more component to the Chaos Game to fully ready us to turn to the myth of Psyche in search of nonlinear wisdom. We already have human players moving towards and away from various vertices without fully arriving according to chance occurrences. All we need to do now is to imagine that it is God in charge of rolling the die (suggested with full apologies to Einstein).

SECTION II: WHOLENESS IN THE PSYCHE

To reverse focus from parts to wholes and to conceive of synchronicity as the norm rather than the exception is to understand open fractal portals between spirit and matter, psyche and universe. In psychological discourse "psyche" usually refers both to conscious and unconscious elements of mind. Originally Freud conceived of the unconscious as a set of defensive mental operations designed to keep unwanted knowledge repressed, pushed beneath a horizontal barrier below the threshold of consciousness. Many question the notion of a repression barrier more recently, opting instead for vertical, dissociative barriers by which aspects of experience become separated and fragmented off from experience. For something to be repressed it must be at least partially within conscious awareness first. By contrast, to be dissociated experience does not necessarily have to have ever been conscious, a key distinction.

Until recently the unconscious has been conceptualized primarily psychologically, as a movement of the mind. Advances in neuroimaging and the brain sciences now lead to a different concept of the neurobiological unconscious, conceived not mentally but materially in terms of brain mechanisms underlying affective, cognitive and social consciousness. For example, researchers (e.g., Libet, 2005) detect specific neural events that actually precede conscious acts of volition. Philosophically many neuroscientists are material positivists who conceive of mental phenomena as side effects of underlying physical processes. Such thinking can carry a subtle Cartesian split by continuing to imply clean separation between inner and outer processes.

By contrast this book posits paradoxical boundaries between self, world and other, with each interpenetrating and co-creating all others. If fractal boundaries exist between subjective and objective levels then implications for the neurobiological unconscious are revolutionary. If self-similarity is nature's way of establishing identity among open, dynamic systems in flux, and if fractal boundaries are rampant at nature's joints, then the neurobiological unconscious extends infinitely in all directions to include no less than the whole of the material universe. In this case, the practical boundary to the infinite would be the time it takes to think about things, for there is not enough time to infinitely render experience. Perhaps the working through process is finite due to the finite boundary of one lifetime.

In Chapter 8, I offered the Klein bottle (see Figure 8.11) as a topological model for an interdimensional object with outsides that completely interpenetrate its insides. The radical idea of the whole in the part as relates to the unconscious also dovetails with the transpersonal element among many Jungians. These psychologists envision the collective unconscious as a single underground pool enveloping all past and future patterns, both at cultural and personal levels, fully accessible to each individual. Furthermore Jung posited the *Unus Munde* as an undivided realm where mind and matter connect through meaning. My own vision extends these ideas even further by fully pulling in the material substrate and context of existence quite directly. Please keep these ideas in mind as we next return to the myth of Psyche. Once again I present the myth in its entirety to refresh the reader's memory.

The myth of Psyche

Psyche was the youngest and most beautiful of three daughters, who took little joy in her beauty without her hand sought in marriage. When Aphrodite learned that men the world over were flocking to Psyche to worship a mere mortal, the Goddess of Beauty became enraged. Aphrodite sent her son Eros, the God of Love, to inflict Psyche with an arrow tying her to the vilest of all men. Meanwhile having received an oracle that predicted her marriage to death, Psyche ceremoniously prepared herself upon a mountain top where she awaited her anticipated doom.

Instead of dying, Psyche was saved by the West Wind, whose soft zephyr transported her to a safe paradise below. There Psyche found herself surrounded by every treasure of the world while promised a life of endless splendor. By day formless voices served her every wish; by night an unseen lover, Eros, son of Aphrodite, visited her bed. All depended upon one condition only: Psyche must never set eyes upon her husband's face.

At first Psyche was completely satisfied with this arrangement. She loved and trusted her night visitor implicitly, by feel. But then Psyche began to feel lonely. She desperately missed and longed to see her sisters. Her husband warned of trouble to come, but loved Psyche so much and hated to see her in such pain, that eventually he gave in to her wishes. Permitting Psyche's sisters to visit, Eros begged his wife not to succumb to their mischief. The same soft zephyr that had transported Psyche now transported her two sisters safely down. Upon beholding the splendor that Psyche lived in and watching their sister command the wind as if a Goddess, the two girls became instantly envious.

Pretending to keep Psyche's welfare in mind, the sisters secretly conspired to take everything away. After noticing Psyche's inconsistent stories about the identity of her husband, they hatched their plot. They warned Psyche that she had married a terrible serpent who must be slaughtered immediately, lest he devour her plus the new life now growing within Psyche's womb. Psyche was instructed to bring a lamp and double-edged blade to their bed. When her husband fell asleep, she must light the joint of his neck and then sever head from body.

Naively trusting her sisters, Psyche grew afraid where before she had felt only calm. In desperation she agreed to the plan, but became unable to carry it fully through. Upon shining the lamp upon her husband's face, rather than beholding a serpent, Psyche discovered none other than Eros himself (Figure 9.4). Mesmerized by the God of Love, Psyche flirted with suicide by turning the blade upon her self. This failing, she began playing with Eros' arrows until she carelessly pricked her finger, only to fall deeply in love with love itself.

In the course of the excitement a drop of lamp oil spilled onto Eros' shoulder. He awakened in pain. Realizing what had happened, Eros flew away without a word, as he had warned. Psyche gripped fast onto Eros' leg, but could not keep hold, eventually dropping to the ground exhausted. Utterly distraught, once again Psyche tried to kill herself, this time by rushing into a nearby stream. Again the suicide failed, as the beautiful girl was gently washed ashore. There she encountered Pan, the cloven-footed god of the countryside. Sitting in the lap of Echo, Pan encouraged Psyche not to give up. Instead she should embrace her fate by using all of her feminine charms to win back Eros' love.

Figure 9.4 German stamp.

Not only is the myth of Psyche at the origin of all "psych"-ological words, but the story has inspired countless artistic interpretations throughout the centuries.

Filled with a new sense of purpose Psyche first returned to her sisters for revenge. One by one she recounted her sad tale to each. She pulled at their heartstrings of greed, separately making each believe that Eros intended to take her instead of Psyche as his bride. When, as Psyche instructed, they arrived one by one at the mountain top prepared to leap into Eros' arms, each jumped to her death instead, when the gentle West Wind failed to appear.

Next Psyche sought the help of various goddesses. None came forward for fear of Aphrodite's rage. Eventually Psyche felt no choice but to face Aphrodite herself. The Goddess responded vengefully by whipping and abusing Psyche and then assigning the beauty a series of four seemingly impossible tasks. The first task was to sort and separate a huge pile of barley, millet, peas, poppy seed, lentils and beans all dropped into the middle of the floor. Seeing such a mess before her Psyche gave up instantly. Luckily Psyche was saved by an ant who took pity on the poor girl. The ant summoned up an army of fellow soldiers who together easily sorted the mess before nightfall.

Psyche's second task was to gather a handful of golden fleece from a herd of wild rams. The girl longed to toss herself into a nearby river instead, but was convinced to do otherwise by a talking reed. The reed told her to wait until sundown, when the animals would become calm and tranquil. Then she could easily gather a fistful of fleece from among the tangled bramble of nearby bushes.

The third task required Psyche to collect a crystal goblet filled with water from a formidable river. The waters ran impossibly high and impossibly low, filling the dreaded Styx, the river of forgetfulness that led to the underworld. Dragons and snakes hissed warnings to stay away. Once again Psyche was helped by an animal friend, an eagle belonging to Zeus, Eros' father. The eagle grabbed the goblet out of Psyche's hand, flew high into the air and nimbly dove towards the river for a sample.

For her final task Psyche had to carry a tiny casket into the underworld, fill it with Persephone's beauty ointment, and then deliver it safely back to Aphrodite. A tower instructed Psyche to bring two cakes to pacify the three-headed dog, Cerberus, plus two gold coins to pay the oarsman to ferry her across the Styx. Along the way Psyche had to resist all the desperate souls who begged for help. Later she must not partake in the feast offered during her stay in the underworld. Once the casket was filled, Psyche was not to peek inside before delivering it to Aphrodite.

Psyche accomplished everything easily until the very end, when she could not resist her own curiosity. Psyche opened the casket upon returning from the underworld. Rather than to behold Persephone's beauty ointment as expected, Psyche encountered an invisible cloud instead that instantly put her into a deathlike sleep. Luckily Eros was close by. The young god revived Psyche and returned the sleep back in the casket so that she could deliver it to Aphrodite.

With all four tasks now completed Zeus and Aphrodite approved of Eros' marriage to Psyche (Figure 9.5). Psyche was made into a goddess and the marriage ceremony was conducted at Mount Olympus where all danced to the beautiful flute of Pan. Shortly afterwards Psyche gave birth to a beautiful baby girl named Pleasure.

A nonlinear interpretation

As discussed earlier, by dropping a literal translation of myths and fairytales to embrace psychological, self-referential ones, Jungian psychologists affected a revolution in thought. Myths became outer tales told about inner events within the myth-makers themselves. In revisiting the myth of Psyche from a nonlinear perspective, I wish to mix a symbolic with literal interpretation. In addition to the intrapsychic level of previous analyses, I offer the concrete, material level of the interobjective realm.

In focusing on the interdimensional zone where mind meets matter, my approach parallels contemporary psychoanalytic thought that posits an underlying intersubjective reality to most psychological events. The majority

Figure 9.5 Psyche and Eros.

After *The Ravishment of Psyche* by Adolphe William Bourguereau, 1895

of therapists today interpret the construction of inner worlds as realistic responses to outer occurrences rather than the result of intrapsychic mechanism and fantasy. Likewise I suggest that the myth of Psyche represents a real story as intuited by the unconscious precisely because the unconscious is plugged into the whole of reality in the first place. In this sense the unconscious "knows" everything because it is everything, even if this knowledge comes so often in and from the dark, where it cannot be verbalized or even enter into direct reflective awareness.

The myth of Psyche has been interpreted by a number of brilliant Jungian analysts, including Erich Neumann (1956) and Robert Johnson (1976) and more recently by feminist Carol Gilligan (2002). Each spins the tale as one of feminine or feminist development, detailing trials and tribulations women endure in order to unite anima and animus, i.e., male and female energies within. As Psyche pines for union with another, she finds Eros, only to lose him again (Figure 9.6). She is ready to reunite with her lover only after facing

Figure 9.6 Psyche's descent.

Courtesy of Georgianne Cowan

a series of tasks that help her to integrate her own feminine with masculine attributes. Only by achieving the inner union of male and female faculties can outer fulfillment through marriage be possible. Certainly this was the case for Puck, even if he is a man.

One reason the myth of Psyche is so often conceived as a tale of feminine development lies in its sharp contrast to the sun-hero myths like Oedipus. Instead of bravely facing and fighting her obstacles, over and over Psyche gives up. She becomes confused, discouraged and even suicidal in the face of what at first appear as hopeless, helpless circumstances. This could be interpreted negatively in terms of women's powerlessness, but has been interpreted more positively as a woman's need to fertilize herself by being still and receptive to inner resources that emerge from the deep, dark womb of her unconscious.

How different from the classic male hero articulated by Joseph Campbell (1949/1973), which calls for active, thrusting stances when facing obstacles. Whether the challenge is to slay dragons or rescue damsels in distress, the classic sun/son hero flexes his muscles and charges directly into battle. He never gives up, but instead musters the courage and bravery to outsmart, overpower and control his nemeses. Such heroism not only reflects the penis in action but also the challenges of male ego development, where the light of consciousness actively distinguishes itself from the dark of the unconscious in order for individuation to occur.

Gilligan's (1982) earlier work suggests relational underpinnings to these gender differences. Consider traditional parenting situations: in order to individuate, little boys must actively break away from their mothers, while the picture is more complex for girls. More recently there is neurobiological evidence (Olesker, 1990; Perry et al., 1995) that infant girls and boys might respond differentially to distress, with girls exhibiting sympathetic hypo-arousal and withdrawal, while boys become hyper-aroused and emit more angry protest.

Though not a Jungian or feminist myself, I admire these gender-related readings of the Psyche myth. I humbly add my voice by suggesting a gender-neutral interpretation positing an interobjective level of description. To me the myth of Psyche can apply equally well to both sexes when understood in terms of the dangers and opportunities that surround everyone's need to make sense, find order and gain self-control within a chaotic universe.

While we long to see clearly that which lies besides us in the dark, if we insist on knowing what we cannot, we only fill ourselves with panic. Just as the words "psyche" and "psychology" derive from Psyche's name, the word "panic" derives from the ancient Greek god Pan. How fitting that Pan's realm of the countryside is that of Nature's unpredictability. How ironic that it is Pan himself who first counsels Psyche to calmly face her fate.

Through nonlinear lenses the myth of Psyche can be approached simultaneously on three different but interrelated descriptive levels, each mirroring an aspect of inner complexity detailed in this book.

Self–self relations

The myth is an intrapsychic tale about the marriage of opposite psychological attributes, one looping outwards, the other looping inwards – masculine/feminine, conscious/unconscious, active/receptive, thinking/intuiting, sensing/feeling, explicit/implicit.

Self–other relations

Here the myth pertains to real relationships in the real world, detailing self-similar attachment dynamics on multiple levels. The tale applies to wholeness of emotional expression and need fulfillment derived from early connection to others. The tale also applies to wholeness derived later in life through marriage to another.

Self–world relations: macro-level

The myth of Psyche is a blueprint for achieving an ordered sense of wholeness through the path of chaos. Nonlinear science offers the notion of open fractal borders between self and world to account for self-similar patterns of destiny. The scale free quality of this order reveals underlying wholeness and hidden pattern lurking beneath seemingly random events on the surface.

Self–world relations: micro-level

The myth of Psyche is a neurobiological tale about experience-dependent brain maturation. It tells of the trauma of negative emotions and dissociation, which are processed through decoupled, separated operations between right and left cerebral hemispheres, plus the triumph of positive emotions and integrated function that emerges from the nonlinear coupling between hemispheres.

Couplings everywhere

With the other descriptive levels well covered by previous thinkers, I focus primarily here on my third area of inner complexity – self–world relations. My neurobiology rests upon Schore's (1997) assertion that Freud's unconscious lies curled within the implicit processes of the right-brain, versus ego consciousness characterized more by the explicit processes of the left-brain. To previous intrapsychic accounts of the myth, I offer the right and left cerebral hemispheres for consideration. Through neurobiological, developmental lenses, Psyche symbolizes the implicit processing of the right-brain, while Eros represents the explicit processing of the left-brain.

Just as Psyche entered the scene first so does the right-brain during infancy. In both girls and boys alike it is the right-brain that comes online initially to navigate the intersubjective field between baby and caretaker. With the infant's emotional and material needs initially regulated through coupled dynamics of the relationship, only in the context of attuned responding by caretakers does the baby's brain self-organize to full potential. Eventually the child gains the capacity to regulate his or her own emotions and needs, with mature self-regulation an emergent property of the dyadic system.

Early right-brain development is critical during the first three years of life, beginning with subcortical limbic structures attached to emotion. Over time higher right-brain cortical functions are added, and especially during the third year of life, the left-brain comes on board, as symbolic, verbal and logical capacities mature. In cases of early maternal neglect, abuse or misattuned response, damage to right-brain structures leaves children at risk later for failed neural integration, both vertically between subcortical and cortical levels, and especially horizontally between the two cerebral hemispheres.

In the beginning of this myth, Psyche felt no joy. Although beautiful she took no pleasure in her looks while longing for union through marriage. With respect to neurobiological underpinnings of joy, recent nonlinear research (Aftanas et al., 1998) suggests that important cortical differences exist between the two hemispheres when processing stimuli related to positive versus negative emotion. Whereas positive emotions require the coupled operations of both hemispheres, negative involves decoupled dynamics, processed primarily within the right-brain.

Aftanas' group obtained these results by comparing EEG measures from different cortical regions in response to emotionally valenced film clips. The negative condition revealed a hospital dressing scene of third-degree burns. The positive condition portrayed antics of a Russian comedy troupe. There was also a neutral condition for comparison purposes involving a dispassionate news clip. The researchers sought evidence for underlying attractors under each of these three conditions using a new dynamical measure, called mutual dimension. Mutual dimension calculates how strongly each EEG electrode is paired to all other electrodes.

For the negative film clip Aftanas' group found evidence for different underlying attractors within the two cerebral hemispheres, suggesting their *decoupled* operations. They found negative emotions, like fear and disgust, were processed primarily in the right-hemisphere, where there appeared greater subcortical involvement that invoked the amygdala, memory and developmentally earlier mechanisms. In the contrasting case of the positive film clip, the mutual dimension was the same for the two hemispheres, indicating a single attractor underlying both. From this experiment, we might speculate that positive emotions like pleasure and love are whole brain, present-centered experiences that require the nonlinear integration between hemispheres versus negative emotions like fear and disgust, which are processed exclusively in the right-brain.

To feel joy Psyche-as-right-brain was in need of her left-brain companion, with her very pleasure dependent upon their nonlinear coupling. In order for infants to experience joy, there is also a concrete level at which this is true, with coupling required at the intersubjective level of emotional exchange, feeding, caretaking, and touch. Through attuned responding the caretaker reaches out to the baby; through pleasure the baby reaches out towards the caretaker. Here we find self-similarity in coupled dynamics at multiple descriptive levels: in the feedback loops of emotional and material exchange between people, as well as in the feedback loops of neural exchange between cerebral hemispheres. I might speculate that self-similarity serves as the mechanism linking these descriptive levels.

The life and death quality of the infant's initial dependency and helplessness puts into context Psyche's initial helplessness and continuing vulnerability to despair and suicidal impulses throughout her tale. Being a right-brain experience these negative emotions signaled Psyche's utter aloneness. But never for too long, as helpers always came. This developmental perspective contextualizes Psyche's repeated reliance on the assistance of others to be soothed and move her beyond helplessness and despair to action based upon a game plan externally supplied. First Pan, then an ant, a reed, an eagle, a tower and finally Eros himself were all instrumental at the most primitive level of Psyche's survival, as they helped her to regulate her emotions as well as organize her actions.

Just as the externally coupled operations between caretaker and infant are necessary for baby's wellbeing, the vertical integration of the right hemisphere as well as internally coupled operations of baby's cerebral hemispheres are necessary to produce positive emotion. If all goes well, later in life a decoupling occurs between child and caretaker as the child increasingly self-regulates and organizes her own emotions and needs. This external decoupling goes hand-in-hand with increased internal complexity and greater coupling between subcortical and cortical areas. While the initial "aha!" experience of sudden insight appears to be a right-brain experience (Jung-Beeman et al., 2004), a wealth of literature (Bekhtereva et al., 2000, 2004; Carlsson et al., 2000; Petsche, 1996; Razoumnikova, 2000) suggests tight inter-hemisphere coordination in creative individuals, while engaged in creative tasks.

Initially the coupling between Psyche and Eros was only in the dark, given that the one requirement for Psyche's eternal bliss was that she not peek at her husband by the light of day. As infants, with the emotional processing of external stimuli, the coupled operations between hemispheres also begins "in the dark," where sensations, feelings and other early experiences are had at implicit, unconscious levels. The light of greater self-awareness becomes possible only as higher cortical levels come on board. We can now interpret the challenges that Psyche faced developmentally as her need for higher cortical levels in the form of vertical integration, plus greater coordination between hemispheres.

Because development requires differentiation of structure to occur before integration of function becomes possible, Psyche must separate from Eros before the two ultimately can unite fully at more conscious and spiritual levels of complexity. Eros represents linear, left-brain functions embodied as conscious thought, language, logic and planning. Activated in service of will power, these are brain to body, spirit to matter, top-down movements of the mind. No wonder Eros is a powerful God who sports the capacity to fly.

As a mere mortal and earthbound creature, Psyche stands in danger of falling from the mountain top where she initially awaits her death according to prophecy. Just like an infant, Psyche is saved from death only through the help of others, as she is carried to safety by the West Wind. In Eros' palace, a paradisical, womb-like place, Psyche is not allowed to see Eros. She must integrate the operation of the left-brain at emotional, implicit, unconscious levels first before turning to higher cortical, cognitive capacities, as symbolized by the lamp and knife of conscious functioning later supplied by her sisters.

Before Psyche's sisters force her separation from Eros, one of his arrows pierces her skin. This causes the beauty to fall in love with love itself, symbolizing the first prick of self-reflection. As self-reference and inner complexity mature, Psyche can now attend recursively to feelings and reflections about feelings. Correspondingly a drop of oil falls from Psyche's lamp to spoil Eros' perfect, eternal lightness. The oil burns a dark hole into the Sun-hero's skin, as if to form a tunnel into his unconscious Psyche as his unconscious, so that he can later feel her presence intuitively and send help to her from afar, before he comes ever closer, ultimately to help her himself during the final of her four tasks.

The piercing of Psyche and Eros, each by the other, can be visualized as a yin-yang symbol, where a spot of black lies nested in the center of the white and a spot of light is curled in the center of the dark side. With this mutual piercing, the seeds of each hemisphere and their integration are planted within the other. This interpretation is affirmed by the incredible neural plasticity of the brain, including the capacity for each hemisphere to compensate for what is often regarded as the primary, if not exclusive, domain and functions of the other in cases of damage from injury or stroke.

To reunite with Eros, Psyche is given four seemingly impossible tasks. Four is the number of stability and materialization, for instance the four winds, the four corners of the earth. By contrast, three is the number of transformation, which is why in fairytales things come in threes, usually foreshadowing change. The number three also relates to chaos theory, whose technical name derives from Yorke and Li's (1975) article, "Period three implies chaos."

Psyche's first task is to separate a pile of seeds and grains, clearly symbolizing the need to make order out of chaos. With the original pile a chaotic mess the task requires logical ordering, typically the domain of the left hemisphere. The ant helpers symbolize Psyche's reliance on implicit operations or natural instincts as they operate beneath conscious experience within the cognitive unconscious. Here we can utilize the material of the outer world without knowing how. Just as horses and crows contain a primitive ability to count (e.g., Tobias and Mazur, 2007) the infant begins life ordering her experiences implicitly, through relatedness to people, without knowing how she does this.

The Chaos Game reveals how acausal connection provides the glue between seemingly unrelated events. Despite rolls of the dice that appear random and unconnected to one another, there are invisible threads connecting them underneath to form meaningful, ordered pattern. In much the same way acausal connection operates, often in the form of synchronicity between inner and outer levels, spirit and world, appearing in ways that cannot be captured by reason or broken by force.

In the myth of Psyche synchronicity appears over and over the form of critical guides. First Pan, then an ant, a reed, an eagle, a tower and miraculously Eros, all there to help Psyche. When the student is ready, the teacher will come. Just as we are all forced to trust in invisible workings of our brains and bodies, Psyche was forced to rely upon the presence of Nature's self-organizing forces. To trust in the meaningful interconnection between inner and outer worlds is both to surrender to the wisdom and healing capacities of our bodies as well as to those "leaps of faith" that Puck initially resisted. This is how we create openings for something of even greater value to enter our lives unexpectedly.

Psyche's second task of gathering fleece has an increasingly fractal element, as we sink beneath the chaos to fractal order. Hair, which grows in chaotic clumps on the surface of beasts, much like pores on skin, also reveals underlying fractal order. Like pores, hair represents a critical boundary zone, a place of transition between inside and outside. Reminiscent of Schroedinger's cat or the Buddhist conception of true essence existing between being and non-being, hair simultaneously is alive at its root cells and dead from root to tip.

Hair symbolizes the power of animal instinct through the essence of the whole. Recall Jason's search for the Golden Fleece or Samson's secret potency through his long hair. In parts of the world where voodoo is practiced, power over enemies is sometimes achieved using bits of hair to fashion and some-time torture self-similar, miniature replicas. Psyche's task to collect a handful of fleece illuminates the power of the fractal part to represent and reflect the whole, sometimes called "pars pro toto" (see Von Franz, 1972).

There is another level of self-similarity lurking within this second task. Recall that it was a talking reed by the river's side that guided Psyche. Reeds, like hair, grow in chaotic clumps that also display underlying fractal order. Reeds may be considered the "hair" of the earth (see Neumann, 1956), or poetically (see Lovelock, 1979/2000), the hair on Gaia's head. Further the reed pipe was Pan's chosen instrument and Pan inspired Psyche to embrace her fate. In yet another self-similar reverberation, Psyche eventually married Eros to the tunes of Pan's flute. From the hair on the sheep, to the reed on the land, to the reed fashioned as cultural artifact and so tamed and curled by human nature, there is self-similarity linking animal with mineral with human culture.

Sound engineer David Sonnenschein (2001) contrasts Pan's flute, made of reeds, to Hermes' lyre, fashioned by the guts of an animal strung across a tortoise shell. Pan's flute works from the "inside out," with the sound of the reed flute borne on the inner movement of breath. Hermes' lyre works from the "outside in," with harmonic vibrations of the lute originating externally in the physical act of plucking. How fitting and resonant with the right-brain workings of the unconscious that Psyche moves by feel more than thought. She faces the pieces of her experience by tapping inwards, into her own inspiration through her resonant wholeness with the cosmos.

Fractal order also emerges out of chaos during Psyche's third challenge. By filling a goblet with the river's raging water, Psyche again seeks to contain the power of the whole in the vessel of the part. Raging rivers are prototypical of nature's chaos, with the Stykes-Navier equations describing turbulent flow. Within water resides the full range of dynamical states – from completely chaotic, as in the local unpredictability of a rapid or waterfall; through its linear state of a smooth, laminar flow, as in pipes; to the completely frozen form found in ice.

The same range, from wild chaos, through the fluid edge of chaos, to rigid order, at the other extreme, epitomizes the range of biological and emotional states. The inner challenges of self-regulation, of facing nature's chaos in the form of wild emotions, to fluidly contain them versus rigidly controlling her fearsome forces, are easily recognized in flood mythology the world over. Whereas Western mythology often opts for control, Eastern mythology leans towards containment. An example is the Chinese tale of Yu, who uses a dragon's tail to dig channels for flooding waters (see Hayles, 1990).

In the myth of Psyche Zeus' eagle symbolizes the flight of the spirit to gather a bird's-eye view of the whole (intuition), again indicative of right-brain operations. With the whole in mind it is easier to face chaotic rivers of emotion. Once more, the goblet of water symbolizes the whole whose essence is contained within a small scale. Consider Psyche's later mastery over raging waters in contrast to her earlier danger of drowning. How to pick our battles is partly an issue of scale: we must choose tasks on scales small enough to succeed, but large enough to provide adequate challenge.

With three the critical number for change, a difference appears with Psyche's fourth and final task. She can no longer rely on her animal and nature friends for completion. Instead a tower renders advice to more concretely (pun intended) symbolize operations of the left-brain in the form of the heights of human culture and intellect. The tower is a central fractal image in religious iconography, portraying the spirit as it reaches towards the heavens (Jackson, 2004). Consider the self-similar spires of a Buddhist temple or the following quote concerning Vairocana's tower: "Within the tower there are hundreds of thousands of towers, each one as exquisitely adorned . . . and each one, while preserving its individual existence, at the same time offering no obstruction to all the rest" (Williams, 1989: 124–125).

With chaos now constrained through fractal order and the instinctual level firmly in place, Psyche is finally ready integrate these unconscious pieces and assemble herself back to wholeness as consciously known. Armed with the power to discriminate order from chaos as well as the ability to fully contain chaotic forces in nature, Psyche must next travel as a vulnerable mortal to the depths of the underworld where she hovers between life and death, before being accepted into the spiritual realm of the gods at the heights of Mount Olympus.

In hero mythology the world over, to visit the underworld is to descend into dark forces of chaos and the unconscious to experience a kind of death through non-being plus re-emergence and rebirth into new order. Once again we find self-similarity of theme. Earlier Psyche was commanded not to look at Eros at risk of loss. Now she is commanded not to look within the casket at risk of death. Again she cannot resist peeking, this time not out of fear but out of natural curiosity to become more fully conscious. Psyche opens the casket, itself symbolic of a little death.

Just as the oracle predicted that Psyche would marry death, during this stage of her marriage to Eros she falls into an unconscious, deathlike state. This echoes the inevitability of regression, of fractal returns to the old in the midst of the new, especially on the threshold of major transition. As therapists, we understand how the stakes grow higher the farther we progress. As we become more aware there really is no going back. Especially surrounding issues of self-expression, the internal conflicts often grow more, not less intense, as the threshold shifts to finer-grained scales and dynamics. So Psyche sinks into a state of unconsciousness far beyond what she experienced before.

Yet Psyche is also further along. She is beyond the subcortical clutches of her amygdyla, and the "lower" motive of fear driving her previous peek at Eros. Now Psyche is more motivated by curiosity, a positive outreaching of emotion already borne of coupled dynamics between left and right hemispheres. Psyche's "higher" state lets her move through nonbeing as a portal to a higher level of complexity. Psyche emerges whole and ready to receive Eros in a final union. She is strong enough to abandon herself to love without inner dissolution. Infected by Eros' arrow, in love with love itself, Psyche embraces love as the conscious, full-brained way to connect to others and the wholeness of the universe at large. And as joy and love tend to beget more joy and love the two give birth to the next generation of Pleasure.

Psyche caught in Indra's net

In Hindu mythology, Indra is the sky God depicted in the *Atharva Veda* (1000 BCE) who brings order out of chaos by conquering the serpent Vritra. Indra inhabits the upper atmosphere, dispensing his own form of chaos through storms as he commands *devas* or "shining ones" (Figure 9.7). In the *Rig Veda* the sky god is described in fractal terms as the model for every other form (Jackson, 2004).

In ancient Indian mythology Indra relates to a stunning fractal image – known as Indra's net – that embodies fundamental interdependency between the whole and its parts. Far away in Indra's heavenly abode a cunning artificer casts a miraculous net. In honor of the extravagant tastes of the deities a glittering pearl is hung in each "eye" of the net. The net is endless in dimensions so that an infinite number of pearls glitter like stars in the sky. To gaze into any single pearl is to see all others reflected in its polished surface. Each pearl, reflected in this one pearl, is also reflected in all others. Every pearl contains not only reflections of all other jewels, but also reflections of reflections of reflections. Indra's wondrous net is infinitely wide, and given its wealth of recursively embedded reflections, it is also infinitely deep.

According to Buddhist scholar Francis Cook (1977) the Hua-yen school of Buddhism was founded in seventh-century China as the philosophical rather

Figure 9.7 Indra on Airavata.

Indra sits on his white elephant Airavata, who was originally churned from the seas and sends rain on the Earth. In his hand Indra holds a natural fractal as a weapon – a lightening bolt, symbol of psychic energy and good ideas.

than practical arm dedicated towards revealing the true nature of things. Hua-yen Buddhism elevates Indra's net to a central image for the universe with infinitely repeated interrelationships among its elements. When Cook published his book in 1977 he believed this image to be foreign to Western thought. Cook saw its resonances glimmering on the intellectual horizon in the form of ecology, which was just recognizing the interconnection between seemingly disparate elements of Nature.

In the current day intellectual climate, nonlinear science prepares us further to meld spirit with heart and intellect as we grasp the beautiful image offered by Indra's net. Like this mythology nonlinear science offers visions of wholeness through fundamental interconnectedness, where each facet of the universe can be understood to determine and sustain all others. Within this non-hierarchical arrangement the tiniest elements can carry as much power as the largest, while all parts embody the infinite expansiveness and depth of the whole.

Pearls symbolize faith and esoteric wisdom, sleeping in dark, hidden spaces, becoming available only through the great effort it takes to pry open an oyster's tightly clenched shell. The struggle is not unlike that of entering the kingdom of Heaven, whose jeweled gates consist of twelve pearls. In the *Dictionary of symbols and imagery* de Vries (1984) describes the pearl in self-similar terms as both the Mystic Centre in relation to the world-oyster, and the human soul in relation to the body-oyster. As with the pearl, so with the human psyche – it can take great effort to pry open the shell sheathing its treasures and wrest secrets of the unconscious into the light of self-awareness. But any psychotherapist privileged enough to witness even one instance of deep transformation knows this effort is worth every bit of suffering and struggle this may entail.

As above, so below: Indra's jeweled net describes the fundamental essence of reality as seen by enlightened minds. It is a fractal image capturing the outside, material world, the interlocking of psyches, as well as the inside psychological one, including the neurobiological bases for consciousness itself. The co-creation of world, self and other means that the subtlest nuances anywhere can carry nonlinear power to affect all else.

As therapists striving towards the highest levels of integration and wholeness, we would do well to remember that each person and event exists as a fractal pearl in Indra's net. To embrace a recursive, nonlinear vision of the universe is to let the whole breathe into the part at every level of existence. Our interdependence, including the material embedding of our psyches, is most apparent as we search for wisdom in one another's eyes, only to find reflections of the whole universe there, including that of our selves.

Conclusion

This book is a nonlinear account of entanglement between self, other and world during psychotherapy. Chaos theory enters our offices through the whole of our selves in relation to our patients' lives that cannot be broken down into neat components analyzed independently from one another. Complexity theory enters through new order that emerges spontaneously and unpredictability in self and other at the edge of chaos. With the patient–therapist dyad representing a single nonlinear coupled entity, fractal geometry helps to sensitize us to scale and self-similar patterns of the whole as appear or do not appear at multiple levels of description.

Clinicians can understand mental health as the preservation of complexity achieved at the edge of chaos. Attention to clinical metaphor represents one important, whole-brain technique enabling us to integrate left- with right-brain processes while blending the known with the unknown, embodied experience with mental images, feelings with words, unconscious with conscious aspects. Fractal geometry appears to be an important source for new models and metaphors within clinical theory and practice. Fractal geometry is the geometry of nature which, due to open borders between world, self and other, applies as much to human psychological nature as to material processes and substrates, and in fact helps to bridge all descriptive levels. Self-similarity represents a newly discovered symmetry in Nature. In this symmetry of identity, Nature's parts carry fingerprints of her wholes. Applied to the psyche, properties of scale-invariance and self-similarity help us to find great meaning in tiny moments, as well as to detect ordered patterns in the disorder we face.

Out of the nonlinear coupling of two brains, bodies, hearts, minds and souls fused together healing in the form of greater complexity can arise spontaneously and unpredictably in both. The highly nonlinear nature both of psychotherapy and its underlying brain processes means that formularized methods based on reductionistic assumptions have severe limitations. While pointing towards important global principles, by reducing the complexity of the whole they are bound to fail as precise algorithms for specific actions.

Nonlinear science is a science of wholeness, and within the context of the whole, being appears more important than doing. At neurobiological levels the brain alters in response to implicit emotional exchanges arising far beyond our conscious capabilities. This highlights the importance of clinical intuition based on emergent aspects of the moment. Within therapists, I have come to believe that the nonlinear emergence of novelty out of attention to the whole enables highest creativity within the blending of science, art and spirit during the practice of psychotherapy.

When all goes well, whole-brained clinical intuition that arises implicitly out of the intersubjective moment will always be a lot smarter and more inclusive than our explicit, rational thoughts. Humanist and Gestalt psychologists recognized this intuitively decades ago. Now we have scientific language to understand the full complexity of our endeavor without resorting to rationalization, trivialization or defensive rejection of science. As interpersonal neurobiology recognizes broadly, a complexity paradigm honors the holistic quality of right-brained, nonverbal, implicit, relational sides that continually operate alongside the left-brain clinical narrative. This book attempts to specify how nonlinear paradigms might alter the clinician's eye. I am hopeful that it contributes to an already rich literature, as well as provides some additional features for others to elaborate upon, test and spin out in creative ways I cannot possibly imagine.

Like a finger pointing towards the moon, this text has woven together words, clinical tales and scientific concepts to nudge readers towards the relevance of nonlinear science to psychotherapy. My subject matter, like life itself, is open-ended, ever in flux, and much too complex to fully grasp. In honor of these features, instead of ending this book with a summary aimed at certain conclusions and convergent awareness, I choose an opposite, divergent path. The following pages consist of twelve computer-generated fractal images created by two fractalists whose passion lies at the intersection of art, math, and science. The first three images are "traditional," derived from the Mandelbrot set. The next nine were rendered at the forefront of fractal innovation. Plates 1, 2, 3, 5, 7, 8 and 10 were created by David Wexler, while plates 4, 6, 9, 11 and 12 were created by Nicolas Desprez. I offer these images as a meditative device and aesthetic springboard to formulate your own summary of the material, by wordlessly gauging where you stand. Do you too share a fractal aesthetic? If you find these pictures pretty, are they just that? Or do you also think fractals are profound?

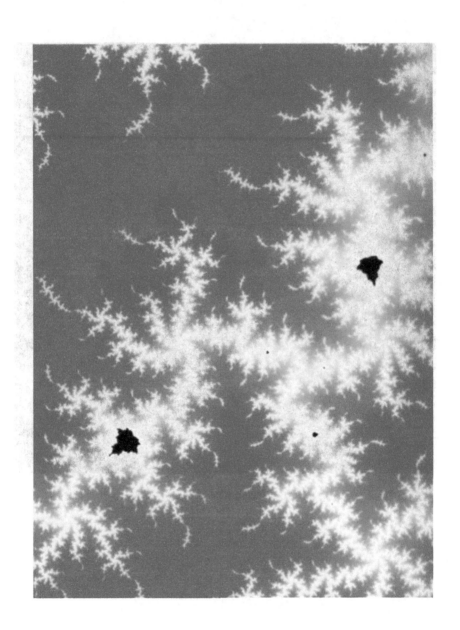

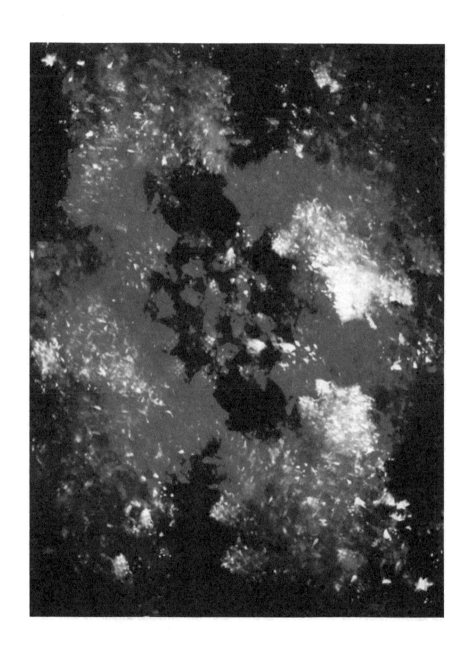

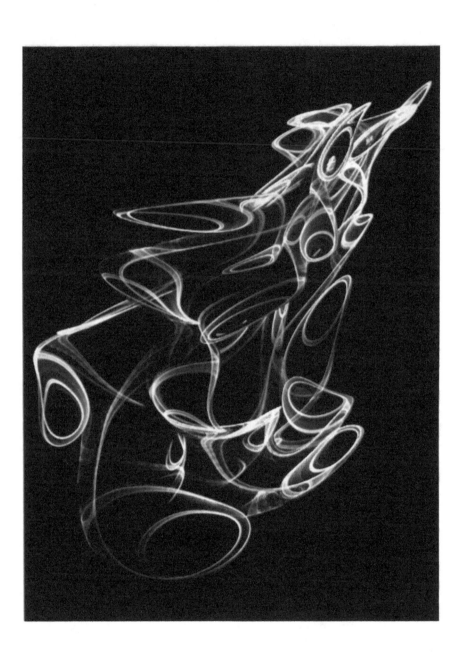

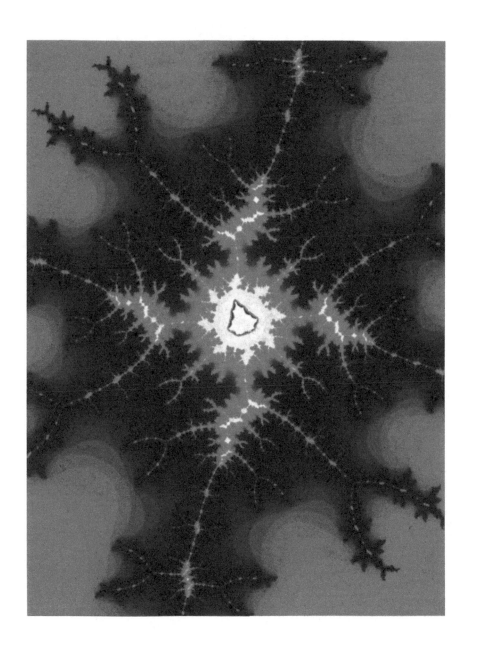

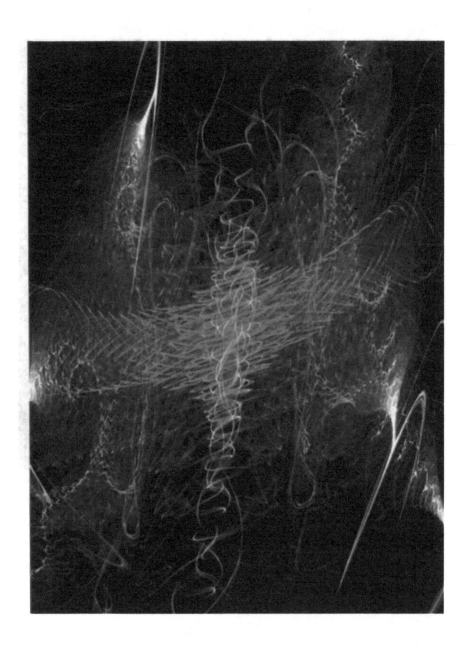

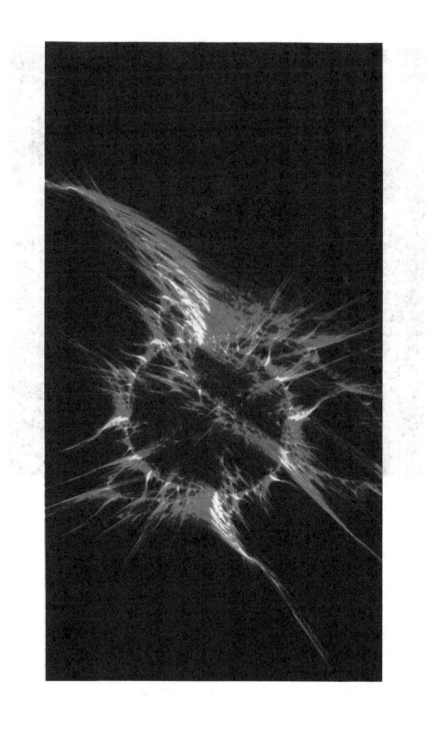

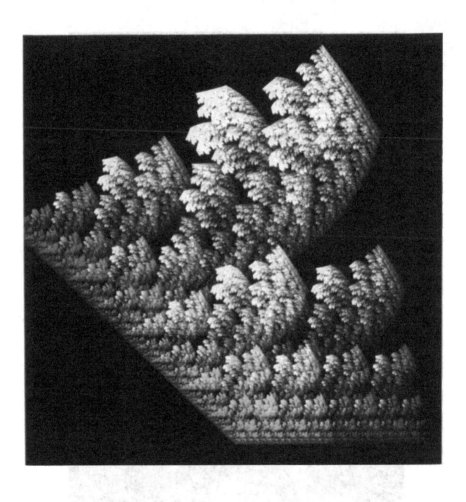

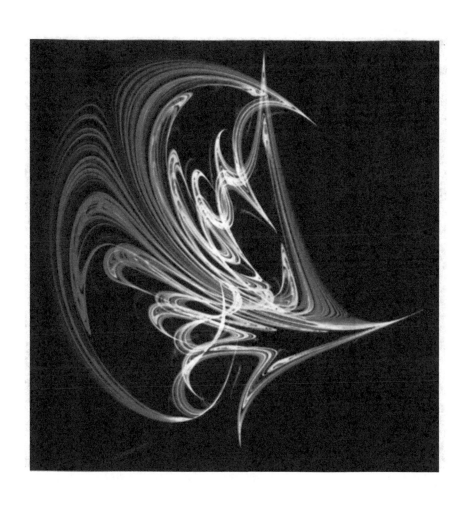

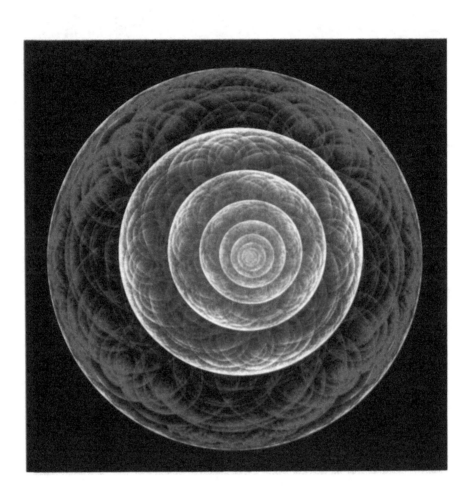

Notes on the artists

Fred Abraham was over-educated at Dartmouth (BA), University of Michigan (MS), Indiana University (PhD), and University of California Los Angeles and San Diego (post-doctoral), and has held faculty positions at California State College San Diego, UCLA, UC Irvine, UVM, University of Washington, and Silliman University. He was a co-founder of the Winter Conference on Brain Research and the Society for Chaos Theory in Psychology. He has proved his ignorance in research, books, articles, lectures, and workshops in psychology, neurophysiology, philosophy, and dynamical systems. His most recent paper, "Cyborgs, Cyberspace, and Cybersexuality" appears in *Everyday creativity* (2007, edited by Ruth Richards). He is active in music (jazz and classical), kayaking, telemark skiing, and in efforts to protect the wilderness qualities of American lakes.

Georgianne Cowan's art reflects her passion for movement, her fascination with mythic and dream imagery, and her reverence for nature. As a visual artist, teacher of dance (Body Landscapes, a meditational movement process), and an environmental performer, her work reflects both the elemental and primal aspects of the psyche. She is the author of *The soul of nature* (Doubleday) and *Earth dreaming* (New Era Media). Georgianne lives in Los Angeles with her husband, Charles Bernstein, and daughter, Serina. gcowan2000@aol.com.

Nicolas Desprez is a 36-year-old Frenchman living and working in the United Kingdom. He is an amateur fractalist whose main interests are fractal landscapes and strange attractors. He is the creator of Chaoscope, one of the few three-dimensional strange attractors rendering software available, and certainly one of the most user-friendly. Desprez is a database administrator by day. His other hobbies include drawing and composing music. http://www.chaoscope.org

Patrick Grim is Distinguished Teaching Professor of Philosophy at the State University of New York at Stony Brook. He has published widely, not only in philosophy, but also in scholarly journals in other fields: theoretical biology, linguistics, decision theory, artificial intelligence, and computer science. He is author of *The incomplete universe*, co-author of *The philosophical computer*, and founding editor of more than 20 volumes of *The philosopher's annual*.

Myrna Katz is an artist whose work essentially involves the ever changing and mysterious dance between the conscious and the unconscious. She has traveled extensively, and has lived and worked nationally and internationally. Presently she resides in California. http://myrnakatzdesigns.com myrna@myrnakatzdesigns.com

Susan B. Krevoy is founding director of the Susan B. Krevoy Eating Disorders Program, a low-cost, intensive, outpatient program. Clinic services include: individual psychotherapy, group psychotherapy, family psychotherapy, nutritional counseling, art therapy, yoga, and cognitive workshops that cover topics such as mind-body healing, self-esteem and body image. Location: 9911 W. Pico Blvd, Suite 720, Los Angeles, California 90035. info@krevoy.org www.drkrevoy.com

Susan Mirow is a neuropsychiatrist in private practice in Salt Lake City, Utah. She is board certified in psychiatry and she has been elected a Distinguished Fellow of the American Psychiatric Association. In addition to her MD, she has a PhD in Anatomy. She is an Associate Clinical Professor in the Department of Psychiatry at the University of Utah, School of Medicine. Along with her practice of psychiatry she conducts clinical research in psychobiological dysregulation and its relationship to disease states. She has innovated and patented measures of physiological variability that can diagnose psychiatric conditions, track treatment efficacy, and even detect psychobiological dysregulation before clinical symptoms are manifest. These ambulatory and noninvasive measurements allow for data collection in naturalistic settings. She will continue to make them available to both clinicians and researchers interested in a holistic approach to the human mind/body interface in both health and disease and ageing. susanmirow@aol.com www.coppertonplace.com.

David Wexler, 22, is a versatile renaissance kid working out of Los Angeles, CA. Besides founding a media production company and think-tank by the age of 21, Wexler has had experimental films shown around the world, in galleries, film festivals, on Turner Classic Movies, and in colleges such as Loyola Marymount University, the Academy of Arts in San Francisco, and Santa Monica College, to help broaden the horizons of film-students. He won the Young Eco Inventors award when he was 7, had his first film accepted into Malibu Film Festival at age 14, won the American Movie Classics Young Filmmaker Award at the age of 15, and had a film accepted into the Telluride Film Festival when he was 21. Academically, he has studied mystical states, philosophy, fractals, video art, astrobiology, and traditional narrative film. www.naturalmediaresearch.com

Megan Williams is a painter who has exhibited solo extensively in New York and Los Angeles. Her works are in the collection of the Museum of Contemporary Art, Los Angeles. A graduate of California Institute for the Arts during its heyday in the 1970s, Williams is considered a pioneer in the use of cartoon imagery in art. The *New Yorker* magazine described her work as "neo-futurist exploding figures," saying that it "breathed new life" into the genre of drawing. Her high octane content draws viewers in, but then debunks the romantic notion of purity. The naughty content is made gargantuan with her current shift in style to large multiple panels which take on a three dimensional effect. Williams has lived and worked in the Los Angeles area for 30 years.

Tobi Zausner has an interdisciplinary doctorate in art and psychology. She is also an art historian and an award-winning visual artist with works in major museums and in private collections around the world. Zausner writes and lectures widely on the psychology of art and human potential and teaches at the C.G. Jung Foundation in New York and Long Island University. She is also an officer on the Board of Arts, Crafts, and Theatre Safety, a non-profit organization investigating health hazards in the arts. Her book, *When walls become doorways* (2007), is about the influence of physical illness on the creative process of visual artists. It shows that instead of stopping artists, physical difficulties transform them, enhancing both their life and their work. A native New Yorker and an avid walker, Zausner wishes there were more trees, grass, and hills in New York City.

Glossary

Acausal connection: a pattern of interrelationship that cannot be explained in linear terms as one event directly resulting in another.

Alexithymia: impaired capacity to experience and/or articulate feelings, desires, fantasies, or other nuances of internal experience.

Attractor: the end-state of a dynamical system moving over time, either represented visually or graphically as trajectories in **phase space**. See also **Cycle attractor, Point attractor, Strange attractor, Torus attractor**.

Attunement: the quality of sensitive understanding in caretakers serving the emotional foundation for secure attachment in relationships. Attunement can occur towards others or towards one's self by sensitively understanding one's own experience and feelings.

Bifurcation: a sudden, spontaneous change in the underlying **attractor** pattern of a **dynamical system**, such as from a **point attractor** to a **cycle attractor**, or from a cycle of period three to a doubled period of six. See also **Feigenbaum universal**.

Bootstrapping problem: the inability of a system to step outside of its own dynamics in order to observe them. The phrase derives from the expression "to lift oneself up by your own bootstraps – a seemingly impossible **paradox**, and a key concept for self-organization.

Butterfly effect: see **Sensitive dependence on initial conditions**.

Castration anxiety: a classical Freudian notion corresponding to the phallic period of psychosexual development, where little boys are thought to harbor a deep-seated fear of their penises being cut off as punishment for sexually desiring their mothers and desiring to kill their rival father.

Cathexis: a term from psychoanalytic drive theory indicating strong emotional attachment to an idea, object, or most commonly, a person, whether conscious or unconscious.

Chaos theory: the study of **nonlinear dynamics** whose trajectory through phase space is sensitively dependent on initial conditions, such that tiny causes can produce large effects.

Classical psychoanalysis: a form of intensive psychotherapy where the psychoanalyst strives to be a neutral, anonymous observer invested with the authority to interpret the **unconscious** motivation(s) of patients through the application of classical psychoanalytic theory. The psychoanalyst in this paradigm is understood as a "blank screen" and the patient develops **transference** to the analyst, which is then used as the data for psychoanalytic interpretation. The analyst's own feelings about the patient are seen as **countertransference**, meant to be either used as data for interpretation, or more classically, factored out of the treatment.

Collective unconscious: the Jungian idea of a transcultural, transpersonal level of awareness or human spirit that extends beyond personal history or cultural specifics to inform universal aspects of psychological and emotional development, for example, the universality of some myths.

Complexity: the hallmark of healthy functioning in **self-organizing** systems arising at the **edge of chaos**.

Complexity theory: the study of **self-organizing, nonlinear dynamics**, where order and novel structure arise from simple rules and many local, often recursive, interactions.

Countertransference: a therapist's emotional entanglement with a patient based on unresolved emotions, past relationships, and the psychoneurobiological states of the therapist. See also **Transference**.

Coupled dynamics: weak or strong linkages between two **dynamical systems**, which share an underlying **attractor**, and may be either symmetrical or asymmetrial and directionally or mutually driven.

Critical point / point of criticality: the attractor point that characterizes many slowly driven, highly nonlinear systems, that operate **far from equilibrium** and are **self-organized** to the **edge of chaos**. At this critical point, the behavior of such systems displays scale invariant dynamics typical of **phase transitions**, where the likelihood of changes of various sizes are governed by **power law** distributions. See also **Self-organized criticality**.

Cybernetics: the study of **feedback** dynamics and control systems within information sciences.

Cycle attractor: a **dynamical system** that terminates in a stable, repeating pattern consisting of two or more fixed points. See also **Attractor**.

Defense mechanism: internal energy directed in the service of self-protection, functioning to constrict experience of feelings or awareness. Several specific defense mechanisms are described in classical psychoanalytic theory, for example **dissociation, projection, repression**, rationalization, intellectualization, denial, sublimation, and so forth.

Degrees of freedom: the countable number of underlying **parameters** upon which the behavior of a **dynamical system** depends.

Determinism (chaotic): The understanding that most **dynamical systems**, even those studied by classical mechanics, may be perfectly deterministic in principle, yet may behave in a manner that is intrinsically unpredictable due to **sensitive dependence on initial conditions**.

Determinism (classical): a philosophical position holding that the future state of some system is completely contingent on its prior states, such that given complete knowledge of past history and current starting positions, the future of a system is predictable in theory.

Dimension: the number of underlying **parameters** of a **dynamical system**, also known as its **degrees of freedom** to move in space.

Dissipative system: a thermodynamically open system operating in **far from equilibrium** conditions in an environment such that there is a continual exchange of matter, energy and/or information across open boundaries.

Dissociation: disrupted integration between elements of consciousness, including feeling, memory, identity, and/or perception of the environment, such that a person has multiple or fragmented "self states" not symbolically or neurobiologically linked with one another. Dissociation is considered to be on a spectrum from normal dissociation – paying attention to a task while excluding extraneous stimuli – to pathological – as in Post-Traumatic Stress Disorder (PTSD) and in the extreme, Dissociative Identity Disorder (DID, also known as multiple personality disorder).

Dynamical system: a coordinated collection of parts that moves in space and/or changes over time.

Edge of chaos: the zone of maximal **complexity** in which **dynamical systems** spontaneously and unpredictably **self-organize**. This zone lies between extremes of totally rigid, static order or frozen states and completely fluid, unstructured states.

Embedding space: the number of **dimensions** in which the **attractor** of a **dynamical system** must be enfolded within **phase space** in order to be reconstructed.

Emergence: the hallmark of **complexity** within **dynamical systems**, where novel and unexpected structure, pattern or processes arise spontaneously during **self-organization**. Emergent phenomena are not predictable in a classically **deterministic** way from the system components, but instead are irreducible properties of the whole.

Enactment: the expression of emotional conflicts or feelings via direct actions rather than words, without conscious awareness of the meaning or origin of such acts, usually occurring within the context of a relationship.

Equilibrium: the tendency of an isolated system that has little or no exchange of matter, energy or information across its borders to maintain **homeostasis**, that is, to tend toward a stable state, or set of stable states.

Euclidean geometry: the earliest known systematic discussion of geometry developed by the Greek mathematician, Euclid, based on a method of proving propositions from a small set of axioms. Euclidean geometry, as commonly taught in grade school, begins with circles, squares, triangles and other objects of plane geometry, extends into spheres, cubes, tetrahedrons, and other solid figures of three **dimensions**, and then was subsequently extended to any finite number of dimensions.

Exteroception: the aspect of the autonomic nervous system providing information about the external world through the six senses of sight, smell, touch, hearing, taste and balance. See also **Interoception** and **Proprioception**.

Far from equilibrium: a system embedded within its environment, often at multiple descriptive levels, such that information, matter and/or energy is taken into the system, converted into work or structure, and waste leaves the system, in continual flows across open boundaries. See also **Dissipative system**.

Feedback: when aspects of an output signal are recursively looped or fed back into a **dynamical system** as new input, serving to control or influence its direction from within. See also **Feedforward, Negative feedback, Positive feedback**.

Feedforward: when a system reacts to changes in its environment in a predetermined way, such as to assert expectations or to maintain some desired state of the system. Feedforward stands in contrast with **feedback**, where order is emergent and not predefined, and the system is better able to handle with novel input.

Feigenbaum universal: a newly discovered constant, equal to 4.669201 . . ., that describes the rate of period doubling **bifurcations** commonly found in a variety of systems in nature as they cascade from order to **chaos**. This same number is also the limiting ratio between successive circles on the axis of the **Mandelbrot set**.

Fractal: multidimensional objects with pattern on various size and/or time scales whose hallmark is both **self-similarity** and **scale-invariance**. Fractal geometry yields the most complicated mathematical objects known to humankind, while also modeling complex repetitive, yet unique patterns of nature at large.

Fractal dimension: the exponent of the number of **self-similar** pieces into which a figure may be broken in relation to its given magnification factor. Many objects in nature possess fractal dimension, such as clouds, branching structures, mountain, and coastlines. When an object possesses a fractal dimension, it exists in the spaces between ordinary Euclidean dimensions. See also **Euclidean geometry**.

Fuzzy logic: a system of multi-valued reasoning that contains an infinite number of fractional terms representing degrees of truth between 0 and 1, the two anchor points for falsity and truth respectively. Fuzzy logic is one of many multivariate systems contrasting with Aristotle's classical system of binary logic.

Holism: a philosophical stance holding that complex phenomena cannot be understood by being broken down into their component parts. Instead the pattern of the whole must be preserved using synthetic rather than **reductionistic** methods.

Homeorhesis: the tendency for a system to regulate itself within a range of functional **parameters** via **positive feedback** and **negative feedback**, as contrasted with **homeostasis** where a system comes to rest at a stable point.

Homeostasis: the tendency for a **dynamical system** that remains isolated from its environment to come to rest at a stable **point attractor**. See also **Homeorhesis**.

Implicit processes: the operation of emotion, memory, learning or cognition through subcortical neurological pathways that operate beneath or outside of conscious awareness. See also **Unconscious**.

Individuation: the lifelong process of developing and integrating all aspects of personality, both positive and negative, to mature into our full potential as human beings.

Interoception: the aspect of the autonomic system that provides feedback on the internal status of the body, including pain and stretching of its organs. See also **Exteroception** and **Proprioception**.

Interpersonal neurobiology: a consilient approach looking for parallel findings from independent fields of knowing, including **chaos** and **complexity** theory, devoted to understanding the interfaces between the mind, brain, body, people, and world.

Intersubjectivity: the shared relational field that extends between two people and is a **nonlinear** product of the coupled subjectivities of both. Intersubjectivity includes conscious and unconscious aspects of the psyche, brain, and body-based components as well. The formation of intersubjective space is considered by many to be a developmental accomplishment or goal of therapy.

Introjection: to take in or internalize some facet of another person's mind. Introjection is sometimes considered a normal and healthy developmental step, as when internalizing the values of parents, and sometimes considered an unhealthy process, as when swallowing information whole without critical reflection.

Iteration: the repeated application of an algorithm, formula or transformation rule, such that the output or product from one round becomes the input or starting condition for the next application.

Klein bottle: a three-dimensional manifold that folds back upon itself within the fourth **dimension**, and as a result, possesses no clear distinction between "inside" and "outside" surfaces.

Linear dynamics: the study of **dynamical systems** whose behavioral output is proportional to their input, such that small nudges results in small changes, while large pushes trigger large consequences.

Mandelbrot set: the most complicated object known to humankind, consisting of a simple, **nonlinear** equation, $z \rightarrow x^2 + c$, **iterated** for each point on the complex number plane. When the Mandelbrot set is rendered visually by computer, the ordered area within the set appears in black, while and the chaotic area outside the set is colored according to how rapidly it escapes towards infinity. The actual set is the infinitely complex zone at the figure's edge.

Mental health: the open, complex, embodied, relational flow of mental energy and information, as extends between one pole of frozen order and another of complete instability. Mental health can extend between people, into the world, across time, and through generations.

Metaphor: Whereas in literature, metaphor is a figure of speech that likens or equates one thing to another, in developmental neurobiology, the concept is more broadly understood as the transfer or carry over experience from one domain into another, such that we understand "this" in terms of "that." As infants, developmentally, we start with an embodied experience of the world; initially through gesture-play and later through the play of words, we bootleg this early experience into more abstract, symbolic forms through metaphor, a capacity that is deeply wired into the right-brain.

Misattunement: emotional insensitivity or lack of relational empathy, which if repetitive and/or remains chronically unaddressed or unrepaired, can trigger insecure attachment in significant others. This concept is sometimes expressed as empathic failure, where repair is the response related to being a "good enough" mother or therapist, versus a "perfect" mother or therapist who is never misattuned.

Möbius Band: within the mathematical field of **topology**, a two-dimensional strip, given a half-twist and then reconnected. The resulting object is interdimensional, in that it is a one-dimensional object extending in two-dimensional space, but with only one side and one edge.

Negative feedback: when the output of a **dynamical system** fed back in recursively as new input serves to reduce, stabilize or linearize its output or behavior or to decrease deviations, as in steering back on course. See also **Positive feedback**.

Nonlinear dynamics: the study of **dynamical systems** whose behavioral output is disproportionate to their input, such that a tiny nudge might cause the system to career off in space or a huge push might result in little impact.

Oedipus Complex: the classical Freudian notion of forbidden sexual attraction to parents of the opposite sex, repressed due to its forbidden nature, and accompanied by envious and aggressive feelings toward the parent of the same sex. The male child, typically, is considered to be in competition with the father over the mother's love.

Paradox: a person, object, or situation exhibiting an apparently contradictory nature. A paradox of self-reference arises if a statement that refers back to itself is self-contradictory. An example is the classical liar, "This sentence is false," which is true only if false and false only if true.

Parameter: an underlying variable that contributes sensitively to the behavior of a **dynamical system**, and which is represented as a **degree of freedom** in **phase space**.

Phase space (also known as state space): within **dynamical systems** studies, the abstract multidimensional representation of all possible system behavior, with each potential state corresponding to a unique point. Phase space can be plotted from **time series** data by displacing the data by one or more points in time (corresponding to the number of **dimensions** needed) and then recursively pairing and graphing results. Although phase space is plotted from measures in time, it is an abstract representation of underlying pattern that exists outside of time and space.

Phase transition: the transformation in a **dynamical system** from one underlying organization to another, often manifesting as an abrupt, sudden change in system behavior, resulting from a tiny change in an underlying **parameter** value.

Point attractor: a **dynamical system** whose end state terminates in a stable, fixed point. See also **Attractor**.

Positive feedback: internal looping within a **dynamical system** by which output is recursively recycled as new input, so as to increase or amplify the system's signal, behavior or deviation. See also **Negative feedback**.

Power law: an asymmetrical, mathematical distribution (1/f), where f is the frequency of an event, that is widespread in nature and indicative of tendencies towards **self-organization** at the **edge of chaos**. An example of a power law is the ratio between frequency and size of earthquakes corresponding to measures on the Richter scale. One can expect a small number of large earthquakes, an intermediate number of mid-sized earthquakes, and a large number of tiny earthquakes.

Process-structure: the maintenance of a complex **dynamical system** from its flow of energy, matter, and information across open borders, where process and structure are seen as interrelated aspects of one another, rather than as dualistically different.

Projection: a **defense mechanism** proposed within classical Freudian theory whereby one attributes one's own unacceptable or unwanted thoughts, feelings or impulses to others. Projection is thought to reduce anxiety by allowing partial, unconscious expression of an impulse or desire.

Projective identification: **unconscious** or **implicit** communication of a feeling, thought or belief such that another person begins to behave as though he or she is actually characterized by those same feelings, thoughts or beliefs. In order for projective identification to happen, one person has to first use projective defenses. For example, a paranoid patient may feel the therapist is part of a conspiracy, which corresponds with the therapist unconsciously beginning to act as if he or she is conspiring against the patient, such as not sharing important information with a patient about a phone conversation with a family member. If unrecognized, projective identification can lead to an empathic failure, treatment rupture, or "negative therapeutic reaction."

Proprioception: the capacity to sense the position and relevant movement of muscles and body parts derived from muscular, tendon and articular sources, providing a foundational level for a bodily based sense of self. See also **Exteroception, Interoception**.

Reductionism: the assertion that complex things in nature can be understood by taking them apart to observe and study their component parts, as contrasted with **holism**, where the whole is perceived as greater than the sum of the parts.

Repression: a **defense mechanism** by which unacceptable ideas, fantasies, affects, or impulses are banished from consciousness, sometimes emerging in disguised form, like slips of the tongue or symbolism in dreams, or accessible through techniques like guided imagery or hypnosis.

Scale-invariance: a hallmark of **fractals** and a concept intimately related to **self-similarity**, such that a feature or property of an object or process remains unaltered with changing size or time scales. This occurs for example in **power laws** where self-similar fluctuations exist on multiple time scales.

Self-organization: the spontaneous, often unpredictable **emergence** of novelty, new levels of integration, higher levels of order or **complexity** within **nonlinear dynamical systems** from simple system components.

Self-organized criticality: a property widely found in nature by which slowly driven, **dynamical systems self-organize** towards a **critical point** at the **edge of chaos** as an underlying **attractor**. See also **Critical point**.

Self-reference: a sentence, formula or other method of expression that recursively loops back in order to refer back to itself through some means of encoding, whether formally or informally in philosophy, mathematics, or everyday language. For example, "This next sentence is false. The prior sentence is true."

Self-similarity: the hallmark of **fractals**, whereby the pattern of the whole characterizes the pattern of the parts, either in space (spatially), e.g., the lung's branches, or (temporally) in time, e.g., fluctuations in EEG bursts that are statistically self-similar across different temporal samples.

Sensitive dependence on initial conditions: the hallmark of **chaotic** states, such that small differences in starting conditions or tiny perturbations carry the capacity to greatly alter the future course of a system's **trajectory**.

Strange (or chaotic) attractor: a **dynamical system** whose end-state is irregular and unstable and is characterized by **sensitive dependence on initial conditions**. Strange attractors have a characteristic shape detectable from multiple trajectories, but no trajectory exactly repeats the path of a prior trajectory, which leads both to unpredictability and ongoing novelty. See also **Attractor**.

Sublimation: the redirecting of sexual energy, or libido, or of aggression into more symbolic expressions, such as writing or movie watching.

Synchronicity: the experience of two or more events whose simultaneous or sequential occurrence cannot be causally or logically explained, but whose co-occurrence feels meaningful as well as suggestive of underlying pattern.

Tangled hierarchy: a multilevel system, often characteristic of the brain, where feedback loops interconnect upper and lower levels in complex ways, e.g., moving up or down through the system leads back to the starting point.

Termination: the usually mutual agreement between patient and therapist to end psychotherapy, which in long-term treatment extends as a stage of treatment for weeks, months or even years.

Time series: a sequence of data points collected at successive time intervals, often analyzed using **nonlinear** methods.

Topographical metaphor: a way to conceive invisible psychological structure concretely as territory with different layers to excavate, with conscious processes close to the surface and unconscious aspects deeper underground.

Topology: a mathematical field devoted to the study of smooth surfaces that can be stretched and folded, but not broken or cut. See also **Möbius Band**.

Torus attractor: a **dynamical system** whose end-state terminates in a semi-regular donut shape, with a slower periodicity wrapping horizontally around the core and a second periodicity wrapping longitudinally around the core. A torus attractor is considered semi-regular because the two periodicities are linked by an irrational number, or a real number that cannot be expressed as a fraction. See also **Attractor**.

Trajectory: the path of a **dynamical system**, either in real space and time or across the abstract **dimensions** of **phase space**.

Transference: the transfer of feelings, wishes, fantasies or thoughts from early significant relationships onto the psychotherapist during therapy. See also **Countertransference**.

Transitional object, transitional space: during an early, developmental stage when a young child begins to differentiate internal from external worlds, a transitional object is the first "not me" possession, such as a blanket or teddy bear, that belongs to the child and occupies the space between mother and child allowing both continued connection and increasing independence. Transitional objects or spaces represent a moving from a self-enclosed sense of self, to an **intersubjective** style of relatedness.

Unconscious: an aspect of the human psyche that operates below the radar of conscious awareness, proposed by Freud and others. Sometimes unconscious functioning can be detectable consciously, in which case it might be called the preconscious. Other times unconscious functioning is totally inaccessible to awareness. See also **Implicit processes**.

Bibliography

Abraham, F. and Gilgen, A. (eds.) (1995). *Chaos theory in psychology*. Westport, CT: Praeger.

Abraham, F., Abraham, R. and Shaw, C. (1990). *A visual introduction to dynamical systems theory for psychology*. Santa Cruz, CA: Aerial Press.

Adler, H. (2007). Toward a biopsychosocial understanding of the patient–physician relationship: An emerging dialogue. *Journal of General Internal Medicine*, 22, 280–285.

Aftanas, L., Lotova, N., Koshkarov, V. and Popov, S. (1998). Non-linear dynamical coupling between different brain areas during evoked emotions: An EEG investigation. *Biological Psychology*, 48, 121–138.

American Psychiatric Association (APA) (1994). *Diagnostic and statistical manual of mental disorders*, DSM IV. Washington, DC: APA.

Anderson, C. and Mandell, A. (1996). Fractal time and the foundations of consciousness: Vertical convergence of 1/f phenomena from ion channels to behavioral states. In E. Mac Cormac and M. Stamenov (eds.) *Fractals of brain, fractals of mind*. Amsterdam: John Benjamin.

Anderson, C., Mandell, A., Selz, K., Terry, L., Robinson, S., Wong, C., Robertson, S. and Smotherman, W. (1998). The development of nuchal atonia associated with active (REM) sleep in fetal sheep: Presence of recurrent fractal organization. *Brain Research*, 787, 2, 351–357.

Arnheim, R. (1977). *The dynamics of architectural form*. Berkeley, CA: University of California Press.

Atwood, G. and Stolorow, R. (1979/1993). *Faces in a cloud: Intersubjectivity in personality theory*. Northvale, NJ: Jason Aronson.

Atwood, G. and Stolorow, R. (1984). *Structures of subjectivity: Explorations in psychoanalytic phenomenology*. Hillsdale, NJ: Analytic Press.

Austin, J. (2006). *Zen-brain reflections*. Cambridge, MA: MIT Press.

Bak, P. (1996). *How nature works: The science of self-organized criticality*. New York: Copernicus.

Barabási, A. (2002). *Linked: The new science of networks*. Cambridge, MA: Perseus.

Barrow, J. (1999). *Impossibility: The limits of science and the science of limits*. Oxford: Oxford University Press.

Barton, S. (1994). Chaos, self-organization, and psychology. *American Psychologist*, 49, 5–14.

Bateson, G. (1972). *Steps to an ecology of mind: Collected essays in anthropology, psychiatry, evolution, and epistemology.* San Francisco, CA: Chandler.

Beebe, B. and Lachmann, F. (2005). *Infant research and adult treatment: Co-constructing interactions.* Hillsdale, NJ: Analytic Press.

Beisser, A. (1971). Paradoxical theory of change. In J. Fagan and I. Shepherd (eds.) *Gestalt Therapy Now.* New York: HarperCollins.

Bekhtereva, N., Starchenko, G., Klyucharev, V., Vorob'ev, V., Pakhomov, S. and Medvedev, S. (2000). Study of the brain organization of creativity: II. Positron-emission tomography data, *Human Physiology*, 26, 5, 12–18.

Bekhtereva, N., Dan'ko, S., Starchenko, M., Pakhomov, S. and Medvedev, S. (2004). Study of the brain organization of creativity: III. Brain activation assessed by the local cerebral blood flow and EEG. *Human Physiology*, 27, 4, 390–397.

Bieberich, E. (2002). Recurrent fractal neural networks. *BioSystems*, 66, 145–163.

Bion, W. (1962). *Learning from experience.* London: Heinemann.

Bion, W. (1983). *Transformations.* Northvale, NJ: Jason Aronson.

Bird, D. (2003). *Chaos and life.* New York: Columbia University Press.

Boden, M. (1992). *The creative mind.* New York: Basic Books.

Bollas, C. (1987). *The shadow of the object: Psychoanalysis of the unthought known.* New York: Columbia University Press.

Bowlby, J. (1969). *Attachment* (Volume 1). New York: Basic Books.

Briggs, J. (1992). *Fractals: The patterns of chaos.* New York: Simon and Schuster.

Briggs, J. and Peat, D. (1989). *Turbulent mirror: An illustrated guide to chaos theory and the science of wholeness.* New York: Harper and Row.

Briggs, J. and Peat, D. (2000). *Seven life lessons of chaos: Spiritual wisdom from the science of change.* New York: Harper Perennial.

Bromberg, P. (1998). *Standing in the spaces.* Hillsdale, NJ: Analytic Press.

Bromberg, P. (2006). *Awakening the dreamer: Clinical journeys.* Hillsdale, NJ: Analytic Press.

Bütz, M. (1997). *Chaos and complexity: Implications for psychological theory and practice.* London: Taylor and Francis.

Bütz, M., Chamberlain, L. and McCown, W. (1996). *Strange attractors, chaos, complexity and the art of family therapy.* New York: Wiley.

Campbell, J. (1949/1973). *The hero with a thousand faces.* Princeton, NJ: Princeton University Press.

Capra, F. (1975). *The tao of physics.* New York: Bantam.

Carlsson, I., Wendt, P. and Risberg, J. (2000). On the neurobiology of creativity: Differences in frontal activity between high and low creative subjects. *Neuropsychologia*, 38, 6, 873–875.

Chamberlain, L. and Bütz, M. (1998). *Clinicial chaos: A therapist's guide to nonlineal dynamics and therapeutic change.* Philadelphia, PA: Taylor and Francis.

Choate, J., Devaney, R. and Foster, A. (1999). *Fractals: A tool kit of dynamics activities.* Emeryville, CA: Key Curriculum Press.

Chopra, D. (1995). *The way of the wizard: Twenty spiritual lessons for creating the life you want.* New York: Harmony.

Combs, A. (1997). The *Radiance of being: Complexity, chaos and the evolution of consciousness.* New York: Paragon House.

Combs, A. and Holland, M. (1990). *Synchronicity: Science, myth, and the trickster.* New York: Paragon House.

Cook, F. (1977). *Hua-yen Buddhism: The jewel net of Indra.* University Park, PA: Pennsylvania State University Press

Cozolino, L. (2002). *The neuroscience of psychotherapy: Building and rebuilding the human brain.* New York: Norton.

Cozolino, L. (2006). *The neuroscience of human relationships: Attachment and the developing social brain.* New York: Norton.

Crutchfield, J., Farmer, D., Packard, N. and Shaw, R. (1986). Chaos. *Scientific American,* 254, 12, 46–57.

Csikszentmihalyi, M. (1990). *Flow: The psychology of optimal experience.* New York: Harper and Row.

Damasio, A. (1994). *Descartes' error: Emotion, reason and the human brain.* Glasgow: Avon/HarperCollins.

Damasio, A. (1999). *The feeling of what happens.* New York: Harcourt Brace.

Dauwalder, J. and Tschacher, W. (2003). *The dynamical systems approach to cognition: Concepts and empirical paradigms based on self-organization, embodiment, and coordination dynamics.* River Edge, NJ: World Scientific.

Delignières, D., Fortes, M. and Ninot, G. (2004). The fractal dynamics of self-esteem and physical self. *Nonlinear Dynamics, Psychology, and Life Sciences,* 8, 4, 479–510.

Deutsch, H. (1942). Some forms of emotional disturbances and their relationship to schizophrenia. *Psychoanalytic Quarterly,* 11, 301–321.

De Vries, A. (1984). *Dictionary of symbols and imagery.* London: Elsevier Science.

Draaisma, D. (1995/2000). *Metaphors of memory: A history of ideas about the mind.* Cambridge: Cambridge University Press.

Edelman, G. (1992). *Bright air, brilliant fire: On the matter of the mind.* New York: Basic Books.

Eglash, R. (1999). *African fractals: Modern computing and indigenous design.* New Brunswick, NJ: Rutgers University Press.

Eigen, M. (1999). *Toxic nourishment.* New York: Karnac.

Eigen, M. (2001). *Damaged bonds.* New York: Karnac.

Ellenberger, H. (1981). *The discovery of the unconscious.* New York: Basic Books.

Elliott, R.N. (2005). *R.N. Elliott's masterworks: The definitive collection,* ed. R. Prechter. Gainesville, GA: New Classics Library.

Erdelyi, M. (2006). The unified theory of repression. *Behavioral and Brain Sciences,* 29, 499–511.

Falletta, N. (1990). *The paradoxicon.* New York: Wiley.

Feder, L. (1974/1988). Adoption trauma: Oedipus myth/clinical reality. In G. Pollock and J. Ross (eds.) *The Oedipus papers.* Madison, CN: International Universities Press.

Feynman, R. (1949). The theory of positrons. *Physical Review,* 76, 6, 749–758.

Feynman, R. and Sykes, C. (1995). *No ordinary genius: The illustrated Richard Feynman.* New York: Norton.

Feynman, R., Leighton, R. and Hutchings, E. (1997). *Surely you're joking, Mr. Feynman! (Adventures of a curious character).* New York: Norton.

Fiscalini, J. (2004). *Coparticipant psychoanalysis: Toward a new theory of clinical inquiry.* New York: Columbia University Press.

Flavell, J. (1963). *The developmental psychology of Jean Piaget.* New York: Van Nostrand.

Fogel, A. and Garvey, A. (2007). Alive communication. *Infant Behavior and Development*, 30, 251–257.

Fonagy, P., Steele, M., Steele, H., Leigh, T., Kennedy, R., Mattoon, G. and Target, M. (1995). The predictive validity of Mary Main's Adult Attachment Interview: A psychoanalytic and developmental perspective on the transgenerational transmission of attachment and borderline states. In S. Goldberg, R. Muir and J. Kerr (eds.) *Attachment theory: Social, developmental and clinical perspectives*. Hillsdale, NJ: Analytic Press.

Freeman, W. (1991). The physiology of perception. *Scientific American*, February, 78–85.

Freeman, W. (1995). *Societies of brains*. Hillsdale, NJ: Erlbaum.

Freeman, W. (1999a). Consciousness, intentionality, and causality. *Journal of Consciousness Studies*, 6, 143–172.

Freeman, W. (1999b). *How brains make up their minds*. London: Weidenfeld and Nicolson.

Galatzer-Levy, R. (2004). Chaotic possibilities: Toward a new model of development. *International Journal of Psychoanalysis*, 85, 419–442.

Gardner, H. (1982). *Art, mind, and brain: A cognitive approach to creativity*. New York: Basic Books.

Gardner, H. (1985). *The mind's new science: A history of the cognitive revolution*. New York: Basic Books.

Gartner, R. (2001). *Betrayed as boys: Psychodynamic treatment of sexually abused men*. New York: Guilford.

Ghent, E. (1992). Paradox and process. *Psychoanalytic Dialogues*, 2, 135–159.

Gibson, W. (1987). *Neuromancer*. New York: Ace.

Gilden, D. (2001). Cognitive emissions of 1/f noise. *Psychological Review*, 108, 33–56.

Gilligan, C. (1982). *In a different voice: Psychological theory and women's development*. Cambridge, MA: Harvard University Press.

Gilligan, C. (2002). *The birth of pleasure*. New York: Knopf.

Gleick, J. (1987). *Chaos: Making a new science*. New York: Viking.

Goertzel, B. (1993). *The evolving mind*. Langhorne, PA: Gordon and Breach.

Goertzel, B. (1994). *Chaotic logic*. New York: Plenum.

Goertzel, B. (1997). *From complexity to creativity: Explorations in evolutionary, autopoetic, and cognitive dynamics*. New York: Springer.

Goldstein, J. (1997). Embracing the random in the self-organizing psyche. *Nonlinear Dynamics, Psychology, and Life Sciences*, 1, 181–202.

Goldstein, J. (2007). Emergence and psychological morphogenesis. In C. Piers, J. Muller and J. Brent (eds.) *Self-organizing complexity in psychological systems*. New York: Jason Aronson.

Gottman, J., Murray, J., Swanson, C. and Ryson, R. (2002). *The mathematics of marriage: Dynamic nonlinear models*. Cambridge, MA: MIT Press.

Gottschalk, A., Bauer, M. and Whybrow, P. (1995). Evidence of chaotic mood variation in bipolar disorder. *Archives of General Psychiatry*, 52, 947–959.

Grabner, R., Fink, A. and Neubauer, A. (2007). Brain correlates of self-rated originality of ideas: Evidence from event-related power and phase-locking changes in the EEG. *Behavioral Neuroscience*, 121, 1, 224–230.

Grim, P., Mar, G. and St. Denis, P. (1998). *The philosophical computer: Exploratory essays in philosophical computer modeling*. Cambridge, MA: MIT Press.

Grisby, J. and Stevens, R. (2000). *Neurodynamics of personality*. New York: Guilford.

Guastello, S. (2001). *Managing emergent phenomena: Nonlinear dynamics in work organizations*. Mahwah, NJ: Erlbaum.

Guastello, S. (2006). *Human factors engineering and ergonomics: A systems approach*. Mahwah, NJ: Erlbaum.

Guastello, S., Pincus, D. and Gunderson, P. (2006). Electrodermal arousal between participants in a conversation: Nonlinear dynamics and linkage effects. *Nonlinear Dynamics, Psychology, and Life Sciences*, 10, 3, 365–399.

Haken, H. (1984). *The science of structure: Synergetics*. Upper Saddle River, NJ: Prentice Hall.

Hannah, T. (1990). Does chaos theory have application to psychology: The example of daily mood fluctuations? *Network*, 8, 3, 13–14.

Hayles, K. (1990). *Chaos bound: Orderly disorder in contemporary literature and science*. Ithaca, NY: Cornell University Press.

Hayles, K. (1999). *How we became posthuman: Virtual bodies in cybernetics, literature and informatics*. Chicago, IL: University of Chicago Press.

Hayman, R. (2001). *A life of Jung*. New York: Norton.

Heims, S. (1991). *The cybernetics group*. Cambridge, MA: MIT Press.

Hellerstein, N. (1997). *Diamond: A paradox logic*. River Edge, NJ: World Scientific.

Herman, J. (1997). *Trauma and recovery: The aftermath of violence – From domestic abuse to political terror*. New York: Basic Books.

Hesse, E. and Main, M. (2006). Frightened, threatening, and dissociative parental behavior in low-risk samples: Description, discussion, and interpretations. *Development and Psychopathology*, 18, 309–343.

Hillman, J. (1979). *The dream and the underworld*. Glasgow: HarperCollins.

Hillman, J. (1996). *The soul's code: In search of character and calling*. New York: Random House.

Hirsch, I. (2003). Psychoanalytic theory as a form of countertransference. *Journal of the American Psychoanalytic Association*, 51, 181–201.

Hoffman, Z. (1998). *Ritual and spontaneity in the psychoanalytic process: A dialectical-constructivist view*. Hillsdale, NJ: Analytic Press.

Hofstadter, D. and Dennett, D. (1981). *The Mind's I*. New York: Bantam.

Hopcke, R. (1998). *There are no accidents: Synchronicity and the stories of our lives*. New York: Riverhead.

Iannaccone, P. and Khokha, M. (eds.) (1996). *Fractal geometry in biological systems*. New York: CRC Press.

Jackson, W. (2004). *Heaven's fractal net: Retrieving lost visions in the humanities*. Bloomington, IN: Indiana University Press.

Jamison, K. (1996). *Touched with fire: Manic-depressive illness and the artistic temperament*. New York: Free Press.

Jardine, L. and Stewart, A. (1999). *Hostage to fortune: The troubled life of Francis Bacon*. New York: Hill and Wang.

Johnson, R. (1976). *She: Understanding feminine psychology*. New York: Harper and Row.

Jung, C. (1973). *Synchronicity: An acausal connecting principle*. Princeton, NJ: Bollingen.

Jung, C. and Jaffe, A. (1961/1989). *Dreams, memories, reflections*. New York: Vintage.

Jung-Beeman, J., Bowden, E., Haberman, J., Frymiare, J., Arambel-Liu, S., Greenblatt, R., Reber, P. and Kounios, J. (2004). Neural activity when people solve verbal problems with insight. *PLoS Biology*, 2, 4, 500–510.

Kahn, D., Krippner, S. and Combs, A. (2000). Dreaming and the self-organizing brain. *Journal of Consciousness Studies*, 7, 7, 4–11.

Kauffman, S. (1995). *At home in the universe: The search for the laws of self-organization of brain and behavior*. Cambridge, MA: MIT Press.

Kelso, S. (1995). *Dynamical patterns: The self-organization of brain and behavior*. Cambridge, MA: MIT Press.

Kerr, J. (1993). *A most dangerous method: The story of Jung, Freud, and Sabina Spielrein*. New York: Knopf.

Klein, M. (1979). On projective identification. *International Journal of Psychoanalysis*, 60, 357–373.

Knapska, E., Nikolaev, E., Boguzewski, P., Walasek, G., Blaszczyk, J., Kaczmarek, L. and Werka, T. (2006). Between-subject transfer of emotional information evokes specific pattern of amygdala activation. *Proceedings of the National Academy of Sciences*, 103, 10, 3858–3862.

Koch, R. (2005). Morphware: Magnetic logic may usher in an era in which computing devices can change instantly from one type of hardware to another. *Scientific American*, August, 293, 2, 56–63.

Koopmans, M. (2001). From double bind to n-bind: Toward a new theory of schizophrenia and family interaction. *Nonlinear Dynamics, Psychology, and Life Sciences*, 5, 4, 289–323.

Kopp, R. (1995). *Metaphor therapy using client-generated metaphors in psychotherapy*. New York: Brunner/Mazel.

Korzybski, A. (1994). *Science and sanity: An introduction to non-Aristotelian systems and general semantics*, 5th edn. International Non-Aristotelian Library. Englewood, NJ: Institute of General Semantics.

Kosko, B. (1994). *Fuzzy thinking: The new science of fuzzy logic*. New York: Hyperion.

Kuhn, T. (1962). *The structure of scientific revolutions*. Chicago, IL: University of Chicago Press.

Kulish, V., Sourin, S. and Sourina, O. (2006). Human electroencephalograms seen as fractal time series: Mathematical analysis and visualization. *Computers in Biology and Medicine*, 36, 291–301.

Kurtz, S. (1989). *The art of unknowing: Dimensions of openness in analytic therapy*. Northvale, NJ: Jason Aronson.

Kvalseth, T. (1992). Fechner's psychophysical law as a special case of Stevens' three-parameter power law. *Perception and Motor Skills*, 75, 3, 1205–1206.

Laing, R.D. (1970). *Knots*. New York: Random House.

Lakoff, G. and Johnson, M. (1980). *Metaphors we live by*. Chicago, IL: University of Chicago Press.

Lakoff, G. and Johnson, M. (1999). *Philosophy in the flesh: The embodied mind and its challenge to western thought*. New York: Basic Books.

Lakoff, G. and Núñez, R. (2001). *Where mathematics comes from: How the embodied mind brings mathematics into being*. New York: Basic Books.

Langer, E. (1989). *Mindfulness*. Reading, MA: Addison-Wesley.

Leibovitch, L. (1998). *Fractals and chaos simplified for the life sciences*. New York: Oxford University Press.

Levenson, E. (1976). A holographic model of psychoanalytic change. *Contemporary Psychoanalysis*, 12, 1–20.

Levenson, E. (1983). *The ambiguity of change*. New York: Basic Books.

Levenson, E. (1994). The uses of disorder: Chaos theory and psychoanalysis. *Contemporary Psychoanalysis*, 30, 5–24.

Levinson, R. and Gottman, J. (1983). Marital interaction: Physiological linkage and affective exchange. *Journal of Personality and Social Psychology*, 45, 587–597.

Lévi-Strauss, C. (1977). *Structural anthropology 1*, trans. C. Jacobson and B.G. Schoepf. Harmondsworth: Penguin.

Lewis, M. and Granic, I. (2002). *Emotion, development, and self-organization: Dynamic systems approaches to emotional development*. Cambridge: Cambridge University Press.

Libet, B. (2005). *Mind time: The temporal factor in consciousness*. Boston, MA: Harvard University Press.

Linehan, M. (1993). *Cognitive-behavioral treatment of Borderline Personality Disorder*. New York: Guilford.

Lipsitz, L. and Goldberger, A. (1992). Loss of "complexity" and aging: Potential applications of fractals and chaos theory to senescence. *Journal of American Medical Association*, 267, 1806–1809.

Lloyd, D. and Rossi, E. (eds.) (1994). *Ultradian rhythms in life processes*. New York: Springer.

Lovelock, J. (1979/2000). *Gaia: A new look at life on earth*. Oxford: Oxford University Press.

Lowen, S. and Teich, M. (1993). Fractal renewal processes generate 1/f noise. *Physical Review E*, 47, 2, 992–1001.

Mac Cormac, E. and Stamenov, M. (eds.) (1996). *Fractals of brain, fractals of mind*. Amsterdam: John Benjamin.

MacLean, P. (1990). *The Triune brain in evolution: Role in paleocerebral functioning*. New York: Springer.

McNeill, D. and Freiberger, P. (1993). *Fuzzy logic*. New York: Simon and Schuster.

Main, M. and Hesse, E. (1990). Parents' unresolved traumatic experiences are related to infant disorganized attachment status: Is frightened and/or frightening parental behavior the linking mechanism? In M. Greenberg, D. Cicchetti and E. Cummings (eds.) *Attachment in the preschool years: Theory, research and intervention*. Chicago, IL: University of Chicago Press.

Mancia, M. (2006). Implicit memory and early unrepressed unconscious: Their role in the therapeutic process. *International Journal of Psychoanalysis*, 87, 83–103.

Mandelbrot, B. (1977). *The fractal geometry of nature*. New York: W.H. Freeman.

Mandelbrot, B. and Hudson, R. (2004). *The (mis)behavior of markets*. New York: Basic Books.

Marks-Tarlow, T. (1993). A new look at impulsivity: Hidden order beneath apparent chaos? In W. McCown, J. Johnson and M. Shure (eds.) *The impulsive client: Theory, research, and practice*. Washington, DC: American Psychological Association.

Marks-Tarlow, T. (1995a). *Creativity inside out: Learning through multiple intelligences*. Reading, MA: Addison-Wesley.

Marks-Tarlow, T. (1995b). The fractal geometry of human nature. In R. Robertson and A. Combs (eds.) *Proceedings from the first conference of the Society for Chaos Theory in Psychology and the Life Sciences*. Mahwah, NJ: Erlbaum.

Marks-Tarlow, T. (1999). The self as a dynamical system. *Nonlinear Dynamics, Psychology, and Life Sciences*, 3, 4, 311–345.

Marks-Tarlow, T. (2002). Fractal dynamics of the psyche. In B. Goertzel and A. Combs (eds.) *Dynamical Psychology, an International, Interdisciplinary E-Journal of Complex Mental Affairs*. Online. Available www.goertzel.org/dynapsyc/2002/FractalPsyche.htm (accessed 10 August, 2007).

Marks-Tarlow, T. (2003). The certainty of uncertainty, *Psychological Perspectives*, 45, 118–130.

Marks-Tarlow, T. (2004). Semiotic seams: Fractal dynamics of reentry. *Cybernetics and Human Knowing*, 11, 1, 49–62.

Marks-Tarlow, T. (2008). Riddle of the sphinx: A paradox of self-reference revealed and reviled. In F. Orsucci and N. Sala (eds.) *Reflecting interfaces: The complex coevolution of information technology ecosystems*. Hershey, PA: Idea Group.

Marks-Tarlow, T. (in press). Alan Turing meets the sphinx: Some new and old riddles. *Chaos and Complexity Letters*.

Marks-Tarlow, T., Robertson, R. and Combs, A. (2002). Varela and the uroboros: The psychological significance of reentry. *Cybernetics and Human Knowing*, 9, 2, 31–47.

Masterpasqua, F. and Perna, P. (1997). *The psychological meaning of chaos: Translating theory into practice*. Washington, DC: American Psychological Association.

Meares, R., Stevenson, J. and Gordon, E. (1999). A Jacksonian and biopsychosocial hypothesis concerning borderline and related phenomena. *Australian and New Zealand Journal of Psychiatry*, 33, 831–840.

Miller, M. (1999). Chaos, Complexity, and Psychoanalysis, *Psychoanalytic Psychology*, 16, 355–379.

Mindell, A. (2000). *Quantum mind: The edge between physics and psychology*. Portland, OR: Lao Tse Press.

Mitchell, S. (1997). *Influence and autonomy in psychoanalysis*. Hillsdale, NJ: Analytic Press.

Modell, A. (2003). *Imagination and the meaningful brain*. Cambridge, MA: MIT Press.

Moghaddan, F. (2003). Interobjectivity and culture, *Culture and Psychology*, 9, 3, 221–232.

Molino, A. (2004). *Culture, subject and psyche: Dialogues in psychoanalysis and anthropology*. Middletown, CT: Wesleyan University Press.

Monte, C. and Sollod, R. (2003). *Beneath the mask: An introduction to theories of personality*. New York: Wiley.

Murray, J. (2004). *Mathematical biology*. New York: Springer.

Neumann, E. (1954/1993). *The origins and history of consciousness*. Princeton, NJ: Princeton University Press.

Neumann, E. (1956). *Amor and Psyche: The psychic development of the feminine*. New York: Harper and Row.

Ogden, P., Minton, K. and Pain, C. (2006). *Trauma and the body: A sensorimotor approach to psychotherapy*. New York: Norton.

Olesker, W. (1990). Sex differences during the early separation-individuation process: Implications for gender identity formation. *Journal of the American Psychoanalytic Association*, 38, 325–346.

Ornstein, R. (1972). *The psychology of consciousness*. San Francisco, CA: W.H. Freeman.

Orsucci, F. (1998). *Complex matters of mind.* River Edge, NJ: World Scientific.

Palombo, S. (1999). *The emergent ego: Complexity and coevolution in the psychoanalytic process.* Madison, CT: International Universities Press.

Panksepp, J. (1998). *Affective neuroscience: The foundations of human and animal emotions.* New York: Oxford University Press.

Peat, D. (2002). *From certainty to uncertainty: The story of science and ideas in the twentieth century.* Washington, DC: Joseph Henry Press.

Peitgen, O. (1986). *The beauty of fractals: Images of complex dynamical systems.* New York: Springer.

Pelton, R. (1989). *The Trickster in West Africa: A story of mythic irony and sacred delight.* Berkeley, CA: University of California Press.

Penrose, R. (1989). *The emperor's new mind.* New York: Oxford University Press.

Perls, F. (1969). *Ego, hunger, and aggression.* New York: Random House.

Perry, B., Pollard, R., Blakley, T., Baker, W. and Vigilante, D. (1995). Childhood trauma, the neurobiology of adaptation, and use-dependent development of the brain: How states become traits. *Infant Mental Health,* 16, 4, 271–291.

Petsche, H. (1996). Approaches to verbal, visual and musical creativity by EEG coherence analysis. *International Journal of Psychophysiology,* 24, 1–2, 145–159.

Piers, C. (2005). The mind's multiplicity and continuity. *Psychoanalytic Dialogues,* 15, 2, 229–254.

Piers, C., Muller, J. and Brent, J. (eds.) (2007). *Self-organizing complexity in psychological systems.* New York: Jason Aronson.

Pincus, D. (2001). A framework and methodology for the study of self-organizing family dynamics. *Nonlinear Dynamics, Psychology, and Life Sciences,* 5, 635–677.

Pizer, S. (1998). *Building bridges: The negotiation of paradox in psychoanalysis.* Hillsdale, NJ: Analytic Press.

Polster, E. and Polster, M. (1973). *Gestalt therapy integrated: Contours of theory and practice.* New York: Random House.

Pribram, K., Nuwer, M. and Baron, R. (1974). The holographic hypothesis of memory structure in brain function and perception. In R. Atkinson, D. Krantz, R. Luce and P. Suppes (eds.) *Contemporary developments in mathematical psychology.* San Francisco, CA: W.H. Freeman.

Prigogine, I. and Stengers, I. (1984). *Order out of chaos: Man's new dialogue with nature.* New York: Bantam.

Putnam, F. (1989). The switch process in multiple personality disorder and other state-change disorders. *Dissociation,* 1, 24–32.

Razoumnikova, O. (2000). Functional organization of different brain areas during convergent and divergent thinking: An EEG investigation. *Cognitive Brain Research,* 10, 1–2, 11–18.

Recordati, G. (2003). A thermodynamic model of the sympathetic and parasympathetic nervous systems. *Autonomic Neuroscience: Basic and Clinical,* 103, 1–12.

Richards, R. (2001). A new aesthetic for environmental awareness: Chaos theory, the natural world, and our broader humanistic identity. *Journal of Humanistic Psychology,* 41, 2, 59–95.

Richards, R. (ed.) (2007). *Everyday creativity and new views of human nature: Psychological, social, and spiritual perspectives*. Washington, DC: American Psychological Association.

Robertson, R. and Combs, A. (eds.) (1995). *Proceedings from the first conference of the Society for Chaos Theory in Psychology and the Life Sciences*. Hillsdale, NJ: Erlbaum.

Rosen, S. (1994). *Science, paradox and the moebius principle: The evolution of a "transcultural" approach to wholeness*. Albany, NY: State University of New York Press.

Rossi, E. (1996). *The symptom path to enlightenment: The new dynamics of self-organization in hypnotherapy*. Pacific Palisades, CA: Palisades Gateway.

Rothschild, B. (2000). *The body remembers: The psychophysiology of trauma and trauma treatment*. New York: Norton.

Schore, A. (1997). A century after Freud's project: Is a rapprochement between psychoanalysis and neurobiology at hand? *Journal of the American Psychoanalytic Association*, 45, 3, 807–840.

Schore, A. (1999). *Affect regulation and the origin of the self: The neurobiology of emotional development*. Hillsdale, NJ: Erlbaum.

Schore, A. (2001). Minds in the making: Attachment, the self-organizing brain, and developmentally-oriented psychoanalytic psychotherapy. *British Journal of Psychotherapy*, 17, 3, 299–328.

Schore, A. (2002). Dysregulation of the right brain: A fundamental mechanism of traumatic attachment and the psychopathogenesis of posttraumatic stress disorder. *Australia and New Zealand Journal of Psychiatry*, 36, 1, 9–30.

Schore, A. (2003a). *Affect dysregulation and disorders of the self*. New York: Norton.

Schore, A. (2003b). *Affect regulation and the repair of the self*. New York: Norton.

Schroeder, M. (1991). *Fractals, chaos, power laws*. New York: Freeman.

Schwalbe, M. (1991). The autogenesis of self. *Journal for the Theory of Social Behavior*, 21, 269–295.

Schwartz, J. (1999). *Cassandra's daughter: A history of psychoanalysis*. New York: Viking.

Seuss, D. (1958). *The cat in the hat comes back*. New York: Random House.

Seligman, S. (2005). Dynamic systems theories as a metaframework for psychoanalysis. *Psychoanalytic Dialogues*, 15, 285–319.

Shelhamer, M. (2006). *Nonlinear dynamics in physiology*. River Edge, NJ: World Scientific.

Shepherd, L. (1993). *Lifting the veil: The feminine face of science*. Boston, MA: Shambhala.

Shockley, K. (2003). Application: Cross-RQA and interpersonal synchrony. In M. Riley and G. Van Orden (Co-Chairs) *Workshop: Nonlinear methods for psychology*. Fairfax, VA: George Mason University and National Science Foundation.

Siegel, D. (1999). *The developing mind: How relationships and the brain interact to shape who we are*. New York: Guilford.

Siegel, D. (2001). Memory: An overview, with emphasis on developmental, interpersonal, and neurobiological aspects. *Journal of the Academy of Child and Adolescent Psychiatry*, 40, 9, 997–1011.

Siegel, D. (2003). An interpersonal neurobiology of psychotherapy: The developing mind and the resolution of trauma. In M. Solomon and D. Siegel (eds.) *Healing trauma*. New York: Norton.

Siegel, D. (2006). An interpersonal neurobiology approach to psychotherapy. *Psychiatric Annals*, 36, 4, 248–256.

Siegel, D. (2007). *The mindful brain in psychotherapy: Reflection and attunement in the cultivation of well-being*. New York: Norton.

Siegel, D. (2008). *Mindsight: Our seventh sense*. New York: Bantam.

Siegel, D. and Hartzell, M. (2003). *Parenting from the inside out: How a deeper self-understanding can help you raise children who thrive*. New York: Penguin/Putnam.

Skarda, C. and Freeman, W. (1987). How brains make chaos in order to make sense of the world. *Behavioral and Brain Sciences*, 10, 161–195.

Smith, L. (2007). *Chaos: A very short introduction*. London: Oxford University Press.

Solomon, M. and Siegel, D. (eds.) (2003). *Healing trauma: Attachment, mind, body and brain*. New York: Norton.

Sonnenschein, D. (2001). *Sound design: The expressive power of music, voice, and sound effects in cinema*. Studio City, CA: Michael Wise Productions.

Spehar, B., Clifford, C., Newell, B. and Taylor, R. (2003). Universal aesthetic of fractals. *Computers and Graphics*, 27, 813–820.

Sroufe, L. (1983). *Infant-caregiver attachment and patterns of adaptation in preschool: The roots of maladaption and competence* (Volume 16). Hillsdale, NJ: Erlbaum.

Stern, D. (1985). *The interpersonal world of the infant: A view from psychoanalysis and developmental psychology*. New York: Basic Books.

Stern, D. (2003). *Unformulated experience: From dissociation to imagination in psychoanalysis*. Hillsdale, NJ: Analytic Press.

Stern, D. (2004a). *The Present Moment in Psychotherapy and Everyday Life*. New York: Norton.

Stern, D. (2004b). The eye sees itself: Dissociation, enactment, and the achievement of conflict. *Contemporary Psychoanalysis*, 40, 197–237.

Sternberg, R. (1990). *Metaphors of mind: Conceptions of the nature of intelligence*. New York: Cambridge University Press.

Stolorow, R. (1997). Dynamic, dyadic, intersubjective systems: An evolving paradigm for psychoanalysis. *Psychoanalytic Psychology*, 14, 337–346.

Stone, R. (1975). *Because a little bug went ka-choo*. New York: Random House.

Sulis, W. and Combs, A. (eds.). (1996). *Nonlinear dynamics and human behavior*. Singapore: World Scientific.

Sullivan, H. (1964). *The fusion of psychiatry and social science*. New York: Norton.

Suzuki, D. (1994). *Zen koan as a means of attaining enlightenment*. Rutland, VT: Charles E. Tuttle.

Taylor, R. (2003). *Art and complexity*. Amsterdam: Elsevier Press.

Taylor, R. (2006). Pollock, Mondrian and nature: Recent scientific investigations. *Chaos and Complexity Letters*, 1, 3, 265–277.

Taylor, R., Micolich, A. and Jones, D. (1999). Fractal analysis of Pollock's drip paintings. *Nature*, 399, 422.

Thelen, E. and Smith, L. (eds.) (1993). *A dynamic systems approach to development: Applications*. Cambridge, MA: MIT Press.

Thelen, E. and Smith, L. (1994). *A dynamic systems approach to the development of cognition and action*. Cambridge, MA: Bradford Books/MIT Press.

Tobias, D. and Mazur, B. (2007). *Number: The language of science.* New York: Plume/ Penguin.

Tschacher, W., Scheier, C. and Grawe, K. (1998). Order and pattern formation in psychotherapy. *Nonlinear Dynamics, Psychology, and Life Sciences,* 2, 3, 195–215.

Vallacher, R. and Nowak, A. (eds.) (1994). *Dynamical systems in social psychology.* New York: Academic Press.

Van de Castle, R. (1994). *Our dreaming mind.* New York: Ballantine.

Vandervert, L. (1990). Systems thinking and neurological positivism: Further elucidations and implications. *Systems Research,* 7, 1, 1–17.

Van Orden, G. (ed.) (2002). *Nonlinear dynamics and psycholinguistics: A special double issue of ecological psychology.* Mahwah, NJ: Erlbaum.

Varela, F. (1979). *Principles of biological autonomy.* New York: North Holland.

Varela, F. and Shear, J. (eds.) (1999). *The view from within: First person approaches to the study of consciousness.* Thorverton, UK: Imprint Academic.

Varela, F., Maturana, H. and Uribe, R. (1974). Autopoiesis: The organization of living systems, its characterization and a model. *Biosystems,* 5, 187–196.

Varela, F., Thompson, E. and Rosch, E. (1991). *The embodied mind: Cognitive science and human experience.* Cambridge, MA: MIT Press.

Volz, K. and von Cramon, D. (2006). What neuroscience can tell about intuitive processes in the context of perceptual discovery. *Journal of Cognitive Neuroscience,* 18, 12, 2077–2087.

Von Franz, M. (1972). *Creation myths.* New York: Spring.

Vonnegut, K. (1973). *Breakfast of champions.* New York: Delacorte.

Watson, D. (2001). Dissociations of the night: Individual differences in sleep-related experiences and their relation to dissociation and schizotypy. *Journal of Abnormal Psychology,* 110, 526–535.

Watzlawick, P. (1978). *The language of change.* New York: Basic Books.

West, B. (1990). *Chaos in medicine.* River Edge, NJ: World Scientific.

West, B. (2006). *Where medicine went wrong.* River Edge, NJ: World Scientific.

West, B. (2007). The average person is truly exceptional. Keynote address, Society for Chaos Theory in Psychology and Life Sciences, Seventeenth Annual International Conference, Chapman University, Orange, California.

West, B. and Deering, B. (1995). *The lure of modern science: Fractal thinking.* River Edge, NJ: World Scientific.

Whitehead, A. and Russell, B. (1910/1927). *Principia mathematica,* 3 volumes. Cambridge: Cambridge University Press.

Wilbur, K. (1982). *The holographic paradigm and other paradoxes.* Boulder, CO: Shambhala.

Willeford, W. (1969). *The Fool and his scepter: A study in clowns and jesters and their audience.* Chicago, IL: Northwestern University Press.

Williams, G. (1997). *Chaos theory tamed.* Washington, DC: National Academies Press.

Williams, P. (1989). *Mahāyāna Buddhism: The doctrinal foundations.* London: Routledge.

Wilner, W. (1998). Experience, metaphor, and the crucial nature of the analyst's expressive participation. *Contemporary Psychoanalysis,* 34, 413–443.

Wilson, E. (1998). *Consilience: The unity of knowledge.* New York: Knopf.

Winnicott, D.W. (1953). Transitional objects and transitional phenomena. *International Journal of Psychoanalysis*, 34, 89–97.

Winnicott, D.W. (1960). Ego distortion in terms of true and false self. In D.W. Winnicott (1965) *The maturational processes and the facilitating environment: Studies in the theory of emotional development*. New York: International Universities Press.

Winnicott, D.W. (1971). *Playing and reality*. London: Tavistock

Wolf, A. (1994). *The dreaming universe: A mind-expanding journey into the place where psyche and physics meet*. New York: Simon and Schuster.

Wolfram, S. (2002). *A new kind of science*. Champaign, IL: Wolfram Media.

Wolstein, B. (1995). Five psychoanalytic metaphors of the therapist's psyche in analysis, and some related issues. Unpublished manuscript.

Yorke, T. and Li, J. (1975). Period three implies chaos. *American Mathematical Monthly*, 82, 985–992.

Zausner, T. (2006). *When walls become doors*. New York: Harmony.

Zukav, G. (1979). *The dancing Wu Li masters*. New York: Bantam.

Index

Note: page numbers in **bold** refer to figures and information contained in captions.